Cruising Ports:
Florida to California via Panama

Captains Pat & John E. Rains

Point **L**oma **P**ublishing

Post Office Box 60190
San Diego, CA 92166
(888) 302-BOAT

This book and its charts and illustrations are to be used for planning and reference purposes only. They are specifically **not to be used for navigation.** Some of this book's charts are taken from the latest DMA and NOAA charts. For the sake of clarity, the authors have deleted some soundings and added new shoreline data, such as marinas, breakwaters and fuel docks. Other charts in this book are created from the authors' own sketch charts. The text has been carefully prepared, based upon personal inspection, official publications and other data deemed reliable, with the objective of making the cruising skipper's voyage more enjoyable. Every reasonable effort has been made to achieve up-to-date accuracy, but the infinite complexities of personal observation and a constantly changing world render total accuracy impossible. Thus, all sailing information and directions in this book must be checked against the skipper's own eyes and latest charts, publications and *Notice to Mariners*.

Every skipper is alone responsible for the safety of his or her crew and vessel, and he or she must plot the safe course. The authors and the publisher must therefore both specifically disclaim any and all personal liability for loss or risk, to persons or property or both, which might occur either directly or indirectly from any person's use or interpretation of any information contained in this book. No publication can substitute for good sea sense.

© 1999 **Point Loma Publishing**
San Diego, California

ISBN 0-9638470-7-4
Cruising Ports: Florida to California via Panama
Captains Pat and John E. Rains

Cruising Ports:
Florida to California via Panama

Captains Pat & John E. Rains

Acknowledgements

We give a hearty thanks to all great folks who helped us update this hugely expanded fourth edition. First, thanks to the hundreds of adventurous boaters we've met along this route; it's for you we wrote this book - and for that next boat coming over the horizon.

We are deeply indebted to many busy Port Captains, harbor officials and U.S. Coast Guard officers for their technical assistance and gracious good will.

Of the 40 charts in this book, 13 were produced by illustrator Mark Sampson from our hand-drawn surveys and sketch charts. Although we took most of the 100+ photos in this book, Susan Canfield gave us three beauties, and Pam Lynd Fink and Stuart Lochner each gave us one. We thank Karl Raggio for the aerial of Marina Vallarta. Thanks to Dick Hansen for his super reporting job. A special thanks to the man who got us started writing about the cruising ports, Louis Gerlinger Sr., former publisher of the Log Newspapers.

Finally, we thank our network of family and friends for not sending out the Coast Guard to find us, when we disappeared from the planet for two months in order to work up this latest edition of "Cruising Ports."

Pat and John Rains

To contact the authors:
Captains Pat and John E. Rains
Post Office Box 81669
San Diego, CA 92138
(619) 222-9028
www.inetworld.net/rains

- Trip consultation
- Speaking engagements
- Reader contributions
  to future editions

- Yacht deliveries
- Crew placement
- Ship deliveries

Contents

Contents

Foreword

Almost two decades have passed since the original *"Cruising Ports"* was published and the world has changed greatly, especially Central America. As a professional yacht delivery skipper I travel regularly between South Florida and Southern California via the Panama Canal. Prior to the first edition of this book, I'd skippered boats on the complete voyage only six times; now I've covered it over 50 times, power and sail. I've learned a lot, and this fourth edition reflects that. It is greatly expanded, updated and reorganized, and it contains many scanned images of selected areas of actual DMA charts. And we've included many new anchorages along the way.

My wife joins me as co-author in this fourth edition. She has made the trip more than 25 times and brings along her powers of observation and organization, her professional editing skills, and - with her woman's point of view - she mellows out my sometimes harsh rhetoric.

I originally wrote *"Cruising Ports"* to fill an information gap, because large areas of shore and sea hadn't been written about. I included them in this book. Each year the number of cruising yachts passing through the Panama Canal increases and so does the need for good practical guidance.

This is a guide to the most vital boating needs in the major cruising ports along the 5,000-mile route. And of course it is designed to be used from either direction, Florida to California or vice versa. For the first time, we've included many of the interesting cruising grounds that lie just off the beaten path, but the thousands of nameless coves in between are still waiting for you to discover.

Our format for each port includes all those things visitors by boat will encounter and seek: approaching the port from either direction; presenting oneself to the authorities; obtaining fuel, water, dockage, repairs and provisions; making transportation connections; and then maybe even having a good time. We've included a brief historical and political background for each country, to give you a feeling for the attitudes of the citizens and perhaps an idea of where the country's future lies.

The flip of a coin determined the East Coast-to-West Coast order for this edition. An equal number of boats travel in either direction, so we wrote the chapters in such a manner that they can be used in both directions. Perhaps the fifth edition will start at California and move toward Florida. It depends on feedback from you, our readers.

The Caribbean section focuses on the cruisers' route, the west end around Cuba. This edition has much more western Caribbean weather and routing information than the previous editions. The eastern route around Cuba is preferred by long-range heavy displacement power boats, so we have merely sketched this route in one chapter. So many of our readers asked for it, so for the first time, we've included the Sea of Cortez in *"Cruising Ports,"* starting with the mainland side, then the Baja California side.

Throughout the text and in one appendix, we have included hundreds of GPA waypoint latitudes and longitudes for the entire 5,000-mile route. Now that GPS or at least satnav are on every cruising boat, these GPS waypoints can save the navigator much time.

Chapter 1
Boat Preparation

~~~~~~

Adequate boat preparation starting right now is absolutely vital to your being able to enjoy many months – or years – of kick-back cruising bliss once you're finally out there doing it, exploring far beyond your current horizons. Just like with any painting or varnishing project, some careful preparation steps are the keys to success. No way can you prepare yourself for every eventuality, nor carry every possible spare part. But a little organization today goes a long way toward safety and fun tomorrow.

How long will it take? The various stages of preparation for a major cruise generally take several months of full-time concentrated effort by everyone who's going along, but a lot depends on how much time, money and energy you're able to devote to each stage.

Fortunately, you can carry out several of these stages simultaneously. Overall, preparation involves choosing and preparing the boat, training the people who will be going (physically and emotionally), and setting up your shore support (family or others who may take care of your affairs in your absence). The first requirement is the boat.

Picking a Sailing Vessel

Most of the pleasure boats making the adventurous cruise between the East and West Coasts of the United States via Panama are sailboats – at least four to one over pleasure powerboats. One of the most commonly asked question at my cruising seminars is, "What characteristics must a sailboat have in order to make this cruise?"

Boat Size: We consider 35 feet to be the minimum length for sail, simply because stowage of all the necessary equipment for this route requires a certain amount of space. The hull has to be absolutely sound, and the design has to be seaworthy. It should have good windward capabilities. Don't forget that once you've made the beautiful, warm downwind sleigh ride to paradise, you'll eventually have to face the music during the return slog to weather.

Motorsailors generally don't sail to weather very well, but a good motorsailor will give you the power and range to more than compensate for it.

The Rig: The sailing rig must be a lot sturdier than the beefiest day sailor. A sloop will always be easier to handle and points better, but a ketch rig offers you more options of sail combinations, which becomes increasingly important in heavy weather. Masts should be stepped through to the keel.

Fuel: We recommend diesel power for main propulsion. To me, gasoline is unacceptable not only because it introduces the potential for explosion and fire onboard, but also because it requires a complex ignition system. Besides, diesel is much more widely attainable in ports throughout the world than is gasoline.

What about dinghy gas? On this route, only a dozen or so of the major ports have fuel docks with gasoline also available. So jerry jugs need to be filled there and carried on deck. In the hundreds of lesser ports and remote villages, you'll have to carry your gasoline jerry jugs inland to the nearest highway gas station. Because you'll probably want to hire a taxi driver to carry your full jugs in his trunk back to the waterfront, it's often easier to engage the taxi as a round trip.

Speed & Range: One of the most frequently asked questions at our seminars is "What kind of speed and range should my boat have in order to make this cruising route?" Choose a diesel engine that's powerful enough to push your boat to windward at six knots under average sea conditions. The Panama Canal requires you to be able to move at a minimum consistent speed of five knots during your entire transit – anywhere from eight hours to 20 hours. Veteran cruisers frequently comment that

– for various reasons – they had to do a whole lot more motoring than they had expected.

If you're planning to cruise from one coast of the United States to the other via the Panama Canal, then having a range of 360 miles allows you to jump from Puerto Quetzal in Guatemala down to Marina Flamingo in northern Costa Rica; this bypasses the Pacific ports in El Salvador, Honduras and Nicaragua. Wind conditions along this stretch range from weeks of zero wind to days of gale force wind. If your built-in tank capacity is insufficient, consider increasing your range by carrying extra fuel on deck. (See "Carrying Extra Fuel" later in this chapter.)

Draft: Deep-draft cruising boats don't generally encounter difficulties in the entrance channels of most of the ports mentioned in this book. However, the exceptions are the jetty entrance to Marina Ixtapa, the curving channel into the back bay at Puntarenas and the entrance bar outside Rio Dulce; in these three places, deep-drafters very often need to stand by inside or outside for the next high tide.

Fresh Water: Most of the municipalities you'll be visiting have drinking water that your body will react to as if it were contaminated. If the sailboat you're thinking of cruising in does not carry a 7-day supply of fresh water, meaning enough for drinking and cooking and personal hygiene for each person onboard, then determine whether or not it can support a reverse-osmosis water maker. Many new 12-volt models are designed for sailboats. Otherwise, you'll constantly be on "short-water rationing" while anchored in paradise – or you'll be tethered to a marina. While you're underway on the high seas or stopped in a pristine anchorage, make all the water you can carry, and top off your tanks before beginning a port call; never make water inside a port.

Fresh Air: Ventilation below decks is an absolute essential, and it gets even more critical the farther you venture into the tropics. Think 5% drenching rain, 95% blistering sun and 100% humidity. Without a dodger, you'll have to keep your companionway closed in rainy weather – or rig an alternative. Any dorades, hatches and opening ports that your prospective boat already has will still need to be supplemented with wide deck awnings, strategically placed sun shades, directional wind scoops and a few 12-volt fans. More about this in "Outfitting" below.

Picking a Power Boat

About 1/4 of the pleasure boats we encounter on the Panama route between California and Florida are powerboats, but each year we're seeing new fuel stops springing up between the old reliable cruising ports, so we expect more powerboats to join the ranks of nautical tourists.

Boat Size: For the route laid out in this book, 40 feet is my minimum recommended length for a cruising poweryacht, but seaworthiness is a more primary consideration. Trawlers and trawler types do very well in these waters, particularly the designs that ride low and have rolling chocks or hard chines to keep the beam roll to a minimum. Larger powerboats should have stabilizers. Larger sportfishers and motoryachts with or without fishing cockpits are quite common travelers along this route. Each year, larger and larger power cruisers are making this route, and more fuel docks make that possible.

Fuel: Diesel is by far the preferred

power propulsion along this route. You will soon get familiar with commercial fuel piers that offer only large diameter nozzles (bring your own reducers) and high velocity pumps (learn how to slow them down) or tank truck delivery in which you must purchase the entire truckload of fuel (plan your fuel stops wisely). In all the major ports, you must complete your round of port clearances before you can begin to make arrangements for taking fuel. In some ports, an additional written permission is required from the Port Captain's office before you can make fuel arrangements.

Speed & Range: Your boat should have a cruising fuel range of at least 360 miles in order to jump from Puerto Quetzal in Guatemala down to Marina Flamingo in northern Costa Rica; this bypasses the Pacific ports in El Salvador, Honduras and Nicaragua. If you cannot extend the vessel's cruising range enough by running at reduced RPMs, then consider carrying deck fuel. (See "Carrying Extra Fuel" later in this chapter.)

A single-screw boat is acceptable if you're a superb engineer and/or have an emergency backup to the main engine. For example, a single-screw vessel may have a hydraulic system that could, in case of a main-engine failure, link the generator to the propeller to provide enough propulsion to make port. The two manufacturers of marine diesel engines for which parts are relatively easy to find in this route outside the United States are Detroit and Caterpillar.

Fresh Water: Most of the municipalities you'll be visiting have drinking water that your body will react to as if it were contaminated. Unless you spend all your time in marinas with filtered water or you don't mind being on "short-water rationing," then a water maker is practically required equipment for this voyage. Most water makers are either 220 or 12 volt. Make all your water while underway on the high seas or stopped in a pristine anchorage, and top off your tanks before beginning a port call; never make water inside a port.

The quality of the municipal water supply in many of the ports covered in this book is often questionable, especially for a week or more after a heavy rainfall. So far, the primary exception is the country of Panama, which still has good water.

Fresh Air: Many powerboats are designed to be buttoned up while underway at sea, so they rely heavily on their air conditioning systems – few of which can withstand the rigors of tropical heat and humidity. Commonly, the compressor fails or the system simply cannot cool sufficiently due to the warmth of the sea water it uses for cooling. Sweating and leaking of air conditioning ducting behind wall coverings and inside overheads is another common problem in the deepest tropics, so be sure your pipes are well insulated.

Install back-up fans and devise methods to keep salt spray and exhaust fumes out while running the boat with some ports open.

Outfitting (for all boats)

While cruising within the boundaries of the U.S., pleasure boaters take for granted their easy access to safe marinas and fuel docks, to well-charted waterways lined with chandlers, repair yards and a thousand marine services. In some of the ports covered in this book you can find the basic supplies required by commercial fishing boats. But in very few places can you buy replacement parts for equipment that is found only on a pleasure boat, and even fewer places can provide yacht-quality services. Boaters undertaking this extensive of a foreign route should be prepared to remain as self sufficient and accident free as possible. Don't expect the Coast Guard Auxiliary or a membership towing service to rush to your rescue.

Ground Tackle: When cruising outside the U.S., most boaters will be sleeping on the hook 80 to 90% of the time. The best insurance policy you can buy is good ground tackle. Don't get cheesy in this department or you'll never get a good

Ground Tackle: You'll be sleeping on the hook more often than not, so a heavy-duty 2-anchor system that's quick and reliable is a good idea.

night's sleep or feel safe leaving your boat.

As your primary tackle, a properly sized anchor with 300 feet of all chain usually covers even hazardous anchoring situations – and you'll have plenty of them. As a bare minimum for smaller and lighter boats, 50 feet of chain with 250 feet of rode (3-strand nylon line) might suffice. This could serve as a ready-to-go backup anchor to the primary all-chain system.

Your primary anchor should be securely mounted in position but ready for instant use. A power windlass with a manual mode as backup is ideal. The pins in all shackles and swivel shackles should be safety-wired with monel. No line should be connected to the chain end of the anchor with less than a 4-tuck splice and a metal thimble.

Danforth-type anchors are good all-purpose anchors, and plow-type anchors are equally good in most conditions except very soft bottoms or reefs. A relatively light grapnel-type anchor with a trip line is handy for rock and reef anchoring. (Please avoid anchoring near coral heads or coral reefs, because even your chain dragging across them can destroy formations that are centuries old.)

The ideal policy is to carry three anchor set-ups: two bow anchors (mounted in place with their chains or lines flaked down in individual below-deck chain lockers) and a stern anchor. The stern anchor need not be as large as the others, and it may have a shorter length of chain with rode, about 2/3rds of the total length.

TIPS: Be sure all hawse holes are of sufficient diameter to make it impossible for the chain to jam. Even if the hawse hole has a metal cap chained on, you could plug the hole with plasticene putty during long passages. Access to the chain locker lets you flake the chain neatly as you take it in (keep a Y-shaped stick for this purpose), *which prevents it from balling up hopelessly during your next bouncy passage.*

Lights: The route between Florida and California follows major shipping lanes in many places. For this reason, it's imperative that pleasure boats have clean, bright running lights placed as high as possible above the water, to make them as easily visible as possible. Even though standard production running lights conform to current U.S. Coast Guard regulations, they often are insufficient for the heavy traffic situations and high seas conditions you're sure to encounter. Don't hesitate to have your lights beefed up.

Although technically not "legal," a masthead strobe light saved us from being run down by several large freighters while we were lying becalmed and engineless one dark night in the shipping lanes off Manzanillo, Mexico. Hardly anything is overkill when you're outfitting your own boat for blue-water travel. So, for your own safety, don't try to get by with the minimum requirements, okay?

For sailboats, a masthead tri-color light is highly recommended to make the boat more visible.

Radar reflectors for sailboats are very important for the offshore portions of this route, especially considering this common scenario: The non-English-speaking helmsman of a Taiwanese fishing boat may not even be allowed to change the settings on his radar, let alone change course, so if your comparatively minuscule yacht didn't show up on his radar screen when 10 miles separated you, you'll never show up as he gets closer – where you're even more likely to be obscured by the sea clutter. Buy the largest, most reflective gadget you can find, and secure it as high as possible whenever you head offshore.

Dinghies or Launches: Since you'll be anchoring most of the time, you'll be using the "dink" on a daily basis. For the cruising route described in this book, an inflatable with a hard bottom (or at least wooden floorboards) and a transom-mounted outboard motor is by far the vehicle of choice by veteran cruising folks. Without a stiff bottom, the trough of each big wave tends to fold the dinghy like a soft taco. To slow down sun damage to the pontoons, treat them with products such as 303, and make a canvas cover in a light color – to protect the pontoons and your family's fannies as well.

What size? Ask yourself how you'll bring it aboard and where it will stow. Realistically, can it seat everyone safely plus a load of groceries? How about in rough waves and surf landings?

Dinghy wheels make landing and launching on hard-sand beaches much easier. We've seen even Baja pangas with wheels. If they're tall enough, they'll help protect the prop and lower end of your outboard. Before you buy wheels for your dink, be sure they're designed for salt water, and consider what's involved in removing them occasionally.

A reliable 10-hp outboard is the minimum essential for tropical cruising, because in many anchorages and ports it's completely impossible to row ashore due to tidal currents, rough water and long distances. Use the largest outboard that's practical for the size of your dinghy. About a third of the way through this route, many cruisers start searching around for a larger dinghy and motor.

We used to say that there's nothing worse than having a tiny outboard that cavitates wildly at each wave crest – only to get its carburetor submerged at the bottom of the next. But then we met a guy in Cabo San Lucas who's wimpy outboard let him down in a 20-knot headwind at Puerto Vallarta, causing him to run out of gas and be swept 400 miles westward. For days, he had no water or food, no shelter from the elements, no oars, and no hope of drifting to land. Fortunately a fishing boat spotted his seemingly deserted inflatable well west of Cabo's longitude, and they diverted to have a closer look – and they were able to revive him from near death.

Since hearing his story, we now recommend not only a dependable outboard, but also an extra fuel tank, pulling oars with dependable oar locks, a spare oar lock or two, a bailer, a small dinghy anchor with rode, an extra PFD or some floatation, a flashlight and a water jug. Stow the loose stuff in a bag tied into the corner that can serve as a seat. If you get into the simple habit of carrying a fully charged hand-held VHF along each time you go off in the dinghy, it could save your life.

When you land on remote beaches, lock your outboard to the transom, have locking cables for the fuel tank and oars, and cover loose items. The VHF cruising nets and the "coconut telegraph" are great for passing warnings about petty theft in specific anchorages. The most common hassle is the occasional beach kid who's fascinated with your dinghy – and can't resist playing fort on it.

We don't recommend towing a large dinghy any great distance, because the towing eye can fail, which is exactly how most dinghy losses occur. But if you have to tow it, make up a 3-point towing bridle to spread the load.

Sails & Rigging (Sailboats only): A good working set of sails should include jiffy reefing on the main, light-wind sails and a pole rigged for downwind work. For severe weather, a storm trysail should have a separate track on the mast – and be backed

Jiffy reefing is a safety factor, because you spend less time struggling with sails in bad weather.

up with a storm jib. Roller furling is safer and more convenient than wrestling sails on a slippery foredeck. Be aware that furling lines tend to chafe fatally, and that furling sails sometimes don't harden up as well in high wind. But if you stay vigilant for chafe and stay in port in stormy weather, then a roller furling system is fine for this route.

Carrying Extra Fuel: If you need to extend your range in order to make a lengthy non-stop passage, you may want to consider these three methods of carrying extra diesel – temporarily but safely. Your boat's natural underway trim must be maintained, or the extra weight may affect its steering and buoyancy. You'll need a portable fuel pump and hoses to transfer the extra diesel to a regular tank while you're at sea – not at a nice calm dock. Avoid leaks, spills and fumes.

One option may be to temporarily sacrifice an internal tank for diesel, such as a cleaned holding tank. Don't put diesel into a potable water tank, because it will

never be fit for potable water again. Rigid PVC tanks may be carried in a separate lazarette, but be sure any internal tankage is well vented overboard.

Carried on deck, flexible bladders are sold in chandler stores and catalogues. If you consider bladders, buy the best quality available; the failure points are the seams and grommets or ties. A bladder should be emptied all at once, because a half-empty bladder is impossible to secure; it wants to creep or launch itself. Never carry a bladder on the bow. Two smaller bladders distributing the weight fore and aft (or athwartship) are better than one larger bladder. One advantage of bladders is that they can be rolled up and stowed.

PVC drums come in 55- and 30-gallon sizes. Check the chandler catalogues, or "barrels" in the yellow pages. If you buy

Deck Fuel: PVC drums or barrels must be lashed in place securely. Never use metal drums on a yacht.

used drums, be sure the bungs and the threads on the bung holes are in perfect condition, and that the insides are absolutely clean and dry. Inspect them with a flash light. Never put steel drums on a yacht; they rust, gouge and leak. Never tie a full drum to a deck stanchion; it throws enough weight to rip a stanchion out by its through-bolts. PVC drums are difficult to secure and stow.

Electronics and Navigation

Autopilot: A reliable autopilot will become your favorite crew member; it doesn't eat much, it can steer the boat all day and all night, and it doesn't talk back. Many boaters give familiar names to their autopilots – like "Mother" or "good old Joe," Before you name a new pilot, however, sea trial it to see how it performs steering downwind in heavy seas. If it becomes overpowered too easily, you'll call it something less kind, because it could cause your vessel to broach.

Larger vessels require heavy duty autopilots that are internally mounted, often hydraulically operated. A smaller powerboat or sailboat could get by on an externally mounted pilot that hooks directly to the wheel. And a self-steering vane for a smaller sailboat is fine, but we would use it as a back-up to the mechanical autopilot; the vane's limitation becomes obvious when the wind quits, as it does along much of this route.

Depth Sounder: It's absolutely essential, and for this route it should read to 100 fathoms in order to navigate the all-important 100-fathom curve. Digital readouts are fine, but a recording depth sounder is top of the line. The depth sounder is one of those items that should have a back up, budget permitting. At least make up a usable lead line, and practice using it. Be aware that the new inexpensive "fish finders" are not a good substitute; many models have a hard time finding the bottom in water less than 100 feet deep, which is exactly where you need it most, although in deeper water they're good at showing targets not attached to the bottom, such as schools of fish.

Radar expands your horizon, literally. Radar is an essential safety device, not just at night or during fog, rain or tossing seas, but also any time you pilot unfamiliar waters – and anytime you need to stay out of the path of other vessels. Even on a minimal 15-mile screen, unseen coastal features are shown as 2-dimensional outlines that, when combined with a chart, should leave little doubt as to your position. Working up a "radar fix" on any coastline is a fast and accurate method for determining your position – no matter what the weather or visibility circumstances may be. Radar gives you your first alert in crossing and head-on traffic situations. Larger vessels have been considered negligent when they didn't "stand a proper watch" – including a constant radar watch.

GPS: The marvelous system of Global Position Satellites sends virtually constant signals to your boat from at least 24 geo-stationary satellites, telling you not only your latitude and longitude to within 100 meters (when dithered) or closer, but also computing your actual course and speed over the bottom, which are essential for determining your set and drift (how far and how fast you're being pushed off course by wind and current).

However, whenever you approach land, navigate by your radar and soundings, because the charts may not concur with your GPS positions. GPS accuracy has showed some areas of earlier NOAA and DMA and

SM charts to be inaccurate by as much as two miles.

Each year, GPS devices come down in price, size and amperage requirements, and they're increasingly user-friendly. GPS is no longer considered a luxury for this extensive of a voyage. Many larger boats stow their back-up hand-held GPS in the ditch kit. (As of early 1999, D-GPS isn't receivable over most of this route.)

CAUTION: We all enjoy using electronic navigation gadgets, but they cannot substitute for your performing meticulous chart work with paper charts, pencils, dividers, rolling plotters or parallel rulers and calculators – and using your noodle. Electronics cannot replace actual navigation. Never rely solely on electronic gadgets, because they fail frequently and suddenly in the marine environment. When (not if) that happens, you'll have to revert to the paper chart and know exactly where you were before the electronics failed – and how to navigate from there with only your noodle.

Communication Radios

Radios are essential safety gear for this route, because on a daily basis they allow you to monitor long- and short-range weather reports so you know of any storms or inhospitable wind and sea conditions that may be approaching your location – or that may stand in your way ahead. Additionally, if you or anyone else gets in trouble, radios allow you to broadcast a loud cry for assistance. Beyond safety, shipboard radios make possible e-mail, business calls and personal chats. The four kinds of marine radios are VHF, ham, SSB, and WX-fax.

VHF (Very High Frequency) radio is essential for safety, even though it's limited to line-of-sight communication. Most of the route in this book lies in or near major shipping lanes where commercial ships constantly monitor VHF channels 16 (distress and hailing) and 13 (ship to ship). If you put out a "May-Day" or "Pan-Pan" distress call on either of these channels, then chances are great that you'll be heard by one of these ships. The most common VHF frequencies are designated as channels 9, 10, 12, 13, 22, 26, 27, 28, 68, 70, 71, 72, 83, 85 and 86.

A hand-held VHF radio is extremely practical. For example, when a couple goes cruising, someone often gets stuck pulling anchor watch while the other gets to go ashore. If the anchor dregs, the boat sitter will want to call the shore bird on the hand-held VHF – to let him or her know at least where to look for the boat if it's been re-anchored. In foreign waters, you may not be able to leave the dinghy ashore unattended, so the shore party gets dropped off, takes the hand-held, and then calls the boat when they're ready to be picked up. The boat sitter invariably forgets to add something to the shopping list, or the shore party cannot locate the right size bearings; the handy hand-held VHF saves the day every time.

As handy as a VHF radio may be, it's merely a local system, not acceptable as the only radio aboard a boat making the voyage described in this book.

Ham radio (licensed amateur radio) is the cheapest yet most versatile world-wide communication system for a yacht. Seasoned "Maritime Mobiles" (cruising hams) will verify that getting a ham license is definitely a worthwhile project before departing on this cruise. Over the long hot summer in the Sea of Cortez, study groups often form to practice for their FCC exams. The tests of Morse code and technical expertise aren't as difficult as they used to be. Since the FCC offered a "no code" entry level license, many weekend crash-course radio schools practically guarantee a passing grade. However, get at least a "general class" license to be able to use the Maritime Mobile Networks. In summer 1999, the Morse code requirement was proposed to be lowered from 13 words per minute to only five words per minute.

On the West Coast, we highly recommend Gordon West's Radio School, 714-549-5000. Computer programs and audio-cassette courses also make getting a ham license pretty easy.

Besides the normal QSOs with ham friends on distant boats, you can jump in on the many amateur radio networks, known as ham nets, that meet on certain frequencies at set times each day, where valuable information is shared. By linking up with other "stations" during the net check-in and then going off frequency with them, cruisers can make free non-business "phone-patch" calls to family and friends back home. Friendly volunteers ashore love to assist us adventurous mariners, and they love to hear our sea stories.

SSB is short for commercial **single side-band radio**. SSB radios are more expensive than ham radios, but they offer good long-range communications and have easier licensing requirements. SSB channel 12-Alpha has a very useful network of boats working their way along the entire western seaboard of Mexico. Our U.S. Coast Guard's weather broadcasts on SSB are extensive and important. Also, you can place SSB phone calls through the WLO High Seas Operator system, especially on a radio with a large number of channels. Even a costly High Seas call is more effective than trying to call from some of the primitive land-based telephone systems you'll find in rural areas outside the U.S.

Many of SSBs will also operate on the frequencies designated for ham, which gives you the best of both worlds. If you invest in an SSB for this dual purpose, just be sure it can receive the lower side-band (for amateur frequencies below 10 Mhz, which provide the best weather information) as well as the upper side-band. New dual-function SSB models come out annually. Three of the many popular brands names are Kenwood, ICOM and Furuno.

An "all-band receiver" can monitor the U.S. Coast Guard weather broadcasts, get information from SSB channel 12-Alpha, as well as pick up the "time tick" and weather from WWV. The time tick is handy for celestial navigation.

Cellular and Satellite Phones: Many cellular phones work in Mexico, Panama and parts of the Caribbean; ask your company in which countries it offers Roam service and what special access codes are required. If you're going to remain in a region very long, go to one of the local cell companies and get your own cell phone temporarily re-programmed for their local network.

Satellite phones are becoming smaller and less expensive. We predict that soon even the smaller cruising boats will carry "sat phones." For instance, Sky Cell has a unit with a low-gain antenna that sells for around $4,000 and that has a "footprint" covering the entire route described in the book. International calls are presently about $2.50 per minute, and we expect the rates to continue to drop.

E-mail: Now e-mail can be sent and received from a vessel in the middle of the ocean via any SSB radio, or Inmarsat A, B, M, Mini-M or C communications. Similar to how you normally set up a computer e-mail account through an internet-access provider, these new companies charge a flat rate for the initial "air time" account plus two to five lines of e-mail text per dollar. One company we've used is Stratos Mobile Networks; for information about international shipboard e-mail service, phone 709-748-4233, or for service in North America, call toll free (888) 766-1313. Visit their website at http://www.stratos.com.ca

A **weather-fax receiver** (WX-fax) prints out a variety of weather charts and satellite photos that are constantly being broadcast from meteorological forecasting offices throughout the world. Like most electronic gadgets, WX-fax machines are now so inexpensive, compact and user-friendly that they belong on most vessels cruising this route. Although port captains sometimes post WX-fax data about hurricanes on the outside their offices, you'll have to go ashore to see for yourself. If you happen to be the only boat with WX-fax in any of the many remote cruising grounds along this route, your new-found friends may consider it your seaman-like duty to share the latest satellite image or tropical report with them.

If you already have a good SSB receiver and a computer aboard your vessel, you can buy a WX-fax program and a black-box integrator for about $150 that let you download National Weather Service and U.S. Coast Guard weather charts and satellite images and make hard copies on your printer.

Additional Navigation Gear
Others required for this voyage are:
✓ A good ship's **compass**, accurately swung and adjusted. Know how to use the **compass error card**.
✓ A **hand-bearing compass.** We prefer the hockey-puck kind because they're

Pat's checking out the latest WX-fax charts and satellite photos. Each year WXfax systems are smaller and easier to program.

more accurate and take less space than the sling-shot kind. The 5-year batteries don't corrode as other kinds do.
✓ A **distance log** makes dead reckoning fast and accurate.
✓ **Binoculars.** The best navigation device you have is your own pair of eyeballs, and binoculars extend that range. For marine use, 7 X 50 power is fine. Personally, we prefer Fujinon. Night-vision helps in making landfall where there are no lights and during night-time passage-making.
✓ A **barometer** that looks nice on an office wall may not be accurate or sturdy enough for onboard use. Don't be cheap. Calibrate your barometer by listening to the local WX report on VHF, which always gives the barometric pressure, then adjust the screw on the back or inside the instrument.
✓ An **anemometer** reading apparent wind strength and direction helps you distinguish true wind speed from boat speed, which is difficult at night when you can't see indicators on the water. Also, an anemometer is useful for dispelling whopper sea stories.

✓A good set of **dividers** has a replaceable **lead** in one end, also a **thumb wheel** that prevents the legs from slipping. Don't try to get buy with the brass ones that come with leather desktop accessories from the stationery store.

✓**Parallel rules** – or a **rolling plotter** – can be made of clear plastic so you can read the compass through them, but they'll need to be replaced as soon as they start slipping, which is probably more often a good steel variety.

✓Your **chart table/navigation area** is the nerve center of the boat, and you'll be doing a lot of critical calculations there. Don't try to make the salon table serve this purpose. A chart table should be dedicated to navigation only, and it should be laid out to handle your charts conveniently. It needs to be out of the wind and spray – yet handy to the helm.

The Galley

The **galley location** should be in the middle section of the boat where motion is less severe, located near a hatchway or main companionway, with good ventilation and light. A compact U-shaped galley may keep the cook from being flung around. If your galley is less encircling, through-bolt two eyebolts for holding a "cook's sling."

Pat prefers to cook on a gas stove, but she has cooked on some strange stoves, including Big Bertha diesel burners during a 5,000-mile voyage, and an Atlantic crossing to Spain with a finicky alcohol stove. Diesel stoves are way too dirty for pleasure boats, and an alcohol burner is awkward to light and its flame is not very hot.

Stoves: Most gimbaled propane stoves come with a sturdy metal rail surrounding the burner top that's designed for securing screw-on pan holder arms, one set for each burner. The back of a gimbaled stove should have counterweights to keep it balanced when the oven door is open, and for really heavy seas, the stove should be able to be secured steady to prevent damage to the gimbal system.

Propane tanks are easily refilled in Latin American and Caribbean ports. Onboard propane plumbing should include a well mounted electric solenoid and safety switch with a red light or clicker to remind you that pressurized gas is in the line. Install a "sniffer" device as well. Turn off the switch and let the flame extinguish itself,

Hearth on the High Seas: A good marine stove is designed with sea rails to make cooking underway safe and easy. The extra grab bar is a good idea.

then close the burner valve; this burns off the gas in the line between the solenoid and the stove, so the heavy gas doesn't find its way into your bilge. Ventilate the bilge with a spark-proof blower several times a day – and before you start the engine or generator. Be scrupulously safety conscious when cooking with propane.

Electric stoves are most common on powerboats. Especially if you have a non-gimbaled electric stove, it should be fitted with a metal rail around the top for securing screw-on pan holder arms, one set for each burner. Have a stainless steel shop fabricate rails for your stove. Built-in stoves are most common on powerboats, but a free-standing stove must be built into the cabinetry. An auxiliary generator usually must run all during the baking. If your generator is shaky, keep a back-up stove for use on deck in an emergency, such as a 2-burner Coleman propane stove or a Sea-Swing kerosene burner. Pat brings a tiny back-packing stove on some of our deliveries, and she has had to use it aboard some very luxurious yachts when their massive generator plants have failed to fire up.

Microwave ovens are very practical in tropical climates, because they create so little heat, and the low-wattage models are increasingly popular for sailboats. But be sure the interior is large enough to hold a standard 9" x 13" baking dish, and be sure to bolt the microwave in place while you're installing it. With a little practice, a good cook can make nearly everything in a microwave – except bread. Convection ovens generate intense heat, but they cook much faster than gas or electric ovens.

Refrigeration: Some form of refrigeration is essential for civilized cruising in the tropics. Powerboats often use household-type refrigerators, but they must be especially well secured into the bulkhead, and the doors should have pin-type keepers. *During a rough passage on one of John's first deliveries, a huge household refridgerator that wasn't secured started waltzing itself slowly but steadily across the galley floor, flapping its doors wildly with each roll, flinging out its entire contents. Within seconds the galley floor was covered in broken glass and olive oil; now the unwieldy fridge threatened to skid and crash through the side of the boat, so glass or no glass, he had to wrestle it back into place.*

Block ice made from potable water is a rare find in tropic cruising ports, and since marine freezer units have become smaller and more efficient each season, refrigeration is an essential – even on sailboats. A fridge box that loads from the top prevents cold air from escaping (Remember all the ping-pong balls falling out each time the box is opened?), even though food on the bottom tends to get lost or squashed. Engine-compressor systems (110-volt) seem to be more efficient and more reliable than 12-volt battery powered chillers and propane-powered refrigerators. To conserve your main refrigeration, keep cold drinks in a separate ice chest that's secured outside the galley.

TIPS: Since you'll be barefoot 98% of the time, you can improve safety and comfort in your galley by installing one large piece of Berber-type outdoor carpet shaped to exactly cover your galley floor; small pieces only skid around. Sinks should be deep double basins, and a cutting-board cover on one side increases counter space – a premium on any boat. Drawers and cupboard doors must latch securely when closed; the cupboard doors that lift out of their hinges can become airborne when the boat drops off a wave top. Louvered doors promote better ventilation. Keep knives stowed flat in a drawer, never left in a heavy wooden block like lethal missiles primed for launching. Anything movable needs a regular stowing place while underway.

Provisioning: Food and outfitting items for this extensive of a cruising route could probably submerge your waterline, but it's manageable if you stay organized. The typical galley barely contain enough stowage room for the food ingredients and cooking utensils that are used on a daily basis, so bulkier staples will need to be stowed in bins, lockers and dry bilge compartments scattered throughout the boat, like squirrel stashes. Make a Master Inventory as you buy foods, leaving space to update it later as you consume and re-provision down south. Make a Stowage Diagram of your stash spots and what's in each one, because it's surprisingly easy to lose things.

For your initial provisioning, CostCo and other discount stores are worth the membership fee. Choose 12 medium cans of something rather than one giant can – unless you have unlimited refrigerator space and regularly feed six or eight people for each meal. Stock up on top-quality paper products in the U.S. (paper plates, towels, TP, tampons, etc.), because elsewhere they're flimsier or unavailable. Food items that may be difficult to find in rural or coastal Mexico, Central America and the western Caribbean are: albacore packed in water, canned chicken, brown rice, whole wheat flour, soy flour, ketchup or peanut butter made without a ton of sugar, canned tomatoes, herbal or seasoned vinegars, plain yogurt, diet sodas or diet drink mixes, instant soup cups and seedless jams. Fresh milk is sometimes sour, but pint and quart cartons of ultra-pasteurized milk are readily available; it doesn't require refrigeration until opened. If you absolutely must have

sun-dried julienned tomatoes packed in extra virgin olive oil, or tangerine chutney, or Scandinavian goose pate, then definitely do stock up on them before leaving your home port.

Re-provisioning is not especially difficult for most boaters, so don't think you have to sink the boat with your initial provisioning. Thanks to free trade, all the major cruising ports now have at least one modern air-conditioned supermarket with a large selection of canned, frozen and fresh foods at reasonable prices. The newer ones have a deli to die for. Commercial Mexicana is the most prevalent chain of food stores, and there's also WalMart, CostCo, Price Club and Ace Hardware. Mom & pop groceries have sporadic supplies but usually good quality.

The best places to plan a major re-provisioning along this route are: Puerto Vallarta, Acapulco, Puntarenas, Balboa, San Andres, Livingston near the Rio Dulce, French Harbor on Roatan Island, and Isla Mujeres.

Most voyagers say they're are interested in expanding their horizons with new cultural experiences, and one of the most interesting we've found is to go shopping in a "mercado central" – one tall roof sheltering dozens of individually run booths or stalls. Every municipality has at least one mercado central, and the shop keepers love to brag about their fresh cilantro, yucca, choyote, membrilla, arroz, carnes and flores. Take along a dictionary plus your own dock cart, woven shopping bags, and bug-proof egg cartons.

Ship Keeping

It's a good idea to have access to one week's supply of potable water on this route. Reverse osmosis **watermakers** transform raw sea water into delicious drinking water, enabling you to cruise longer and farther between port calls. So they're almost an essential for long-range cruising. Especially after heavy rains, the tap water in many ports contains bacteria that your gastro-intestinal tract probably won't like. Even if it hasn't rained lately, it's a good idea to arrive in Cabo San Lucas and Acapulco with your water tanks full.

Most 5-kw generators can handle the power draw, but the watermaker system should be professionally installed and plumbed. Many sailboat alternators can run the newer 12-volt watermakers, setting them free from the marina hose. The additional ultra-violet (UV) step has proven worthwhile; if it's plumbed to treat the water moving from your tanks to the faucet, it will purify any contaminated public water you may have to take onboard. Carry extra spare parts and filters, because they're difficult to find down south. Never ever make water inside a town harbor. Even when making water off shore, be sure there's no oil on the surface or any natural sealife contamination – such as the beginnings of a red tide or coral spawn.

If you don't have a water-maker, plumb salt water and fresh to the galley sink with foot pumps to encourage fresh water conservation. Wash and rinse everything with salt water, then do a second rinse with fresh water. Using raw sea water inside any of the larger harbors is inadvisable.

Chlorine Treatment: Chlorine is the most common treatment for iffy fresh-water tanks. Pat uses from 1/8th to 1/4 cup (about three to six tablespoons, or nine to 18 teaspoons) of Clorox bleach per 100 gallons of fresh water, depending on how suspect the water is. Put a few teaspoons of chlorine bleach into the fill tube every few minutes while you're filling the tank. Never add chlorine all at once to the top of a full tank: it can't reach the bottom, and the high concentration of chlorine can corrode pipe connections and destroy the sensor inside your water heater. Immediately after treating a tank with chlorine, you need to let most of the chlorine gas escape, so scrub away any spills from around the deck fills, then leave the deck caps open for 12 hours or so – until the bleach smell disappears from the deck fills and also from water flowing from the faucets inside.

TIP: To improve the flavor of water in a chlorine-treated tank, add one bottle of white wine.

Linens: Getting adequate sleep aboard a moving vessel (or even an anchored one) takes some practice – and special **bedding**. A 4- to 6-inch mattress

21

made of high-quality foam-rubber absorbs the constant motion and allows you to sleep more safely; an inner-spring mattress accentuates even the slight motion of being at anchor. Adding a 1-inch layer of "egg-crate" foam beneath the sheets ventilates them, keeping you cooler, and cradles you better. Sheets should be fine gauge 100% cotton to wick moisture from your body – thus helping to cool you.

Mildew: To kill the spores without using toxins, spray and wipe musty surfaces with an ammonia solution or plain white vinegar, then air out dank spaces often. To protect bread loaves, mist them lightly with cider vinegar and let dry before wrapping.

Bugs: To prevent cockroach infestation, never allow cardboard boxes to come on board; they conceal live critters and their eggs. Instead, unload grocery cartons in the dinghy and take the cartons back to shore right away. If you do get cockroaches, one non-toxic killer is finely powdered borax. Sprinkle the powder along roach routes; their feet and feelers get coated, and they ingest it while cleaning themselves. To kill weevil eggs hidden inside packages of dry flour-type mixes, microwave each package on high for 5 minutes. Avon brand's Skin So Soft lotion serves well as a non-toxic repellent of biting sand flies and the dreaded (but infrequent) no-see-'ems. To repel mosquitoes from belowdecks without using poison, try smudging small chunks of clean coconut husk (the brown outer fibers) in a deep ceramic bowl; the light smoke smells rather nice to humans. The "mosquito coils" that burn link green incense all night are fairly effective but slightly toxic; if you lose the coil holder, break out the center inch of the coil, prop the remaining coil over the narrow neck of a glass soda bottle, and place it in the sink to burn safely overnight.

Air conditioning is greatly appreciated in the tropics, especially for powerboats. Powerboats are seldom designed with natural ventilation in mind. However, the abundant humidity can cause the drip pans to overflow pretty regularly. Clean the drains regularly or they'll plug up. If the AC piping behind the interior walls or ceiling hasn't been properly insulated, it can sweat heavily, stain the interior and breed mildew. No air conditioning? Mount small **electric fans** in the galley and berthing areas to make life possible in the tropics.

Deck awnings and wind scoops on sailboats can bring down the interior temperature by 10°F or more. Rain awnings over the companionway and deck hatches let you breath during the warm downpours. For a powerboat, the windshield needs an exterior sun screen that snaps on whenever you're not underway. For all other interior windows, the translucent kind of 2-ply shades constructed like a honey-comb are excellent for keeping the heat out without darkening the cabin too much.

Safety & Engineering

One very wise old salt stated, "A boat can't have too many bilge pumps." To that we can add only, "Amen!"

Bilge Pumps: Depending on the size and kind of boat, two or three electric Rule-type pumps with built-in strainers are fine for normal use, and a great accessory is the solid-state circuitry bilge alarm that indicates when water is rising past a pre-set depth. A bilge pump with a float switch needs a red light mounted on the control panel or near the helm station to indicate when it's running; when the red light comes on, you'll know that pump's working. But if the red light stays on, you'll know you have either a high-water situation – or you have a jammed float switch that should be unjammed before the pump burns itself out.

Install a back-up pump, too. A manually operated, double-diaphragm bilge pump should be permanently mounted and plumbed, ready to go, with easy access during high water. If the handle is removable, mount the handle's special bracket or clips next to the pump. Carry a spare handle.

For serious emergencies, the clutch-geared engine-driven pumps generally move the largest amount of water most efficiently. Powerboats can often rig their engine water pumps to double as bilge pumps, but it's a good idea to also plumb a strainer in line so it's only a matter of turning a valve to begin de-watering the engine room.

Fuel System: In the engine room, a well designed fuel filtration system will help eliminate water and dirty sediments, which are the major contaminants in southern waters. Dual Racor filters should be plumbed so that if one filter needs to be changed, the second filter can then be brought on line without shutting down the engine. This second filter can then be changed. Vacuum gauges on the filters will show you how quickly the filters are clogging up, so you'll have a good idea in advance of when they'll need to be changed. The process of bleeding the system is speedier with an electric fuel prime pump than it is with a manual fuel pump. (Learn how to bleed your engine injectorsfuel while you're still at your own dock.)

If you're going to be schlepping fuel in jerry jugs from remote villages, then take along a "Baja fuel filter." Many cruisers make their own, and they're marketed in Southern California and South Florida. Basically, a Baja fuel filter is just a box-shaped funnel with two or three compartments and screens to filter out water and dirt while you're fueling – before it goes into your tank. However, diesel is generally clean at Turtle Bay, San Carlos in Mag Bay, Cabo San Lucas and La Paz – places that once were known for their dirty fuels.

Electricity: Depending on your requirements for current, you need at least two batteries. One should be isolated to serve ONLY as your emergency-start battery. A third battery, disconnected but charged, can be held in reserve to start the engine with jumper cables when all else fails. Have a battery-test indicator and monitor it as part of your daily routine. Some boaters have permanently mounted photo-voltaic panels in their cabin tops to serve as trickle chargers. "Hot battery insurance" in any form is highly recommended.

Generators: Having 110-volt electric current makes cruising more like home. Main engine-driven "cruise generators" are adequate for sailboats, although they are troublesome. Accurate construction of the mounts is important, and the voltage and cycles must be regulated carefully. For smaller boats, Honda makes a small gasoline portable generator that, combined with a battery charger, helps get the engine started in a tight spot.

For larger boats, a separate diesel generator is preferable to a cruise generator, and the best idea is to have two separate generators. This lets you either split the load or let one generator cool down while you run each generator only on alternate days.

Medical Kit: Most of the first-aid kits sold in marine stores are hardly more than Band-Aid kits. But some doctors in the Florida and California boating communities have put together advanced medical kits that are complete and well organized. Some of these doctors can even be reached by high seas radio for emergency consultation.

Otherwise, you can put together your own medical kit as outlined in the well-known book "*Advanced First Aid Afloat*" by Dr. Peter F. Eastman. It's the best and most compact medical manual I've found. Study it before you depart and take it along.

Consult with your own doctor, too, and be sure to get written prescriptions to take along. Unless you require rare, experimental or non-generic drugs, you'll probably be able to get your prescriptions filled a "*farmacia*" in any port in Mexico and Central America – probably at a lower cost, too. If you need an experimental drug or one that's extremely new on the market, ask you doctor to research its foreign availability for you.

Unlike the old days, doctors and nurses (*medicos*) are generally available at rural clinics, and most villages have at least one *farmacia* with a person licensed to write non-narcotic prescriptions.

Inside the medical kit, keep one photocopy of each written prescription (except for over-the-counter drugs), because you could be asked to show it during routine boardings and inspections.

Aside from your serious Medical Kit, keep the following item handy for everyday use: waterproof bandage strips, antiseptic ointment and liquid wash, eye wash, aspirin or other OTC pain/fever reducers, plus your favorite sea-sickness pills and cold remedies.

☑ Outfitting Check Lists

John has used this following set of check-lists as the basis for outfitting and preparing more than 100 different pleasure and commercial boats that he's then delivered along this exact route.

Each vessel has its own unique inventory of brand-name devices, and each gizmo has its own list of factory parts; but you can easily adapt these lists below to your vessel's specific needs.

☑ Safety Equipment

- all the equipment required to pass U.S. Coast Guard inspection, including the proper size bell for your vessel and your placards for pollution control and garbage management.
- fire extinguishers, proper number and type, within date.
- PFDs for all onboard plus guests, with whistle and/or strobe attached.
- man-overboard system. (Perform surprise M.O. drill.)
- safety harnesses that clip into jack lines.
- jack lines or special life lines to lead forward, aft.
- flare gun and fresh flares.
- radar reflector (sailboats only).
- heaving line.
- emergency tiller.
- duct tape.
- collision kit including bungs (tapered wooden plugs for hull).
- automatically inflatable life raft, freshly certified.
- EPIRB (emergency position indicating radio beacon), fresh battery.
- strobe light.
- signaling mirror.
- ditch kit.

☑ Spare Parts Lists

Main engines
- 1 complete rebuild kit for raw-water pump, plus two impellers.
- 1 fresh-water pump.
- 1 injector per engine (minimum).
- 1 complete set of belts.
- 1 complete set of engine gaskets.
- 1 starter (correct rotation), or solenoids

and brushes.
- 1 spare fuel pump (optional).
- 1 alternator, if only way of making electricity.
- hoses and clamps of needed sizes for fresh and salt water.
- engine fuel filters, 2 cases per engine.
- engine manuals: shop, operator, repair.
- filter cores (Racor), 1 case per engine.
- lube oil filters, 2 cases per engine.
- spare fuel lines, flaring tool.

☑ **Generators**
- 1 injector per generator (minimum).
- 1 complete set of belts per generator.
- 1 generator starter, or at least solenoid and brushes.
- 1 generator shut-down solenoid.
- 1 complete raw-water rebuild kit per generator, plus 2 spare impellers.
- 1 case Racor filter cores.
- 1 case oil filters.
- 1 complete gasket set.
- 2 engine fuel filters per generator.
- hoses and clamps for fresh and salt water.

☑ **Tools**
- Craftsman socket sets in ¼ inch, 3/8 inch, ½ inch.
- box end wrenches, ¼ inch to 1-¼ inch.
- two items of above in metric if applicable.
- 3 crescent wrenches: 6- 10- and 16-inch.
- 3 pair channel locks (water-pump pliers), small, medium, large.
- 2 vice grips, small narrow jaw, medium wide jaw.
- 1 side cutters (dikes).
- 1 good quality wire strippers/crimpers.
- 1 set Allen wrenches, small to large.
- 1 set feeler gauges.
- 1 ball-peen hammer.
- 1 good cold chisel.
- 1 center punch.
- 2 regular punches.
- 2 pipe wrenches, medium & large.

- 1 electric 3/8-inch drill motor, plus 2 sets metal bits.
- 1 hack saw, two coarse blades.
- 1 razor knife, spare blades.
- 1 12-volt test light.
- 1 multi-meter tester with alligator clamps.
- 1 pair pliers with wide jaw.
- 1 good quality filter wrench.
- 2 sets of screw drivers, Phillips and slot head.

☑ **General**
- prop, shaft, and puller
- distilled water and battery hydrometer (unless gel cells).
- bilge pump and float switch.
- fresh-water pump, or repair kit and back-up motor for burn out.
- refrigeration belts, freon, drier, solenoid valve.
- assorted nuts, bolts, washers, screws.
- spark plugs for outboard motor.
- lube oil.
- shaft packing material in proper width.
- wooden bungs for through-hulls (fastened near each through hull).
- hydraulic fluid.
- diaphragms or seals for steering system.
- long jumper cables.
- come-along.
- underwater epoxy.
- gasket material, sheet and liquid.
- electrical wire, black tape, assorted lugs, connectors, switches, fuses, breakers.
- soldering gun, solder with flux.
- light bulbs for 110- , 12- and 24-volt.
- light bulbs for running lights and navigation lights.
- autopilot relays and connectors.
- paper for WxFax.
- PL-259 connectors, RG-58U cabling, SWR bridge.
- fuses for all electrical devices, check each manual for spares recommendations.

Cruising Ports

☑ **Deck Gear**
- 3 very large fenders (ball or teardrop type, not tubular).
- 4 Panama Canal lines (with eyes, 125-ft. each) or 600-ft. spool of 3-strand.
- flashlights, spare batteries and bulbs.
- back-up anchor with at least 35 feet of 3/8-inch chain (if no 2nd anchor).
- monel seizing wire for anchor shackle pin.
- leather or rubber chafing gear.
- dinghy and motor, chocks and tie downs, covers.
- hose, nontoxic (shipping water & washdown).
- washdown bucket, brush, chamois.
- materials: paper towels, cotton rags (diapers), Murphy's oil soap for wood, furniture polish, Simple Green or deck soap, stainless steel polish, Parson's ammonia cleaner, denatured alcohol, tar remover, toilet cleaner & brush, exterior & interior paints & brushes, paint thinner, teak cleaner & oil, varnish, sand papers, brass wool.

☑ **Sailing Gear**
- 2 complete turnbuckles in each size found onboard.
- cotter pins or cir-clips for standing rigging.
- 1 wire forestay and 1 backstay, made up with fittings on one end.
- Nico-press swedge tool, thimbles and zincs in size for stays above.
- 2 halyards, made up with fittings.
- 2 spare winch handles.
- mast tangs, or flat stock to fabricate replacements.
- sail cloth and repair kit.
- sail hanks and slides.
- shackles: assorted swivel, snap and pin.
- line: assorted braided and 3-strand.
- rigging blocks: assorted.

☑ **Official Stuff**
- ensign, staff, flag halyard.
- foreign courtesy flags for each country (Mexico, Grand Cayman, Honduras, Guatemala, Colombia, Panama, Costa Rica; also perhaps El Salvador and Nicaragua).
- Q-flag (yellow quarantine flag).
- ship's papers (document, registration, bill of sale, captain's license, crew list, passports and visas, fishing permits and licenses, port clearance papers, permisso letters, etc.)
- photocopies of ship's papers, especially the document and one of each passport.

☑ **Navigation Gear**
- hand bearing compass.
- sextant and chronometer.
- WWV weather-radio receiver.
- binoculars.
- hand-held VHF radio.
- parallel rulers or rolling plotter.
- dividers (lead in one end for radar plotting).
- #2 soft lead pencils, sharpener, erasers.
- ship's log book.
- nautical almanac.
- *"Sailing Directions"*
- *"Sight Reduction Tables"*
- *"Tidal Stream Atlas"*
- *"Tide Tables"*
- *"Light List"*
- *"Reeds Nautical Almanac"* for Pacific and Caribbean. (Reeds contains the five publications listed above.)
- *"Mariner's Guide to Single Side Band"* Frederick Graves.
- *"World Wide Weather Broadcasts"*
- *"MexWX: Mexico Weather for Boaters"* John Rains.
- paper charts.

The next two chapter discuss preparing the mariners for this adventure and the official paperwork requirements. Then we'll jump into the actual cruising ports and some intermediate stopovers – from Florida to California via the Panama Canal.

Chapter 2
Self Preparation

Some people spend all their time working on their boats, and then they immediately take off on their long cruise – only to discover that they themselves aren't adequately prepared.

Have you given yourself the skills to navigate unknown waters, to predict the weather, to fix their mechanical equipment, to treat medical emergencies, to communicate with Spanish-speaking officials and locals -- all on a daily level without undue stress?

Cruising Skills

Although every member of the crew should posses some kind of specialized "cruising skills" or training (even guests), it's always the skipper's position that carries the most responsibility on board any vessel. In the boating world, this cruising voyage is usually his or her fondest dream, but it's a dream that demands extensive planning and self preparation. The crew's lives will depend on the depth of the skipper's skills and knowledge.

Read the Literature: Mankind has been going to sea since it was there. He's been writing about it since before the pyramids were built. Davie Jones' Locker would burst with the books and publications dealing with sea-related subjects that are available today. In one of our Appendices, we've recommended some of the publications we think are most helpful for boaters making this adventurous voyage. Whether you're a green boot or a 4-striped old salt, this great storehouse of nautical information will serve you well.

One of the most important books you can study is Rules of the Road – the international code of conduct (rules for maneuvering vessels to avoid collisions, how to read buoy systems, etc.) that every skipper is expected to know by heart and obey. Most importantly, it tells you what all those weird running lights signify on each kind of vessel you'll be encountering, so you'll know which direction it's heading (Toward you? Crossing your bow? Collision course?), whether it's engaged in fishing or dredging, whether it's anchored or drifting, etc. – not just which vessel has the right of way and what your action should be.

Advanced Boating Classes: Besides independent reading, we strongly recommend that you (skipper and crew) complete as many as possible of the excellent boating courses offered by the U.S. Coast Guard Auxiliary, the U.S. Power Squadron, your local chandlers, yacht clubs or community colleges. Start with a course (or series of courses) in basic coastal navigation – and master this vital craft thoroughly before you move on. The theory of coastal navigation is easy to comprehend in the classroom, but it's tough to actually practice. A complete and agile command of coastal navigation is vital to your safety and comfort on the route described in this book.

Although celestial navigation is highly recommended – and it might be useful on some smaller boats making the passages between Cabo San Lucas and Puerto Vallarta, between Key West and Cozumel, between Puerto Madero and Marina Flamingo, between Roatan and Providencia – it's only a supplement to your coastal navigation skills.

Weather Wisdom: Deciphering the vagaries of day-to-day weather offshore or in unfamiliar waters becomes much easier when you first understand the basic principles of meteorology. That's exactly why John wrote "**MexWX: Mexico Weather for Boaters**." Radio buffs will recognize WX (pronounced "wex") which is radio short-hand for "weather."

Also, many community colleges offer summary classes on meteorology, especially in coastal regions of the U.S., while introductory meteorology courses available through 4-year universities may be geared more toward a career in meteorology. We've encountered remarkably little severe weather in our sea-going experience, but we must attribute this good fortune to three things: we've garnered a pretty good understanding of the principles of meteorology, we work hard every day to monitor all available weather data, and we try to "pick our weather" – meaning we try to avoid going where the bad weather is when it's really bad.

Medical Savvy: Because vessels often travel many days beyond the reach of professional medical care, the skipper often

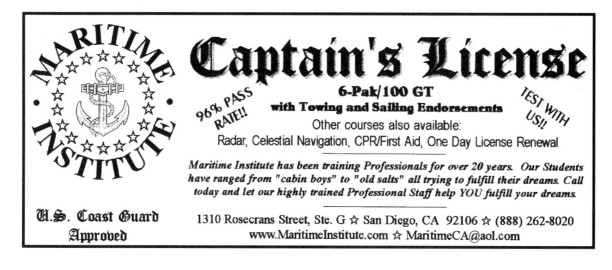

becomes the ship's doctor, too. If not the skipper, then at least one person on board must complete a good First Aid & CPR class, such as those given by local Red Cross organizations. It's not uncommon for the whole crew to take such classes together.

People who are frail due to age or who have serious health problems probably should not undertake this entire cruising route without first getting professional medical training specific to their problems. Look into a medical evacuation service, and take along any special equipment you may need.

Language Skills: Learn as much Spanish as you can before embarking on this route, because after you pass the first few easy-access "resort ports" such as Cozumel or Cabo San Lucas, you'll be traveling in places where little or no English is spoken. Sure, anyone can order "*mas cervezas, por favor*" in a beach palapa – but can you understand the VHF storm report that's broadcast by the Port Captain? Can you explain to a mechanic that your transmission seals were replaced just after the noise started, not before? Can you ask whether or not the doctor had received your last message yet? Can you find out whether or not the bus you're boarding comes back the same day? (See the Appendices for Spanish boating terms.)

In Southern California and South Florida, there's a growing trend for small groups of boaters who are planning to cruise Mexico and Central America to form their own Spanish-language classes by hiring a local teacher; the curriculum can be tailored especially for their own needs. Our recommendation is that you become fluid

(not the same as fluent) in at least the present tense plus know when NOT to use the familiar forms of address – before you head south.

Buddy Boating: An extra advantage from taking all these cruising-skills classes mentioned above is that you'll meet other folks heading south. Classmates often develop friendships or become "buddy boats" within the annual flotilla heading south.

Being a buddy can range from simply giving the other folks the "high sign" as they finally make a major departure - to paying attention to the fact that they did or did not arrive safely in the anchorage - to maintaining a regular VHF radio schedule during passages. But it should feel right for both boat-loads of buddies.

Boaters link up for various reasons: "Their boat and our boat travel at about the same speed, so we're both going to start this next offshore passage on the same day." "They have the weather fax and we have the scuba gear, so we're going to spend the summer in Costa Rica together." "Our kids have become inseparable buddies, so we decided to stop together in some of the more remote destinations."

But it's also a good idea for buddy boaters to retain their option for occasional independence and privacy.

Sea Trials Will Breed Self Confidence

Give yourself and your entire crew plenty of sea trials before you head south. You can't overdo practicing your navigation, seamanship and anchoring skills within your local waters. Work on all your at-sea techniques: Plot your position every 15 minutes with running fixes and radar fixes; practice setting and retrieving a drogue; get out into a shipping lane and then call one particular ship on VHF (giving your latitude and longitude) to see whether they can see you.

Develop your own hand signals between the helm and bow, then switch places and let the first mate up anchor and get the boat underway. Practice anchoring in various weather conditions and awkward locations where you must use bow and stern anchors. Such sea trials will quickly point out which skills still need a little polishing, and – with practice – will breed that indispensable sense of mutual trust and individual self confidence.

Get used to being underway at night. Many folks we've met while cruising southern waters are afraid to be underway in the dark, and they always try to be settled into a safe spot before sunset. We consider that to be nearly impossible, because it forces you to enter anchorages that are dangerous or marginal at best. In those cases, you'd be much safer to remain at sea throughout the night.

Veteran cruisers will concur that some of their fondest memories were created during the long hours of a night's run – phosphorescence glowing beneath the hull, stars singing above, and just your boat's own sounds keeping you company. Besides, it's impossible to bypass some of the less pleasant ports along this route within a single day's run.

Develop your cruising confidence by making some overnight mini-cruises that require staying off shore all night long as well as entering a lighted port in the dark. This should teach you about using the Rules of the Road, as well as to distinguish the critical navigation lights from a busy background. This actually gets much easier the more you practice it. (If you absolutely cannot cope with night voyaging, you should probably rethink the idea of extended cruising.) Building sea time isn't work, it's fun.

Personal Preparations

Cruising Clothing: Once they embark on the tropical voyage this book covers, most boaters live in shorts and T-shirts on a daily basis. Pure cotton and mostly-cotton blend fabrics are most successful. Flip flops and sports shoes suffice for shore. In really hot weather you might often dress for the entire day aboard your boat by putting on a swimming suit. A sun dress or tank top and non-iron broom skirt are typical attire for everyday cocktails in your neighbor's cockpit, while some men dress up for these non-occasions by switching to a non-holey T-shirt. All this is fine within the narrow yachtie community.

But for a trip to the Port Captain's office or other local authorities – or going downtown in the bigger cities or to big airports, being dressed so casually is taken by the locals as a sign of social disrespect to them. For such occasions, we recommend that men wear their most presentable shorts or long pants, and shoes rather than sandals. For women, either longer shorts, longer skirts or slacks are much better than short shorts or short skirts.

For passagemaking, your rain gear jacket should be light-weight (yellow or bright red for safety) and well ventilated. When the rain is so warm most folks don't bother with the bottoms – just a safety harness over the jacket. A windbreaker and a few cotton sweaters serve for rare cool evenings on the hook.

$$$

Money: Most of the countries covered in this guidebook have instant cash machines located inside banks, larger stores and even on the grounds of the Acapulco Yacht Club. You can get a cash advance against your Visa/MC or

American Express card. So ask your home-port bank how you can access your accounts from abroad. Visa and Master Charge are widely accepted for payment; some others are not. Often at marinas and fuel docks, you can use your credit card to pay your bill.

However, this requires that you've already designated some reliable person back home to promptly pay your monthly credit-card bills. One late payment and you'll probably be denied access from outside the U.S. Read "Keeping the Home Fires Burning" on the next page.

Start off with some cash. Unfortunately, $100 bills can be very difficult to break, because they must be in perfect condition (no bent or missing corners) and because no one ever has change. Take plenty of $20s in good condition. When arriving in a new country, make a bank visit to convert to the local currency. Otherwise, if you change dollars on the street, you'll lose money value in the conversion process. Travelers checks are often accepted in larger stores and exchange houses – but seldom in smaller shops. Clerks usually want to write your passport number on each cashiers check.

Telephones: If you aren't careful, you can get stung by the rates in the phone booths that advertise they'll just bill your Visa/MC or AmEx credit cards for calls to the U.S. Many of us *Norte Americanos* are so used to using phones without first asking for the rates that we're often aghast when our enormous bill for that simple call finally arrives a few months later. Always ask first. Be aware that a collect call to the U.S. is cheaper than paying for the call locally, due to local taxes.

Pre-paid telephone cards are becoming the rule rather than the exception. They're sold in almost every corner store, in specific denominations, like 50 and 100 pesos. You'll need them even to place a local call, because many phones no longer accept coins. However, before you buy a packet of phone cards, find out what geographic area they're good for within that country; a card purchased in Ensenada may not work in Cabo San Lucas.

On some phones, you can access your home-port long-distance carrier, like AT&T, MCI, Sprint, by using your home-port long-distance carrier credit card, which is certainly more convenient. But to do this, you must ask that carrier for access number for each country.

Cellular phones and satellite phones are increasingly practical for long-range cruisers venturing outside the U.S. Read the section on Communication Radios in Chapter One.

Keep the Home Fires Burning:
Even free spirits have to keep the gears of their home world spinning away smoothly. In fact, the more smoothly your financial and familial affairs back home continue to operate, the more free you'll be during your cruise.

Get all your financial affairs in top order before you depart, hopefully so that they can continue to function without major changes or decision requirements for up to a year at a stretch – even though most cruisers fly back home at least once a year.

It's a good idea to designate one very capable, responsible and trusted person to act with your **"power of attorney"** – freeing you from worry about daily details. This is not a simple favor to ask. Perhaps you'll specifically limit him/her to (a.) opening all your mail, (b.) fielding all your phone calls, (c.) forwarding all important stuff to you at designated ports, and (d.) accessing one of your bank accounts solely for the purpose of making all your deposits and paying all your bills. Spell out the duties clearly, and try to address unanticipated problems. Then ask your favorite attorney to help you and your designee draw up a simple Power of Attorney.

It's probably a good idea to designate one person as your **social liaison**, and, once you're traveling, to regularly phone him/her directly, so that one person will always know (a.) your present whereabouts, (b.) your next port, and (c.) at least two alternate routes in case of bad weather or mechanical breakdown. This makes it much easier and less confusing when friends and family try to link up with you – off in the wild blue yonder in places they can't pronounce or find in the Atlas Britannica, places the travel agents don't believe exist. And if you should ever "go missing," it will certainly hasten your rescue – or prevent a needless Search & Rescue Operation when you're simply following your pre-designated Plan B.

Some very sociable friends of ours (let's call them the Smiths) planned to cruise from Florida to Cuba and then to Mexico during December and January one year. They forgot to cancel some very tentative plans to maybe meet one of their adult children in Havana sometime around Christmas, and when, by January 10th, the kids still hadn't heard where the family rendezvous was to take place, they panicked. They called every one of their parents' friends across the U.S., each person becoming more worried – and calling more friends. A request for on-air information about the Smiths' whereabouts was emailed to one of the cruising ham radio nets

covering that area, but no response was ever heard. Just before someone reported to the U.S. Coast Guard that the Smiths were obviously "missing at sea somewhere near Cuba," they arrived in Isla Mujeres and called home. Key West had been too crowded and they hadn't liked Cuba enough to stay very long, so they decided instead to explore the Yucatan coast without guests.

Unless you're completely cut off from family and friends back home, having one person act as liaison about your whereabouts is usually more than worth the tiny effort on your part.

Mail Forwarding: This is similar to what your power-of-attorney person would do for you, but it's usually a considerably less personal service. You forward your home and or office mail via the post office to your hired mail forwarder, and they hold it all until you  reach your next major port, and they send it all in one big package by FedEx, DHL, Estafeta or one of the international express shippers. Some services will receive your return package full of letters and bill payments to be stamped and sent out for you.

The Firearms Issue: This controversy rekindles itself each fall when the fleet of cruising boats heads south. Our recommendation is not to carry firearms on board your boat while you're cruising along the route described in this book, most of it outside U.S. waters.

Our reasons are many, but the most obvious is that Mexico, which sits astride the water route between Florida and California, now strictly enforces its gun laws. Their laws make it impossible for your vessel to legally carry a gun while transiting their waters. Remember, that right to bear arms starts and ends at the U.S. border.

A gun will usually get you into more trouble than it could ever keep you out of. They can back fire, literally and figuratively. Introducing a gun into a volatile situation presupposes that it will be used (pushing it to lethal proportions), and it might not be used by you. In many cases, the presence of a gun has turned a living robbery victim into a murder victim. Also, the corrosive marine environment is murder on a gun's delicate firing mechanisms, making a gun more prone to misfire or backfire in your face.

In Jimmy Cornell's book "Ocean Cruising Survey," he asked 100 skippers who were long-distance cruising in the Pacific about this hot topic. Although the majority were firmly against the idea of carrying guns onboard, 38 of them did so anyway.

Each country has its own rules, and when you're boarded at sea, one of the the first question they ask is "Are there any firearms on board?" Then they search. In many countries, having undeclared weapons is a major crime punishable by immediate imprisonment, do not pass GO.

In other countries, you must provide a sturdy lockable built-in gun cabinet to hold all your weapons and ammo. They'll place their Customs seal over the lock, to be kept in place until they remove it when you check out. Or, they'll confiscate all firearms and ammo until you come back to that port to check directly out of that country, which usually isn't a practical itinerary for you.

Alternatives for Security: Lots of effective security measures can be take without firearms.

✓ Easiest, don't take your boat to places known for smuggling trouble, and always pay attention to what's going on around you, because innocent bystanders fall prey. Smugglers ply anything from drugs to designer jeans to refrigerators.

✓ Pet dogs are one of the most effective deterents. However, check out the local quarantine laws first.

✓ Day or night, keep theft-prone items stowed below decks, especially when you enter a new port. Once desirable items have been visible on deck, they attract thieves who will return even after they're stowed below. Such items are outboard motors, dinghy gas tanks, small generators and power tools, fishing rods and reels, tool boxes, spools of yacht braid, hand-held VHF radios and GPS units.

✓ When anchored at night, pull in the boarding ladder and fenders, close the life lines. Josh Slocum sprinkled tcks on deck, and we've seen folks string treble hooks on fishing line around the perimeter of their boat.

✓ An electronic motion sensor with a laser light and loud alarm can be installed pretty easily on any boat. It's probably best to set the trigger on the boat's main entrance to the cabin area, but exclude anything that normally swings as the boat floats, such as loose drapery, gimballed electronics or hanging lamps.

✓ One inexpensive alternative to such a sophisticated system is the battery-operated motion-detector plastic frog that's made for keeping pets out of the garden. It will croak loudly if an intruder enters your main salon, or even if a pelican lands on your deck. They're found in garden supply shops.

✓ For personal protection, a flare pistol and a spear gun are formidable deterrants, and they're normally carried on board anyway.

✓ Pepper spray comes in a wide variety of delivery devices, ranging from things that look like flashlights to paperback books to hand guns.

✓ Mace stings longer than pepper spray and in some places requires a safety-class certificate in order to purchase it.

✓ The newer toy water guns that pack a whallop and shoot a good quart of water in a hard blast would certainly surprise an intruder.

✓ Our choice is a sling shot and a handfull of marbles.

Chapter 3
The Paperwork Cha Cha

Traveling the world in a boat can be very exciting. If you haven't experienced crossing international borders on your own before, you're likely to be surprised how much paper shuffling and rubber stamping is involved. Years ago, when we began writing for varioius boating magazines about the vessel clearance process in foreign countries, there were always so many variables and confusing steps involved in this bureaucratic dance that we began dubbing it the "Paperwork Cha Cha." As long as you allow the bureaucratic process plenty of time, it's just another dance.

As with all citizens of the world, you, as the captain, are required to "present yourself" and all the ship's official paperwork each time you enter and exit any foreign country, and each time you enter or exit a major cruising port. And sometimes the officials come to you, aboard your boat. This is called the port clearance procedures. You'll have to visit several different governmental offices in a specific order. Each office has its own special forms and procedures, and from time to time, a country

or port will change ("streamline") its forms or procedures. The main reason they do this is to keep the authors of cruising guidebooks on their toes.

The 5 Basic Steps of the Paperwork Cha Cha:

1.) Whether you're entering a new country or a new port, the first step is always a visit to the Port Captain's office. The building in which his office is located is called the "Capitania." The Port Captain is like God in that port, and he'll tell you in which order he wants you to visit the other governmental offices in that town. In larger ports, vessel clearance may be handled by an assistant Port Captain. If it's a port that requires a special permit to take fuel, it has to be issued by the Port Captain.

2. & 3.) The second and third steps alternate between the offices of Migacion (Immigration) and Aduana (Customs) – the exact order varies from port to port. In some smaller ports, the

Port Captain:
In each port you enter with your boat, the Port Captain is the "jefe grande" or big boss of all shipping, fishing, fuel docks, yacht harbors, marinas, anchorages - and you and your boat. Some Port Captains wear uniforms, others don't.

Port Captain may wear more than one hat; he might handle Migracion or Aduana papers as well. Migracion is generally interested only in your passports and tourist cards. The Aduana, who also represents treasury and tax agencies, usually wants to see every paper you've got – and at least one you don't yet have.

4.) If you're arriving from another country, many ports now have a new health and agriculture inspection, which would be the fourth step. They might send a navy officer or other port official to your boat to inspect your refrigerator and produce locker – and to see if anyone onboard appears to be ill. Not all ports require this fourth step.

5.) The final step is normally a return to the Port Captain's office, after which you're officially cleared in (or out).

Ships' Agents: In some places (Colombian ports, for example), private yachts are required to hire a "ships' agent," an agency or person who is locally licensed to act as the liaison between the officials (local, state, federal or military) and the boat's owner. In ports where the use of an agent is mandatory, we've listed the names of people with whom we've had good experience. Elsewhere, hiring an agent is optional.

The agent's first job is to clear the vessel's official papers, and for this their basic fee ranges for $10 to $600. Beyond that, most agents can also smooth problems and negotiate local business dealings on the vessel owner's behalf, such as arrange for a fuel truck and a dock, gather prices from local repair shops, arrange an emergency haul-out, oversee Customs clearance of repair parts being flown in. Their wealth of local knowledge can be quite valuable: where to safely anchor or tie up, which restaurants won't poison you, which grocery stores have fresher bread and better provisions.

In Mexico, thanks to ever-increasing nautical tourism, it's becoming much easier, less expensive and more popular to hire a local ships' agent to handle all your port-clearance procedures for you. Every marina mentioned in this guidebook offers such a service for its slip guests, and some extend the service to non-guests.

TIP: Just because some locals may happen to speak English and ingratiate themselves to you – that doesn't mean they're qualified ships' agents. We've even seen scam artists with bogus letters of recommendation. Always ask the Port Captain to verify that this person has his current permission to work as a ships' agent for you.

When to Start: Local laws require that – immediately upon entering your first foreign Port of Entry – you alone as the captain must take your ship's papers, listed below, to the Port Captain's office. (In some ports, however, the officials come to you.) Technically, the boat's captain is the only person allowed to off the boat, and only for the purpose of clearing the papers. Everyone else must stay aboard the boat until the job's done. If you don't show up at the Capitania as soon as is reasonably possible, some Port Captains are famous for sending out a well armed Navy patrol boat to board newly arrived yachts – demanding that the captain come ashore to begin clearance procedures "pronto." So save the celebrations until after the Paperwork Cha Cha is completed.

TIP: The Paperwork Cha Cha can keep you hopping for half a day or more, so be sure to ask what time each office closes for siesta (including the bank), what time they close for the day, and if they're going to be open tomorrow. You may not be aware of local holidays: The Monday after a Sunday fiesta sometimes turns into another holiday, called San Lunes (Saint Monday), meaning few folks show up for work Monday morning.

TIP: Hiring a taxi to shuttle you around saves you lots of time and shoe leather, and the local taxistas know where each office is located.

Quarantine: In your Port of Entry in each new country, until the clearing-in procedure is completed, your boat is officially quarantined; you must fly the yellow Q-flag from your port flag halyard and your courtesy flag to starboard. This means no visitors are allowed on board, no crew are allowed off the boat. Some ports are more lax about enforcing quarantines than others, but it's the law. As soon as this Port of Entry clearance is completed, you can drop the Q-flag – and go find the nearest welcome wagon. (For some reason, the west coast of Mexico doesn't enforce the Q-flag custom.)

TIP: Even though you may already have hired a ships' agent to handle your Paperwork Cha Cha, no one on your crew list can depart that port until the clearance procedures are completed. Just because a guest or crew member has a plane to catch doesn't mean they can excuse themselves from the rest of the official dance program. In the U.S., there's a $5,000 fine for jumping ship, levied against the boat owner and the vessel. Other countries have stiffer punishments. We've seen it happen many times. So if someone has an emergency, make sure the ships' agent and the Port Captain understand your situation.

Papers & Documents

Here's our current list of official documents and papers that are required of pleasure boats taking the route covered in this guidebook. Besides clearing in and out of foreign ports, you will invariably be boarded at sea by the local Navy or Coast Guard, and each boarding party will also want to examine your ship's paper.

Keep a supply of at least 12 clear copies of each document onboard; you'll be passing them out three and four at at time with each office you visit during each clearance procedure. And some will be used during high-seas boardings. If you don't have sufficient copies for each boarding official who shows up, the entire process will halt while you and the official make a special trip to shore – just to make more copies.

TIP: Stow all your ship's ducuments and papers in a watertight safe place on board. Whenever you carry a few documents or papers off the boat, first place them inside a large plastic zip-type bag. Don't laminate anything.

Passports: Especially in light of recent security problems abroad, we highly recommend that you and everyone on board your boat carry a valid passport whenever outside your home country. In most Central American countries, you won't be allowed off your own boat if you don't have a valid passport. Besides the copies mentioned above, keep at least two photocopies of your passport's data pages with photo in a separate location. Side trips inland are an essential part of this cruise, so take your passport plus a copy of the data/photo page.

Obtaining a passport can take 30 days or more, so start early. If your city's main post office doesn't contain a passport annex, then call the toll-free number listed under Passports in the U.S. Government pages of your local telephone book. You'll need to give them a certified copy of your birth certificate (usually issued by the Recorder's Office of the city or county in which you were born) plus two recent "mug shots" (often available in one hour from Passport Photo shops nearby). A U.S. passport is usually valid for 10 years.

If you already have a passport, check the expiration date; if it's going to expire before you return to the U.S., get a new one before you depart. If the back pages of your old passport are nearly filled up with stamps, turn it in for a new one before you depart on this voyage;

otherwise some Central American official may refuse to let you get off your own boat.

Vessel Documentation or Registration: The U.S. Coast Guard issues a "Document," and each U.S. state issues its own "Registration." Some boats have both forms of vessel identification. In order to make this voyage, your boat must have one or the other. Same for your dinghy or other motorized vessels. They must be valid when you enter each new country. If your "sticker" expires before you return, you'll need to buy a new one when the boat returns to home waters.

For most cruising boats with a Document, the upper left-hand corner of the paper will list the vessel's purpose as either "pleasure" or "recreational." State Registrations also designate the vessel's primary purpose. No matter what form of vessel identification you have, the "pleasure" or "recreational" designations have proved to be the simplest, easiest way to go for all of us who are in fact being nautical tourists in other countries. In most countries, charging guests on your boat is called "chartering," and that requires at least a "commercial" designation.

If your vessel's Document or Registration lists "commercial," then, even if you're just passing through, you'll be required in most ports to hire a ships' agent to clear your papers.

Tourist Cards and Travel Visas: In order to issue you a Tourist Card (valid for up to six months), Mexico requires either a valid passport or some official equivalent of a birth certificate. Blank tourist cards are readily available in Southern California and South Florida, from travel agents and from the many fishing tackle shops that also sell Mexican fishing permits and licenses. Fill out the

Tourist Card, but don't date it until you're ready to clear into your first port (Port of Entry) – where it will be stamped and validated. Request the maximum length of time, presently 180 days, by explaining that you are cruising extensively on your own boat.

Make several copies that show this validation stamp and date, and stow them away. Tuck the validated original inside your passport, and keep all passports inside a waterproof container, along with all the other ship's papers. You'll need to present these to a round of officials each time you clear in and out of a major cruising port. If you're still cruising Mexico when this tourist card is about to expire, you have to leave the country and get a new one upon re-entering.

Costa Rica's tourist cards are currently issued for only 90 days, even though boats can stay longer. Cruisers simply take a bus or fly to nearby Panama and get new tourist cards when they re-enter Costa Rica. Panama's visa requirements are changing, so obtain them when you arrive in country.

Crew List: In Spanish, it's called the *"Lista de Tripulantes,"* meaning List of Crewmembers. The blank form is written in Spanish and addressed to the Port Captain – and you fill it out in Spanish. (See below for a sample Crew List.)

Besides the date, the Crew List tells the Port Captain (a) a few details about the boat, such as its name, what kind of boat it is, the name of its owner, its home port, its registration or documentation numbers, and its gross and net tonnage, (b) about your route, such as your last port, and (c) about each person on board: name, age, position on board, nationality and passport number.

Each time you enter and leave a port that has a Port Captain's office, you'll need

to fill out a new Crew List (and six plain-paper copies) to give to the local officials while you're performing your port-clearance procedures.

TIP: All changes to your crew roster must be shown on your Crew List: if a guest wants to join your boat for a passage to the next major port, his or her name must appear on your out-going ("Salida") Crew List before you clear out of the port where they join you. A guest is listed as either a "marinero" or "marinera." When that person leaves to fly home, if you haven't formally taken them off your Crew List – and if you show up in your next port minus one person – the Port Captain and the Navy will want to know exactly where you dumped that missing person's body overboard.

You can generate your own Crew Lists on a shipboard computer, filling them out on the computer with fresh information for each port you come to, then print out as many as you need.

Turn to the Sample Crew List example at the end of this chapter. List as many as three intermediate ports, giving yourself the option to stop almost anywhere along that route. Don't get cute with your crew positions, such as "imperial majesty," "deck ape" and "galley slave;" the internationally recognized positions are Captain, First Mate, Navigator, Cook, Engineer and Mariner. There's only one Captain, and for a non-commercial vessel or pleasure yacht, everyone else on bord, including temporary guests, can be listed as a Mariner - Marinero or Marinera.

Import Permits: Currently, Mexico offers a 20-year Import Permit. It allows you as the boat's non-resident owner to enter Mexican waters with your boat – and then to leave your boat behind while you depart Mexico, coming and going any number of times over a period of time not to exceed 20 years. This is a vast improvement over the single-entry Import Permit, which is invalidated the first time the boat's owner crosses a border out of Mexico.

It's almost invariable that boaters will want to park their boats safely in some marina while they fly out of Mexico – to pick up duty-free replacement parts, visit friends and relatives, or spend part of the summer in cooler latitudes. So the 20-year Import Permit is the only practical option.

Before you jet away without your boat, however, be sure that you and the marina both have several copies of your 20-year Import Permit as well as copies of the Tourist Card with which you arrived. (Remember, you'll have to turn in your old Tourist Card when you leave Mexico, and you'll be getting a new Tourist Card when you come back in to rejoin your boat. If you have a single-entry Import Permit, you'll be in deep yogurt with the Port Captain, Aduana and Migracion when you try to clear out of that port with a Tourist Card that's different from the one with which you cleared in.)

Import Permits are issued to boaters by Aduana when they "clear in" in their very first Port of Entry. They'll ask you to specify how many years you expect to have your boat in Mexican waters (up to 20 years) before you move it to some other country. Veteran cruisers suggest adding at least two years to your first estimate.

Fishing Papers: Mexico and Costa Rica are the only countries along the route described in "Cruising Ports" that currently requires fishing papers. Mexico is much more strict in its enforcement of fishing licenses than is Costa Rica.

The two kinds of fishing papers for Mexico are (A.) Boat Permits and (B.) Individual Licenses. Even if you don't plan to fish while you're in Mexican waters, you must get both these papers, which are issued by Mexico's SEMARNAP (formerly Pesca) agency. If you don't have these papers when you get boarded by the Mexican Navy or visit the Port Captain, you're in violation of Mexican law. Fines and temporary seizure of boats are possible.

(A.) The owner of each "pleasure" or "recreational" vessel is required to purchase one Boat Permit for their primary vessel and another Boat Permit for its tender or dinghy. You'll have to fill out an Application and show either your "Document" with current sticker or your valid state "Registration" (or a clear copy of either if you're applying by mail). It should state either "pleasure" or "recreational" usage, not "coastwise" or "commercial" or multiple use. A Boat Permit is valid for 12 months from its date of issue, not for a calendar year. The fee scale for a Boat Permit is based on three categories of boat length: (under 23' – 23'00" to 29'11" – 30' or more).

If your primary boat is 30 feet in length or more, your Boat Permits and Individual Licenses must be issued from the sole SEMARNAP agency in the U.S., which is located in San Diego. Phone or fax them to request an Application.

SEMARNAP
2550 Fifth Avenue, Suite 101
San Diego, CA 92103-6622
phone (619) 233-6956
fax (619) 233-0344

The 1-page Application is for Boat Permits and Individual Licenses, and it comes with instructions and the current fees in U.S. dollars – which change every six months according to the current peso : dollar ratio. Unfortunately, they can't accept plastic or a personal check, so you'll need to pay all fees with a cashier's check or money order for the correct amount, along with one business-sized SASE and your filled-out Application.

If your primary boat's length is 29 feet 11 inches or less, then you can get an Application for your Boat Permits and Individual Licenses at any of 35 authorized fishing businesses located around Southern California and Arizona. Call or fax SEMARNAP for the complete listing. Going through one of these sub-agencies often takes longer.

(B.) Each person on board must have an Individual License in his or her name – even kids and temporary guests – whether or not they fish. You can get an Individual License either for one week, one month or one year. Most long-range boaters making the route covered in "Cruising Ports" will opt for the 1-year licenses for each person on their crew – so they'll start and end on the same date as their Boat Permits. The weekly and monthly licenses can start at any time you specify. The fee in U.S. dollars for an Individual License also varies; it's based on the ever-changing peso : dollar ratio. New prices are posted on the first of January and June.

(If you expect temporary guests to join your boat after it's already in Mexican waters, you can go to the nearest Port Captain or SEMARNAP office to apply for additional Individual Licenses for your guests. In this case, the weekly or monthly licenses are fine.)

I've heard of folks trying to squirm out of the requirement to buy fishing papers by pleading that they're deathly allergic to fish, that they're only going to be spear fishing, or that they don't have even one tiny fishing hook on board – not even in their life raft and ditch kit. Of course, none of these excuses has worked or will work, but they're creative. The fee amount will vary of course, but it's not a budget buster. As we go to press on the 4th edition of this

book, the annual fishing fees for a 30-plus foot boat with a registered dinghy and two people on board would total less than $150.

Insurance Policy and Travel Endorsements: Most marinas and some Port Captains who are responsible for municipal anchorages now require a copy of your vessel's Proof of Liability Insurance – or a copy of the pages of your insurance agreement that show your name, boat name and identification numbers, and the time period and location for which the liability coverage is valid.

Equipment and Serial Number List: More frequently, some but not all Port of Entry officials are requesting a listing of all the vessel's equipment and a serial number for each item. Guatemala is one that does. As unrealistic as this may at first seem, it's actually a good idea. The purpose is to discourage theft from boaters, to help you recover items if they are stolen, and to help you get reimbursed from your insurance company.

Before you embark on this voyage, make a thorough inventory of your boat's electronics, dinghy, motors, tools, and anything of significant market value, including a serial numbers beside each item. Get an engraving tool and carve your boat's name and your own inventory number on items that don't already have serial numbers. Give a copy to your insurance company and keep several copies on board, in case officials ask for one. Even if you aren't asked for such a list, you never know when you might need it.

Additional Papers

The following documents are requested by port and boarding officials only under certain circumstances.

Tourist Tax: As we go to press, Mexico plans to start a $15-per person tourist tax, but there's so much static about it, we don't know if it will stick for long.

Professional Captain: If a professional captain clears a vessel into a country without the owner present, the captain has to have a notorized letter in Spanish from the vessel's legal owner stating specifically that he/she gives permission to the named captain to take that boat into that country for a specific time period. If the vessel's legal owner is a corporation, the letter must be on corporate letterhead stationery, and a list of the corporate officers must accompany the letter. (This could occur even if the captain is also the owner – if the vessel is documented to a corporation. In that case, the captain had to have a corporate letter from himself.) Officials often request a copy of this original letter to take with them and keep on file. Their purpose is to discourage boat theives from hiding out in their waters.

Here's what goes into your Professional Captain letter in Spanish:

Fecha (date)
A quien corresponda,

Yo, (vessel owner's name), *propetario del crucero de placer,* (vessel name), (vessel doc/reg number), (gross tons), (home port), *ortorgo que* (captain's name), (passport number), *transporte la embarcacion de* (name of starting port, country) *a* (name of ending port, country) *entre las fechas* (starting date) *y* (ending date) *por el Canal de Panama y puertos intermedios como necesario.*

Firma, (signature of boat owner)
(address and phone number)
NOTARY SEAL & DATE

Minor Child: If a minor is traveling without both parents, the one parent who is present has to show the officials a notorized letter from the other parent stating specifically that he/she gives permission to the other parent to take that named minor into that country, specifying a time period. Officials often request a copy of this original letter to keep on file. Their purpose is to discourage kidnapping for ransom or child-custody disputes.

Sample Crew List: On the next page is our copyrighted version of the Crew List used in all Spanish-speaking countries. For more about this important document, refer to the 4th item mentioned under Papers & Documents earlier in this chapter.

We're happy to give permission to the purchaser of this book to make as many copies as he or she needs for clearing ports - for FREE!

*However, we think that anyone who tries to **SELL boot-legged copies** of our Crew List for money is a dirty low-down whale-breathed scum bag.*

"Cruising Ports" by John & Pat Rains
Sample <u>Crew List</u>
for Spanish Speaking Countries

Estimado Capitan de Puerto

Presente _____(boat captain's name)_____, Capitan del yate de placer ____(boat name)___, de la matricula de ____(home port)___ del porte de ___(gross tons)___ toneladas brutas y de ___(net tons)____ netas de arqueo, declara:

Que el dia de hoy zarpara con destino al puerto de ____(destination port, state)_____ con escala en los siguientes puertos de ____(intermediate ports, states)_____ siendo la tripulacion de este yate como sigue:

Nombre	*Nacionalidad*	*Cargo a bordo*	*Edad*	*# de Pasaporte*
(name)	*(nationality)*	*(crew position)*	*(age)*	*(passport #)*
(name)	*(nationality)*	*(crew position)*	*(age)*	*(passport #)*
(name)	*(nationality)*	*(crew position)*	*(age)*	*(passport #)*
(name)	*(nationality)*	*(crew position)*	*(age)*	*(passport #)*

Comprende este Roll los asientos de ___(total # of people)___ personas y es de mi satisfaccion, como Capitan que soy, manifestar que me obligo al exacto cumplimiento de todo cuanto disponen las Leyes y Reglamentos actualmente en vigor.

____(month, day)___ de ___(year)___.

El Capitan _____(boat captain's signature)_____.

Visada de conformidad por esta Oficina de Migracion con ____(total # of people)___ tripulantes inclusive su Capitan; se hace a la mar con destino a ____(destination port, state)___ escalando puntos intermedios.

____(month, day)___ de ___(year)___.

El Jefe de la Oficina de Migracion

____(to be signed by Immigration Officer)_____.

Habiendo cumplido su escala en este puerto, el yate _____(boat name)_____ en esta fecha despachese para _____(destination port, state)____ escalando todos los lugares que se mencionan, con _____(total # of persons)_____ tripulantes inclusive su Capitan.

____(month, day)___ de ___(year)___.

El Capitan de Puerto
____(to be signed by Port Captain)____.

Fort Lauderdale, Florida

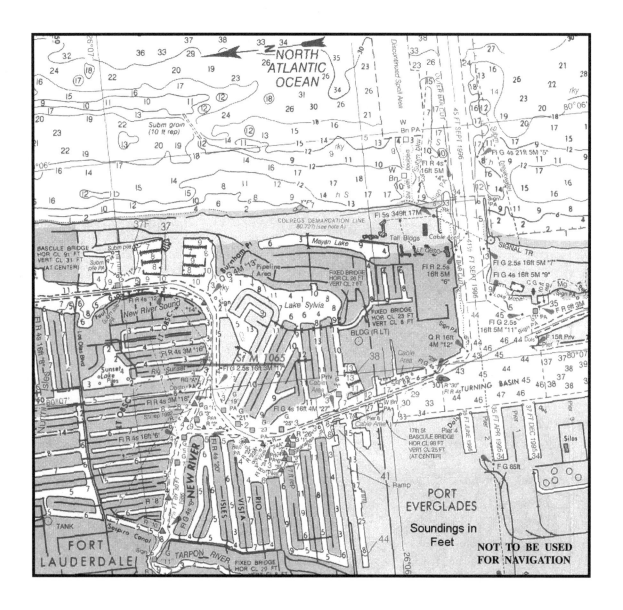

Chapter 4
Fort Lauderdale

∿∿∿∿∿∿∿∿∿∿∿∿∿∿∿∿∿∿∿∿∿∿∿∿∿∿∿∿∿∿∿

This guidebook is meant to be used by boaters traveling in either direction, east to west or vice versa. In this chapter, we'll begin the first of our long list of "cruising ports" – or, for boaters traveling from the U.S. West Coast to the East Coast, the final destination after a long adventure.

Either way, Fort Lauderdale has lots to offer to long-range cruising boaters.

Fort Lauderdale

Fort Lauderdale is the largest yachting center in the entire United States. Broward County alone has 44,000 registered boats. And the boating tourist population swells to who knows what during the winter. Everything a yachtsperson could want is found here, making it an ideal place to begin (or end) a long journey. Sometimes it is jokingly referred to as Fort Liquordale.

The inlet to Ft. Lauderdale passes through Port Everglades and is one of the safest and most widely used inlets in Florida. It was formed in 1765 by the discharge of the New River into the sea, a recent occurrence by geological standards. Man aided nature by building breakwaters, dredging the channel and installing buoys. It's an easy entrance in all but heavy east winds.

Approaches: From well out to sea you'll see a 18-story condominium complex on the north bank of the inlet. At 1.2 miles south of the harbor entrance you'll see the conspicuous tall red-and-white striped stacks of a Florida Power and Light plant. At night they show red aircraft lights.

The sea buoy's racon flashes "T." From the sea buoy (26°05.4'N by 80°04.7'W), the approach is a single straight-in shot on the range marker (269.5° True), a good time to check your compass deviation. At the breakwater the mean tide range is 2.6 feet with an average tidal current of 0.7 knots. Maximum current is three knots on the flood and four knots on the ebb. Once inside, you find yourself in the large turning basin of Port Everglades, a deep-water port of little interest to yachtsmen.

Cruising Ports

Port Clearance: If you're entering Florida for the first time from a foreign country, you must check with U.S. Customs by phone. Call them immediately upon your arrival at the first dock you touch. Their phone is (800) 432-1216. A convenient place to do this is the fuel dock of the Lauderdale Marina. It's on the west bank of the ICW just north of the 17th Street Bridge. They have a direct phone line to Customs. On the phone the Customs officer will ask the particulars of your crew and the nature of your voyage. If you are all U.S. citizens on a U.S.-flagged vessel, the officer may give you a clearance number – and that is all there is to it. Otherwise, he or she may ask you to remain where you are, and Customs officers will come down for a physical inspection.

Local Services and Marinas: If you're entering Ft. Lauderdale only for fuel, an excellent place to fuel is just north of the basin and before the 17th Street Bridge, because it doesn't require passing under the bridge itself. Adjacent to this fuel dock is the Marina Inn and Yacht Harbor. Dockage is much cheaper here than in marinas on the other side of the bridge, but it is exposed to the boat wakes from the ICW.

The 17th Street Draw Bridge is being rebuilt to a vertical clearance of 55 feet and is scheduled to be completed in November, 2000. Meanwhile, a temporary draw bridge has a clearance of 25 feet – and opens on the hour and half-hour between 0700 and 1800. Watch out for a strong tidal rip under the bridge, because it flows in either direction depending on the tide. Around 1600 on Sunday afternoons, this bottleneck is a nautical zoo.

Immediately inside the bridge are the main staging areas for boats arriving or leaving on long trips. Pier 66 on the east bank is the plushest with modern facilities including fuel dock. The Marriott Marina and Lauderdale Marina, both with fuel docks, are on the opposite bank and have the advantage of being in walking distance of just about anything your heart desires.

Southport Shopping Center on the west bank contains Bluewater Books and Charts, which has the region's best selection of charts and all other nautical publications. Their phone is (954) 763-6533. Charlie's Locker, a marine supply store is next door to Bluewater. Publix grocery nearby is one of the primary chain grocery stores (Winn Dixie, WalMart and CostCo being the others), and this one is a handy place to do the bulk of your provisioning. They will provide boxes, if requested the night before,

Lauderdale Marina is located on the west bank of the ICW.

to simplify loading of provisions. The market is generally crowded, so shop early in the morning.

Just beyond the northwest corner of Southport Shopping Center is the Southport Raw Bar, an inexpensive place to eat and drink, full of sometimes raucous boat crews from all over God's watery creation. The bar has slips to tie up your dinghy while you eat.

The entrance to the New River is approximately a mile north of Pier 66 on the ICW. This river passes through the old part of Ft. Lauderdale, so you can cruise by stately homes and into the center of town itself, site of numerous restricted bridges.

The New River in Fort Lauderdale is one of the great yachting centers of the world, for power and sail.

East of the Andrews Avenue Bridge and on the south bank is the City Dockmaster's office, at 14 South River Drive. The city rents dock space first come, first served. Call ahead for information: (954) 761-5423.

Further up the river and past the town's center you'll find a number of boat repair facilities. River Bend Boat Yard allows do-it-yourself work and Bradford Marine is one of the world's finest. Due to its location, Bradford's is considered at the head of navigation for most boats.

Continuing north on the ICW past the New River entrance and around the bend, on the east bank is Lake Sylvia, a free anchorage with stays limited to 24 hours. Check the charts and watch your depths.

Opposite the entrance to Lake Sylvia, you'll see the famous Bahia Mar Marina. On this ancient site, the Indians used to portage their canoes the short distance between the inland water and the open ocean. Now it's a full service marina including maids and valets if required. The Bahia Mar is where author John D. McDonald's fictional character Travis McGee lived aboard his houseboat, the Busted Flush.

Ft. Lauderdale's main beach is just across the street. Within walking distance is a business strip with many restaurants, shops and bars including the Elbow Room that was made famous by the movie "Where the Boys Are."

Immediately south of the Las Olas Street Bridge on the west bank is the only designated anchorage in the city. Pick up any empty mooring, and the dockmaster will stop later to collect the fee, or call ahead to reserve a space. The phone is (954) 761-5423. An owner may rent one for no more than 30 days in any 12-month period. A dinghy landing is located on the cove's north shore.

The other major area for boatyards is down the Dania Cutoff Canal. This canal's entrance is 1.7 miles south of the Port Everglades entrance, and the yards are .9 miles west into the canal. The Dania Cutoff Canal is my favorite area for visiting yachts, because it has a deep-water approach with no bridges. The canal's entrance is 1.7 miles south of the entrance to Port Everglades, and you'll find marinas, fuel docks and yards only 1 mile west down the canal. Harbor Towne Marina lies at the end of the canal. Their phone is (954) 926-0300. It has a small ship store, travel lift and fuel dock. For access to Lauderdale's chandlers, it's a quick dash up Highway 1 past the Ft. Lauderdale International Airport.

Though chandlers are scattered throughout Ft. Lauderdale, the main area is from the intersection of Federal Highway and State Route 84 – and west for a few blocks along SR 84. West Marine is at 2300 South Federal Highway; they have van pickup available 0900 to 1700 by calling (954) 527-5540. Farther west on SR 84 past the railroad tracks on the north side of the street is MacDonald's Hardware, the best stocked hardware store with a nautical orientation in Lauderdale. Their phone is (954) 463-2000.

You can get the cheapest rates on fuel by ordering a delivery by truck from Port Petroleum. Their phone is (954) 522-1182. If you're bound on a foreign voyage without stopping at another U.S. port, ask Port Petroleum if you may be able to buy fuel without paying sales tax. Check with your dockmaster about fueling rules, and check with Port Petroleum about the length of their hose. You may have to find another dock to take fuel.

History and Ambiance: Although the New River was first mentioned in the 1575 memoirs of a visiting Spaniard, little happened for centuries. Major William Lauderdale established a fort, circa 1837, for protection during the Seminole Indian War. A stage-coach ferry crossing and camp was set up in 1893, and a navigable waterway between Bay Biscayne and Lake

Worth was completed in 1895. After the railroad was completed in 1896, wealthy Northeasterners began coming down to escape bitter winters. Development got into high gear after World War II. Many swamps were dredged and the resultant canals and building lots created the Venice of America.

Ft. Lauderdale is full of entertainment, though the pace is considerably subdued in hot summer months. Many pleasurable hours can be spent cruising the 150 miles of waterway by motorized launch. You'll see every type of watercraft imaginable.

To get from the Miami entrance to the Ft. Lauderdale entrance, you may go outside the ICW (20 miles) or use the ICW if your mast height is under 56 feet. Inside, the sight-seeing is great, but many "no-wake" zones and bridges make it difficult to make good time. However if the winds are blowing outside, the ICW usually offers excellent protection.

The ICW adjacent to Baker's Haulover is subject to frequent shoaling to less than the 8-foot control depth of the ICW, so grounding is always possible. Before making a trip between Ft. Lauderdale and Miami, be sure to check recent ICW conditions in the vicinity of Baker's Haulover.

Chapter 5
Miami

Miami is one of the greatest yachting centers in the world. Because its character is more Latino than Anglo, Miami is also considered to be a major Latin American vortex. If you plan to head south with your boat, spending time in Miami is a good introduction to a vibrant Latin culture. If you're returning from the south, Miami's Latin ambiance will cushion the culture shock.

Approaches: The tall buildings of downtown Miami, five miles inland from the entrance, can be seen well out to sea. Coming from the north, you will be paralleling the high-rise buildings on Miami Beach. They end just north of the breakwater entrance. You will see a prominent tank close by on the north side of the entrance. Coming from the south, you will see the tower and light at Cape Florida and a tall stack and light on Virginia Key.

Since Miami is a major port, its ship channel offers an easy entrance from seaward. From the racon "M" sea buoy (25°46.1'N by 80°05'W), line up on the range markers to buoys number 5 and 6,

and then make a dog-leg to starboard to enter through the breakwaters. The tidal range is 2.5 feet in the breakwater and two feet in the bay. The entrance can have breaking waves in strong northeast winds and on an ebb tide.

Local Services and Marinas: The first channel inside to the northward takes you to Miami Beach Marina, which offers berthing, fuel and a quick in-and-out via deep water access; (305) 673-6000. This marina is handy for activities in the renovated Art Deco district of South Beach, dubbed the Hollywood of the East Coast.

Directly opposite the channel to Miami Beach Marina is Fisherman's Channel leading to the south side of Dodge Island. This channel also gives you access to the mouth of the Miami River and Miami Marina (also known as Miamarina) without having to pass beneath any bridges. You may encounter car ferries crossing at right angles to the channel traffic.

Continuing west down the 30-foot dredged main channel, you'll pass a measured mile on the north bank. Courses

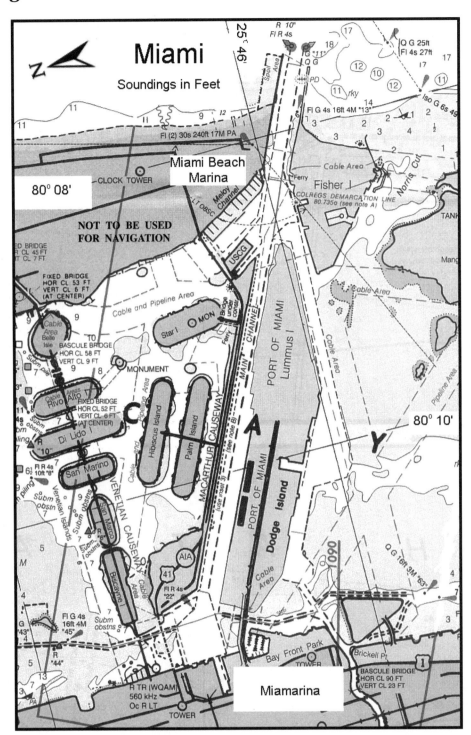

for the range are 115.5° True and 295.5° True. Three miles from the entrance you enter the Intercoastal Waterway (ICW). At this junction you may turn north to various anchorages or south to Miamarina.

Miami's designated anchorage areas are only for vessels able to operate in six feet of water. From the turning basin, turn north, pass under the MacArthur Causeway and turn to starboard before arriving at the Venetian Causeway, a short distance away. You'll find two anchorages, one on each end of Hibiscus and Palm islands. The noise from the

Many bridges span the busy Miami River. We try not to be underway during rush hour, while many major street bridges remain closed.

MacArthur Causeway is bothersome.

Miami Marina, also called Miamarina, is south of the ICW junction and in the heart of downtown Miami. To get to the marina, cross the turning basin, turn to the south and pass through the three Dodge Island bridges. The first is a fixed highway bridge with a 65-foot clearance. The railroad bridge with 22-foot clearance is usually open, and the old highway bridge is always left open.

Miami Marina lies just south of the bridges, and it would be the next best choice for a vessel entering from deep water for a short stay. Their phone is (305) 579-6955. It's within walking distance of Miami's night life. If you plan to see the sights of downtown Miami, from here you'd have good access and public transportation via the Metromover and Metrorail.

You may also get to this marina without having to go under these bridges. Take the aforementioned channel that branches to the south just after entering the breakwater, pass south of Dodge Island, and then turn north in the ICW.

Miamarina has modern facilities including good security for more than 200 yachts up to 125 feet. A neon-studded shopping center surrounds the marina. Bay Front Park is next to the marina. It was the sight of an ancient Indian village and now contains a public library, auditorium and amphitheater.

A short distance south of the marina you'll see the entrance to the Miami River, which is navigable for four miles to 36th street. The river is a pleasurable place to sight-see by launch. You pass many inter-island freighters from all over the Caribbean. Who knows what cargo they might be unloading? The river contains most of Miami's boating service centers.

to avoid the commuter rush hours, because the bridges are closed to bigger vessels.

You'll find other anchorages and marinas south of the Miami River entrance. Take the ICW south and through the fixed Rickenbacker Causeway Bridge. You are now in Biscayne Bay. Just east of the south side of the bridge entrance is a good anchorage in the lee of Virginia Key. This anchorage is off a very good swimming beach and near the Seaquarium, Crandon Marina and several restaurants.

About three miles further south is another anchorage on the east side of Key Biscayne between ICW marker 28 and 30. It is quieter than Virginia Key and well protected. Directly west of this anchorage and on the opposite shore is the Dinner Key marina area for vessels up to 6 1/2 feet of draft. Dinner Key is another major pleasure-boating center with some of the best spots to buy boat supplies in Miami. A marina and an anchorage give access to the popular and stylish suburb of Coconut Grove with its many restaurants.

For a short stay away from the bustle of Miami, try anchoring at No Name Harbor in the State Park near the tip of Cape Florida. Far from town, it is very quiet and surrounded by a forest. The boats around you are likely to be leaving in the morning for Bahamian ports through the marked channel south of Cape Florida, which has a 7-foot maximum draft.

Chapter 6
Skirting the Florida Keys

〰〰〰〰〰〰〰〰〰〰〰〰〰〰〰〰〰〰〰〰〰〰〰〰

The 150-mile voyage between Miami and Key West skirts just outside the spectacular Florida Keys. The Keys are mostly low coral formations covered with dense mangrove growth, though some are wooded with pines and coconut palms. Most of the major Keys are connected by U.S. Highway 1, the Overseas Highway. The taller of the bridges connecting the Keys can be seen from out at sea.

Three Routes

For your run from Miami to Key West (or vice versa), you can choose from three routes: outside the reef; the Hawk Channel; or the inside waterway.

Inside: The inside passage has a questionable 5-foot controlling depth but is in totally protected waters. It is not recommended without local knowledge. I once had a professional captain, a veteran of 30 years in South Florida, tell me I ought to use this channel on a delivery of a 57-foot powerboat with a 4¾-foot draft. He said, "You'll have only one shoal spot to worry about, but if you are sure to be up on a plane, no sweat." I could visualize hitting a coral head at 18 knots, so I decided to go outside. The inside channel is a scenic milk run, complete with nice scenery and lots of stops.

Hawk Channel: Running the Hawk Channel shortens the distance to 127 miles, and the channel is semi-protected by off-lying reefs. When running in the Hawk Channel, you'll find yourself in turquoise water with the deeper water off to port, and the deep Caribbean blue sky overhead. Though it can be choppy in a blow, the Hawk Channel won't be as rough or as long a passage as going outside the reef in the Gulf Stream. The channel is well marked and has an 8-foot controlling depth, but it's much deeper in most places. During lobster season, thousands of floats from lobster pots are waiting everywhere to foul the screws of the unwary. If you navigate outside the confines of the channel, be aware of the many unlit and unmarked reefs as well as remnants of the old overseas railway. These hazards can be spotted in calm water during the day with high sun, but not at night.

Outside the Reef: I recommend the outside route for settled weather, for night-running and for making good time, but you'll need precise navigation and a good lookout for the heavy shipping traffic and numerous pleasure craft in the Florida Straits. The Keys are flanked by a chain of dangerous reefs and shoals lying an average of five miles from the shoreline of the Keys. The reefs are hazardous because they are not marked by breakers in smooth weather, and only a few reefs show above the water. The bottom comes up abruptly on their outer edges and between the reefs.

Navigating by Color

On the seaward approach to the reefs, you are warned of their proximity by the change in color of the water, from deep blue to light green. In clear weather the lights and day beacons make navigation along the reefs easy, but in thick weather, soundings should be relied on for safety. Fifty-fathom soundings indicate a distance of two to three miles from the reefs. Fog is not frequent in the Keys.

The usual color of the water on the reefs is turquoise or greenish blue, and the shoal patches show dark, shading through brown to yellow as they approach the surface. The shoal sand patches show as a bright green. At depths of 10 to 15 feet, grass patches on the bottom look quite similar to rocks. When piloting in this area, chose a time when the sun will be astern, and con the vessel from aloft or from an elevated position forward, because then the line of demarcation between deep water and the edges of the shoals will be displayed with surprising clarity.

You will find this navigating technique for clear shoal waters very useful throughout the Caribbean. However, after stormy weather, shallow water always becomes milky and therefore impossible to read. White or brown sand from the bottom is stirred up, even by surge action from storms 100 miles away.

Techniques for Skirting the Florida Keys

Depending on which way you're headed, the tactics or techniques to use for skirting the Keys will differ.

Southbound Techniques: If you are southbound on the outside route, the closer you hug the reef, the less Gulf Stream current you have to fight. Due to the proximity of the shoals and to your need to make constant course changes to starboard, this southbound voyage calls for very precise navigation. The navigation aids are reliable, but you should be sure to identify each light, tower and buoy as you see it, and then check it off as you pass by. Because you're constantly turning slightly, it's very easy to get confused.

Northbound Techniques: If you are northbound on the outside route, stand three to four miles off the numerous lights marking the edge of shoal water. This puts you out in the Gulf Stream current for a free escalator ride.

Local Services and Marinas: In case of trouble you can head for any number of marinas and fuel docks in the Keys, but deep-draft vessels have a limited selection. Enter at night only in dire emergency. The background lights can be very confusing, so expect to see vehicle traffic on the Overseas Highway and many lighted motels and clubs.

Caloosa Cove Marina is the deepest draft Marina (6-foot depth) and is about at the halfway point on the run, 79 miles from Miami. The marina is located on the southwest corner of Lower Matecumbe Key, five miles past the large tower of Alligator Reef when Key West-bound. Head for the Channel Two bridge. The approaches to the marina are well marked, but watch for a strong current that flows under the bridge. It can set you out of the channel just as you are turning into another channel that parallels the highway. The marina has 32 slips and offers full services including fuel and on-duty mechanic. Their phone is (305) 664-8057.

For larger vessels (7-foot maximum draft), another option is Boot Key Harbor on Marathon. Approach from deep water near Sombrero Key Light, and once clear proceed on a heading of 076⌐M for 4.3 miles. There you'll pick up the day markers #1 and #2 just south of Knight Key. Follow the well staked channel on in. Once inside, you're well protected from the weather. Down the narrow channel are numerous marine facilities, haul-out yards and marinas. I recommend Faro Blanco, the most well appointed; their phone is (305) 743-9018. Beyond Faro Blanco is a bridge that opens on demand between 0600 and 2200. There the channel opens up into Boot Key Harbor, which provides free anchoring in seven feet of water – if you can find a spot between Thanksgiving and Easter.

The Florida Keys are a great cruising ground within themselves. Some of our favorite spots are here. Scuba divers, snorkelers, water skiers, shellers, kayakers, bird watchers, sun-bathers and fishermen all find plenty to keep them happily occupied on the water and in boats.

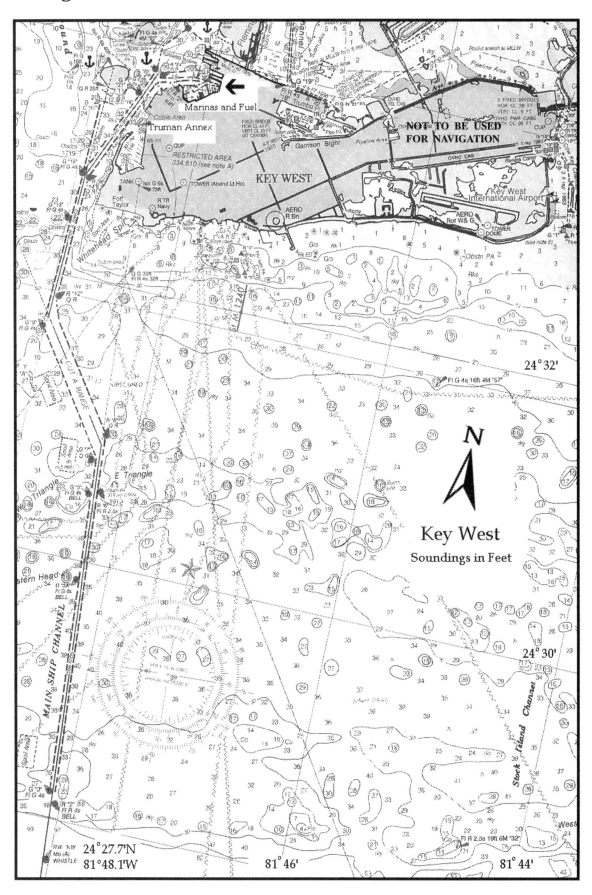

Key West

Soundings in Feet

Chapter 7
Key West

∿∿∿∿∿∿∿∿∿∿∿∿∿∿∿∿∿∿∿∿∿∿∿∿∿∿∿∿∿∿∿

Key West is the southernmost city in the United States, and the island itself is bathed by the warm waters of the Gulf Stream. This tropical paradise is the jumping off and arrival point for cruisers visiting the Western Caribbean. Key West has a fair number of yacht facilities, though not as extensive as the Miami-Ft. Lauderdale area to which it is connected both by air and overseas highway.

Approaches: If you're approaching Key West from the east, you'll see two white radar domes at Boca Chica Key, then the white dome of the National Weather Service and the aerobeacon at Key West International Airport. A 300-foot radio tower stands near Fort Taylor on the southwest corner of Key West.

The Key West "Main Ship Channel" is used by large and small vessels and is well marked. After you arrive at the seabouy (24°27.7'N by 81°48.1'W) proceed up the channel by lining up on the range markers.

If you're approaching from the south or west, you'll first see the prominent Sand Key Light rising 109 feet above the water. It's shown from a square brown pyramid-shaped skeleton tower that encloses a circular stairway and a square dwelling on a pile foundation. You can no longer see the stacks of the city's electric plant on Key West Bight. When arriving from the southwest, you might think of using the Southwest Channel as a short cut. But use this only during daylight after you have a good fix on your position and have picked up the right navigation aids as you passed into shallow water. Pick up the unlit Buoy "A" on Satan Shoal (81°58.8'N by 24°26.6'W) and follow the buoyed channel to the southwest tip of Key West, where it joins the Main Ship Channel. The Southwest Channel has been swept to a depth of 23 feet. In case of doubt, stay in deep water while passing Sand Key to port, continue to the seabuoy and then take the safer option of the Main Ship Channel.

Anchorage at Key West: The most popular anchorage is east of Wisteria Island (known locally as Christmas Tree Island) at the northwest corner of Key West.

Cruising Ports

Several marinas line Key West Bight, off the island's southwest side.

The bottom is mud and fair holding ground, but the anchorage is exposed to weather, and strong currents sweep through the area. In strong northeast winds, you may get better protection close in the lee of Fleming Key. The main advantage to these anchorages is that they are close to the downtown area. In rough weather, getting ashore via the dinghy can be anywhere from very wet to impossible. One alternative is the Key West Water Taxi that runs from 0600 to 0230. Call them on VHF channel 68. The taxi boat disembarks at the foot of Williams Street and charges $5 per person one way.

Port Clearance: Upon arrival from outside the U.S., either anchor out or check into a marina. Then immediately call U.S. Customs at 296-5411 or (800) 432-1216. After you answer a few questions, they may give you a clearance number over the phone and you are cleared in. Or they may come down to the boat and do a full inspection. Very often, at least one Agriculture Officer will come down to inspect your meats and produce, something they rarely do when you enter at Ft. Lauderdale. If Customs doesn't come down to your boat and you don't have a User's Fee decal for the current year, then you'll have to get one. The Customs Office is at the beautiful old Depression-era post office (now the Federal Building) about a 3-block walk from Key West Bight. In fact, if you're leaving the U.S. and returning the same year, you may save yourself an inspection by getting the decal before you leave on your trip.

Local Services and Marinas at Key West Bight: The Galleon is a plush marina and hotel in Key West Bight. They have guest slips up to 110 feet on floating docks with good security. Guests have access to the swimming pool, spa and private beach. Right next door is the smaller, older A&B Lobster House Marina. Both marinas are within walking distance of the heart of Key West. This can be an advantage if you want to explore the busy tourist shops, but a lot of excursion boats come and go from Key West Bight all day and early evening. You would do well to call ahead to make reservations: Galleon (305) 292-1292; A&B (305) 294- 2535. You can also reach them on channel 16.

Key West Seaport Marina is on the opposite bank of Key West Bight. Their phone is (305) 269-3838. They have non-floating docks and a fuel dock. Directly ashore is the Half Shell Raw Bar, a good casual eatery. Across the street is Key West Marine Hardware, and two blocks away is a West Marine.

Slips are expensive and hard to come by in Key West, especially during winter/spring. Another option is Key West Hilton Marina in the former Truman Annex, the first entrance to starboard when you're coming in from the Main Ship Channel. Their slips are subject to surge.

Local Services and Marinas Elsewhere on Key West: Key West's Garrison Bight also has marinas, but it is a long way to deep water down a tricky, shallow channel. A favorite easy-in, easy-out spot for deep draft vessels is Oceanside Marina on Stock Island. Oceanside Marina is five miles from downtown Key West, which makes it much more relaxed and quiet than Key West Bight, and Oceanside's prices differ from downtown, too.

To enter Oceanside from the Gulf Stream, follow Stock Island Channel to the well-staked entrance to the marina. You will find no bridges or overhead wires, and they have docks for vessels to 145 feet. The modern facility has gas and diesel, repair service, ship's store, rental cars, 110 volt and 220 volt shore power, dockside telephone and TV. Call ahead for reservations, (305) 294-4676. They monitor VHF channel 16.

Safe Harbor shares the same entrance channel with Oceanside Marina. It is the home of the shrimp fleet and has ship yards if you need to haul out. It can be a rowdy and dangerous place.

The Dion Oil Company operates a fuel facility in the southwest corner, and they have had good prices on larger quantities. Their phone is (305) 296-5411.

History and Ambiance: Key West's people and history are very colorful. Though Ponce de Leon first sighted the Florida Keys in 1513, Key West had no permanent settlement for another 300 years. Its name is derived from the Spanish words Cayo Hueso, meaning Bone Key. Early Spanish visitors noted a large number of human bones scattered – the remains of large battles between feuding Indian tribes. The English, in their inimitable manner of twisting foreign words, came out with Key West. It does fit, however, because it is the most westerly of the inhabited Keys.

Florida was ceded by Spain to the United States in 1819, and the Stars and Stripes were hoisted over Key West in 1822. Shortly thereafter the Navy established a base here, and Commodore David Porter had the mission of getting rid of the pirates known as the "Brethren of the Coast" who frequented the entire Keys area. After the successful completion of Porter's mission, settlers moved in from the southern states, the Bahamas and Cuba. A combination of wreckers, pirates and commercial fishermen formed the unique core of Key West's society, which became known as "Conchs" (pronounced Konks) after the plentiful shellfish that were a staple in their diet. Conchs are still eaten throughout the Florida Keys, but the term also refers to a person born in Key West.

The conch people became famous

Oceanside Marina lies about five miles east of downtown Key West.

– or infamous – for their lucrative marine salvage businesses fed by the numerous wrecks that occurred on the Key's dangerous reefs. Local legends say that some of these ships were deliberately lured onto to reefs by fake lights and crooked skippers. Whether the wrecks were accidental or deliberate, their salvage still made Key West the most prosperous city per capita in the U.S. by 1830. By 1890 it was Florida's largest city.

Some of the treasures as well as construction materials from the wrecks went into beautiful homes that are still standing in town. The unique architecture called Eyebrow is a blend of New England and Bahamian that takes advantage of tropical breezes. Many of these homes became very run down over the years, but in the last decade wealthy Northeasterners have bought and restored them. The local gay community spear-heads the town's on-going restoration and preservation campaign.

Ernest Hemingway was one of Key West's most colorful citizens. His mansion home has been turned into a museum. You can almost feel his powerful presence as you roam the grounds that include Key West's first swimming pool. There's also a Spanish-tile urinal that he stole from Sloppy Joe's Bar. Hemingway wrote a number of novels in Key West including "To Have and Have Not." His home became a salon for literary socialites until his move to Cuba, which he attributed to "U.S. taxes, no privacy and a lousy divorce."

Key West is a rowdy town for a community of 50,000 permanent residents, and the nightlife goes on until dawn. Since most of the Navy left, tourism is the town's number one industry. Sloppy Joe's on Duvall Street was Hemingway's favorite hangout. There he partook of bare-knuckled fist fights for the fun of it and brought photos of record marlin he boated. The original location of Sloppy Joe's is now called Captain Tony's and was frequented by contemporaries such was Tennessee Williams and Truman Capote. Popular singer Jimmy Buffet, a conch, dubbed his town "Margaritaville" and made a million with the song. He likes to drink at Tony's and to lounge on the Embarcadero – where he used to sing and play for tips.

Key West is well known for its fine seafood restaurants. One favorite informal spot for cruisers is the Half Shell Raw Bar (mentioned above) located on Key West Bight. Years ago when we first visited Key West, its patrons where mostly shrimp boats crew who drank beer, listened to country music, and duked it out. Now the shrimpers have been replaced by sun-burned tourists. It's not posh, but it's a good place to get the flavor of Key West while sitting at picnic benches and eating raw oysters. Be sure to buy one of their famous "Eat It Raw" T-shirts.

Though Key West is tropical and therefore hot and muggy much of the year, it can get cold snaps in the dead of winter. During one such spell while we were waiting out a Norther, the wind-chill factor hit 26 degrees. We shivered for days because we didn't have warm clothes with us. We didn't think it could ever get that cold here. However these snaps happen only once or twice a winter, and between them temperatures are as delightful as late fall and early spring.

Chapter 8
Caribbean: *Weather & Routing*

∿∿

As the crow flies, a straight line from South Florida to Panama goes directly across Cuba. Since we're not crows, we must decide whether to go around the east end of Cuba or the west. (For more about visiting Cuba, see the end of the next chapter.) The routes that mariners choose are based primarily on weather and sea conditions that will be encountered at different times of the year. Because this guidebook is used by mariners who are coming and going in various directions, we'll look at all the options.

East vs West around Cuba

Both directions around Cuba total the same distance, but in my opinion, the west-end route is far superior. It offers better weather conditions, safer political considerations, more fuel stops and rest stops – and less open ocean.

I can think of only two circumstances in which a vessel might use the east-end route in passing from Florida to Panama. The first is a long-range, very sea-worthy power vessel going non-stop to the canal. The second is a large, well-powered motor sailor making this voyage in the late spring. The first because it avoids the adverse currents of the Gulf Stream and attains better fuel consumption. The second because, although the first leg is dead to windward, once you have turned the corner in the Windward Passage, the rest of the passage is likely to be a fine reach into the Panama Canal.

Northbound: If you're coming up to Florida from Panama, avoid the east-end route via the Windward Passage between Cuba and Haiti. It is a long, rugged, open-ocean passage often dead into the wind, and the Windward Passage offers notoriously bad weather. MAY AND NOVEMBER ARE THE BEST MONTHS FOR NON-STOP PASSAGE-MAKING BETWEEN FLORIDA AND PANAMA.

Seasonal Considerations

The two principal seasons in the Caribbean are wet and dry. Normally, the dry season starts in December and ends in

May. The wet season holds sway the balance of the year. Rainfall is generally in the form of thundershowers, and though more common in the rainy season, they may occur in all seasons.

The Northeast Trade Winds dominate throughout the year. In winter they have a more northerly component with higher wind velocities. In spring and summer they change to the east and southeast with lower velocities.

Northers (*Nortes*) are the dreaded winter winds. They are most violent in the northern Caribbean, but at times they reach all the way south to the coast of Panama. They are caused by Arctic cold fronts moving out of the continental United States into the Gulf of Mexico and Caribbean waters. Periods of strong winds can last several days and attain speeds of 60 knots in the Gulf of Mexico. Sailing and powering are particularly dangerous wherever these northerly winds blow exactly contrary to the northward-flowing Gulf Stream currents, because the result is very steep and rough seas, especially in the Yucatan Channel.

Although the winter Trades are strong and seemingly last forever, their strength is cyclical and affected by low-pressure systems passing well to the north. As a low-pressure cell moves to the north, it is often preceded by a warm front.

Weather Windows: In the Gulf of Mexico this can actually create southerly winds on the surface. Farther south in the Caribbean this often causes the Trades to decrease in intensity, but not die, and to shift to an easterly and sometimes southeasterly direction. If you happen to be holed up somewhere waiting for a break in the weather, this is the pattern to look for. The window of opportunity may not last long, so go for it. As the low-pressure system moves eastward, the trailing cold front enters the Caribbean, and then a Norther blows.

On some occasions a cold front may overtake a warm front and form an occluded front in which the Trades will be lighter for a longer period of time. Likewise, a cold front moving into the Gulf of Mexico may stall out and then begin to move north as a warm front. Good weather information is dispensed by HF radio stations WOM and NMC, and weather fax station NMG. (See Appendix).

Hurricane Season: Fierce tropical cyclones can form from late June through November, but they rarely occur south of 15°N (about Cabo Gracias a Dios). September and October are the most dangerous months, because they bring the highest frequency of storms, highest wind speeds, and fastest forward speeds. Between these storms, the weather is normally hot with light easterlies and some occasionally strong thunderstorms with high winds. These localized storms are of short duration, and radar is useful in maneuvering to avoid them.

Well-found power yachts with long range, with speeds over 10 knots and those operated by weather-savvy, vigilant captains can make their calmest Caribbean passages in June and July. If you don't fit into this category, hurricane season can be dangerous.

During hurricane season the trick is to travel between tropical waves. Weather fax is a key to this trick. The most important chart that shows tropical waves is station NMG's 24-hour and 36-hour wind/sea forecast at 0030Z and 1230Z. See the Appendix for full details. These charts will show the predicted positions of tropical waves in the next 36 hours.

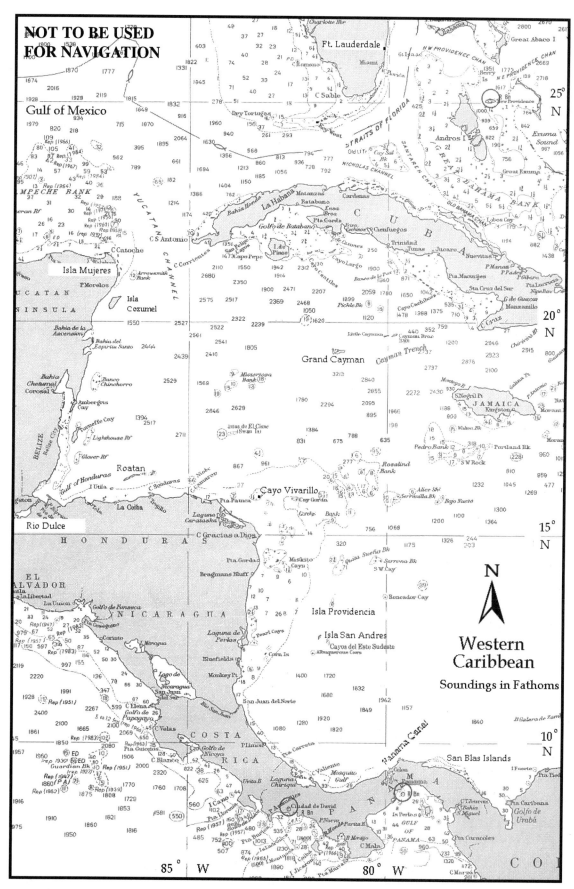

Planning Chart for Chapter 8 through Chapter 19

Tropical Waves: A tropical wave is a northward bulge of the isobar lines, and that bulge travels from east to west in the Trade Wind belt. Ahead of a tropical wave, the weather is partly cloudy with wind from the northeast. As the wave passes over your position, the cloud cover increases, rain comes more frequently in squalls, and the wind shifts to the southeast. If upper atmospheric conditions are just right, a tropical wave can develop a closed circulation of its own and create a tropical depression capable of reaching hurricane force.

Only a small percentage of tropical waves ever become depressions, but each one must be watched carefully. Since a period of only a few days separates their passage, the trick is to travel in between two moving waves – and then to arrive in a safe port and remain there while the next wave is passing over you. This requires reliable propulsion and your constant vigilance to all sources of weather reporting.

Key West to Panama Canal (1,096 miles)

I mention this long direct-route option first, because – even though it offers few cruising hang-outs and would be difficult or impractical for many cruising yachts – the fact is that every wise skipper should first understand this basic direct-route possibility and then plan to add his/her own pleasurable side trips and gunk-hole diversion to it. As a delivery captain, I prefer to make this passage as quickly as possible, and it's quite practical plan for long-range boats.

The Waypoints: From Key West head for Waypoint #1 (23°06'N by 84°21'W). This is abeam of Cayo Jutias, Cuba. The direct route to Cabo San Antonio would skirt Cuba's barrier reef, so this waypoint constitutes a dog leg that keeps you far enough off shore. Do not allow yourself to be set to the east of the rhumb line between these waypoints.

Now head directly for Waypoint #2 (21°52'N by 85°16'W). This is a watery point 18 miles due west of Cabo San Antonio, which is the very western tip of Cuba.

When rounding Cape San Antonio (21°52'N by 84°57'W), make sure you don't get set into Cuba's 12-mile perimeter. The temptation is to try to cut the corner and save yourself a few miles. The Gulf Stream current is strong and variable around this cape, so check constantly to make sure you're not getting set east. This is a major waypoint for shipping throughout the Caribbean and Gulf of Mexico, so traffic will be heavy. Allow yourself room to maneuver without getting forced too far east.

The leg to Waypoint #3 (15°45'N by 81°00'W) is a very long, open passage of 440 miles. This waypoint is between Rosalind Bank to the northeast and Gorda Bank to the southwest. The narrow slot between these banks has water deeper than 100 fathoms. During night hours, keep in this narrow strip to avoid the many lobster pots and fishing boats on the banks. During daylight hours when you can see these pots, you can pass safely over either bank. The edges of these banks are fabulous fishing grounds, especially for tasty dorado and huge yellowfin tuna.

In case of bad weather along this stretch, you could divert to Georgetown, Grand Cayman (19°18'N by 81°23'W). Cayman is a very pleasant stop with no political or racial troubles, and fuel is available. However, prices on Grand Cayman are high.

This leg takes you right past Swan Island (17°25'N by 83° 56'W), also called

Isla del Cisne. Consider it a stop only in case of dire emergency. Swan Island, a former U.S. possession, was given to the Honduran government in the early 1980s.

From Waypoint #3, you can head straight to the Cristobal breakwater (09°23.3'N by 079°55.3'W), a distance of 385 miles. This leg will take you in between Quito Sueno Bank and Serrana Bank. Both banks should be considered extremely dangerous; they're littered with the wrecks of ancient Spanish galleons and more recent shipwrecks. If possible, pass them during daylight hours and only after verifying your position with good GPS coverage. Though the banks are low, they might show up at close range on a well-tuned radar if it's flat-calm and no seas clutter your screen. Stand well off both these banks, but favor the side of Serrana, because the wind and current usually set you toward Quito Sueno.

Both these banks and Roncador Cay have anchorages. They belong to Colombia and have Navy personnel stationed there. Be sure to call on VHF channel 16 first, to request permission to anchor.

This non-stop route can be used in the exact reverse order by vessels bound from Panama to Key West.

Western Cruising Routes

This route is for people who wish to cruise between the Panama Canal and Key West or for those wishing quick passage across the Western Caribbean but lack the fuel range to go non-stop.

The Waypoints: Follow a route from Key West to Waypoint #1 and then to the Cozumel-Cancun-Isla Mujeres area. From Cozumel head straight to the west end of Roatan. From Roatan head to Waypoint A (16°20'N by 82° 35'W) with a course of 090°T, for 235 miles. This waypoint will keep you safely 10 miles north of the reef called Hobbies.

From Roatan going eastward can be a major ordeal of bashing into strong winds and square waves. Columbus was the first European to experience this tribulation when it took him one month to cover the distance. He named the point Cabo Gracias a Dios (Cape Thanks to God), because, after a month of beating to weather, he finally rounded it and encountered fair winds. However, going westward from Cabo Gracias a Dios in a sailboat is a delightful sleigh ride.

Now head to Waypoint B (15°25N by 81°38'W), 77 miles. The closest point of approach (CPA) to danger is nine miles away, at Farral Rocks.

Turn toward San Andres (12°35'N by 81°42'W) where fuel is available. You'll finish crossing the extensive shallow banks between Nicaragua and Honduras and then cross the 100-fathom curve very dramatically into deep water. On this leg you will pass close to Quito Sueno Banks. They are low and dangerous, so use extreme caution. You may wish to stop at Isla Providencia (13°21'N by 81°22'W), which is a beautiful cruising stop but not a reliable fuel source.

Now that the political situation has generally improved in Nicaragua, we can once again safely use the Moskito Channel. This is the most direct route across the bank from Roatan to the Panama Canal. The channel runs very close to the Nicaraguan coast and is protected from heavy Trades weather by offshore reefs.

To use the Moskito Channel, head from Roatan to Cayo Vivarillo (15°50'N by 83°18'W), a convenient anchorage to break up the long leg across the bank. Anchoring in the lee of the cay offers fine protection from the Trades. The tiny, coconut-palm-covered island is an idyllic, remote paradise to visit.

Use extreme caution rounding Cabo Falso (15°12'N by 83°20'W) and Cabo Gracias a Dios (15°00'N by 83°10'W), because they are low, difficult to spot and have sand shoals extending well to seaward. Once you're south of Punta Gorda and clear of the shoals to the east, turn directly toward the north end of Isla San Andres. From Isla San Andres you have a straight shot to Panama.

Northbound Route (for cruising sailboats): Sailors may take advantage of a route used by the Spanish galleons who loaded treasure in Porto Belo in present-day Panama and then sailed to Cartagena, Colombia. Their route took advantage of a favorable wind shift from east to north along the northeast shore of Panama, allowing even those unweatherly square-rigged vessels a good slant to Cartagena. From there it put them in a more upwind position to sail northwest through the Yucatan Channel and then on to Spain.

Modern cruisers sail out to Panama's palm-studded San Blas Islands, where the Cuna Indian women are famous for their colorfully embroidered "molas," and then onward to Cartagena. Although Colombia's mainland shore is rife with smugglers, the city of Cartagena has been a fairly safe refuge for cruising boats, provided you sail straight in, stay together in the harbor, and sail straight out – without skirting or stopping anywhere else on the Colombian coast.

From Cartagena, most sailors head on a starboard tack to Isla Providencia, then downwind to Cayo Vivarillo, Roatan and into the Rio Dulce cruising grounds – where they spend the hurricane season. The best months to sail northwest from Cartagena are May and November. From Rio Dulce,

sailors can work their way northward inside the reef of Belize, then on to Isla Mujeres, Mexico, where they jump off to Florida.

Eastern Routes via the Windward Passage

To move a boat south from Florida to the Panama Canal, the least desirable route is through the Windward Passage, which is the pass between the east end of Cuba and Haiti. Because pleasure boats use the Windward Passage route only infrequently, I will describe it only briefly. (However, if you plan to explore the Eastern Caribbean islands, Hart and Stone's book "A Cruising Guide to the Caribbean" best depicts the Eastern Caribbean.)

For the first leg, you would depart Ft. Lauderdale nearly due east and out through the Northwest and Northeast Providence Channels of the Bahama Bank, and turn toward the south, passing just west of San Salvador, through the Mira Por Vos Channel. From there, head to the Windward Passage and directly to Panama. For comments on the route and possible deep-water fueling stops, read on.

Northwest & Northeast Providence Channels: When crossing the Gulf Stream to Great Isaac from Ft. Lauderdale, you'll want to pick your weather well for departure and allow for the strong Gulf Stream current on the starboard beam, ranging from three to six knots. Once Isaac is on your starboard hand, you are out of the stream, but you'll still have a strong tidal set toward the bank. The channel is deep, and it's a major shipping lane. Traffic usually stays to their right side of the channel. However I have encountered small native inter-island ferries that are crossing the channel at right angles, paying no attention to other traffic – let alone "Rules of the Road" – particularly at night.

Shallow-draft vessels may cross the Bahama Bank and then move down Exuma Sound, which is more sheltered. This should be done in daylight only.

Nassau: This is slightly out of the way but offers easy deep-water access and a number of first-class marinas with full services and fuel. The harbor entrance may be closed out two or three times a year in strong Northers, but during such a "Rage at the Bar," a prominent red light is shown at Fort Fincastle.

Great Inagua: The natural jumping-off place before heading into the Windward Passage, Matthew Town, has an open rodestead anchorage that is protected from northeast to southeast prevailing winds – but is open to surge. An artificial basin just to the north offers facilities to fuel by tank truck if you draw six feet or less. The island has a good hospital and air connections to the U.S.

Windward Passage: This infamous passage has strong currents and winds, besides the political problems of Cuba and Haiti, the countries on either side. Stay right in the middle of the channel, pass Navassa Island, then head directly to the Panama Canal. In a dire emergency you might consider Mole Saint Nicholas, a huge and magnificent natural harbor that lies just inside of Cap Du Mole, the northwest tip of Haiti. Here you will encounter not only incredible poverty but also the problems that go with it. You will certainly be boarded for the inspection of your cruising permit. In any anchorage in Haiti, an all-night anchor watch must be maintained to guard against armed thieves or the deliberate cutting, slipping or fouling or your set anchor.

Jamaica: The large island nation of Jamaica is a good stop in case of an emergency or for fuel. The well-protected Port Antonio on the northeast coast is the preferred stop. Its picturesque twin harbor is divided by Tichfield Peninsula. Take the west channel between the peninsula and Navy Island toward Boundbrook commercial pier and turn to port. You may anchor out off the market area or ask for a berth at the East Jamaica Angler's Club (EJAC).

The EJAC has wooden docks with eight feet of water alongside. Med-mooring is most common. The club has 110-volt and 220-volt electricity, water, fuel dock, clubhouse and showers. Captain Bligh once brought a shipment of his beloved breadfruit to Port Antonio from the South Pacific. But this occurred after the infamous mutiny of the *Bounty* and on a different ship.

You may also stop at Port Royal, which lies on the approaches to Kingston, and thus avoid the urban problems of Kingston. In Port Royal you can get fuel, repairs and moorage at Morgan's Harbour Yacht Club right in the middle of the most famous pirate lair of centuries past. Port Royal is very near the island's main airport, which you can get to without passing through Kingston. Check in advance, as political situations change rapidly.

Panama to (from) the Eastern Caribbean

The tactics to use to cross the Eastern Caribbean will differ, depending on which direction you're traveling.

Westbound: From anywhere in the Eastern Caribbean, you can go straight into the Panama Canal region. Particularly for cruising sailboats, this route offers one of the finest sleigh rides in the world. You may often be reefed way down and surfing with white knuckles firmly glued to the wheel. Not so, the other direction.

Eastbound: Bad timing and wrong routing are the two biggest mistakes cruisers make when they try to head upwind and upcurrent from Panama to the islands of the Eastern Caribbean. Many cruising boats summer over in Costa Rica and then move through Panama after hurricane season, but from there they try to head east in the winter. Wrong.

During the winter months, the Northeast Trades blow the strongest. Offshore of the Guajira Peninsula, which is the northern-most tip of South America, the Trades often blow at gale force for days. This is not caused by cyclonic activity; it's a reinforced Trade Wind "breeze." The worst winds begin in mid December and are known locally as the "Christmas Trades." Even 2,000-ton tuna seiners bound from Panama to canneries in Puerto Rico have great difficulties trying to make this leg in winter. <u>For 99.9 percent of all yachts, especially sailboats, that route is virtually impossible in winter.</u>

Every winter, I watch cruisers bravely depart through the Cristobal breakwaters, northeast bound. They have heard from others that the weather is difficult, but they are determined that they will just "hunker down and go for it." By the time they get five miles from the seabuoy, they find out how impossible it is and turn back to the protected anchorage – where they must wait months for the wind to subside.

A Better Plan: Strong motor yachts and well-powered sailboats have a chance to win the long uphill battle from Panama to the Eastern Caribbean, but only at the proper season. The route that works

includes: a stop in Panama's lovely San Blas Islands; a passage at least 100 miles off Colombia's pirate-ridden coast; a stop in Curacao, Venezuela; then on to Grenada. Its final reward is to work north through the Lesser Antilles.

The best months are either May or November, because the Trades have either begun to drop off considerably (sometimes going flat for days) or they haven't picked up yet. The trip is possible during the entire summer/autumn season, because the route lies beneath the normal hurricane-formation belt. However, in abnormal weather years like strong El Ninos, hurricanes have formed that far south.

Though the Trades are down, you'll probably encounter heavy thunderstorms and their accompanying high wind and big seas, but these are of short duration. Some groups of cruising boats spend their remaining summer months in Venezuela and then move on.

An Alternative: An alternative route from the Panama Canal to the Virgin Islands is to head east from Colon to the San Blas Islands, then cross north to Jamaica. From there work your way close inshore on the south side of the islands of Hispaniola and Puerto Rico. This tactic takes advantage of the land/sea breeze effect of the islands on the Trades. May is the best month for this plan. November is next best, but there still persists some danger of late hurricanes. From December through April it is impossible because of the winter Trades.

Chapter 9
Key West to the Yucatan

The 330-mile crossing from Key West to Mexico's Yucatan destinations of Cozumel, Cancun and Isla Mujeres (and vice versa) demands close attention to both the weather and navigation. Spring is the best time of year to make this crossing, because winter's Northers blow against the Gulf Stream current to create big square waves.

Southbound

To look for favorable trends, monitor the weather and Gulf Stream reports for several days before your planned departure. In the winter, watch for strong cold fronts moving off the Texas coast, because these are what cause Northers when they reach down into the Yucatan Channel. In winter, perhaps the best time to leave is right after a Norther has just blown itself out but before the next one begins. Don't leave if your forecast is questionable. The Gulf Stream current varies in intensity and direction, further complicating navigation. Because your landfalls on both ends are on low islands, you'll rely on your GPS and radar.

Southbound from Key West, we lay a course for the Isla Mujeres Light, even though we're heading for Cozumel, so that we can have a good fix and then coast along by the high-rise hotels of Cancun and head directly for the northwest corner of Cozumel. The high-rise hotels of Cozumel will appear out of the haze first.

Northbound

If you're northbound through the Yucatan Channel, you'll aided by the Gulf Stream current. Late spring is the best time for this leg. At that time of the year, you may even be so fortunate as to have the wind southeast, which might give you a beam reach the whole way to Key West.

In a dire emergency such as a violent Norther, you could take shelter in the lee of Cabo San Antonio, the west end of Cuba. But, if you come within 12 miles of Cuba's reefs or land, do call their Guarda Costa on VHF channel 16 to request permission to enter their waters. And then expect to be boarded by the Cuban Navy.

Cruising Ports

Via Cuba

Either direction, the route between Key West and the Yucatan Channel destinations will skirt right along the north coast of Cuba. Stay outside Cuba's 12-mile limit.

Each year, many cruising yachts visit Cuba, and they report that the locals are friendly. For making the route covered in this guidebook, a stop over on Cuba is quite logical, and we look forward to being able to include a chapter on Cuba in our fifth edition. But as we go to press with this fourth edition, the U.S. still has not relaxed its restrictions on visiting Cuba.

If you do plan to stop in Cuba, fax the Office of Foreign Assets Control at (202) 622-0077 to request a list of the regulations regarding a visit to Cuba. Many cruisers interpret the regulations to say that you can visit Cuba but cannot spend any money there – specifically at Marina Hemingway, the well appointed marina just west of Havana to which most visitors head. It has been reported that the "spend no money" clause is not often prosecuted – except in obvious cases, such as coming straight from Havana to Key West and leaving a receipt from Marina Hemingway laying on the chart table for U.S. Customs inspectors to have trouble not seeing.

To visit Cuba when you're coming from South Florida, you must get the U.S. Coast Guard permission to depart the security zone. The form is available any Coast Guard station in South Florida. Read it, fill it out and sign the back.)Reading the fine print of this form may discourage you from going at all.) Then fax it to Key West Coast Guard Station at (305) 292-8739, and they will fax you back the authorization form.

If you're traveling from Key West and planning to cruise the Yucatan Channel destinations, you could enter Cuba at Marina Hemingway (23⌇05.4'N by 82⌇30.6'W). Do call their Guarda Costa on VHF channel 16 to request permission to enter their waters. Then, staying behind the reef that protects Cuba's north coastline, you could work your way westward from anchorage to anchorage. Your jump off at Cabo San Antonio would leave you only 90 miles from Isla Mujeres, Mexico.

Chapter 10
Yucatan Channel Cruising Grounds

Isla Mujeres, Cancun and Isla Cozumel are the cruising boaters' favorite tropical destinations in Mexico along the Yucatan Channel, and because they're not far away from each other, we've combined them into one handy chapter.

Isla Mujeres

Literally translated, this means Women Island. With the construction of a new marina, Isla Mujeres has become the yachting center of the east coast of Mexico. The island is on the Caribbean Coast of the Yucatan peninsula, 330 miles southwest of Key West, Florida. It lies only 3.5 miles off the Mexican mainland and 4 miles north of the mega-resorts of Cancun. Cancun has the airport, the high-rise hotels and the boogey-woogey night life. Isla Mujeres (population 10,000) is its laid back, peaceful companion, a favorite of knowledgeable world travelers including the British Royal Family.

Northern Approach: The island is low. Coming from the north you will first see a high-rise hotel standing alone on the north end of the island. A reef runs 400 meters north of the tip. On the north end of the reef is a post and tower with green light. Pass this light on your port hand with 0.392 n.m. berth, then turn to 190⸗M. Ahead you will see a buoy, and it marks the entrance channel to the harbor. Keep this off your starboard bow and pass along the shore. This approach has a minimum of 8-foot water depth. Be careful of a brown looking shoal on your starboard side. You can see it with high sun. Then, keeping the entrance buoy to starboard, turn around to port, keeping the low white sandy point on your port side. Pass close along the shore and pass another buoy on your starboard side. This marks a shoal to starboard. To avoid it, keep close along the shore.

Southern approach: Pass between (Becket Rock) Roca La Bandera (21°10'N by 86°44'W) and the southern end of Isla Mujeres, heading to just west of the Bajo Pepito buoy (21°12.5'N by 86°45.3'W). A considerable reef area lies between this buoy and the island, and a very strong

Cruising Ports

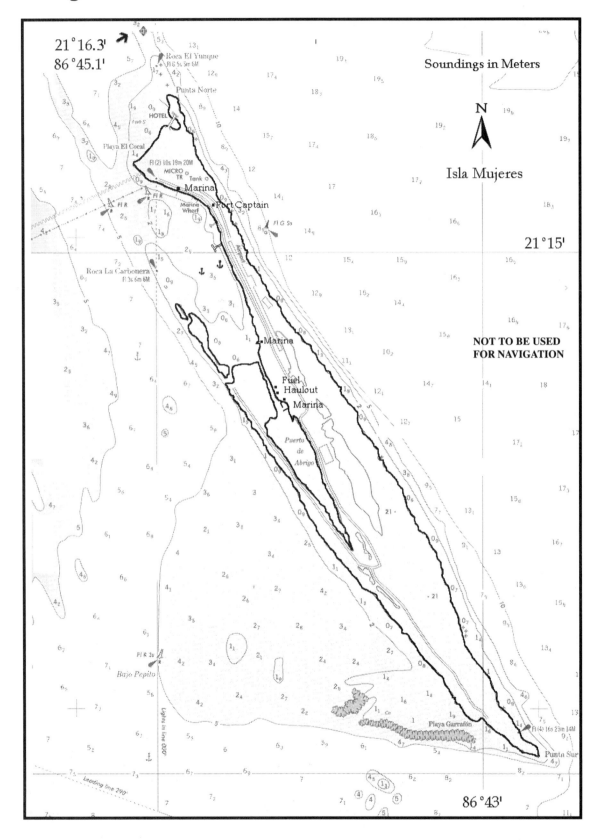

current sets you toward it, so give the reef a wide berth. When rounding Pepito in three fathoms of water, you will see two lights in range due north marking the entrance to the harbor. Keep these off your starboard bow at 2.5 miles until you pick up the channel buoys. Stay north of the channel buoys as you enter the harbor to avoid an uncharted shoal in the center.

Inner Harbor: Continuing south along the shore you will pass the docks of the Club de Yates, the ferry landing in the middle of town, the Navy docks, a long concrete T-head pier, a half-mile of sand beach and coconut palms and, farther south, the Paraiso Marina.

You may anchor south of the concrete T-head pier, but the Port Captain requires that the channel into the Laguna Makax be kept clear. Because the prevailing wind is easterly, anchoring along the eastern shore is calmest. If there is a spot, anchor in as close to the beach as your draft will allow. Otherwise anchor just west of the channel. The anchorage is very protected in all winds, but becomes choppy in a Norther. The bottom is sand with patches of grass. Try to find a spot clear of grass or it will be difficult to set the hook. Do not anchor too far to the west because of shoaling. You may land a dinghy at the concrete T-head pier, which gives you access to downtown.

At the south end of the anchorage you'll see Marina Paraiso on the eastern shore. Then you will see a narrow canal (minimum depth 10') entering into Laguna Makax. Puerto Isla Mujeres Marina is just south of this canal where it widens up and is on the port side. There is also a very narrow entrance from Bahia Mujeres into the south end of the northern harbor called the Chute de Chute pass. It has eight feet of water but because it is twisty, narrow and has a swift current I wouldn't recommend it.

You may also anchor in the north central part of this lagoon in about 10' over sand and grass. However, it is a long way to town. This anchorage has all around protection, but in strong winds you tend to drag because of all the grass on the bottom. It is also farther from town than the northern anchorage. The lagoon shoals in the southern part.

Port Clearance: For port clearance come into port flying your Q-flag to port and courtesy flag to starboard. Go ashore (captain only) with five copies of your Crew

Puerto Isla Mujeres Marina: This modern marina is a major destination for pleasure boats and the center of activity of the Yucatan cruising grounds.

List, ship's document and passports. The Capitania, Aduana and Migracion offices are conveniently placed along the malecOn (beach front avenue) near the ferry pier. Start first at the Port Captain's office. He can issue a cruising permit (small daily fee). that allows you to come and go in the area without having to clear in and out each time.

This area lends it self to local cruising, providing easy visits to favorite local dive spots, Cancun and Isla Contoy. Throughout the Yucatan area there are new anchoring regulations being enforced to protect coral reefs which involves heavy fines for violators. Ask the Port Captain where you may anchor and where you may not. Then go on to Migracion (Immigration) where you'll be give tourist cards to fill out. Then to Aduana (Customs). You may also be required to visit the health clinic for a health clearance. Now you can go back to the boat and lower your Q-flag.

Marina Puerto Isla Mujeres: This marina was built inside Laguna Makax, which is a hurricane hole entered through a narrow channel with a 10-foot minimum depth. Deep-draft vessels should hug the eastern bank. A modern fuel facility is located along the eastern shore of the channel. It has a non-floating wooden dock approximately 200-feet long. They sell low-sulfur centrifuged diesel. Next door is a haul-out facility with a 150-ton travel lift run by Derekor Gunnel of Ft. Lauderdale.

The marina is adjacent to the yard. In front of the marina office, you'll see Florida-style docks, which are wooden pilings and non floating wooden docks. Just south of that are California-style floating docks. They have several size docks which can handle from megayachts on down. You can make reservations in the U.S. at 1-800-960-ISLA or in Mexico 52-987-704-39, email <<isla@cancun.rce.com.mx>>. The

docks have 110/30amp and 220/50 amp. The voltage holds up very well, better than most Mexican marinas I have been in, or even some in the states for that matter. We could easily run our air conditioning and washer/dryer. Dockside water is chlorinated and hard. They have telephone hookups, the only Mexican marina I know of to do so for temporary guests. The system works well. Laundry service is pick up and return; there's no do-it-yourself laundromat on the premises. Guests may use the pool and restaurant bar of the adjacent resort. A convenience store with limited supplies is one block from the entrance to the resort.

Marina Puerto Isla Mujeres has a launch service that can take you directly to the embarcadero in Cancun, and they offer a package deal: launch and taxi to and from the airport, which is several miles south of Cancun. A marine parts and hardware store on the embarcadero is open, and you can also order many Lewis catalog parts to be shipped down from Florida via the dockmaster.

Dockmaster Pierre Sanchez is ever present for help and advice. A U.S. citizen who is equally fluent in English, Spanish and French, Pierre can arrange your port clearance, which involves a visit to the boat from Migracion and the Port Captain. There are no charges for this service, but a $15 to $20 gratuity to the officials is common for the service of them coming to you – as opposed to you going to them.

Hurricane Hole: As mentioned earlier Laguna Makax is a hurricane hole. However the bottom of the lagoon is covered with grass and therefore very poor holding. During a hurricane watch Puerto Isla Mujeres Marina accepts vessels on a first come, first serve basis. Because the marina is so heavily constructed and especially with the heavy pilings, vessels can be heavily moored. Unlike marinas in the states, their liabilities in reference to insurance are: if your vessel damages their docks, their insurance pays for the damage, and likewise, if damage happens to your vessel from their docks, they are not liable. Vessels in this marina survived a hit from mega-hurricane Gilbert several years ago.

Marina Paraiso: The 24-slip Marina Paraiso has 7-foot average depths alongside their wooden non-floating docks. They have 110- and 220-volt shore power, security, swimming pool, washer and dryer, showers and an international telephone. Manuel Gutierrez is the owner/manager; their phone is (987) 7-02-52.

Enrique Lima's Marina: Enrique's is the first facility you come to upon entering the harbor. It has slips and is in the middle of town. It is rarely used except when all the rest of slips on the island are taken up at the height of the season around Easter. This location is exposed to boat wakes and fetch from southerly winds.

Local Services: The Super Betino is the largest grocery store on the main plaza. Isla Mujeres' farmers market is at the north end of Matamoros for fresh produce. Arrive early for the best selection. Supplies are somewhat limited on the island and if you need to do a major reprovisioning you should do it at the big WalMart store in nearby Cancun. (See Cancun below.)

We have had occasion to use the emergency medical services of English-speaking Dr. Antonio Salas and we were quite pleased. His phone is (987) 7-00-21 or 7-04-77.

The national underwater park of Garrafon Reef occupies the southwest corner of the island. Hurricane Gilbert damaged but didn't destroy this delicate coral formation, but Garrafon and Manchones reef is still a good place to scuba and snorkel in Isla Mujeres' clear waters.

Fast ferries leave Isla Mujeres' downtown dock for Puerto Juarez near Cancun on the mainland every half hour. The ride is very inexpensive and takes 20 to 30 minutes. A car ferry also runs to Punta Sam farther to the north.

Cancun

Although the sprawling city of Cancun on the Yucatan mainland is not as popular a spot for cruising boaters, it is more well known to land-based tourists. You can visit Cancun in your own boat, but the anchorage is indifferent and can be uncomfortable when the wind is north through east. The anchorage is on the northeast corner of Cancun fronting the hotels. If you anchor in 15 to 20 feet on a sand bottom, you're in a wonderful place to swim. You can go ashore by landing on the sand beaches.

Cancun has an interior lagoon with three marinas west of this anchorage, but don't be fooled. The lagoon is suitable for only very small craft. Its main limitation is that you must pass beneath a low bridge (15 foot vertical clearance) into the lagoon, which has questionable depths of six feet. Just before you come to the bridge, you'll see a concrete pier used by tour boats.

The ferry dock at Puerto Juarez is just north of but adjacent to Cancun City. About a half mile north of Puerto Juarez is Marina Hacienda del Mar (Tel. 80-1070) with 150 slips, fuel, electrical hookup, cable-TV, 24 hour security, and laundry. The marina is placed on a lee-shore from the prevailing easterlies. It's protected by a breakwater, but still subject to surge in high winds. It does give access to the tourist amenities of Cancun without having to take a ferry ride.

75

Cancun City (as opposed to the tourist district) is a large city with many stores. Visit the brand new enclosed air-conditioned shopping mall, the Plaza Las Americas. It's as nice as any mall you'll find in the U.S. You can take in the latest run movie, eat at one of many restaurants and then go shopping at Sears, Ace Hardware and the Commercial Mexicana, a well-stocked grocery store.

The regional airport 20 minutes outside Cancun has flights to Houston, Miami, and Mexico City. It's a fairly expensive cab ride.

Side Trips: Cancun makes a good place to leave the boat, rent a car and explore the magnificent Mayan ruins of the Yucatan. Tulum, south of the islands, is the most dramatic because it is located on the coast. You can also visit it and many of the inland ruins such as Chichen-Itza by tour buses which you can join at Cancun.

Isla Cozumel

The small island of Cozumel (20°30'N by 86°58'W) is situated eight miles from the Yucatan peninsula of Mexico. For cruising boater, Cozumel offers an anchorage off the town center plus two small marinas. It is known to scuba

The narrow entrance to Puerto Abrigo is difficult to see.

divers the world over for its credibly clear waters and black coral. Sportfishing is a big draw, too.

Northern Approaches: The Gulf Stream is strong and variable around the island. The current is at least three knots over the Arrowsmith Bank on the northerly approaches to the island. On one powerboat passage from Isla Mujeres to Cozumel, we were making 10 knots through the water but only four knots over the bottom, because we were fighting a whopping six-knot current!

The Trades blow strongly around Cozumel Island, keeping it relatively cool but making for wet sailing. In winter months a strong wind known as the *Nortada* must be reckoned with. When this wind blows across the opposing current, some wicked seas stack up. In the summer Cozumel is a frequent target of the West Indian hurricane. In fact the Yucatan Channel was the first place to be nicknamed "Hurricane Alley."

In 1988 we arrived on Cozumel two months after it had been savaged by Hurricane Gilbert, a class five hurricane – the worst classification. The perimeter of the whole island looked like it had been fire-bombed, because all that lush vegetation had been killed by the salt inundation. Sunken boats were strewn all over the marina. The island's highest point at the center of this little island is only 60 feet above sea level. It's a miracle that no one on Cozumel was killed.

The only chart covering Cozumel is Mexican Chart No. S.M. 926. The island is low and blanketed with 70-foot trees. When approaching from the north, a few high-rise hotels will appear first out of the haze. Use caution on approaches to both the north

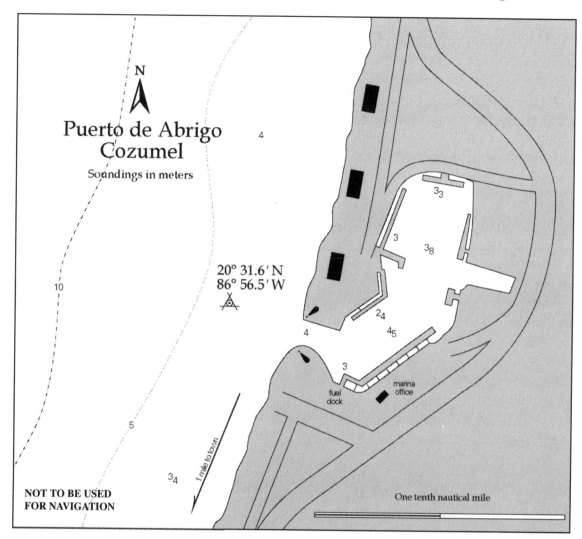

Puerto de Abrigo
Cozumel

Soundings in meters

N

4

20° 31.6′ N
86° 56.5′ W

10

3_3

3

3_8

2_4

4_5

4

3

marina office

fuel dock

5

1 mile to town

3_4

**NOT TO BE USED
FOR NAVIGATION**

One tenth nautical mile

end of the island and the south because of extensive reefs. Pass west of them in deep water.

Marinas: Puerto Abrigo, a man-made yacht harbor, is about a mile north of the municipal pier on the east side of the island. It was formerly a coral limestone quarry and was made into a yacht basin by dynamiting out the seaward wall. The hard-to-spot narrow entrance is marked by a light tower and barber pole-like structures that carry red and green lights at night. During the day you might see the tuna towers of the many sportfishing boats inside before you spot the entrance itself. "Abrigo" means overcoat, signifying that this basin is well

protected. But when the larger yachts nose in to take a look, they usually think it means straight-jacket.

Puerto Abrigo is very crowded during the winter/spring season, because it is a favorite of sportfishermen who come down from South Florida and Houston. Several big- money tournaments take place here, so with such high rollers around, the marina is expensive. Call ahead for a reservation: Club Nautico de Cozumel, telephone 20-11-8.

Only the pier in front of the marina office may be used by visitors. All the piers are non-floating concrete, and you must Med-moor. This procedure can be tricky, because the wind often blows on the beam, setting you down on the neighboring boat. The bottom is limestone and coral gravel over hardpan, so it is difficult to get an anchor to set or even to find a place to put it down, as the bottom is crowded with the anchors of other boats. Fortunately the water is so clear that you can see the placement of other anchors. It's probably a good idea to dive on your anchor to make sure there won't be surprises.

Puerto Abrigo is usually well protected, but when a Norther is blowing, some surge makes it inside the harbor, and it can be rough at the guest piers. Make sure your stern is well fendered in case your anchor drags and your stern is thrown into the concrete pier.

Port Clearance: Once you're moored inside and flying the yellow "quarantine" flag, announce your arrival at the marina office, so they can notify the authorities. Remain on board until someone from the port captain's office comes down to the boat and clear you. Unlike the relaxed *laissez faire* attitude of Mexican officials in Pacific ports, these authorities take a very dim view of your disembarking before you have been inspected. In some respects, the

port clearance procedure here is almost like a different country compared to the Mexican Pacific. Here, requests for "tips" for which receipts are not given (a sure sign of "mordida") are far more common. Try not to arrive or clear on a weekend, because overtime charges for *"servicios extraordinarios"* are "muy expensive."

To clear out, visit the Capitania, the Port Captain's office which is a two-story white building located a good walk south of the marina, which lies on the north edge of town. The immigration office, Migracion, is in a federal building a few blocks south of the municipal pier, and the Aduana or Customs is at the airport, for which you'll probably need a taxi. As in most of Mexico, the smaller taxis usually charge less than the full-sized ones. For an extra charge the marina will handle your port clearance, both in and out.

Fuel Stop: The Club Nautico sells centrifuged diesel. The fuel pier is immediately to starboard upon entering the harbor. You may tie alongside to fuel, but if a Norther is blowing, it can be rough here. Even under prevailing conditions, you'll notice the surge and need plenty of fenders.

Space is tight inside Club Nautico, located inside Puerto Abrigo on Isla Cozumel. Fuel dock is along right side of photo.

Cozumel's municipal ferry dock is busy with shore boats from cruise ships and local excursion boats.

This fuel pier's tanks are frequently dry, meaning you'll have to wait a day or two for a truck to fill them.

Anchorage: If you don't wish to use the marina, you can anchor off the huge concrete municipal pier in the open rodestead. Though generally protected from the prevailing easterly Trades, it offers no protection from Northers. To clear with the authorities you may be asked to come alongside this pier, but don't do so unless you are asked and given a schedule. This pier is always busy with commercial off-loading, fishing boats, local excursions, and shore boats from ocean liners that make port calls here. The pier is also subject to a great deal of surge, so you'll want to remain alongside only long enough to clear. If you use the pier to land your dinghy, you'll be right in the middle of town.

Bahia Caleta is three miles south of the pier, just north of the El Presidente Hotel. It's a natural harbor but often crowded with local boats, so it's hard to find a place to anchor. The cove entrance is 30 feet wide, marked by a 20-foot metal tower on each bank lighted red and green. The depth of the entrance is 6.5 feet. As you enter and reach the place where the cove opens up, hook to the north to avoid a large submerged rock. Vessels Med-moor to the shore. Many of the local boats leave during the day but return to their same spot in the evening, so ask first if there's an open spot.

Town Services: Cozumel's only town, San Miguel, is small but does offer plenty of good restaurants that cater to visitors who arrive by boat. Two grocery stores on the town square have a modest selection of foods but lots of interesting miscellany. Cozumel's airport has direct flights to Miami, Merida and Mexico City. A ferry also runs to several point on the mainland, one of them being Cancun.

Renting an inexpensive motorcycle is a good way to explore here. Outside San Miguel, the island is sparsely populated. The paved road that encircles the island takes you past the best beaches which are on the southeast corner. Nice hotels here cater to divers.

On the northeast side of the island, a rugged dirt road runs out to the lighthouse on the point. This road winds through uninhabited jungle and past the roaring surf, allowing you to explore overgrown Spanish and Mayan ruins in solitude. If you think of taking this little side trip, tell the rental agency, so they can fix you up with an extra jug of gasoline from the island's only gas station.

The entire west side of the island is usually in the lee of the prevailing Trade Winds and therefore serves as an anchorage. Exploration by boat gives the best access to diving on the island. Air and diving supplies are available at several dive shops in San Miguel and at most hotels.

History: Cozumel was first inhabited by the Mayan Indians whose ruined temples and cities are still scattered throughout the jungle. The Spanish discovered the island of Cozumel shortly before the beginning of their Mexican conquest. The Conquistadors held the first Catholic mass in Meso-America atop one of the Mayan pyramids. The descendants of the noble Maya people still comprise the bulk of Cozumel's inhabitants. Today, the living coral reefs that form this island's spectacular scuba diving spots is in danger of being silted over and killed – by the turbulence from the giant props of all the visiting cruise ships. When you anchor anywhere around the island of Cozumel, be sure your anchor and chain do not come into contact with any of the delicate coral heads.

Puerto Aventuras, just down Mexico's mainland coast from Isla Mujeres and Cozumel, has received lots of press lately. Some small local fishing boats are based there. Unfortunately, its only entrance is still somewhat dangerous due to lots of shallow water on the outer approaches and some large shifting shoals that must be avoided on the inner approach to the entrance jetty. For those reasons, we cannot yet recommend it as a cruising port for the larger long-range cruising boats or U.S. sportfishing boats.

Chapter 11
Grand Cayman

∿∿∿∿∿∿∿∿∿∿∿∿∿∿∿∿∿∿∿∿∿∿∿∿∿∿∿∿∿

The island of Grand Cayman (19°18'N by 81°23'W) lies almost at the center of the Western Caribbean. Although it lies off the usual sailing routes, it could be a vital fueling stop for power cruisers. Grand Cayman is always a good place to keep in mind in case of emergency.

The island is a British Crown Colony, and despite its facade of sandy-beach resorts, it is primarily an off-shore banking center. Prosperity is much more evident on Grand Cayman than on most islands of the Caribbean, but consequently prices are higher here than on its nearest neighbors. Because Grand Cayman never had large plantations, slavery did not figure prominently in its history. The many races here are mixed through marriage, and racial tensions are nearly non-existent.

Approaches: From either direction, your first visual clue may be an increase in pleasure craft traffic. Cayman is such a low island that you often don't see it on radar until 10 miles away, and you can't see it with binoculars until you're right

on it. Call Port Security on VHF channel 16 to announce your arrival.

Anchorages: The primary anchorage is off the center of George Town, on the southwest corner of the island. Drop the hook just to the northwest of the pier. The bottom is a mixture of coral and sand, so pick out a sandy spot in the incredibly clear water.

George Town is not much of a harbor, because it is protected only from the east. Yes, this is the prevailing wind, but any wind or swell from other quadrants is definitely felt in the harbor. During a Nor'wester, which happens several times a winter, this anchorage becomes a lee shore. The season for Nor'westers is from November through April. These storms can strike with little or no warning, sometimes out of a blue sky. The presence of a swell out of the west may presage a storm. When visiting here, stay tuned to weather from NMN, and pay close attention to the portion for conditions in the Gulf of Mexico and the Northwest Caribbean. Remember that the colder the forecast for

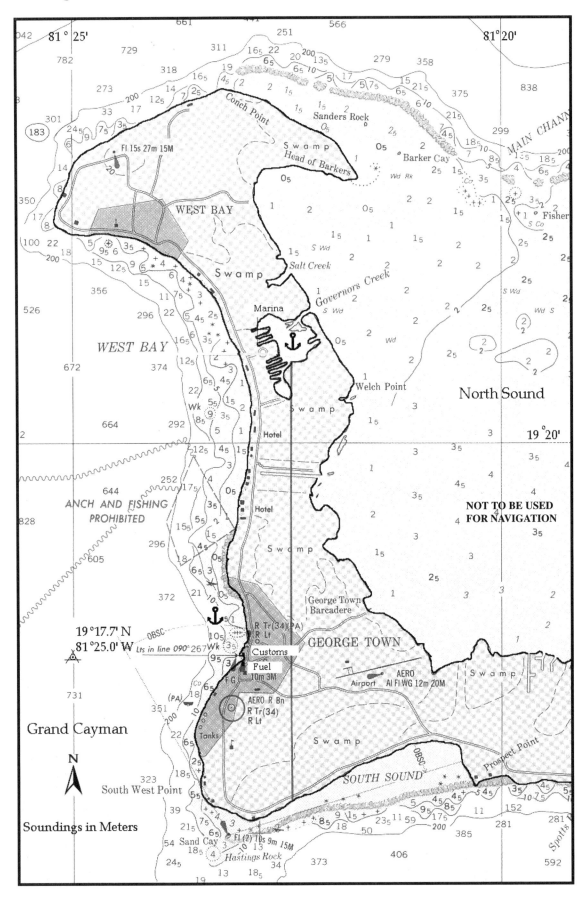

Miami, the more violent the storm.

The best shelter from a Nor'wester is in Southwest Sound. Come in as close as your draft will permit between Spot Bay and Prospect. If you see a general exodus of local boats in that direction, by all means follow suit.

Once you get anchored call Port Security again. They will instruct you when to come to the pier for boarding. I have tried to convince them to come out in our launch, but they won't. I don't like this pier, because it was designed for commercial ships and the surge is bad. It may seem calm for hours, but then a severe surge will hit from nowhere. Unfortunately, everyone who enters the islands must dock at the pier; it's the rule. Make sure your vessel is well fendered.

Port Clearance: In my experience, Grand Cayman is the easiest, least expensive and friendliest place in the Caribbean to clear official papers. The officials board your boat at the pier, and you fill out a few simple forms and present passports. Be sure to declare your firearms. This is true wherever you go but even more so in British or former-British possessions, especially nearby Jamaica. Grand Cayman has very strong gun laws. If you declare your arms, no problem. They take them off and store them, (and when you are leaving, you return to the same pier and they bring them back to your boat). Once the officials have cleared you in, you are free to leave the pier.

To clear out, you walk a few steps to the Port Authority Building. Your first office is Customs, where you fill in a clearance form and pay a $3-fee. However, the do charge a $50-overtime fee after 1600 weekdays, after 1200 on Saturdays, and anytime on Sundays. Then you walk upstairs to Immigration, where they put an exit stamp in your passports and clearance form. That's it.

George Town's Customs Pier looks over the quaint waterfront.

Fuel Stop: To make fuel arrangements, call Beffer's Fuel Pier on VHF channel 16. Beffer's own private pier lies on the south side of the bight, only 100 meters away from the municipal pier where you cleared in; this one too suffers from surge but isn't as jagged. Beffer's pier has its own tanks and pumps, and good drinking water is available. As on most Caribbean islands, both fuel and water are expensive. Cayman uses Imperial Gallons (1.0 ImpG = 1.2 U.S. gallons) and Cayman dollars (1.0 Cayman = 1.2 U.S. dollars). The metered drinking water is about 10 cents per gallon.

Local Services: You may land your dinghy at the dock used for cruise ship launches, which is right in the center of town. Nearby are banks, restaurants, banks, grocery shops and more banks. (If you hadn't heard before, you'll quickly see that Grand Cayman is a banking center.) At the head of this dock is a wondrous device, a telephone booth with an instant link to the U.S. via AT&T. You may also land a dinghy a few hundred yards north of the pier where you'll see another wonder, a Burger King. This was the first Burger King in the world at which you can arrive by launch.

You may also anchor north of George Town in West Bay, along a beautiful white- sand stretch of beach called Seven-Mile Beach, which is lined with hotels and is actually only four miles long. To rent a car or grab a taxi, anchor off the Holiday Inn at 19° 20.3'N. North Sound is very well protected by a barrier reef. If your draft is six feet or less, you can enter through the Main Channel using your now acute visual coral-piloting skills. Inside you'll find a large marina with alongside berthing at Governor's Harbour, a Florida-style development with waterfront homes. Mosquitoes are voracious here. There is plenty of room to anchor, and it's also a snug place to ride out a Nor'wester.

In the south end of the North Sound is Harbour House Marina with a fuel dock and 40-ton haulout facility, but be aware that this area gets a bad chop in Nor'westers.

Surge is often a problem at Beffer's fuel pier, so plan to fender well.

Chapter 12
Isla Roatan

∿∿∿

Roatan is the principal island in a group called the Bay Islands of Honduras, which are the best cruising grounds in the Western Caribbean. The lovely but poorly charted island of Roatan lies 28 miles from the north coast of mainland Honduras, 625 miles from Key West.

In 1502, Roatan had the distinction of being one of the islands that Columbus "discovered," and beginning in the 17th century, Roatan was used as a base for English pirates raiding the Spanish Main. Their English-speaking descendants as well as the descendants of blacks they brought with them from Jamaica still inhabit these islands. However they have turned to the less blood-thirsty pursuits of fishing and tourism. Pirate treasure has been secretly dug up and smuggled off the island, so the authorities here take a dim view of treasure seekers.

Coxen's Hole (16°18'N by 86°35'W) on the southwest end of the island is the Bay Islands' governmental center. The Port Captain is located here, so you can enter here, but yacht facilities are few. More conveniently, you can also enter at French Harbor or the nearby Fantasy Island Marina, if you wish to pay the officials to drive down-island in a taxi.

Approaches to Coxen's Hole: When approaching the harbor from the west end of Roatan, stay fairly close to shore, because two reefs lie to starboard. We line up on the clock tower, because it takes us right to the municipal pier which has six feet of water at its head. At the foot of the pier is the white Customs and Immigration building. Once you tie up at the pier, for which there is a charge, the officials will arrive immediately.

If you anchor, drop the hook in two to three fathoms to the west of Big Cay. It is good holding ground on a mud bottom, but swinging room is restricted by a large sunken vessel. The rules here state that the captain alone should go to Customs to notify them of the arrival.

Port Clearance: You may clear your own papers. If you plan a short stay, clear papers from the last port, mentioning

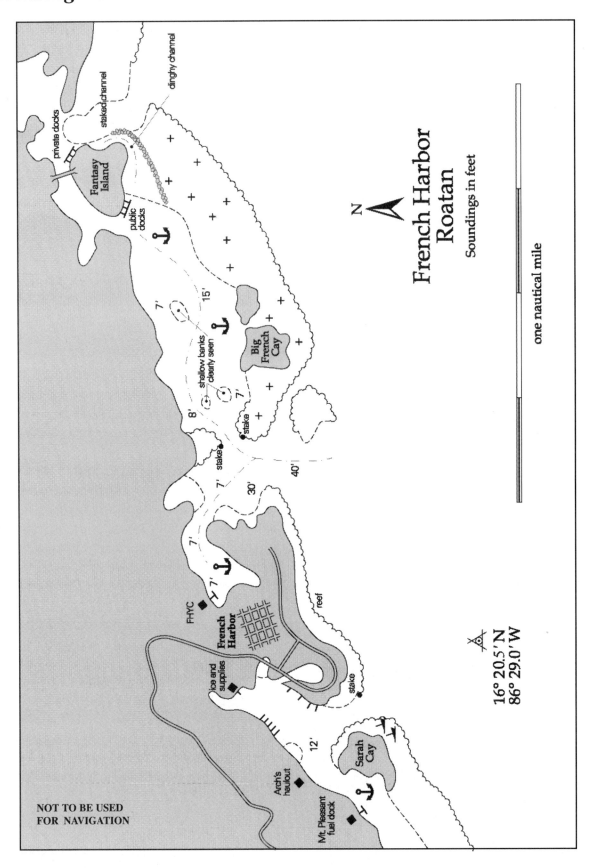

French Harbor
Roatan

Soundings in feet

N

one nautical mile

16° 20.5' N
86° 29.0' W

NOT TO BE USED
FOR NAVIGATION

private docks

staked channel

dinghy channel

Fantasy
Island

public docks

15'

7'

shallow banks
clearly seen

7'

8'

stake

Big
French
Cay

stake

7'

30'

40'

7'

7'

reef

FHYC

French
Harbor

ice and
supplies

stake

Arch's
haulout

12'

Sarah
Cay

Mt. Pleasant
fuel dock

Roatan as an intermediate stop only. This gives you a transient status, making it less expensive to clear. However the "run around" and *mordida* are the order of the day. To avoid all these hassles, you may wish to use a ship's agent. If so, try Beatman Ebanks; his phone is (504) 45-12-71. He answers to "Lady V" on VHF channel 16. Beatman is an energetic native English-speaker who is experienced in dealing with yachts and has a good working relationship with the officials.

Local Services: While waiting for the clearance, the captain can walk around town and get the flavor of the place. Things are a bit primitive and services are few, but a well-stocked grocery store (Warren's) stands near the head of the pier. There's a bank nearby, and although dollars are frequently accepted, you can trade them here for the local currency, which is the lempira.

Fuel Stop: A new dock with fuel is found on the other side of Warren's. Take fuel from its north side. Because this fuel has had a reputation for being dirty, Jackson's in French Harbor is a better fuel stop. BJ's is an excellent restaurant on Big Key. An airline office and airstrip offer daily service to La Ceiba on the Honduran mainland, where you can make connections to the rest of the world.

Once papers are cleared, you can move a few miles east to French Harbor with its commodious, well-protected harbor. At the entrance you find a stake to starboard with a white triangle on it marking the edge of the reef. Keep to the starboard side of the entrance to avoid the unmarked reef to port. There is 60 feet of water in the center of the channel. Once inside, be aware there is another reef dead ahead and marked by another stake.

Anchorages: A turn to the left will take you to a well-protected anchorage away from the bustle of French Harbor. Mt. Pleasant is a well-stocked grocery store along this section of shoreline, and they also fill propane bottles. A turn to starboard takes you into French Harbor, the home of a large shrimper fleet. For cruisers, French Harbor has a haul-out facility, Seth Arch's yard. It is a center for wooden boat-building and repair, because it has access to good woods and cheap labor. At Jackson's Fuel Dock you can get gas, diesel, water and ice chips.

You can make arrangements to tie alongside the pier of Romeo's Restaurant. From here you can watch the comings and goings of harbor traffic and be near this

French Harbor Yacht Club lies inside one of the Caribbean's best hurricane holes.

Fantasy Island's marina is clean, modern and well built.

small community's center. The Buccaneer is another fine dining establishment which was founded by Romeo's father. It is run by his widow Rita, who also runs a travel agency next door.

The area between Big French Key and Fantasy Island is frequently used as a well protected all-weather anchorage by cruisers.

Marinas: French Harbor Yacht Club shares the next entrance east of French Key. You head north between Big French Key and the main island, entering into what is one of the island's best hurricane holes, and then turn northwest a short distance. The Yacht Club is a small 9-slip cruisers' hangout with 7- to 8-foot depths. It has water and 110-volt power only. They have a pool, restaurant and small grocery store. The Yacht Club has the advantage of being closer to town than Fantasy Island. The French Harbor Yacht Club's phone is 455-1478 and 455-1460. Their fax is 455-1459.

Fantasy Island Resort, on Ezekiel Cay a mile east of the FHYC, is Roatan's most luxurious and modern facility for pleasure boaters. You can take 12-foot draft vessels up to this marina, which monitors

VHF channel 19. To get to the eastern side of Fantasy Island, you enter the same way as for French Harbor Yacht Club (above), but after clearing Big French Key, you turn east nearer the shore of the big island, watching out for coral heads in the incredibly clear water, and head for Fantasy Island docks. It has non-floating wooden piers, water, power (110-volt, 30 amp and 220-volt, 50 amp), cable TV, and the fuel dock has diesel and gasoline. Being a guest of the marina gives you access to the resort's facilities: tennis, laundry, swimming and free use of wind surfers. During the winter and spring season, Fantasy Island fills up, so reserve ahead. The marina's phone is (504) 45-11-91 and fax is 45-12-68.

Another entrance to Fantasy Island is immediately to the east between the resort and Coco View Island. This narrow channel is well staked, but this side of the marina has fewer slips than the western side.

Oak Ridge, another community a few miles east of French Harbor, has a Shell fuel dock, excellent protection and a large fishing fleet, but it's not as picturesque as French Harbor.

The island of Roatan has two new medical clinics, a public one in Coxen's

Hole with Spanish-speaking doctors and a private clinic in French Harbor with English- speaking doctors.

Columbus named the country Honduras, meaning deep, because he thought that deep waters were the cause of the rough seas he encountered. Actually it was rough because the water was shallow. Perhaps the Admiral's depth sounder had blown a fuse.

The Trades can blow strongly around Roatan, especially in the winter.

In the summer, hurricanes pose a danger, though Roatan lies on the southern fringes of hurricane tracks and is hit only on rare occasions. Hurricane Mitch of 1998 devastated mainland Honduras and flattened the nearby island Guanaja. Many vessels found safe shelter along Roatan's south side, and, fortunately, the hurricane never crossed the island. If the ill-fated wind jammer Phantome hadn't left Roatan, she might not have disappeared with 31 crew members aboard. But second guessing a hurricane is never an easy thing to do.

Spring and early summer are the most delightful seasons. Radio Belize (830 Khz) gives news and weather forecasts in English for the area at 0100, 0300, 1300, 1500, 1700, 1830, 2100 and 2300 Zulu.

The Bay Islands area is one of the best cruising grounds mentioned in this book. With its dozens of beautiful, closely spaced anchorages, you could spend many months exploring the region.

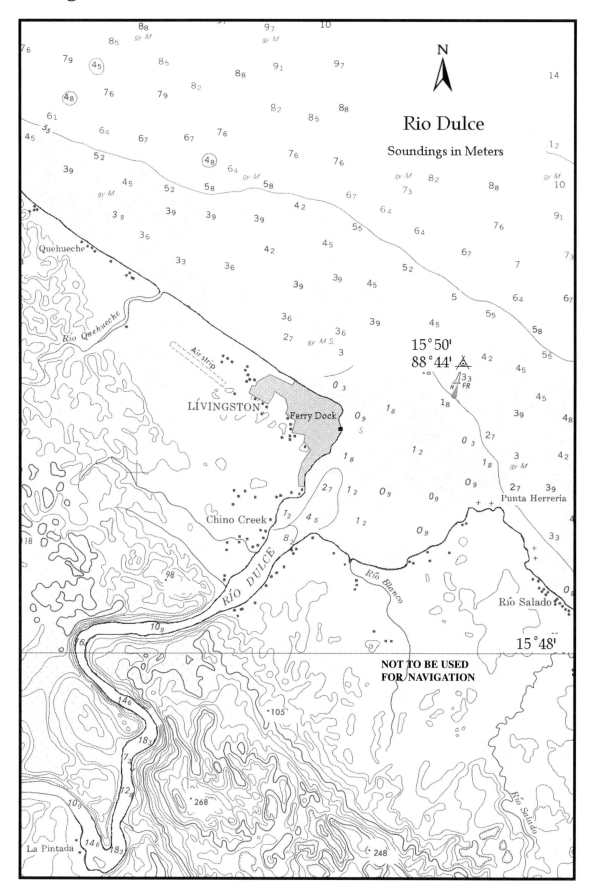

Rio Dulce

Soundings in Meters

Chapter 13
Rio Dulce, Guatemala

In the last few years, the Rio Dulce region of Guatemala's Caribbean coast has become one of the most popular cruising grounds along the route covered in this book. The Rio Dulce (sweet river) cruising region is more than just one river. The mouth of the Rio Dulce opens up a huge expanse of the country's interior to delightful exploration by yacht. The lower portion of the 6-mile river has carved a sinuous gorge between huge limestone cliffs that are draped with lush jungle foliage. Going upstream, the Rio Dulce leads you into the 10-mile-long El Golfete Bay, and it has lots of tributaries and side trips. As you proceed upstream, the main channel compresses and twists between two frontier towns, where most of the boating places are located, then it finally spreads out onto Lake Izabal, which is 25 miles long and 10 miles wide.

Waterfalls, hot springs, Mayan villages, beautiful jungle scenery, friendly locals, and many miles of inland waterways protected from tropical storms are just some of the attractions. Several marinas, fuel docks, haul-out yards and marine supply stores also help draw several hundred cruising yachts each year. That doesn't mean Rio Dulce has already been overrun by jet-set tourists, because, remember, we're talking about wild toucans and monkeys – and the developing nation of Guatemala. The indigenous Mayan tribes welcome the chance to sell their native

Many waterfalls flow into Rio Dulce's Lake Izabal.

foods, colorful *huipile* handicrafts or marine services to the visiting boaters, which are still pretty much a novelty. A hundred cruising yachts could comfortably lose themselves inside Rio Dulce's many separate regions and not see each other for weeks, unless they want to meet for socializing at one of the yachtie watering holes.

Hurricane Hole: Because the inner reaches of the cruising grounds are relatively protected by two mountain ranges (Sierra de Santa Cruz and Montanas del Mico) and the entrance lies behind the peninsula of Punta Manabique, the inner reaches have long been considered a hurricane hole. During the devastating Hurricane Mitch, many cruisers fled into Rio Dulce, using it as an effective hurricane hole. Many boats summer over here. However, this region does lie slightly within in the latitudes that can be raked by tropical storms and hurricanes. If you are visiting the many reefs and cays offshore of Bahia de Amatique when tropical storms threaten, it would certainly be advisable to scoot up river for protection. Exactly where would depend on the direction, speed and intensity of the storm.

Only this non-descript bluff marks the entrance to the Rio Dulce cruising grounds.

Approaches: When approaching the mouth of Rio Dulce from Belize, depart Punta Gorda on a course of 16⌖ True to the Rio Dulce sea buoy (15°50' N by 88°44' W). This 16-mile approach is free of hazards.

When approaching from Honduras, round Cabo Tres Puntas and head 218° True for the sea buoy 10 miles away. To time your arrival at Livingston in the daytime, you can anchor in the lee of the cape. Ox Tongue Shoal in the middle of Bahia Amatique is marked by a radar reflector and has a minimum depth of 10 feet.

The entrance to Rio Dulce can be difficult to spot, being obscured in the backdrop of surrounding hills, but the red tile roofs of Livingston stand out easily from the green vegetation.

Crossing the Bar: The river mouth has a shallow bar that stretches a half mile wide, hut with a uniform depth of six feet of water over it. If this presents a problem for your boat, the best time to cross the bar is whenever the afternoon sea breezes coincide with high tide, which add more depth. The on-shore flow of air retards the out-flowing river water. Check with the Port Captain's office (VHF channel 16) for the exact time of approaching high tides. If needed, a tug from Livingston can assist your vessel over the bar.

Pass 200 yards west of the buoy. Then take a bearing of 225° True, you'll see two things in range: the high point of the bluff in the background and the tip of the east bank of the river. Also, a conspicuous metal pier juts out from the west bank of the mouth of the canyon. Keep it to starboard. Continue in on the range of the bluffs on a course of 225° True. Expect to make course corrections due to the current, which will set you east toward the shoal. Boats that do go

Clear in here at Livingston before moving up into Rio Dulce.

aground can call the Port Captain to arrange for a tow off.

Move on in until you're off the Texaco dock in about nine feet of water, which is slightly south of the concrete municipal pier. You can then anchor in about eight feet of water southeast of it.

Port Clearance: You may clear into Guatemala from any of three places on Bahia Amatique: Livingston, which is usually the easiest for yachts, or Puerto Barrios, or Puerto Santo Tomas. Although it has Port Captain, Migracion and Aduana offices, Livingston is a tiny, remote town whose 2,000 inhabitants are mostly Mayan tribes, Mestizo and Black Caribe descendants. Its Anglo name came from a Louisiana lawyer who wrote Guatemala's penal code and helped introduce the democratic trial-by-jury process, at the request of Guatemala's President Morazan in 1823. Livingston has several good restaurants.

Hoist your yellow Q-flag and announce your arrival to the Port Captain on VHF channel 16. If the ferry is not in and not due back in soon, you might be able to tie up alongside the concrete ferry dock. Otherwise, remain at anchor until you are cleared. If no one responds or turns up after an hour or so, the captain alone may go ashore to search for the officials.

An unofficial English-speaking ship's agent named Philip can help you by

notifying the officials. He may be able to sell you a Guatemalan courtesy flag if you don't have one.

Five different offices will send someone to board you. Immigration takes all your passports. Customs takes your Zarpe or clearance from your last port, crew lists and ship's papers. The Port Captain will ask for any firearms. He will give you a receipt and take them away for now. The police are likely to give your boat a good search, and finally, the health inspectors may pay you a visit.

If you can begin this whole process in the early morning, you may be able to get all your papers and leave the same day. From Customs you need your boat permit. Immigration stamps your passports and issues you visas. From the Port Captain you need a cruising permit. The visas and permits are usually valid for 90 days. If and when you want to extend them, you must travel to Guatemala City, an interesting land journey many cruisers make anyway.

Rio Dulce Cruising Grounds

The major marinas of the Rio Dulce are about 20 miles up stream. Since there's an unfortunate lack of charts available for this region, it's comforting to know that deep draft vessels have been navigating this river for three centuries with frequent soundings and peeled eyeballs. Expect an

A sailboat motors up the narrow gorge just inside the entrance on the Rio Dulce.

current of ½ to one knot, increasing during rainy season when you also have to keep a watch posted for floating or partially submerged logs.

The first six miles of the river runs through a spectacular gorge with steep limestone cliffs soaring to 300 feet almost overhead. As the river bends, stay toward the outside, because it tends to shoal on the inner sides. The exception is the hairpin turn where you favor the outside of the turn. But then cut across toward the north bank immediately after the turn to avoid the shoal on the south bank. The edge of this shoal may be marked with stakes.

Once out the gorge you enter El Golfete, the 10-mile long bay. Depths here average 12 to 15 feet. The route begins by passing Cayo Grande island to starboard. (Fine anchorage can be taken north of Cayo Grande.) Cross El Gofete on a course of 230° True down to Cuatro Cayos island, taking that on your starboard as well. A well marked dog-leg takes you into the Rio Dulce marina area.

Marinas: In this next 5.5-mile section of the river channel is clearly marked. It's four miles to the bridge, which has a center-span clearance of 80 feet. You'll find several marinas to choose from in this area, and three to get started on are Mango Marina, Mario's Marina and Suzanna's Laguna Marina. Mango and Mario's are both located to starboard just after you enter this section of the river. Clustered near the bridge banks on both sides you'll find rustic towns of Fronteras and Relleno, which have fuel docks and repair services. Suzanna's marina is after you go under the bridge, in a small side bay. All the marinas monitor VHF channel 68. Compared to the U.S., prices for dockage are very reasonable. All of them have dock power, shower power, good bars, restaurants and security. You can safely leave a boat under the watchful eye of the marinas, often for months at a time. You can arrange to have your boat aired out, bilges checked and the machinery run periodically. Mario's Marina fax is (502) 332-4885, and Suzanna's Laguna Marina fax is (502) 369-2681.

After passing the narrow spot below the Castillo San Felipe, the river opens out into 25-mile long Lago Izabal. It has numerous places to visit for weeks at a time.

Fuel Stops: Livingston has a diesel dock, but you may choose to take fuel inside the river. Before the bridge, there's a Shell fuel dock (VHF channel 70) adjacent to Hotel Marimont in the side bay to port, and a Texaco fuel dock (VHF channel 64) is

One of the fuel stops on the Rio Dulce is the Esso dock near the bridge at the entrance to Lago Isabal.

almost under the bridge, also on your port side. There's also an Esso fuel dock on the south bank of Rio Dulce, and other fuel docks sprout up and close from year to year.

Local Services: You can get all kinds of repairs made by other cruisers who have settled there. Listen to the local cruisers' net at 0730 daily on VHF channel 69, or ask at the marinas. A colorful local bus from Fronteras will take you to Morelos, a larger town with a greater selection of supplies. From Fronteras you can take a bus to La Ruidosa at the crossroads to the main highway to Guatemala City. From here you can catch a nicer express bus into the capital (a 5-hour trip). You may also charter a light plane owned by the Catamaran Hotel.

Side Trips: Other places to visit in while based in the Rio Dulce region of Guatemala are: Chinchorro Bank, Lighthouse Reef, Belize's Barrier Reef, Glover's Reef and the Sapodilla Cays. Also see the chapter on Roatan, Honduras.

Language School

The Spanish language immersion schools in Antigua are excellent, and, in our opinion, the best one is Proyecto Linguisitico Francisco Marroquin (PLFM for short), a nonprofit school that works hard to preserve the disappearing native languages of the region. Guatemalan Spanish is desirable because it is free of local dialects and slang. You and your private teacher spend six hours a day talking, talking, talking – all in Spanish – and studying at whatever level you need to learn. Classes are held in the rooms or courtyards of lovely private homes scattered around town. Afternoons can be spent either in class or sauntering around the historic cobble-stone streets of the town engrossed in conversation with your instructor. Tuition is about $100 per week. The school locates families for you to live with, so you learn about the culture and society from real-life situations, not merely from books. Room and board with a family ranges from about $40 to $60 per week.

Antigua has other language schools, and so do other towns, but PLFM has the best teachers and is the only school in Guatemala that can give the Foreign Service Institute Exam (FSI Exam) required by our State Department for diplomatic postings.

We have both attended this school on several occasions for at least a month each visit, and at the end of our last visit John passed the FSI Exam and is certified fluent. We can recommend PLFM highly.

For more information, contact the Director of Students, at 011-52-9-0320-406. Or write to PLFM, Apartado Postal 237, Antigua, Guatemala, C.A. (Central America, not California).

If you fly to Guatemala City, the school can have a van or taxi pick you up and bring you to Antigua. If you arrive in Antigua from either the Rio Dulce or Puerto Quetzal side of Guatemala, just ask any taxi driver where the PLFM school office is located.

For current information about Guatemala, contact the Guatemalan Consulate, 57 Park Ave., New York, NY, 10016, or phone (212) 686-3837.

San Felipe Castle overlooking Lago Izabal offers an interesting view of Rio Dulce's history.

Chapter 14
Islas Providencia & San Andres

~~~~~~

We'll combine these two lovely Caribbean islands in one chapter, because they are located only 55 miles apart and both belong to distant Colombia – although they are much closer to Honduras and Nicaragua. If you're coming north from Panama toward Florida, you'll come to the larger Isla San Andres first. You can make your Port of Entry clearance at either place.

Isla Providencia

Providencia Island is about 55 miles north-northeast of San Andres, and although you may first think of these islands as beautiful twins, we agree with the locals who tell insist that Providencia is the more laid-back twin.

A reef extends about eight miles from the north end and two miles on its south and east sides. The main anchorage at Isla Providencia, Catalina Harbor, is very protected. It lies off the main village of Isabel, which lies on the northwest quadrant of the island. The harbor is sheltered from northerly winds by the smaller Catalina Island, and although the anchorage is open to the west, only very rarely does the wind blow from the direction here. Both islands are mountainous, and the highest elevation is 1,190 feet.

Approaches: Around 1996 buoys were installed on the approaches, making it much easier to enter the reef-strewn passage. Approach the island most safely from the north or west, due to more extensive reefs on the other sides. Come to the Isla Providencia sea buoy at GPS position 13°23.95'N by 81°23.75'W. Then come to a heading of 143°M and pass between the pairs of buoys that take you close aboard of Catalina Island and Morgan's Head, the rocky prominence that looks like the infamous pirate who raided from this island.

On the bow, you'll see a prominent cleft in the ridgeline of the main island; the charts call this Split Hill, but the locals call it Morgan's Ass. After the last set of buoys you may anchor anywhere in the harbor not blocking the channel, but watch your depths.

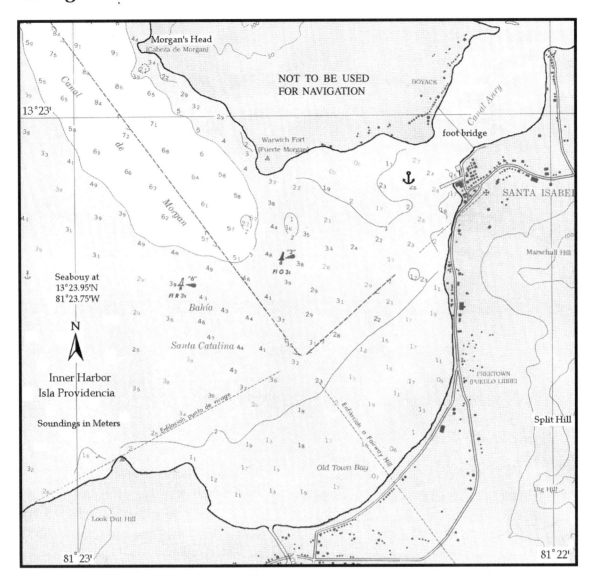

NOT TO BE USED
FOR NAVIGATION

Seabouy at
13°23.95'N
81°23.75'W

N

Inner Harbor
Isla Providencia

Soundings in Meters

Port Clearance: Use of a ship's agent in mandatory but the charge for this service is very reasonable. Call the Bush Agency on your approach on VHF channel 16. If you're unsure about your approach, Bush can talk you in over VHF. His phone is 4-80-50. Mr. Bush speaks English; it's the island's primary language because it was settled by English Puritans. Bush will inform the Port Captain of your arrival and give you instructions as to whether to anchor (smaller boats) and dinghy ashore north of the pier, or (for larger boats) to bring your vessel alongside the town's municipal pier.

If you're instructed to come to the pier (9-foot depth alongside), it requires a turn to port. Because of a shoal, you need to keep slightly right of a straight line between the pier and the last set of buoys.

The Port Captain monitors VHF channel 24, and he has a repeater on the islands highest peak with a range of 60 miles, enabling him to communicate with Isla San Andres. Port clearance is easy and inexpensive, and the officials were very friendly.

Fuel Stop: You can fuel at Providencia, but you shouldn't be in a hurry.

Isla Providencia's Municipal Pier, viewed from north end of the anchorage.

All supplies come into the island by barge or boat from Isla San Andres, 55 miles to the south, so you might have to wait a couple of days. They will bring it down to the pier by tank truck or you can jerry jug smaller quantities.

When you first step off the boat and walk down the pier, you'll probably be smitten by how genuinely friendly all the people are. "Welcome to our island" you'll hear frequently. With its population of only 4,500, this island is a tropical paradise unspoiled by tourism, a very rare thing in the Caribbean these days.

Local Services: At the head of the pier is a bank, but it doesn't exchange U.S. dollars, and traveler's checks are not

Friendliest people in the Caribbean: cargo is unloaded at Isla Providencia's municipal pier, the center of boating activity on the lovely island.

accepted anywhere on the island. They do have a cash machine and accept Visa/MC for cash advances. We have exchanged U.S. dollars for Colombian pesos with various merchants. The few grocery stores have limited supplies because of the island's remoteness, but by visiting all the stores you can get by just fine. For instance vegetables come in by boat from Costa Rica once a week. A handful of restaurants dot the harbor – none of them great but the price is right. The island has a paved airstrip 1,500 meters in length with daily flights in small planes to Isla San Andres where you can connect to Miami once a week. Rented motor scooters are a quick and easy way to tour the whole island of Providencia in a couple hours.

Take a walk for about a mile and visit the ruins of the old fort that protects the harbor. Cross the foot bridge to Santa Catalina Island and head west along the waterfront to the end of the path. Then climb the hill through the jungle. Old cannon still overlook the entrance channel.

Diving: Almost the entire eastern side and half of the west side of this island are encircled in 15 miles of coral reefs, and the snorkeling and scuba diving are absolutely superb – lots of colorful reef fish and exotic fauna not found elsewhere. Providencia's reefs have recently been declared an Underwater Nature Preserve, so look and take photos, but don't hunt. Only locals may take the delicious native conk (*strombus gigas*), lobsters (*panulirus argus*), and only during certain seasons.

Isla San Andres

Like Isla Providencia, the offshore location of Isla San Andres (12°35'N by 81°42'W), lying directly on the Western Caribbean route between Florida and the Panama Canal, makes it another logical stopover and port of refuge.

San Andres (pronounced "ahn-DRAYZ") is as beautiful an island as will be found anywhere in the world. Its green-covered hills are surrounded by coral reefs beneath transparent blue-green waters and isolated cays fringed with tall coconut palms swaying in the Trade Winds. However, because yachts must use a ship's agent and pay stiff harbor charges, it is the most expensive port on the route. Total clearance fees are approximately $200 as of this printing.

History: Henry Morgan used this island, like Providencia, as a base from which to raid the passing Spanish treasure ships. San Andres was first settled in 1629 by English Puritans and later by planters and woodcutters who brought slaves from Jamaica. The descendants of the latter are the majority of present inhabitants. San Andres island was awarded to Spain in 1786 and then strangely, after the Spanish-American Wars of Independence, it became part of Colombia in 1821. I say strangely, because the island is only 110 miles from Nicaragua but 440 miles from Colombia.

Until the last few decades, Colombia's mainland government had little to do with these two islands. Their residents remained English-speaking and Protestant. However in recent years the government has banned island schools from teaching in English, so the language is slowly dying out. There even exists a political contingent of English- speaking separatists who would like to secede from Colombia and join the U.S.

Although the ocean currents are strong is the vicinity, the island is relatively easy to find thanks to its height, the city lights at night, a strong radio beacon, and an aero beacon.

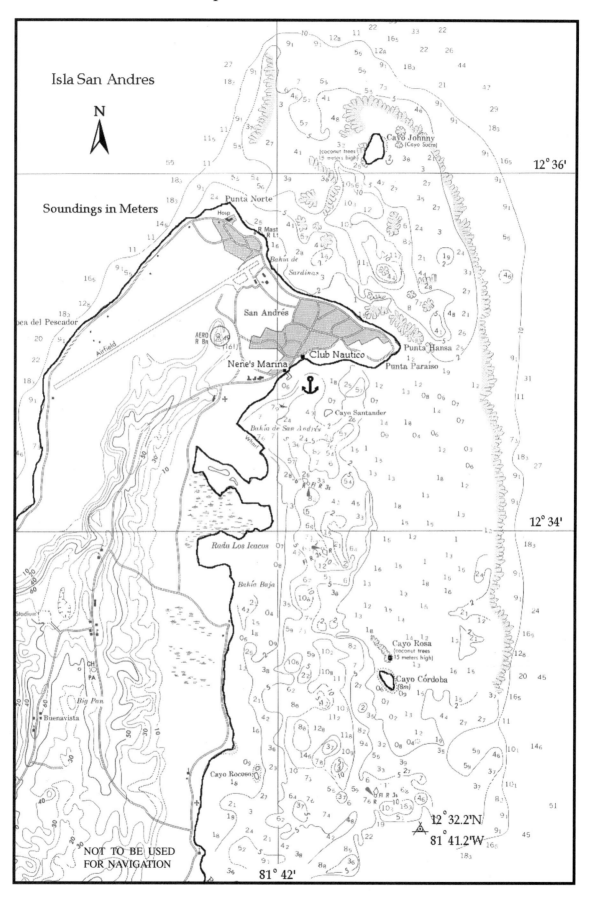

Isla San Andres

N

Soundings in Meters

12° 36'

12° 34'

12° 32.2'N
81° 41.2'W

NOT TO BE USED
FOR NAVIGATION

81° 42'

Cruising Ports

From Nene's Marina in the northwest corner of San Andres harbor, it's only a short walk into town. Rental scooters circle the island in an hour.

Approaches: The harbor is on the northeast corner of the island, but if you're coming from the north, be aware that an approach from the north is dangerous, because a large reef encircles the northeast end of the island. Several wrecks sitting high and dry on San Andres Reef are a good reminder, as well as a good visual landmark. No matter which direction you're traveling, an approach from the south end of San Andres is a much safer route to the sea buoy.

Pilotage is no longer required at San Andres Island. And in spite of what the latest DMA charts show, the entrance channel is now well marked.

Port Clearance and Ship's Agent: Using a ship's agent is mandatory. Though there are several to choose from and they all charge the same price, I recommend only: Thomas Livingston, Agencia Maritima, Isla San Andres, Colombia, telephone 32-34.

Thomas' mother tongue is English,

of which he is quite proud, but he is equally fluent in Spanish. He has close contacts with the American Consul on the mainland of Colombia. The Consul uses him for any official business they need done on San Andres, and the Consul meets with Livingston whenever visiting the island. In a country known for its drug-related political turmoil, such official connections are very important for the honest cruiser. Thomas is not only good at his job, he is a friendly and interesting man. He is a descendent of the first Protestant missionary who came to the island in the early 19th Century from the southern United States. I suggest you contact Thomas Livingston before departing for San Andres to learn the current local conditions.

Make sure that all your ship's papers are in order, or you may have trouble with the port authorities. You must have a "zarpe" from your last port listing San Andres as your destination. If you make an unplanned stop at San Andres, even for weather or mechanical problems, you'll need a letter in Spanish (and several copies) explaining the reason for your unscheduled port call at Isla San Andres.

Contact Thomas on VHF channel 16. Since he carries a hand-held VHF when away from his office, you may have to be close and on the east side of the island in order to reach him. He will arrange for port clearance, fuel, and whatever else your vessel needs.

Fuel Stop: If you have a deep draft, anchor east of the municipal pier. In this case, when you fuel you will probably have to go to the municipal pier. This is a busy commercial wharf with small inter-island freighters and fishing boats alongside. The prevailing wind pins you strongly down against the pier, so you will need fender boards and fenders to avoid damage. Undocking against this breeze calls for expert boat and line handling.

Shallower draft boats can fuel at Nene's Marina.

Nene's Marina: If you draw about six feet or less, you can moor at Nene's (pronounced "NAY-nayz") Marina on the north shore of the anchorage. You'll probably have to Med-moor, but this gives convenient access to town and is only two blocks from Livingston's office. Nene's has standard shore power hookups. The marina's fuel hose now reaches anywhere in the marina. Near Nene's you can rent motor scooters or cars to tour the island.

TIP: Do not leave a vessel unattended here. Allow no one but officials and known friends to come on board. The open use of drugs such as cocaine and marijuana is widespread but certainly not legal. Keeping strangers off your boat is the best protection against problems.

Local Services: The town abounds in restaurants, hotels and casinos. It is a resort used by wealthy mainland

Nene's fuel dock is along the seawall just south of the marina, where you must Med-moor, but the hose reaches to any slip in the marina.

Colombians who come out to vacation and take advantage of the duty-free shopping bargains. Some boat supplies, repairs and parts are available. The island has one weekly airline flight directly to Miami. The rest of the week you can connect to Miami through other Central American capitals like Tegucigalpa, Honduras.

Anchorages: Besides this main harbor, there are several other places to anchor to get away from the busy port. But first you must obtain permission from the Port Captain to move anywhere else.

The most pleasant anchorage is between Cayo Rosa and Cayo Cordoba. It is a beautiful place to swim and dive, and you can go ashore to explore Cordoba. From the main anchorage you can visit Johnny Cay and the northern part of the island.

On the southwest side of the island is a small but very protected anchorage, Rada Cove. At the cove's landing dock, a Colombian Army sentry routinely searches visitors. Apparently smugglers would also like to use this cove.

Side Trips: For longer-range cruising, try Cayos Albuquerque to the south. To the north lies Isla Providencia (described above), which is less developed and even more beautiful than San Andres. Boaters do not need to check in at San Andres before stopping to visit Providencia; Providencia has its own Port Captain and Navy base. Also check out the cays of Roncador Bank, Quito Sueno Bank, and Serrana Bank.

Chapter 15

Panama Canal
History & Uncertain Future

‿‿‿‿‿‿‿‿‿‿‿‿‿‿‿‿‿‿‿‿‿‿‿‿‿‿‿‿‿‿‿‿‿‿‿‿‿‿‿

The Panama Canal is by far the most critical and controversial place discussed in this book. From a visiting boater's standpoint, the canal is the most important facet of Panama. It's what makes this cruising route possible, and despite some difficulties, transiting the Panama Canal is the "short cut" – it's certainly more feasible than circumnavigating the South American continent. And to the Panamanians, the canal is important both economically and politically. A glance at Panama's people and history will aid the cruiser in understanding this complex situation.

Crossroads: Being located literally at the crossroads of the world, Panama's people are a diverse ethnic mix with very interesting demographics. Two thirds are *Mestizos,* which is Latin America's predominate blend of Spanish, Indian and African. In urban areas many races are represented: Chinese, Arab, East Indian and a significant number of English-speaking Blacks whose ancestors came from the West Indies to work on the canal. Only five percent are pure New World Indian (approximately 100,000), and they live mostly in the lowland jungles and coastal areas. Ten percent are considered Caucasian, and they have historically and zealously guarded their heritage by marrying within their own race and class. This segment (*los Rabiblancos*) is considered to rule Panama and is one of the most tightly knit oligarchies in Latin America. One percent of the population owns more than one half of the non-government land.

"Panama" is reportedly an Indian word meaning an abundance of fish. Rodrigo de Bastidas found his way to Panama in 1501. In 1502, Columbus noted the gold ornaments used by the Indians – a discovery that soon led to their demise. The Spanish in their lust for that metal soon began a settlement. Vasco Nunoz de Balboa crossed the steamy jungle of the isthmus to "discover" the Pacific Ocean in 1509. The hated Pedrarias (The Cruel) became governor in 1519 and founded Panama City, now the oldest city on the continent. From that base, Pedrarias sent out Francisco

Pizarro to conquer the Incas of Peru. Inca gold was shipped to Panama, then transported by mule across the narrow isthmus to Portobelo, where it was stored until it could be shipped to Spain. It was then that the dream of a canal was born.

The Spanish gold shipments were later harassed by the English Navy and pirates. Panama was attacked many times by Sir Francis Drake. He died while cruising off the coast of Panama and was buried at sea in a lead coffin near Portobelo. Henry Morgan sacked and burned Panama City in 1609. Unable to properly defend itself, Spanish shipping was forced to use the long and dangerous route around South America's Cape Horn. Panama went into a long period of decline in commercial importance.

Gold Rush: In the mid-19th century, gold once again put Panama on the map, but only because would-be prospectors from Europe flocked across the isthmus in 1849 bound for the recently discovered gold fields in California. American investors hoped to capitalize on this traffic, so they completed a trans-isthmus railroad in 1855. They were paying a $250,000 annual subsidy to the Colombian government, of which Panama was then a part.

The French became involved in the region when Lucien Napoleon Bonaparte Wiese obtained a concession to build a canal and then sold it to Count Ferdinand de Lesseps, builder of the Suez Canal. This location was not geographically the best for a canal, but it was chosen because the railroad tracks, which followed the old Spanish mule trail, were already in place and would aid greatly with construction.

French Efforts: The 75-year-old Count de Lesseps began construction in 1881. As with the Suez Canal, the French were attempting a lockless, sea-level canal. For 12 years they tried and failed for a variety of reasons including weather, corruption, poor design, lack of technology, grossly underestimating the amount of excavation required, and rampant disease that took the lives of 16,000 to 20,000 workers.

Then entered the most controversial character of the episode, Phillipe Bunau-Varilla, who was the successor to the count. In his successful efforts to sell the failed Panama Canal Company to the U.S. in order to minimize French losses, Bunau-Varilla tainted relations between the U.S. and Panama to the present day.

The U.S. began to realize the importance of a canal only after the Spanish-American War, when it had to send warships from the West Coast to the East via the long Cape Horn route. A commission headed by Admiral John Walker determined that the best canal route was through Nicaragua, up the Rio San Juan, through Lake Nicaragua, and that country was quite amenable to the construction of such a canal.

Political Pirates: Bunau-Varilla engaged an influential New York lawyer, William Nelson, for the then enormous fee of $800,000 to assist him in an intense pro-Panama Canal lobbying effort in Congress. The French lowered their original asking price from $109 million to $40 million, and Nelson convinced Congress that the Nicaraguan route was dangerous because of volcanoes and earthquakes. In 1902 Congress made known that it would buy the French company, and it commenced negotiations of a treaty with Colombia that would give the U.S. only administrative rights over the former French canal. But Colombia dragged its feet on the negotiations. Time was running out for the French, because their concession was about to revert automatically to Colombia. Bunau-Varilla fomented a revolution.

By guaranteeing U.S. support, he convinced Panamanian business leaders to take over their territory, even though he did not have permission to offer U.S. support. He also agreed to pay them $100,000 for appointing him ambassador to the U.S. – if their revolution was successful. With the arrival of U.S. warships in Colon, the revolt began, though the fleet played only a passive role. When Colombian officers demanded passage on the U.S.-owned railroad to put down the rebellion, the U.S. Army colonel in charge of the railroad secretly separated the officers' cars from those of their troops and shunted the top brass ihto Panama City. They arrived in the waiting hands of the rebels, who immediately placed the Colombian officers under arrest. The bloodless coup was over quickly, and the U.S. immediately recognized the new government.

Bunau-Varilla paid the $100,000 to the *junta* which was still not pleased at having a foreigner as its first ambassador, but it needed the money to pay its revolutionary troops. When he rushed to New York to negotiate a new treaty for the canal, Bunau-Varilla changed a provision of the junta-written treaty to give the U.S. sovereignty over the canal zone in perpetuity. It was quickly signed by a surprised Secretary of State John Hay, just hours before the arrival of the Panamanian delegation. This delegation was angered about losing sovereign rights, but it was bullied by Bunau-Varilla into signing the treaty. The new Panamanian government desperately needed the $10 million from the U.S. which would virtually guarantee their independence from Colombia.

This sovereignty issue has remained

Giant gates of the Panama Canal chambers swing open, linking the Atlantic to the Pacific.

the main diplomatic thorn in Panama's side over the decades to follow. The Panamanians maintained they were coerced into the agreement and had no idea what they were giving away. However, there was some indication of Panamanian popular support for the treaty at the time of its signing. Lacking a political forum such as a legislature, the junta canvassed the opinions of the municipalities of the new nation and found their approval to be unanimous.

U.S. Efforts: The U.S. purchased 550 square miles of property at fair market prices from individual owners. Later in the 1920s they paid Colombia $25 million for what was described as "Canalimony," additional damages to them as a wronged party.

In the summer of 1904 the first U.S. construction began. The biggest obstacle to success was eliminated by the largest sanitation campaign in history. Col. Wm. Gorgas was responsible for wiping out yellow fever and causing great declines in the number of deaths from malaria and bubonic plague. Three major construction projects were involved: a dam at Gatun, three sets of locks, and the massive excavation of the Gaillard Cut through the Continental Divide. The total investment was $380 million, and the work was done by 40,000 laborers.

The first vessel to transit was the *U.S.S. Ancon* on August 15, 1914. The canal still stands as one of man's greatest achievements and ranks with putting a man on the moon in our modern age. It is a monument to U.S. ingenuity, organization, management and technological development.

The U.S. never intended to recover its initial investment and held down transit rates to self-sustain the maintenance of the canal only – in effect, subsidizing world shipping. Due to inflation, the first rate increase since 1914 occurred in 1973 (19.7 percent) and then again in 1976 (19.5 percent). A third rate increase came in 1998, when yachts began paying a flat fee, based on boat length, that covered admeasurement and transit fees.

Controversy: Panama had long felt that substantial increases in canal charges would greatly benefit their economy. The U.S. felt additional increases would drive shipping to other more profitable routes.

Continuing friction between Panama and the U.S. led to a treaty implemented in 1979 during the Carter administration. The treaty called for a gradual transition from U.S. control until by the year 2000 Panama has total control. The treaty also provided a large subsidy to Panama above the toll collections that had already self-maintained the canal.

General Manuel Antonio Noriega, commander of the Panamanian Defense Forces, had iron-fisted control of the country in the late 1980s. His indictment in the U.S. on drug trafficking charges led to tense years in Panama. With his ouster

and conviction after the U.S. invasion in December, 1989, the country again became a safe place to visit.

When some of the non-lock operations were turned over to Panamanian control, they were at first given no maintenance, but some improvement has been seen in recent years. As we go to press, most lock operations are still running smoothly.

Future for Yachts? Hutchinson, a mainland Chinese shipping corporation, has recently received long-term leases on the port facilities on both ends of the canal, Balboa and Colon. They have plans for major expansion of container facilities in Colon that entail eliminating the tiny Panama Canal Yacht Club, which has long been a vital staging spot for transiting yachts on the Atlantic end of the canal. As we go to press, no workable alternative has appeared on that horizon. The PCYC remains open on a day-to-day basis.

On the Balboa end of the canal, the dilapidated wooden building that housed the Balboa Yacht Club burned to the ground one night, saving its owners the expense of tearing it down. That left the BYC's adjacent moorings area with no shore base.

Fortunately, plans had recently been unveiled for a large new marina with 600 slips to be built nearby, to be run by a major hotelier. Ground was broken for the new marina's location along the north side of the narrow isthmus bordering the approach to the Panama Canal. By land, that's just northwest of the old Balboa Yacht Club. We hope the new marina will provide a safe and convenient staging area for transiting yachts, at least on the Pacific side of the Panama Canal.

Chapter 16
Panama: Atlantic Coast

~~~~~~

This chapter covers the Atlantic or Caribbean side of Panama at the canal area, including Colon or Cristobal, plus two auxiliary regions of Portobelo and Isla Linton.

Colon

The town of Colon and its waterfront area known as Cristobal (named for Christopher Columbus) are both very important to vessels about to transit, or having just transitted, the Panama Canal.

Approaches to Colon and Cristobal: When you are within VHF-range of Colon or Cristobal, call "Cristobal Control" on VHF channel 12 (pronounced "kris-TOE-bahl"), and tell them your boat's name, length and type, and tell them your ETA at their main breakwater (09°23.8'N by 079°55.1'W). This is the more westerly of the two entrances through the Colon breakwater; the newer eastern entrance is only for container ships.

Cristobal Control will respond to your call, and ask you to call again when you arrive within five miles of the entrance.

Blinding rain or thick haze can often limit your visibility and your radar picture in these waters. If you are uncertain of your position as you make landfall from the north, deliberately aim farther east of the canal, because the eastern landfall is much higher than the land right at the canal or west of it. Therefore it should appear out of the haze first and is a much better radar target. Also, a racon marks this jetty entrance.

Several shipping lanes converge as you approach the breakwater encircling the canal's inner anchorage, so the traffic is dense. Large ships may be anchored outside the breakwater as well as inside. Two tall, square skeleton towers flank this entrance through the breakwater. They are marked red to starboard and green to port and are highly visible. Once through the breakwater, you're in the Main Ship Channel.

Anchorage: Cristobal Control manages the considerable traffic in and out of the inner harbor which is large and deep.

Cruising Ports

PCYC fuel dock: Yachts from around the world meet at the Panama Canal Yacht Club, on the Atlantic side of the canal.

After anchoring, notify Cristobal Control on VHF that you are there, then wait for the officials to arrive and inspect your boat. After being cleared by these officials, you may stay anchored for free. Or, if the nearby Panama Canal Yacht Club is still open, you can ask permission from Cristobal Control to move over to the yacht club, which is really just a small marina.

As you're entering, they may give you directions and instructions to proceed to anchor in Anchorage F, also known as "the flats," which is reserved primarily for yachts and small ships.

This anchorage is easy to find. Proceed south on the Main Ship Channel until abreast of the control tower atop the last covered pier to port. The flats anchorage is on your port, the same side of the channel as the control tower. It is marked by yellow buoys and yellow lights, and it is bounded to the north by the Cristobal piers, to the east by the ships' fuel bunkers, to the south by lush grass and tree-covered land, and to the west by the Main Ship Channel leading to Gatun Locks. In the winter the wind often blows 20 knots or more in the anchorage, and the bottom is soft mud and poor holding. The wind can make for a wet ride in a launch to the nearby Panama Canal Yacht Club.

TIP: The Panama Canal Yacht Club is scheduled to be closed, but the exact date is in dispute. Meanwhile, the PCYC is staying open in Colon on a day-to-day basis to assist visiting yachts. By the time you arrive in Colon, it may have been closed.

Yacht Club Docks:

To move from the flats to the yacht club, head east into the side channel between the fuel bunkers and the Cristobal piers, then turn south and proceed a short distance. The club's piers and dozens of yachts are on your left.

The piers directly in front of the club are handiest and have plenty of depth. The non-floating wooden piers have tire fenders, and the tidal range is minor. The tire fenders are coated with the creeping crud, which makes its way onto clean topsides. Good drinking water is available, and the 110-volt electrical current is sufficient for lighting and battery chargers, but not enough for air conditioners, freezers, etc.

These slips are usually full, so you may have to Med-moor off the sea wall immediately to the south of the club, just beyond the launch ramp. It has the same services, but since only Med-mooring is allowed here, it lacks the convenience of being alongside. Some folks prefer this dock, because it is quieter at night than being close to the bar and restaurant.

TIP: The Med-mooring area is not the safer choice. Although the club has a night watchman, teams of knife-wielding robbers have been known to attack the

110

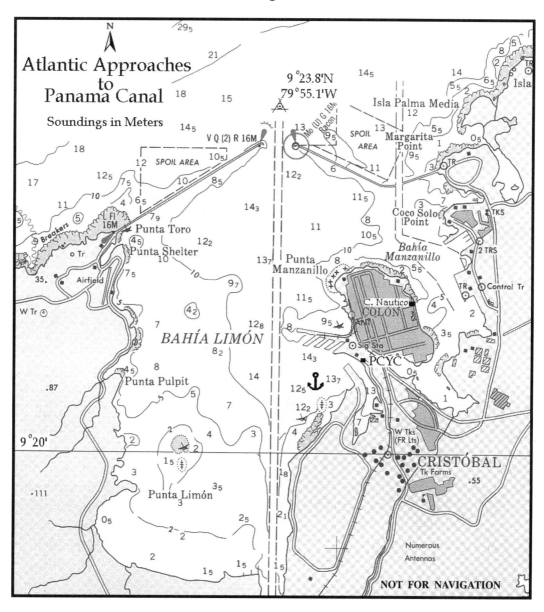

Atlantic Approaches to Panama Canal

Soundings in Meters

9°23.8'N
79°55.1'W

BAHÍA LIMÓN

Punta Toro
Punta Shelter
Airfield
Punta Pulpit
Punta Limón

Isla Palma Media
Margarita Point
Coco Solo Point
Bahía Manzanillo
Punta Manzanillo
C. Nautico
COLON
PCYC
CRISTÓBAL
Tk Farms

Numerous Antennas

NOT FOR NAVIGATION

boats that are Med-moored farthest from the club house.

Even if you remain anchored out, you will probably want to use the club's dinghy dock, just south of the main club house, right alongside the launch ramp. Soon after arrival, you should check in with Panamanian Immigration officials; they have a tiny annex office in the south end of the club's shower and laundry building.

Fuel Stop: The PCYC offers a small fuel dock, a patio restaurant, an air-conditioned bar, a small coin laundry, rustic showers and do-it-yourself haul-out facilities for vessels of 10 and 25 tons. Make arrangements for fuel at the club office. Although the PCYC is an actual yacht club, you don't have to be a member of an affiliated yacht club to use their services.

TIP: The fuel here is usually much cheaper than at the Balboa Yacht Club on the other side of the canal.

Local Scene: The small town immediately adjacent to Cristobal is Colon. It was built in the middle of the last century by the French during their unsuccessful

111

Cruising Ports

The PCYC's Med-mooring docks, located south of the clubhouse and fuel dock, are for guest yachts about to transit.

attempt to build a canal, so Colon's architecture is reminiscent of old New Orleans. Spanish is the primary language, but English is widely spoken because of the large West Indian population.

The fence that used to separate the yacht club from the town has been torn down. Walking the streets of this city is dangerous. Unemployment hovers at about 50 percent, creating a large number of desperate people who mill about aimlessly. Colon is a powder keg when the heat factor rises. Riots, stabbings and muggings are very common.

Always take a cab wherever you go outside the yacht club grounds. Do not walk anywhere. The Panamanian Police will tell you this, and they often turn pedestrians away from certain sections of the city – for their own protection. Carry money in your shoes and wear no jewelry, not even a cheap watch. If you carry a purse, fanny pack or back pack, you're asking to have it taken violently, often with a knife, gun or gang attack.

The only hotel we can recommend is the venerable Hotel Washington, which has landscaped grounds and colonial

architecture. The rooms are tolerable though expensive, and gamblers may be pacified at the hotel's casino.

Colon is not a good place to dine out. The Restaurante VIP just north of the train station has had decent food about half the times we've been there. Across the street from there, you'll find a Chinese restaurant, and one block farther north is a pizza place.

Replacement parts are available on a very limited basis. For anything major you will have to go to Panama City. Mechanics, electricians, yacht electronics technicians and a sail maker are available locally. Ask about them at the PCYC office.

Club Nautico: The Club Nautico, outside the canal zone, extends a cordial welcome, primarily for local trailerable boats to launch. It is located on the east shore of Colon, and it has depths of six feet over the bar to its approaches. The anchorage is 75 yards east of the dock, and a sand-and-mud bottom makes good holding ground in two fathoms. There is 6 1/2 feet of water at the dock. Gasoline and fresh water are available, but for diesel you must make a special order. Up the Folks River, one mile south of the club, is a marine railway capable of hauling 100 tons with drafts to 10 feet.

Provisioning: Aside from the dangers of going ashore, Colon is a fairly good place for reprovisioning, mostly because the PCYC's docks make loading stores easier than when you're anchored out in Balboa. To provision here, take a cab to the El Rey market just south of town but not far from the club. Have the cab driver wait for you. The selection is interesting,

Portobelo: Cruising boats anchor in same spot Columbus did.

but goods imported from the U.S. are expensive. Ask to have fresh meat ground or cut while you do other shopping, because the age of the prewrapped meats may be questionable. The El Rey has some handy hardware items, but its vegetables sometimes aren't crisp. Instead, excellent fresh produce has been available at an open-air farmer's market a few miles away on the Panama City Highway at the turn off to Portobelo.

Portobelo

Be sure to visit the bay and village of Portobelo, 18 miles northeast of Cristobal's breakwater. It is a perfect natural harbor that was once used as the Pacific shipping port for stolen Inca gold on its way to Spain. Here you will be surrounded by maritime history in an idyllic tropical setting. Several centuries-old forts still have their original cannon pointing seaward. Most of the walls of the famous Customs House are still standing, and some preservation work has helped. A few hundred residents, mostly West Indians and aborigines, live a simple existence surrounded by the fort ruins. For awhile, a tiny artist community flourished in Portobelo. Fantasy sculptures still line some walkways through the village.

It's easy to imagine yourself surrounded by the ghosts of Christopher Columbus, who anchored in this same spot, and Sir Frances Drake, who was buried at sea a short distance off the harbor entrance.

Portobelo is a natural stepping stone anchorage for boaters planning to visit the many anchorages along this stretch, leading out to Isla Linton and the fabulous San Blas Islands.

Isla Linton

Located 22 miles northeast of the canal, Isla Linton is a cruisers' hangout. As the PCYC closes, Isla Linton has to serve as a staging area for thousands of yachts, either preparing to transit toward the Pacific or preparing to enter the Caribbean. The name Isla Linton doesn't appear on charts; look instead for Juan Joaquin Island. A good GPS approach waypoint is 9°37.35'N by 79°35.5'W. However, you must use caution, because several submerged rocks and tiny islets lie along the approach. After arriving from the west, you then turn to port and anchor inside the 200-yard slot between Juan Joaquin Island and the mainland. Anchor in about 20 feet of water over sand – snug as a bug in a rug. We've counted 20 cruising boats in here at one time, and a international group we were: North American, German, French, Swiss, Spanish and Canadian to name a few.

Cruisers gather here, surrounded by dense jungle, to get away from it all – but not too far. Ashore is a tiny community where you can get fresh water and catch a bus that runs three times daily to Colon. Isla Grande, the next bay over (a 1.5-mile dinghy ride), has a Chinese market that can supply limited groceries and jerry-jug diesel. Overall, the Isla Linton anchorage has almost everything a boater needs for a long stay.

TIP: The members of the Panama Canal Yacht Club are forming a satellite club house here, so by the time you arrive in Panama, Isla Linton may be their new home.

Cannon among the ruins of the Spanish fort and Customs House are reminders of Portobelo's former significance in the New World.

Chapter 17
Panama Canal Transit

~~~~~~

We'll look a pleasure boater's general procedures upon entering the Panama Canal area and making arrangements for transit. Then we'll explain the actual transit in terms of what to expect while up-locking and down-locking – and entering a different ocean.

General Procedures

Official procedures for a yacht transiting the Panama Canal are undergoing continual change while the Panamanian government gets used to controlling all the daily operations of the canal. What you find when you arrive in Panama may be slightly different from what is described here, but any major changes affecting pleasure boats are sure to be reported immediately over the cruising nets and then in the nautical magazines.

Arrivals: When you're within VHF range of either end of the canal, call on VHF Channel 12 or 16 to give your boat's name, length and type, and to announce your ETA at the sea buoy, which marks the beginning of the entrance channel toward the Panama Canal. On the Caribbean side, you will make this call to "Cristobal Control." On the Pacific side, call "Flamingo Signal." Upon your arrival at the sea buoy, call again to announce that fact. Be sure to fly a yellow quarantine flag from your port spreader and the Panamanian courtesy flag to starboard.

TIP: The star on the luff of Panama's flag goes on top, not on the bottom. Don't fly it incorrectly.

Pleasure boats usually request permission to move to the yacht club docks, but understand that this may be denied; you may be told to anchor in a certain location and wait several hours for a boarding party.

When the officials board, they inspect the vessel and give you papers to fill out. Turn over your last port clearance, fill out a crew list, and present all passports. After inspection by the officials, you are free to lower the Q-flag, and hopefully to move to the yacht club if there's room.

Transit Equipment & Personnel

Go over this checklist and get each item and person completely squared away before you make any moves toward getting a transit date. All this is at the Port Captain's discretion, and he has the final authority about any questionable equipment or personnel you may have.

1. Steady and reliable <u>propulsion</u>: Each vessel must have either an onboard engine capable of pushing your boat at the 5-knot minimum, or you need to hire a canal tug, which is very expensive.

2. <u>Panama Canal lines</u>: You must have four 120-foot lines of a diameter suitable for your vessel. Consider the tremendous shock and strain of your boat being dashed toward a concrete wall during up-locking. (Yachts transiting "center chamber" were having problems with 100-foot lines, so the minimum line length was recently increased to 120 feet.) Poly-line is not acceptable, because it slips too easily.

TIP: It may be possible to rent canal lines from ship's agent Pete Stevens; see below.

Your four 120-foot canal lines must be all of one piece, that is, no joints of two lines. The end of each 120-foot line needs an eye splice with a 3-foot opening in order

On board line handlers have a big job once the gates close and the water rushes in.

to fit over the huge bollards. A large bowline is an awkward but acceptable alternative to an eye splice.

TIP: Your cleats must handle the diameter of these lines in a figure eight that won't slip off. Test them ahead of time. Having a line slip could cost you your boat.

3. <u>Chocks and bitts</u>: Before you can transit, the Panama Canal Commission's Port Captain will require you to sign a waiver releasing the PCC from liability for any damages that may result from your inadequate bitts and chocks. Because of the extremely steep angle of the lines during transit, your boat needs to have four closed chocks. And due to the extreme turbulence, it needs four very sturdy bitts.

Open chocks are not acceptable, so you may be required to have steel bars welded on top, to close them. Flimsy cleats may have to be replaced or have sturdy backing plates through-bolted below decks.

4. <u>Adequate fendering</u>: If your fenders fail during transit, then obviously they were not adequate. Use the absolute biggest, strongest fenders you can find, because they are your best insurance against damage. Yes, do buy special fenders just for your transit. Smaller boats can keep them deflated and stowed until reaching Panama, inflate them and test for leaks before transit, then after transit perhaps sell them to other boaters who arrived unprepared. We've never found adequate fenders sold in Panama stores. For large yachts, we recommend using four of the spherical balls that measure about three feet across when not inflated. Tubular dock fenders are useful only for between rafted boats, not for protection from the chamber walls.

5. <u>Onboard line handlers</u>: Each boat needs four very strong people to serve as its onboard line handlers, one to constantly work each of the four 120-foot Panama

Canal lines throughout the entire transit. Everyone handling lines should know exactly what's going on, and be able to keep the boat from smashing into the concrete walls. This is not a place for light-weights. Line handling requires stamina, a strong back, tall stature for leverage, and callused hands (wear sturdy gloves). During up-locking, the turbulence can be so great and the sudden shocks so strong that few women or small men possess the strength and stamina required to keep the lines under control while they are being hauled in. If one line slips, the hull can be thrown against the concrete walls or steel gates. For this reason, pick muscular line handlers. While you are transiting center chamber (see below), line handlers cannot set down their lines to take pictures, eat, rest or get out of the sun or rain. It's a job that must be taken very seriously. On larger boats, having an extra body to tail each line handler may be a good idea, but smaller boats get way too crowded for extras.

If you don't have enough of your own crew, fellow cruisers with different transit days enjoy helping each other out by serving as line handlers. Your first choice should be someone who has worked as a line handler at least once before, preferably three or four times, because each transit involves a different set of circumstances.

Professional line handlers are a good option. Each of the yacht clubs has a list of local line handlers who work full or part time handling lines for yachts in transit. But get a strong recommendation from someone at the club, and then interview them before hiring. The going rate has been $50 per day, plus about $5 bus fare back from the end of the transit, plus plenty of food and liquids, access to a bathroom, shelter from sun and rain, and a place to sleep if you are required to overnight in Gatun Lake.

6. Your own helmsman: You (or your helmsperson) will steer and maneuver your boat through the locks and channels of the Panama Canal, so your helmsman cannot also be a line handler. (This means you'll have at least five people in your crew.)

Although a PCC Pilot or Transit Advisor comes on board and directs your course and speed, he or she is not required to steer your boat. Transit Advisors usually have worked their way up from being the captain or mate on one of the many PCC tugs. Yachts over 65 feet get a regular PCC Pilot. They have more experience in general, but unfortunately much of their time has been on big ships; pilots often are uncomfortable with delicate yachts.

Transit Paperwork

Before transiting, you must obtain a Panamanian Cruising Permit from the office of "Consular y Naves." Make sure you have a copy of the vessel's document and the serial numbers of your engines. The fee for this permit is about $30. Panama uses U.S. dollar bills for its own currency, which is called the Balboa. Visit the Panamanian Immigration offices to get a visa stamped in the passports for all your crew members. This costs $10 per person. If you have access to a Panamanian Consulate in the U.S., you can take care of this for free before you leave on your voyage.

When you think your boat is completely ready to transit the canal, you start the official ball rolling by visiting the Admeasurer's Office to make an appointment to be admeasured. They may schedule it for tomorrow or a week from tomorrow. If the boat has been through the Panama Canal previously and no structural changes have been made, tell the Admeasurer now – because you may be able to avoid being admeasured again. To be admeasured, a crew comes onboard with tape measures and goes through every compartment measuring internal volume and structural stuff, which later goes into an obscure formula.

TIP: Due to changing rules, by the time you reach Panama, it's possible that yachts may not need to be admeasured.

Transit Fees: Once you've been admeasured, you can take your papers and visit the Port Captain's office, where you'll do more papers and pay the flat fee (cash only). Although this fee has gone up recently, yachts still get a good deal, considering how much is involved in getting each one transited – and considering the alternative of going around South America. The flat fee includes admeasurement and transit (cash only), and it is based on the boat's length in feet:

Center Chamber nested or rafted requires excellent line handling.

PCC Flat Fee as of July 1999
For pleasure boats 50 feet or less, the fee is   **$500.**
For pleasure boats 50 to 80 feet, the fee is   **$750.**
For pleasure boats 80 to 100 feet, the fee is   **$1,000.**
For pleasure boats 100 feet or more, the fee is   **$1,500.**

Methods of Transit: You must be prepared and equipped to transit in all three possible modes before you get out the other side. During the paperwork phase, you will be asked what method you prefer; limiting your choice to one choice, and the three choices are:

1.) "center chamber" means holding position by your engine and four 120-foot

lines. Going center chamber is usually the safest mode, but it demands more maneuvering experience from the helmsman and is much more demanding on your onboard line handlers. An offshoot of this method is called "nested" meaning rafted alongside other pleasure boats or a small ship – to form a raft in the center of the chamber.

2.) "tug tied" means side-tied to a large PCC tug boat if one happens to be transiting that chamber at the same time and isn't already being used. Transiting by going alongside a tug is most convenient for your crew, and it's safe for the boat IF you have excellent fendering, chocks and bitts – and if you don't let the tug maneuver you. Unfortunately, tugs are not always available for lockage.

3.) "side wall" means side-tied along the vertical concrete walls of a chamber. Going sidewall during the turbulence of the up-locking process can damage a yacht's topsides and maybe even its rigging, so when you sign your papers, you should reject this as a preferred method of transit.

TIP: However, if you're well fendered and if the winds are calm, going side wall is often okay for the less turbulent process of down-locking. Half

Alongside a tug, or tug tied, is a nice treat, but tugs aren't always available when you arrive.

way through your transit, you might speed things up by telling your Transit Advisor that you'd now be willing to down-lock by going side wall.

Transit Time: If your boat is in fact found to be ready to transit, the Port Captain will schedule your date and time for transit. Reconfirm this time by telephone the night before your transit. (If your pilot or advisor shows up, and if at that time you can't keep your transit appointment, or if you get started transiting and discover that you aren't as ready as you thought, you may be assessed a huge hefty fine.)

Currently yachts may begin transiting on any day of the week, including Saturdays and Sundays. Paperwork processing may be delayed, however, because the fee collectors work only two

hours on Saturdays and Sundays. If not enough pleasure boats are available to make it worth the canal's time, they may keep delaying a yacht's transit date until sufficient boats warrant it. Waits of up to two weeks are not uncommon.

Meanwhile, you, your boat and all your onboard line handlers must remain ready to transit. Yachts under 65 feet are sometimes scheduled to take two days to complete the transit, anchoring overnight in Gatun Lake.

Ship's Agent: If you are in a hurry or simply don't wish to spend all your time chasing around on the hot and dangerous city streets, you should hire a ship's agent. If you let your agent know in advance when you're going to arrive or when you want to transit, he or she can get you a transit time within 24 hours. Agents charge their fees, but they provide a large package of services – depending on your particular needs. The only ship's agent we recommend in Panama is: Mr. Pete Stevens
Delfino Maritime Agency
(Agencia Maritima Delfino)
Tel. 011-507-261-35-54
Fax 011-507-261-39-43
We have hired Pete Stevens many times and always find his services top drawer. If you hire Pete Stevens to handle your clearances and transit arrangements, and if you don't have four of your own 120-foot canal lines or large fenders, Pete may rent them to you just for your transit; you return them on the other side.

He can locate qualified technicians and mechanics for your repairs. If you need to hire a few professional line handlers for transit, ask Pete Stevens first. He can provide airport pick up for your guests, secure round-trip transportation for your provisioning or side trips, or, if you make advance arrangements, he can even have your provisioning order brought to your dock. There are many other agencies in Panama City, but Pete Stevens is the only one specializing in helping yachts – and has such a sterling reputation. And his rates have been right in line with others.

If you hire an agent, they will meet with you and then stay in contact via VHF, cell phone or in person. The agent brings papers to you for your signature, schedules the various onboard inspections by local officials, and makes all your transiting arrangements with the PCC offices in accordance with your preferences.

Panama Canal Transit

After you've gathered all your transit gear and people, after all your paperwork is in order, you'll be assigned your PCC Pilot or Transit Advisor. If your boat is under 65 feet, the PCC supplies you with a "transit advisor" who acts as your pilot while you are in transit. Your Transit Advisor gives helm instructions and coordinates all transit activities by radio, but he or she does not actually drive your boat. Your transit normally runs through breakfast, lunch and dinner, so you must feed your advisor, too. (Now there're at least six people on board.) By the time you pop out the other side, you'll be exhausted and elated.

Typical Transit: Let's examine a typical transit from north to south (Cristobal to Balboa) aboard a 70-foot motorsailor. Our assigned PCC Pilot comes aboard at 0700 at the yacht club, and we offer coffee and breakfast. He checks our bitts and chocks and sees that we untwist and lay out our four canal lines properly. After the Pilot gets the word on his hand-held VHF, we move out into the main channel and down the jungle-lined distance to the first set of locks, called Gatun Locks.

Gatun is the easiest lock to get through, because all three locks are connected in one set. They raise us to the highest elevation (85 feet). Once lines are made fast to the wall, we are walked from one chamber to the next by PCC line handlers, after up-locking.

In Gatun, we find out that we are going "center chamber." Ahead of us, our first lock partner, a Liberian freighter, moves into the first chamber (each chamber is 110-feet wide, 1,000-feet long) which begins at sea level filled with sea water. After the freighter is secured, we enter behind him, so we're very close to his stern. The PCC line handlers on both sides of the lock walls throw their monkey-fists and tarred-marlin heaving lines on board – in order to receive our 120-foot canal lines. (In spite of the many stories, I don't believe they deliberately knock out windows and spot lights, but it does happen by accident. You could be knocked senseless by a monkey-fist if you don't pay attention.)

Once their four heaving lines are received on board (two fore and aft starboard and two fore and aft port), our line handlers tie them to the eyes of our four canal lines, and the PCC line handlers haul them up to the tops of the lock wall and put our four eyes on four giant bollards. Now, by adjusting our canal lines, we must get hull centered exactly in the center of the 110-foot width, and we must keep our bow and stern parallel to the side walls. The lock gates will already have closed behind us, so as soon as all four canal lines are properly adjusted and secured, the 52 million gallons of fresh water begins rushing in from below. Our ascent has begun.

Up-locking is more difficult than down-locking, because the strong currents welling up from the lock floor create a great deal of turbulence and violent action on the boat hull. Water pushes up on the rudder and hull surfaces, which is NOT like steering up or down a river. The chamber master has two choices: fast or slow. In a fast ascent, which has more turbulence, the up-locking takes about 15 minutes in each chamber. A slower ascent takes about 25 minutes per chamber, and the turbulence is somewhat less violent. In this first chamber at Gatun, we have the added factor of all that fresh water trying to force its way upward through all that salt water. This mixing of fresh and salt water compounds the turbulence.

Prop Wash: When up-locking behind a large ship, be prepared for sudden turbulence from its props.

As helmsman, John assists by trying to keep the boat centered, but he can't go very far forward or back, due to the constraint of the lines. Because of their maneuverability, twin screw boats have a better time of it.

Each onboard line handler must constantly keep hauling in the rapidly slacking lines, in a coordinated way, never cleating off a line. They must keep the boat exactly on station: the bow and stern lined up with the centerline of the chamber, not drifting or twisting. If anyone hauls in too fast or too slow, the boat can get cross-wise or get tossed violently against the walls or gates. It requires lots of muscle and instant communication. The Pilot or Transit Advisor seldom warns you if you're getting crooked; it's up to the captain and crew.

After we reach the maximum height, the gates open and our giant lock partner is hauled into the next chamber by electric locomotives, still called mules. To help get moving, that Liberian freighter's helmsman gives a few turns of his screw.

LOOK OUT! The prop wash sets us back on our lines. It's at this point that most accidents occur. You can help ease the strain by going slow ahead with your lines still secured. Don't allow anyone let go their lines until well after the visible prop wash has passed.

Pleasure craft under 65 feet may have been assigned to "nest" or raft together into a flotilla, sometimes as many as five boats wide, depending on their size, configuration and speed. And depending on how many boats were scheduled to transit that day. Be careful to position the hulls so their rigging won't tangle when turbulence gets everyone rolling. Fender well between hulls, but use the biggest and sturdiest fenders outboard. One yacht, preferably a twin-screw power boat placed in the center of the raft, will act as the engine. The four outside corners of the raft are where the 120-foot lines are worked from, so the best cleats, chocks and bitts should be positioned there. Only four of the onboard line handlers are required to work, but since the job is now complicated by their being farther apart, the extra folks can help with communications. It's always a good idea to let extra bodies tail the big lines and keep the lazy ends flaked out. Two or three rafts may transit in the same chamber, and they may also share the chamber behind a dreaded Liberian freighter.

After the chamber is filled, our 120-foot lines are cast off the lock walls, and we haul them in with the marlin heaving lines still attached. The other ends of the marlin lines are still being held by the PCC line handlers. As we power slowly forward into the next lock, the PCC line handlers walk the heaving lines forward into the next lock. Then our heavier lines are hauled back up and re-secured to the bollards in this second chamber.

We repeat this entire procedure in the second and third chambers until the line handlers cast us off and we enter Gatun Lake, the man-made, freshwater lake 85 feet above sea level. Gatun Lake spreads over 163 square miles, and it's one of the most picturesque parts of the Panama Canal. Here's where line handlers can get their camera, eat, take pit stops, spell the helmsman, etc. We pass through the island-dotted lake for 23½ miles until we reach the anchorage area known as Gamboa.

If we are under 65 feet, we will come to anchor here. The Pilot is taken off by one of the canal boats (PCC boats can transport only PCC employees.), and we spend the rest of the day and the night on the hook with our line handlers. The rules specify that boat owners must feed their line handlers and provide them a toilet and place to sleep. Small boats may have to bunk their extra crew on deck, but it often rains at night here. Via VHF radio, all arrangements are made for a different Transit Advisor to arrive the following day to complete the transit.

Since we are over 65 feet, we don't have to stop for the night, nor anchor at Gamboa. We can continue the same day into the Gaillard Cut, the narrowest part of the canal, where we motor across the Continental Divide. Because of a geological weakness on the Pacific side, two sets of locks had to be built: Pedro Miguel and Mira Flores. This means the process of taking lines must be repeated twice through three chambers.

At Pedro Miguel, we enter the lock ahead of our lock partner (because we are now down-locking), and we go alongside a tug that has already secured to the lock walls. Getting alongside is tricky maneuvering, because the strong current is now behind us, and we are looking over the top of the chamber gate – it's 31 feet straight down – into the next chamber, which is empty. We'll use our own bow and stern lines and crossed spring lines, giving the tug hands our eyes, so we retain control of our destiny as much as possible. Dock lines

Gaillard Cut:
This narrowest part
of the Panama Canal
cuts across the
Continental Divide.

are seldom sturdy enough for this, so use the 120-foot canal lines for bow and stern. Fender well on the tug side, but reserve one big fender for the open side, just in case an accident puts you against the far wall.

Descending is much easier – for two reasons. We don't have the prop wash from the large ships, because they usually down-lock behind yachts. And the violent up-welling isn't present. Someone in the control booth just pulls the plug and down we go, like a toy boat in a really big bathtub. On the other side of the tug, their hands are paying out its canal lines, which lead almost straight up to the top of the chamber walls by the time we've completed this descent. (If a tug had not been available, and if we'd been down-locking sidewall, our 120-foot lines would have been leading straight up; if our chocks had not been completely closed over the top, we couldn't have kept them from popping out.)

We take back our lines from the tug hands and move away, being prepared for some wash from the inward opening of the gates. Never let a tug get underway with you still alongside. This is not a service; much damage occurred to yachts when this practice was still widely used.

We then enter Mira Flores Lake and traverse the short distance to the last set of locks, called Mira Flores. We learn that we will again go center chamber in both chambers. While going down 54 feet at Mira Flores, my four line handlers slacken the lines slowly and evenly. The last of these chamber doors open into the Pacific Ocean. As in Gatun's first chamber, John is prepared for the mixing of fresh and salt water, but this time it occurs after the gate has opened.

We go beneath the Bridge of the Americas and approach the Balboa Yacht Club where we have obtained prior permission to moor. The launch driver greets us and assists in making us fast to a mooring, and the pilot boat arrives to take off our weary Pilot. Any line handlers or guests going ashore will use the BYC's shore boat.

Leaving the Canal: To obtain a port clearance out of the former canal zone, go to the Panamanian offices near the Port Captain's Office on either side. If you are transiting and remaining in the canal area on the other side, do not do this until you're ready to leave from the other side. You fill out a simple form stating how many people arrived, disembarked, and how many are sailing. Then they type your *zarpe*. All these offices at both ends of the canal are constantly being moved, so once you arrive in port, get the current locations from fellow boaters who have just finished their paperwork shuffle. On either end, some cab drivers who frequent the yacht clubs will drive you around to all the offices – for a highly negotiable fee.

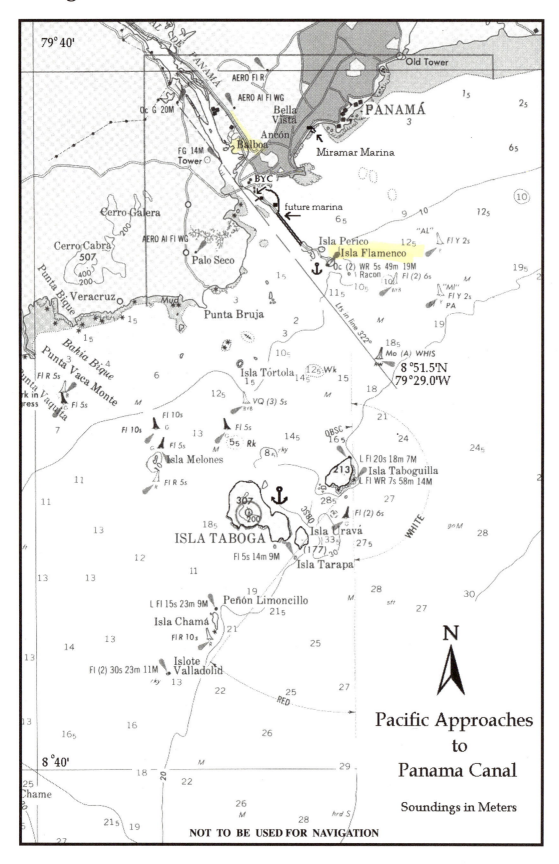

Pacific Approaches
to
Panama Canal

Soundings in Meters

NOT TO BE USED FOR NAVIGATION

Chapter 18
Balboa, Panama

〜〜〜〜〜〜〜〜〜〜〜〜〜〜〜〜〜〜〜〜〜〜〜〜〜〜〜〜〜〜〜〜〜〜〜〜

Balboa is not actually a town, it's the name of the area within the former U.S. Canal Zone that contains the administrative and port facilities on the Pacific side of the canal. The town of Panama City is adjacent to Balboa and is considerably larger.

Approaches: If you've just finished your transit of the Panama Canal, the port authorities will already have asked you of your plans and will have given you permission to proceed to a mooring, presumably at the Balboa Yacht Club, or at the new marina it and when it's built.

If you are arriving in port from the Pacific Ocean, when you are within VHF range, call "Flamenco Signal Station" on VHF channel 16 or 12 to request admittance to the area. Tell them your boat name and kind of boat (i.e. 36-foot sailboat, 120-foot motoryacht, whatever), and tell them your ETA at the Balboa sea buoy (8°51.5'N by 79°29'W). Call Flamenco Signal Station again when you actually arrive at the seabouy, this time to request permission to proceed to the Balboa Yacht Club or other

marina. They may require you to anchor near Flamenco Island to await a boarding party, or they may let you come in.

NOTE: As we go to press, the moorings, fuel dock and gangway of the Balboa Yacht Club are still functioning, but the dilapidated wooden structure ashore has burned to the ground. Ground has been broken for a 600-slip marina on the west bank of Fort Amador. If and when this marina is open, its location should provide pleasure boats with better shelter and less wake-action than on the BYC moorings. However, the opening date is anyone's guess. If in fact the new marina at Fort Amador is opened, pleasure boats will get there by going around the west side of Flamenco, Perico and Naos Islands, not along their east sides as you do to get to the BYC moorings.

Once you get permission to move to the BYC moorings, go down the Main Ship Channel until abreast of the long high gangway to starboard. A moorings area flanks the gangway, and a floating fuel dock is visible at its seaward end. Head for the red nun buoy out in front of the

Cruising Ports

Bridge of the Americas

Balboa's mooring area and fuel dock are just south of the bridge, adjacent to the entrance to the Panama Canal.

floating fuel dock, which sits at the end of this giant gangway.

Don't try any shortcuts to the club outside the ship channel, because a mud flat just south of the mooring area is exposed only at low water. Stand by in the fairway near the red nun and wait for the club launch. The launch service monitors VHF channel 06. The driver will direct you to an available mooring and assist you in picking up the lines. Watch for the current caused by tides as great as 16 feet. Only mooring buoys are available, no anchoring, but the largest ones will handle vessels over 90 feet. The only alongside berth is exclusively for fueling.

You must take the club launch to the fuel pier, because you are not allowed to use your own dinghy. Launch service is free and available 24 hours a day. Though technically against the club's rules, you had better tip the launch drivers or they will become blind, deaf and dumb the next time you try to summon them out to pick you up.

At the head of the landing pier, check in with Immigration, even if you've just finished transiting. The yacht club accepts Visa/MC for moorage and fuel, and if you ask they'll give you an information sheet containing a list of useful businesses and stores and their phone numbers.

Fuel Stop: If you need fuel, you must arrange with the BYC fuel dock in advance, anticipate your needs and prepay. The pump is very slow. On one large vessel, it took us all day and into the wee hours of the morning. This diesel is the most expensive to be found anywhere on this entire route. Fender well against this dock, because ship wakes from the nearby canal entrance can be quite heavy.

Nearby Services: The remains of the club and the future marina are located inside the fences of Balboa, the well-manicured enclave that is no longer separate from the adjacent Panama City. A one-mile walk from either will take you to the Cable and Wireless office, a good place to make international phone calls in air-conditioned comfort. Most of Panama's public telephones use prepaid phone cards, which are good for local calls and long distance. You should purchase several, because many phones don't take coins.

Close to the phone office is an area of stalls that sell local handicrafts and Cuna Indian women's famous "molas." A mola is made of several layers of hand-cut and hand-stitched reverse-appliqué panels of brightly colored cotton. Originally the Cuna women wear their molas as the front and back panels of their traditional blouses, but

126

visitors have found that they make attractive wall hangings and gifts when framed. We buy a few on each trip through Panama and always wish we had bought more. Mola prices here are one tenth of what you would pay for them in the U.S. The Cuna women also string beaded anklets and bracelets that are becoming collectable, too. If you speak Spanish, bargaining with the women is fun, but don't try to take their pictures.

A few blocks north of Cable and Wireless office, you'll find a mediocre Chinese restaurant and a Chase Manhattan Bank across the street. Continuing north two blocks you come to the Post Office. Across the street from the stoplight is Isla Morada, a chart store with the best selection of charts south of Miami. A half block from there is a convenience store for limited food and snacks.

City Services: Panama City has horrible traffic congestion, but it has some very cosmopolitan and beautiful sections. We rent cars and drive around, but it is not for the faint of heart or the uninitiated. Many of the main streets change names without notice, and several are unmarked one-way streets. It's very easy to make a wrong turn onto a one-way street, then find brightly painted buses coming at you four abreast, belching black smoke.

Cabs are relatively inexpensive and are a good idea until you learn your way around. The smaller cabs are less expensive than the large older American-make cabs known as "tourist cabs." The English-speaking tourist cabbies that operate within Balboa can be real hustlers, so you may feel like walking from the yacht club to the main exit from Balboa, where you can flag down a smaller city cab to take you into Panama City. When you come back into Balboa in these smaller cabs, the fare will be less than it was when you went out in the big one.

Many parts and supplies are available in this large capital, though parts specific to a yacht may be difficult to find. This is the best place out of the U.S. for electronics repairs, contact Marco Electronics.

Via Espana is a major east-west thoroughfare through Panama City. Along it and surrounding the Hilton Hotel is an upscale area of shops and restaurants. Our favorite formal eatery is El Cortijo, which has excellent Iberian Spanish food.

The Miramar Hotel's marina lies inside a breakwater-enclosed yacht basin at the east end of the Panama City's downtown

Miramar Hotel's marina on the east shore of Panama City is pretty shallow.

malecon. It has floating docks for boats up to 50 feet, but no moorings or anchoring. Diesel can be taken off a fuel barge that's docked in the far end of the marina basin. However, because of the area's extreme tidal range, most cruising boats can enter or leave this basin only at high tide, and many boats actually sit on the mud bottom at every low tide. There are no plans to dredge this marina.

Provisioning: For a fast major provisioning, take a taxi to the newer Price CostCo mega-store, one block south of the intersection of Via Espana and Via Brasil. It's closer to the waterfront than the original store near Tocumen airport. Costco has good selection and reasonably low prices.

For fresh meats, the closest Casa de Carne store is in Punta Paitilla on Avenida Balboa. Two blocks away is a huge Arrocha Pharmacia. If you're hungry for fresh fish while stuck in the canal area, try Mercado de Mariscos, a good fish market on the west side of Avenida Balboa.

For anything left over that you couldn't find, or for a smaller provisioning, go to the El Dorado shopping center. Here you can do a good reprovisioning at the large El Rey supermarket. It has a good selection, but American brands are expensive. This shopping center also has an excellent green grocer and a good hardware store.

Some of the cabbies may know of other "American" grocery stores that pop up from time to time; although they may carry a few gourmet items you thought you'd never see again, their prices are usually so exorbitant that these shops close down as fast as they sprout up.

Side Trips: On the eastern edge of town, you can walk around inside the colonial ruins called Ciudad Vieja (Old City), the original site that Henry Morgan sacked and destroyed. It's impossible to visit Panama without becoming intrigued with its colorful history and pirate lore.

A short drive north of Balboa is Parque Soberana, a magnificent national park of old-growth trees, lush jungle, flowers, birds and waterfalls along hiking paths.

Excursion boats and ferries run out to Taboga Island several times a day, so boaters anchored at Taboga can have fairly easy access to town services. If you want to check out the Panama Canal operations before taking your own boat through, you can book a local excursion boat and come back by bus to Panama City, or vice versa from Colon.

Las Perlas Islands in the eastern half of Panama Bay are a popular cruising ground containing nearly 24 islands and 75 islets. Contadora Island, the most populated, has several hotels. Boaters spend several months in this region. The beaches are not quite as lovely as those of the San Blas Islands on the Caribbean side.

The Darien Jungle east of Las Perlas is one of the most pristine tropical rainforests in Central America - much of it a biosphere reserve. But if you go more than a mile or so into these maze-like bayous, be sure to hire a local Indian guide. Some will transport you by cayuco or panga up river to the remote villages where the Embera and Wounaan tribes live in open thatch-roofed huts on stilts over the water. Tribal men carve tagua nut and cocobolo wood into delicate sea creatures and jungle birds, while the women weave baskets and bowls so tightly that some hold water. As with the Cuna of San Blas, some handicrafts are made just for selling to visitors.

Chapter 19
Panama: Pacific Coast

~~~~~~

Depending on how much cruising time you want to spend on this coast of Panama, you can see below your options for traveling directly on to Costa Rica – or lingering awhile in this vast and undulating reaches of Panama's jungles and islands on its Pacific coastline.

Non Stop: Panama to Costa Rica

Many boaters depart from the Panama Canal area and move directly to southern Costa Rica. If you plan to do this, you'll pass close aboard and just to the east of Isla Taboguilla (8°49'N by 79°31'W) and Isla Bona (8°35'N by 79°36'W), round Punta Mala (7°28'N by 80°00'W), skirting the southwest coast of Panama. Pass one mile south of Isla Jicarita (7°13'N by 81°48'W), turning for the first time to the northwest. You've just passed the most southerly point along the route covered by this book. Stay west of Isla Montuosa (7°28'N by 82°15'W), being careful of the reef that extends to the northwest of it, and then head toward Punta Burrica (8°02'N by

82°52'W), the peninsula that is half in Panama and half in Costa Rica.

The wind and current will generally be in your favor, so you'll probably move right along and encounter little difficulty with the voyage to Costa Rica. However if you leave so soon, you'll be bypassing a pristine and seldom visited paradise for cruisers and sportfishers alike.

Cruising: Panama to Costa Rica

Cruising toward Costa Rica's Pacific side from Balboa, Panama, is easier than going the other direction, because you're likely to have the wind and weather in your favor. If conditions are pleasant, you may decide to stick around and explore Panama's Pacific sportfishing and cruising grounds before moving on.

On the other hand, if you're going from Costa Rica toward the Panama Canal, you're likely to encounter some adverse winds and sea conditions. In this case, you may seek a few relief stopovers, so we'll look at the possible stops in Pacific

Panama as you cruise from Costa Rica toward the big canal.

Puerto Armuelles: Puerto Armuelles is an oil port on Panama's northwest Pacific coast near the border with Costa Rica. It's a possible Port of Entry, and if you have a mechanical emergency, you may locate help here. But Armuelles is not recommended as a pleasant cruising port. Super tankers carrying Alaskan oil transfer their cargoes here into a trans-isthmus pipeline. The Port Captain is reported to levy large port fees on small yachts.

However, between Puerto Armuelles and Punta Mala lie several islands and mainland anchorages worth visiting for their deserted beaches and jungle.

The winds in this region are generally light and variable. But in January and February the Caribbean Trades can sometimes blow across the isthmus and reach the north side of Coiba Island. This winter wind does not usually reach gale force, but it can make for wet travel. During the rainy season the wind and swell tend to be southwesterly.

Cabanas Parida: This little harbor on the east side of the northern tip of Isla Parida (8°07.8'N 82°19'W) is a cruisers' hangout run by Dave and Sharon Simpson; their phone is (507) 774-8166. Cabanas Parida has ice, diesel, propane, restaurant, bar and a store. About 20 miles southeast are the Islas Secas, Dry Islands, known for their good diving. Isla Cavada is the preferred spot.

Bahia Honda: Bahia Honda is a well-protected natural harbor favored by cruisers, located on the mainland. Several spots on the west side of the bay have good protection and holding, including Playa del

Sol (7°45.9'N by 81°31.7'W) which is a yachtie hangout. The village on Isla Talon in the center of the bay has very basic supplies.

Coiba Island: Isla Coiba is the largest of these islands, and it has many coves and bays, sometimes shrouded in mist. English pirates and raiders like Sir Francis Drake and Commodore George Anson hid for months from the Spanish while using the copious island resources to reprovision and re-outfit their vessels. More recently, the sparsely populated north end of Coiba was a prison territory in which the prisoners roamed free. The prison was closed several years ago, but as we go to press, five particularly dangerous prisoners who evaded capture are still at large. In 1996 a cruising sailor was murdered aboard his vessel by escaped prisoners. Patrol boats still circle the island and warn visitors to beware of the escapees.

Coiba's best anchorage (07°37.8'N by 81°43.6'W) is 2.5 miles southeast of its very northern tip. The anchorage is surrounded by two additional tiny islands: Rancheria and Islas Cocos. The shore vegetation is very lush, and dense foliage grows right down to the water's edge. Because this area is only 7° N of the Equator and within the Inter-tropical Convergence Zone, the weather is normally hot and calm. However, in the winter a north wind sometimes blows and can make the anchorage rolly for a few days. If such is the case, anchor in the southeast corner of Rancheria in 15 to 20 feet of water over sand with good holding properties. Rancheria has a small seasonal hotel.

The sportfishing on Coiba ranks with the finest in the world. Fronting the anchorage on the big island is a remote, fly-in sportfishing resort. In late 1998 we anchored in front of the resort to wait out some bad southerly weather. An armed Panamanian policeman came out in a launch and inspected our boat. He told us about the escaped prisoners and said that anchoring directly in front of the resort was okay, because he could keep an eye on us for our own safety. But, according to the local guards, it's unsafe to anchor anywhere else on this large island.

Naranjo Cove: Naranjo Cove (7°16.5'N by 80°55.6'W) is a marginal anchorage just north of the southwest corner of the Panamanian mainland Peninsula of Azuero. Naranjo and Roncador Islands lie just off shore of the anchorage, which is open to the west. Holding is poor, and swell at high tide can make it rolly. It helps to put out a stern anchor, to keep your boat's head into the swell. From Naranjo to Punta Mala is 56 miles along the beautifully rugged and steep-to coast of the Azuero.

Punta Mala: Or Cape Mala, this major headland (7°28'N by 80°00'W) is aptly named. It's the point at which you turn north into the Gulf of Panama for the last 100 miles to the canal. The powerful navigation light on this point is very reliable, as are most lights in Panama. The current, an offshoot of the counter-Equatorial current, runs from north to south along this side of Panama Bay, and the wind blows at times strongly from the same direction.

Many Pacific shipping lanes converge here, as do local fishing vessels. All the traffic, frequent heavy rain squalls, and the fact that nobody seems to observe the Rules of the Road, cause the Punta Mala area to be dangerous. "Might is Right" seems to be the rule, so stay out of the shipping lanes. We recommend that no boat should go through this area at night without radar.

Benao Cove: From late December through March the Caribbean Trade Winds blow strongly across the low isthmus of Panama in a condition similar to that of the gulfs of Tehuantepec and Papagallo. If you're sailing or powering from the canal toward Costa Rica, it can be fine, but if you're coming the other direction and trying to round Punta Mala, it can be rough going into head winds and seas. In that case, you can find shelter at Benao Cove (7°25.5'N by 080°11.3'W), 12 miles west of Mala. Benao is easy to locate, because two prominent offshore rocks called Los Frailes lie just to the east of it. A small hotel may be seen on the beach at Benao, and a paved road connects it to the outside world. You can get fresh water from a well in a garden near the anchorage, as well as some very basic food from the small restaurant.

The wind blows hard off the hills, but the bottom is good holding ground. Do not be deceived by the wind in the anchorage. Often it will be blowing hard inside the anchorage but only moderately around Punta Mala. You'll have to poke your nose out to give it a try. During the rainy season, however, Benao Cove is a lee shore – not an anchorage.

Rounding Mala: The main shipping lane between Cape Mala and the Panama Canal sea buoy (8°53'N by 79°30'W) is several miles offshore. You can avoid this intense traffic by staying closer to shore. Round Punta Mala no farther out than two miles, then lay a course straight for Isla Bona (08°35'N by 79° 36'W). This will give you a course parallel to, but west of, the shipping lane. Though you'll constantly have shipping on your starboard horizon, rarely will you have to change course for big ships. However, always be on the lookout for fishing boats doing the same tactic.

Cruising Ports

During daylight hours you may pass between Isla Bona and Isla Otoque (pronounced "oh-TOE-kay"), being careful of a rock between the two. Favor the passage toward Otoque. On the south side of Otoque is a good anchorage. Though you are only 17 miles from the sea buoy for the Panama Canal, you may find this anchorage to be a good respite if you're fighting a Norther. A small fishing village is on the north side of Isla Otoque.

Sailing skippers might take advantage of a favorable slant from Punta Mala by reaching out to visit Las Perlas Islands. This puts them in an advantageous position to then sail on into the canal on the other tack with aid from the current.

Islas Las Perlas: The Islas Las Perlas are made up of more than two dozen islands and nearly 200 islets - ranging in size from quite small to large. Except for a few localized resort developments, the rest of Las Perlas are considered pristine cruising ground. Accurate pilotage is needed among their numerous and not very well charted rocks and reefs. The islands were at one time a rich pearling ground, and though this is no longer true, it still remains a fantastic spot for fishing and diving, and it offers many secluded anchorages. Be cautious in secluded places, however, because there are reported to be marijuana plantations on the Perlas, and these islands are rumored to be used for drug-smuggling operations.

Cruising is safe at Contadora, a 220-acre resort and intimate gambling casino. An airport at Contadora offers 15-minute flights into Panama City.

Taboga Island: Taboga (8°47'N by 79°33'W) is a small island only 5.5 miles from the sea buoy. A favorite getaway among cruisers, Taboga's anchorage is on the eastern side in deep water, so you need lots of ground tackle. Cruisers who prefer to remain here away from the bustle of the busy canal use the twice-daily ferry into Balboa to take care of ship's business. The town of Taboga is a resort for Panama's mainlanders. The island's breezes are relatively cool, so it has been thought of as a place to recuperate from tropical fevers since the earliest days of the Spanish. No cars are allowed on Taboga, so it's very quiet. The tiny church here is the second oldest in the Americas. Francisco Pizarro set sail from Taboga to conquer Peru.

Chapter 20
Central America: Overview

~~~~~~

For our definition, Central America includes the countries of Costa Rica, Nicaragua, Honduras, El Salvador and Guatemala. (Mexico is part of North America.)

To Stop – or Not to Stop?

Although the general political climate has improved in most of Central America, we still recommend that recreational boaters (cruisers and sportfishers) bypass the countries of Nicaragua, Honduras and El Salvador. Due to recent hurricane damage and the legacy of decades of civil unrest, the poverty that still grips most sea ports along this stretch makes them inconvenient stops – and especially for what locals see as luxurious yachts full of rich vacationing foreigners. Most of the people who live and work on or near the water do not comprehend the idea of recreational boating, so pleasure boaters are not appreciated in these areas. With the possible exception of the Gulf of Fonseca, there are no cruising grounds in

which to hang out. Port clearance procedures are set up with commercial vessels in mind, not pleasure craft or boat-based tourists, so port clearances can be very expensive and awkward. If and when this picture changes, we'll be among the first to encourage boaters to visit here. Weather-wise, boaters crossing between southern Mexico and northern Costa Rica will face wind and sea conditions similar to the dreaded Gulf of Tehuantepec – not a place to hang out.

In other words, our advice is: No, do not plan to stop in Pacific Nicaragua, Honduras or El Salvador. Our recommendation is to go as directly as possible from northern Costa Rica to southern Mexico, or vice versa if you're southbound from the U.S. West Coast.

In this chapter, we'll look first at the how-to logistics of making this direct route, and then, because you should always know what's over the horizon, we'll take a brief look into each of the Central American countries.

Cruising Ports

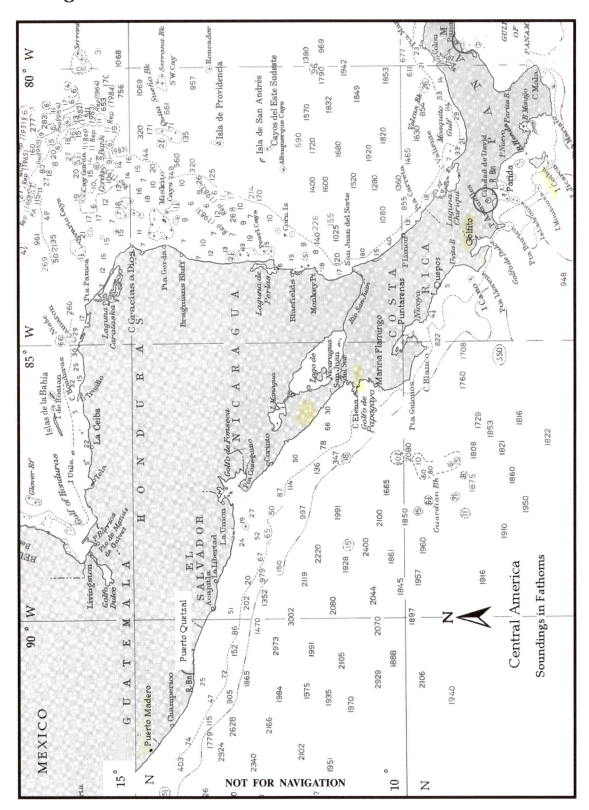

Planning Chart for Chapter 20 through Chapter 23

Direct Route:

Costa Rica to Mexico

The 500-mile stretch between Marina Flamingo, Costa Rica and Puerto Madero, Mexico offers very little in the way of services for yachts. With the exception of Puerto Quetzal and the Gulf of Fonseca, we recommend not stopping unless you're having an emergency.

On this crossing, boaters face the Gulf of Papagallo, which has weather similar to the dreaded Gulf of Tehuantepec. In Chapter 8 on Caribbean Routes and Weather, look at the chart for the western Caribbean. During the winter months (January is the worst), cold fronts reaching down into the Caribbean increase the force of the Northeast Trades, and these winds bridge over the backbone of Central America at its lowest spot and blow strongly into the Pacific.

That low spot is the Rio San Juan Valley on the Nicaragua-Costa Rica border. The wind is strongest at the head of the Gulf of Papagallo, but it affects the entire area between Cabo Velas and El Salvador. Though no weather warnings are given on any commercial high seas radio station, the east wind frequently reaches gale force and blows for several days.

Weather Wisdom: Listen to voice weather from NMN or fax station NMG (see Appendix) for weather in the Caribbean. If a cold front is passing and the Trades are blowing northeast at 25 to 30 knots in the southwest Caribbean, then chances are good for wind in the Papagallo. Listen also to the Central American Breakfast Club (ham net) at 1300Z on 7.083 Mhz lower sideband, though this net doesn't give specific weather reports.

The last week of May is the official beginning of hurricane season in the eastern Pacific. The Gulf of Tehuantepec is the primary hurricane formation area, though they occasionally form farther south, including this stretch south of Puerto Madero. Costa Rica itself is south of the hurricane belt and consequently is a favorite summering-over spot for long-range cruisers. Summer occasionally brings intense thunderstorms with lightning and waterspouts to Costa Rican waters, though never of hurricane strength or long duration.

To be truly safe, vessels that have summered over in Costa Rica shouldn't leave to return north until November 1. However, fast power boats with long cruising range can and make this leg during the summer months. The trick is to travel between easterly waves. Since these waves move from east to west, a vessel traveling from Costa Rica to Mexico has the best chance of staying between waves.

A boat traveling in the opposite direction has to be much faster, because it will be closing with these waves at a rapid rate, with very little time in between them. If you're southbound from Mexico, you should be in northern Costa Rica before the last week in May. Review the section on easterly waves in the chapter on Mexican weather. Or read "MexWX: Mexico Weather for Boaters" which contains chapters on the gulfs of Tehuantepec and Papagallo.

Routing Waypoints: The route you choose should depend upon the time of year. In April through December 15, you can usually proceed directly across the Gulf of Papagallo. From five miles abeam of Point Guiones (9°49'N by 85°44'W), which is the northwest tip of Costa Rica, head for a waypoint off Guatemala (14°04'N by 91°52'W). Or if you're departing from the Playa del Coco (10°34'N by 85°43'W) area, proceed directly to this same waypoint off

Guatemala. This is a 440-mile open-ocean crossing with a slight current that generally sets you toward the beach.

The waypoint off Guatemala takes you outside the 10-fathom curve. Do not pass closer than this because of shoaling southeast of Champerico and much shrimp-boat traffic. We've often been boarded by the Guatemalan Navy 30 miles offshore. They have been courteous but dead serious. They've always inspected us and then let us proceed. From this waypoint you can proceed directly to Puerto Madero (14°42'N by 92°27'W), the first port in southern Mexico.

Northbound: If you're northbound in a power boat, the ride can sometimes be a little rough and rolly. If you're in a well found sailboat, the wind and current are generally in your favor, so you should have a fast sail.

From December 15 through March, you'll need to take a route closer to shore. At the waypoint five miles offshore of Pt. Guiones, turn north into the Gulf of Papagallo and stay close to the shore (except for charted rocks and reefs) to avoid gale force winds. You can stay anchored or slipped comfortably in the area of Marina Flamingo and Playa del Coco until the wind drops somewhat.

In 40-knot winds, we have continued hugging the irregular shoreline through the Gulf of Papagallo, cutting inside the Islas Murcielagos, around Cabo Santa Elena, and then paralleling the Nicaraguan coast two to five miles offshore. The wind carries lots of spray and sand, but being in this close keeps the seas flat. We head to a waypoint off northern Nicaragua at 12°40'N by 87°35'W, then turn straight to the Guatemalan waypoint (14°04'N by 91°52'W). This leg takes you off shore of the Gulf of Fonseca. Do not transit

closer inshore than the rhumb line.

Southbound: If you're southbound from Mexico toward Costa Rica, this passage is more difficult, because the wind and current will be against you.

In the winter months, take the inshore route as described above. Sailboats will get wet and bounced around, but power boats will be down right uncomfortable. This is when stabilizers really pay for themselves.

During other times of the year, you may proceed directly off shore on the southbound route.

Countries of Central America

Boaters leaving Panama and bound for Costa Rica – or boats leaving Mexico and bound for Costa Rica – need to know as much as possible about the small Central American countries whose waters they are traversing. So we'll take a glimpse at each country in geographic order, from south to north on the Pacific side.

Costa Rica

Costa Rica – covered extensively in the next three chapters – is very friendly to North Americans and is very safe for boaters to visit, both along the coast and inland. Costa Rica enjoys Central America's highest per capita income, highest level of education, and a history of successful democratic institutions. Costa Rica has long been the shining light among its sometimes struggling neighbors.

Columbus' first visit to Costa Rica was in 1502, but Costa Rica had no gold, silver or exploitable native labor force, so the Europeans who settled here had no way to amass fast fortunes. They had to work the land themselves, and with this lack of absentee landlords, an egalitarian atmosphere was created that hindered the rise of strong class distinctions.

Costa Rica has a unique racial composition for Central America. Due to a scant aboriginal population, the "Ticos" as they call themselves are largely of European descent, 80 to 85 percent. The balance are *Mestizo* and Antillean Blacks. The populace is proud of its 90% literacy rate that creates their high degree of economic and social mobility.

Since 1948 Costa Rica has had very little political or social unrest, and it has pursued a course of democracy, social welfare, freedom of the press and respect for human rights. The country is unique for not having a standing army, although it has a national police force and a coast guard. Oscar Arias Sanchez, who was Costa Rica's President from 1986 to 1990, received the Nobel Peace Prize for his Central American Peace Plan which was largely responsible for ending hostilities in Nicaragua. Most of Costa Rica's subsequent presidents have carried on Arias' intentions.

The country is faced with rampant inflation and saddled with a huge foreign debt. However, because of a very favorable exchange rate between the U.S. dollar and Costa Rica's monetary unit, the Colon, prices for most items are still very reasonable for *norteamericanos*.

Sportfishing tourism is a thriving and rapidly growing industry on both Costa Rica's Pacific and Caribbean coasts, but largely on the Pacific. Sportfishing for bill fish, tuna and local species is world-class in quality. Many small and medium sized hotels supply their own sportfishing fly-in guests with open day-boats or cuddy cabins.

Sport scuba and snorkel diving enjoys a similar but smaller popularity, mostly involving small hotels and local fishing boats. Air and limited diving supplies are available in almost every small community near the coast. Sport diving and yacht cruising are also on the increase in Costa Rica.

Nicaragua

Civil war is over here, and the region is more politically stable than it has been in decades. For that reason, it is now considered safe to visit Nicaragua by private yacht. However, stopping in a Nicaraguan port is still monumentally inconvenient for private yachts. Consider stopping only in case of an emergency – such as strong Papagallo winds. After years of civil war, the "Nicos" are still very impoverished, totally unaccustomed to the needs of pleasure craft. We discovered that making arrangements for fuel in quantities larger than what can be carried in jerry jugs is ponderous, and the high fees collected by the officials are highly "negotiable."

Corinto

With a population of 7,000, Corinto (12°27'N 87°11'W) is Nicaragua's main commercial port and has the best all-around protection of anywhere on the country's

Corinto is a commercial port, best reserved for emergencies.

Pacific coast. The port is primarily used by large ships, so its approaches are well buoyed. The harbor lies in a protected lagoon behind barrier islands, and distinctive volcanic cones are visible inland.

Approaches and Anchorage: Enter the channel with Isla Cardon to starboard and the cranes of the commercial wharf to port. Call to the Capitania on VHF channel 16 (Spanish only) to announce your arrival. You may be directed to anchor just north of the commercial wharf, directly abeam of some burned and rusted out petroleum tanks ashore. (These tanks were blown up by agents of the CIA during the Contra War, when they also mined the harbor and damaged several ships.) You anchor in about 20 feet of water on a soft mud bottom, so you need plenty of scope out to keep from dragging in the strong tidal flow. This is one of those places where you need to allow room to swing, because you'll do so at the turn of each tide.

Port Clearance: Use your launch to pick up the port officials and bring them out to the boat. They'll take your Zarpe (sailing document from the last country), stamp your passports and give your boat a thorough inspection. Our experience here was that the officials were friendly and helpful while clearing us in. They do not speak English.

Once cleared with these guys, you're allowed to go ashore. You can land and tie your dinghy on the north side of the commercial wharf, where it remains under the watchful eye of port security. Enter the town through the wharf's main gate. To clear papers ashore, first visit Migracion, just outside the fiscal wharf area on the south side of town. Here they exit stamp you passports and collect $50. (This was negotiated down from a much larger figure after which a receipt was given.) Then you go to the Port Captain's office, a block and a half from the main gate of the wharf, and get your Zarpe for another $50.

Local Services: Nicaragua is the poorest country in the Western Hemisphere, and that is immediately apparent as you walk through the main gate. The people are very desperate, beggars and hustlers abound. As we walked around town, we were much stared at, as if we had just landed in a spaceship from Mars. The central market, on the southeast corner of the square, is one of the most impoverished places imaginable. Forget provisioning; if you need anything beyond rice, beans and bananas, you're out of luck.

The only bank in town is adjacent to the Capitania. Nicaragua's monetary unit is the Cordoba, and you'll have to check the current exchange rate. U.S. dollars are accepted in small bills on the street, but usually for less than at the bank. The telephone office where you can make long-distance calls is nearby.

Fuel Stop: If you need fuel in jerry jug quantities, go to the gas station across the street from the bank. Delivery of larger quantities is difficult to arrange, because they're not used to yachts stopping here. You have to get permission from Port Operations to come alongside the wharf; Port Operations offices are on the fiscal wharf. You do this by making a written request in Spanish, then making 10 copies. Then you pay a highly negotiable fee in advance. We paid $122 only because we told them we were forced into port by "arribo forzoso" – bad weather. Otherwise the fee would have been much higher. Water is a small additional charge. If all goes well, you'll then be given an appointment to come to the dock.

All this has to be coordinated with the arrival of a fuel truck. Contact Petronic on VHF channel 16. They deliver diesel at a reasonable price for Central America. You must take it only in 500-gallon increments and pay for the whole load – whether or not you can take it all on board. First you have to meet a company representative at the bank to pay in advance, and pay in Cordoba. Then they'll load the fuel truck, seal the compartments, and meet you at the pier. The fuel is gravity fed.

If you wish, you can hire an English-speaking ship's agent to make all these arrangements for you. However he will be expensive, not familiar with the needs of yachts, you'll become secondary to any other ships he has in port, and, in the end, his fee may be higher than he said in the beginning. Call Kenneth Dash on VHF channel 16.

All in all, we can't recommend Corinto as a cruising stop. However, since it is located in the Gulf of Papagallo, an area notorious for bad weather, we wouldn't hesitate to seek shelter here or cruise in the lee of the land to get out of the wind. And besides – how many people do you know who visited Nicaragua?

Gulf of Fonseca

The Gulf of Fonseca, which has numerous islands, bays, rivers and swamps, is bordered by Honduras, Nicaragua and El Salvador. Small ships and commercial fishing boats use the Gulf of Fonseca. If you are crossing the mouth of this large gulf, try to do so in daylight hours, because local vessels may operate without lights, let alone radar.

Strong Papagallo winds sometimes find their way across the narrow land mass and into Fonseca Bay. From October through February the Gulf of Fonseca is affected by strong northerly wind storms

that last up to a week, a condition known locally as the "Burro Gacho."

Honduras

Honduras has only a tiny coastline on its Pacific side, and that bit falls entirely within the Gulf of Fonseca. For the present, do not visit the Pacific coast of Honduras because of the physical and economic devastation wrought by Hurricane Mitch.

(However you can safely visit the prime cruising grounds of the Bay Islands off the Caribbean coast of Honduras. See Chapter 12 on Roatan Island.)

Between 1855 and 1932, Honduras had 67 heads of state. The period from 1932 to 1954 was marked by greater stability but little social progress. In 1957 Ramon Valleda Morales embarked on a program of improvements of roads, schools, public health, social security, labor and agrarian reform which lasted until 1963. After being accused by the *Wall Street Journal* of taking a $1.25-million bribe from the United Fruit Company to lower the banana export tax, President Osvaldo Lopez Arellano was deposed in 1975.

In 1982 Honduras returned to civilian rule after 18 years of military governments. It has been the U.S.'s staunchest ally, and U.S. troops have been stationed on Honduran soil. However, small waves of violent anti-American demonstrations sweep the capital from time to time.

Puerto Ampala

Puerto Ampala in the north end of the Gulf of Fonseca is the only Honduran port accessible from the Pacific. This more or less abandoned commercial port lies on the northwest side of the large volcanic Isla del Tigre, and it offers good protection when entered through its narrow western channel. The town's 500-foot-long commercial pier has about 11 feet of water at its seaward end. Ampala is a Port of Entry for Honduras, and you must clear in with the Port Captain and other federal authorities.

Alternately, the north end of Isla Meanguera and the northwest part of Isla Zacate Grande both have vessel anchorages. Bahia San Lorenzo has a small loading port seven miles from Isla Raton. Moneypenny Anchorage is a well-sheltered area spreading about 2.5 miles long by six miles wide.

El Salvador

El Salvador is the smallest, most densely populated Central American country. For 2.5 centuries after the Spanish conquest, El Salvador remained a sleepy backwater country because it lacked gold, silver and an easily exploitable indigenous population. Salvadorans are predominantly *Mestizo,* and their cultural heritage is practically free of the sad struggle between Indian and *Mestizo* so evident in their neighbors.

El Salvador's political history is the familiar battle between liberals and conservatives. Both parties consisted of wealthy Creoles but with opposing ideologies. In 1931 a popular revolution removed General Maximiliano Hernandez, followed by a 50-year succession of rulers who tried to maintain the status quo. When neighboring Nicaragua was run by the Sandinistas in 1979, El Salvador became a hotbed of guerrilla and terrorist activity. In October of 1979, Salvadoran Carlos Humberto Romero was ousted, and a military-civilian *junta* was installed. They nationalized the banks and export houses and redistributed some large estates to rural workers. Both the political Left and Right tried to sabotage this land reform, and thousands were killed by violence on both sides of the war.

In 1984 Centrist Jose Napoleon Duarte became El Salvador's first constitutionally elected president in 50 years. His presidency had a moderating influence on the nation, though guerrillas continued to operate in rural areas. When Duarte was diagnosed with severe cancer and was replaced in elections by the Rightist Christiani, violence again flared up for a short time. In the 1990s, a treaty was signed between the government and the rebels, peace prevailed for several years, and things are relatively normal for Salvadorans.

You may transit near shore while passing El Salvador, but beware of many small unlighted fishing vessels in the night.

Acajutla and La Libertad: Acajutla and La Libertad are the El Salvador's two major ports on the Pacific coastline, but both are merely open rodesteads offering very little to zero protection from the Pacific swell. Acajutla has a small breakwater but the anchorage is fouled with sunken vessels and cables. The Rio Lempa is a large navigable river, but of little importance.

La Union: The port of La Union, located about 20 miles up inside the Gulf of Fonseca, is El Salvador's most protected port because it has an almost land-locked harbor. Enter west of Isla Conchiquita. The only anchorage for this non-tourist town is just past the Navy pier. You must clear in with the Navy and then the Port Captain and other port officials. The only fuel is via jerry jugs from a gas station on the north end of town.

Alternately, Bahia Jiquilisco offers good anchorage between Isla Pajarito and Isla Tortuga. A marina is planned at Tamarindo, but the developer is still having problems obtaining permits.

Guatemala

Guatemala is the most populated of these Central American republics. Its highland interior, where most of the people live, is stunningly beautiful and is the site of Mayan and Spanish colonial ruins. Fifty percent of the population is pure indigenous natives, non-Spanish-speaking, and struggling to maintain their cultural identity. Until very recently, their way of life had not changed in centuries.

When Guatemala was conquered by Pedro Alvarado, one of Cortez's lieutenants, it was the center of an advanced Mayan culture. Thereafter it became the Spanish capital of a large region covering what is now Chiapas, El Salvador, Honduras, Nicaragua and Costa Rica. Guatemala was the capital not only politically but culturally, economically and socially. Immediately after Mexico's independence from Spain, the Mexican Emperor Iturbide dispatched an army to Guatemala and forced it to become part of his empire. Though that empire lasted only a year, it permanently soured Mexican-Guatemalan relations, because Mexico retained the large state of Chiapas.

The ensuing political history was the classic struggle between liberals and conservatives, and Guatemala was ruled by a succession of dictators. Dictator Jorge Ubico was overthrown in 1944 by a leftist coalition of students, liberals and dissident military officers. In the 1950s Jacabo Arbenz Guzman, a successor to that revolution, was duly elected. Fearing that he would hand the country over to the Communists, right wing Col. Carlos Castillo Armas overthrew Guzman with the help of the U.S. CIA.

The 1980s saw leftist guerrilla activity in the rural mountains and the slums of Guatemala City. The guerrillas were fought by the Guatemalan army and the dreaded Mano Blanco, a right-wing terrorist group said to secretly operate with government sanction. The gang systematically murdered left-wing opposition leaders in a campaign similar to the very effective Phoenix program which murdered suspected Communists during the Vietnam war. The U.S. cut off military aid to Guatemala because of these death squads. Peace accords were signed in January 1998, and the country has been returning to normal.

Puerto Quetzal

Puerto Quetzal is Guatemala's main port on the Pacific coast, and it may be of service to pleasure boats passing by.

This small port was created by dredging a lagoon and laying in sea walls. Puerto Quetzal is a well-sheltered artificial basin with protecting breakwaters. The northern half is a shipping dock, and the western half is a Navy base. The small

Puerto Quetzal is a secure place to leave your boat, if you want to explore Guatemala's highlands.

dinghy dock

anchorage

Navy fuel pier

anchorage for pleasure boats is accommodated in the Navy's western half. Pleasure boaters may find several reasons to stop at Puerto Quetzal.

First, it's situated between the only two secure and reliable fuel stops in this region, which are Puerto Madero in Mexico and Marina Flamingo in Costa Rica. The rest of the ports in Central America are to be considered for emergencies only. On the other hand, we don't recommend Puerto Quetzal as a fuel stop for quantities larger than you can carry in jerry jugs, because the diesel is very expensive and the procedures are inconvenient.

Second, when you're southbound and the weather ahead in the Gulf of Papagallo looks iffy, Puerto Quetzal gives you a place to duck in and wait for your next weather window.

Third, as we go to press, Puerto Quetzal is a secure place to leave your boat and visit the beautiful and historic highland interior of Guatemala.

Approaches: The immediate coastline is low and swampy; lagoons stretch behind the barrier beaches. Farther behind several miles of lowlands, the terrain rises rapidly to the rugged Guatemalan mountains. The most distinctive landmark in the area is the perfect cone of the inactive Volcan Agua (Water) lying 30 miles inland. The more irregularly shaped Volcan Fuego (Fire) lies just west of Agua, and you often can see smoke rising from it during the day and glowing lava at night. The GPS position of the entrance to the breakwater is 13°54.90'N by 90°47.03'W, which we found to be very accurate on Chart #21483.

Puerto Quetzal is only about two miles mile east of the old port of San Jose, which consists of an unprotected pier jutting out into the open Pacific. A tank farm lies just west of this pier. Do not confuse the entrance to Puerto Quetzal with the entrance to tiny Istapa Lagoon. The latter lies one mile to the east of Puerto Quetzal and is much more shallow and narrow.

Port Clearance: All vessels are required to announce their arrival to the Capitania on VHF channel 16 and request permission to enter the port (in Spanish only). Tell them you're a yacht (as opposed to any kind of commercial vessel), and you'll be instructed to anchor in the west basin just northeast of the end of the Navy pier. This anchorage is well protected, and it has about 17 feet of water over hard black volcanic sand and mud, and the holding is very good.

The port and navy officials come out to your anchored vessel in their own launch to clear you. They usually consist of a Guatemalan Navy lieutenant, the Migracion officer and a military policeman. They ask for your *Zarpe*, which is your international clearance from your last port of your last country. Because you are anchored in a military facility, the MP gives your boat a very thorough inspection and asks you for *facturas*, meaning copies of receipts for the vessel's appurtenances. Port charges are $100 for the first five days (whether you stay that long or not) and $10 for each additional day. This $100 includes the fee for your entrance and exit papers. This fee may seem steep to some cruising budgets, but the Port Captain's office gives efficient service, and you also get excellent security of armed guards patrolling a fenced perimeter. In Guatemala this is a real benefit.

Fuel Stop (Sometimes): Ask the boarding officer how you can make fuel arrangements. Fuel is expensive when delivered by truck to the Navy pier, and you must take it in 2,300-gallon increments –

Antigua, Guatemala: For language school or historical sights, this makes an interesting side trip.

and pay for it all whether you can take it all or not. You must supply your own hoses and reducers from a 2-inch fill. All arrangements and negotiations are in Spanish. If the Navy happens to have extra fuel on hand, which is not always the case, they sometimes will let you buy large quantities directly from them. But don't count on it.

Small quantities of gas and diesel can be jerry-jugged by taxi from a gas station about a mile away.

Local Services: You can land your dinghy at a low floating dock in the northwest corner and leave it safely there. A nearby palapa with picnic tables is a nice place for beach picnic. A nearby military clubhouse with snack bar was being renovated, and it is hoped that visiting boaters may be able to use it, too. The Port Captain's office is the 3-story blue and gray building within sight of the anchorage.

Outside the Navy's main gate, you can catch a taxi or bus to San Jose, which lies two miles to the west. The town has the better markets, but San Jose itself is dirty and otherwise uninteresting. About a mile to the right from the gate is a convenience store call Mercado 24 Horas, signifying that

it's open day and night, but it's not. We've seen it open about 16 hours a day, which is fairly remarkable in Guatemala. This is not a place to reprovision.

Side Trips Inland: Thanks to the good security at the port and because Guatemala's beautiful highland interior is so close to the port, many boaters leave their vessels while they travel inland by public bus or rental car.

If you do this, we recommend a visit to Antigua, only about 1.5 hours away. Antigua (meaning ancient) is the original colonial capital of Central America and home of the best Spanish language schools in all the Americas. We recommend P.L.F.M. for excellent immersion in Spanish with the best teachers in town.

With the signing of peace accords, Guatemala is once again a fairly safe place to travel. Exceptions are the poor barrios of Guatemala City and some of the very remote Mayan villages. Ask about personal safety when you arrive, because hot spots can pop up from week to week – politics and volcanoes both.

Istapa Lagoon

The area just off shore of Puerto Quetzal has excellent fishing for almost all bill fish, especially sail fish. The handful of fly-in sportfishing hotels are located inside the tiny Istapa Lagoon, and many have been featured in U.S. sportfishing magazines. They are all gated, guarded, guided – and do not serve non guests.

The entrance to Istapa Lagoon lies less than a mile east of the Puerto Quetzal breakwater entrance. It lies behind a long barrier island. We'd recommend that visiting boats do not attempt to use Istapa's narrow entrance until they have somehow gained a whole lot of local knowledge, because this murky entrance shoals severely, and the surf over the bars can be large. The zig-zag path changes every few hours, due to heavy silt accumulation and the state of the tide.

However once inside, you turn right, and the main channel leads east to the fishing village of Istapa. The tiny fuel dock on the inland side is used by pangas, shrimpers and local sportfishing boats alike. Beyond here, smaller tidal canals lead inland.

The village of Istapa is a historic curiosity. Here, Juan Rodriguez Cabrillo built the ships that he used to discover California. They were built of local hardwoods (now mostly gone), but all the iron works were forged in Spain and trans-shipped across Guatemala from the Caribbean side. The village is still small and primitive, probably little changed from the time Cabrillo was here.

Istapa's inner lagoon is home to a sportfishing fleet, but visitors must brave the difficult lagoon entrance to reach this tiny fuel dock.

Chapter 21
Costa Rica: South Pacific Coast

For a boater's purposes, Costa Rica's long and enormously beautiful Pacific coast is easily thought of in three distinct regions – southern, central and northern. So in this chapter and the next two, we'll look at these three regions in geographic order – from south to north. (If you're entering Costa Rica from the north, skip ahead to Chapter 23.)

Golfito & the Golfo Dulce

Hundreds of nameless coves and pretty rodesteads line the sinuous coastline along the southern portion of Costa Rica's Pacific coast, but when you're ready for a break from all that solitude, Golfito (8°38'N by 83°11'W) is this region's primary port for services.

Golfito also happens to be one of the most pleasant ports to visit in all of Costa Rica. Located in a landlocked bay 15 miles up the east side of the Golfo Dulce near the Panamanian border, Golfito and the smaller villages on Golfo Dulce fell upon hard times after the United Fruit Company closed down their Golfito operations. So tourism is more important than ever before.

Approaches: When you're coming in from the south, stand off the eastern shore because of a shoal at the mouth of the Rio Coto which empties into the Golfo Dulce just south of Golfito. The narrow entrance to Golfito has a steep jungle-covered hill on the north side and a lower sand spit to the south. Both sides have deep water close to shore until just inside. When the bay widens out, stay in the middle of the channel to avoid mud shoals on both sides, and then head straight in for the large commercial pier on the northeast shore. The entrance channel is buoyed, and the buoys are paired. But the port authorities must have gotten a good deal on red paint, because all the buoys are painted red – regardless of which side of the channel they mark. And because their lights seldom work, they can be dangerous at night; take care not to run over them.

Port Clearance: Port clearance is fairly easy. Take temporary anchorage off the large commercial pier to await the arrival of authorities. You are required to announce your arrival as well as departure to *Base Naval* on VHF channel 16 (Spanish

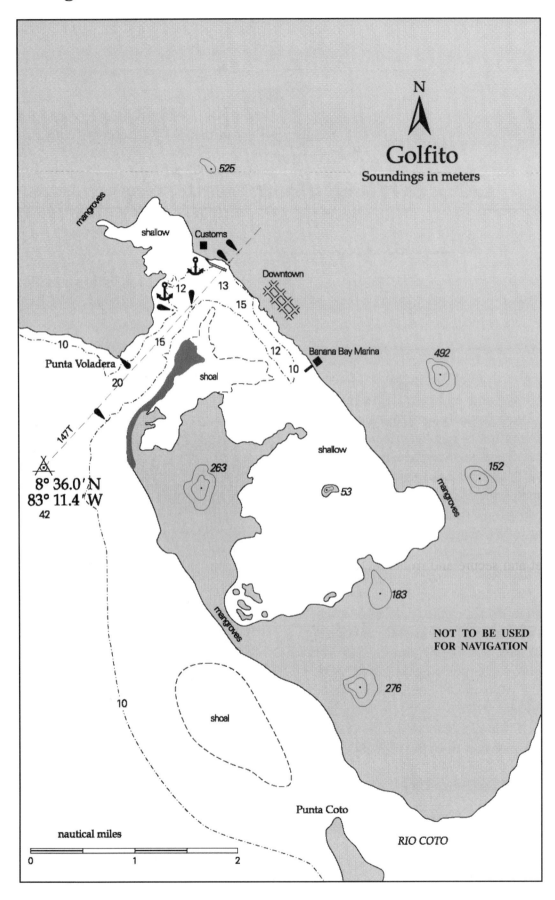

N

Golfito

Soundings in meters

525

mangroves

shallow

Customs

Downtown

12   13

15

10   15

Punta Voladera   12

20   10   Banana Bay Marina

492

shoal

147T

shallow

8° 36.0' N   263   152

83° 11.4" W   53

42

mangroves

183

NOT TO BE USED
FOR NAVIGATION

mangroves

276

10

shoal

Punta Coto

nautical miles   RIO COTO

0   1   2

only so *buena suerte*). Follow the radio instructions of the Port Captain as to clearance. Most often they require you to pick them up in your dinghy so that they can come out and inspect your boat. For clearance out, Customs is located in a large two-story building near the pier. The Port Captain and immigration offices are in another two-story building about two blocks south of Customs on the coast road.

Ship's Agent: The use of a ship's agent isn't required for pleasure boats here. However, if you wish to use the services of an English-speaking agent for port clearance, or for solving any little glitches, call agent Raul Callejas on VHF channel 16 or (506) 775-0097. He specializes in taking care of the needs of yachts.

Fuel Stop: If you need to take fuel in Golfito, arrange it with the Port Captain. Diesel is usually taken by truck off the banana pier.

Anchorages and Marinas: Once cleared, you may anchor in the northwest corner just inside the bay. This anchorage is quiet and secure and fronts the famous Captain Tom's place. You can easily spot the anchorage by a conspicuous gray powerboat high and dry on the beach. This was Tom's "Shipwreck Hotel," the smallest hotel on the Pacific ocean. But Captain Tom has since sailed on to Snug Harbor.

The town of Golfito lies across the bay, and its ferry landing is in the center of town. Just south of town is the Banana Bay Marina owned by Bruce Blevins (506) 775-0838 who monitors VHF channels 16 and 12. The marina has floating docks, large individual slips and one long pier for Med-mooring.

Metered dock power (30-amp, 110-volt and 50-amp 220-volt) is reliable but expensive. Security is good, but you should lock your dinghy at night; petty theft is a problem and Golfito is known for dinghy thefts.

Local Services: Sea and Land yacht services is run by Katie Dunkin and Tim Leechman, former cruising couple who like to help other cruisers. Call them on VHF channel 16 either as "Tierra y Mar" or "Land and Sea" or by their boat name "Caribee." Operating out of an office in a house across the street and up the hill from Banana Bay Marina, their services include phone, fax, e-mail and lots of handy local information. And they're getting licensed as ship's agents for Golfito, too. Their front room is a good meeting spot.

The best grocery store is near the old banana pier and has a fair selection. A meat market and green grocer are in the center of town. The Samoa Restaurant lies between the commercial pier and downtown, and it has good French cuisine.

A small airport offers regular flights inland to San Jose, the country's capital. An efficient bus system runs to San Jose and other towns. Costa Rica's phone system is excellent.

Banana Bay marina has floating docks.

Some cruisers like to anchor off the village of Santo Domingo under the protection of Punta Arenitas. It's located eight miles southwest of Golfito on the eastern shore of the Golfo Dulce, but it has no Port Captain or other services.

Isla del Cano

On the run north outside the Golfo Dulce, you may wish to pay a visit to Isla del Cano (8°43'N by 83°53'W), 40 miles northwest of the entrance to the gulf. Be careful of Roca Corcovado, 1.75 miles offshore between Punta Salsipuedes and Punta Llorana. Give this navigational hazard a berth of at least a mile outside. Do not attempt to pass inshore. (Pay heed; salsipuedes means leave if you can, and llorana means she who cries. The story about La Llorana is a popular myth, like the boogie man.)

The flat-topped and heavily wooded island of Cano is a good radar target and also has a 12-mile light on shore. The island offers an indifferent anchorage, but the prevailing weather here is quite calm. The preferred anchorage is on the north side, but as always it depends on the swell and sea conditions.

All of Isla de Cano is a biological preserve and prior permission must be obtained in Puntarenas before visiting the island. Rangers in boats patrol the waters around the island to insure you have a permit and do not anchor over coral. The best place to anchor and land a dinghy is in front of the tiny ranger headquarters is on the north shore, because two rock spurs sticking seaward give it protection from the swell. Just east of the headquarters you'll find a fresh-water lagoon behind the beach. This is an idyllic setting surrounded by coconut palms and exotic tropical birds.

Quepos

Another potential stop on the route through Costa Rica's southern cruising grounds is Quepos (9°24'N by 84°10'W), pronounced "KAY-pohz." This town is a small loading port for fruits of the sea and land: bananas, pineapples and swordfish.

Quepos offers only an indifferent anchorage, but this entire coast is in the lee of mountains and massive volcanoes, and the wind is generally calm. A small breakwater protects the loading pier, but the swell is bad. A lagoon entrance north of the pier is very shoal and breaks wildly. Local skiffs brave it only at high tide.

Port Clearance: You must go through formal clearance procedures with the Quepos Port Captain if you need fuel here. To take diesel, you must Med-moor off the north side of the high pier. Diesel arrives via fuel truck. This is inconvenient enough not to be listed as a fuel stop.

Bill fishing along this portion of the coast is said to be among the best in the world. At least one major sportfishing charter operation has set up shop here. Two small hotels and a few restaurants line the town's four or five paved streets. Quepos is just northwest of Manuel Antonio National Park, which claims to have the most beautiful beaches in Costa Rica. This is quite a statement for a country known for its magnificent shoreline, but most visitors agree. You can use Quepos as a base and anchor off these nearby beaches.

Chapter 22
Costa Rica: Central Pacific Coast

In this chapter, we'll examine the central portion of Costa Rica's long Pacific Coast, specifically what's of interest to recreational boaters: Puntarenas and its vicinity, and the Gulf of Nicoya and its pleasant anchorages.

Puntarenas

For pleasure boaters, Puntarenas (9°58'N by 84°50'W) is the major cruising port on the central Pacific coast of Costa Rica. Puntarenas means sandy point in Spanish. The town of Puntarenas grew up on the long sandy peninsula that you will find 26 miles up into the large Golfo de Nicoya, which is the main geographic feature of Costa Rica's central Pacific coast. The peninsula of Puntarenas nearly bisects the huge bay, and today nearly 50,000 people live in this thriving port.

The Gulf of Nicoya is a vast cruising ground with many gunk-hole anchorages, either uninhabited or near remote jungle villages. For all the private cruising vessels that ply this region, Puntarenas is the primary service center.

Much of Costa Rica's cargo shipping has recently been moved from Puntarenas to the renovated commercial port of Caldera a few miles east, so expect to see a lot of freighters as you go through the Golfo de Nicoya. Caldera has little to offer a yacht, and Puntarenas now enjoys more tourism from pleasure craft, less harbor congestion and more land tourists to its beautiful beaches. Puntarenas has recently rebuilt its main pier, and cruise ships are now calling.

Approaches: Try not to approach Puntarenas at night on an ebb tide, because logs wash down into the gulf from dozens of rivers that empty the forested highlands. Dead heads and debris are especially numerous in the rainy season.

The main small-craft harbor is in a lagoon on the north side of the peninsula, but it is quite shallow, so enter only at high tide. First head for the municipal pier on the south side of the spit, 1.25 miles form the west end. Call "Puntamar" on VHF channel 16 to announce your arrival, and they will notify the authorities for you. If

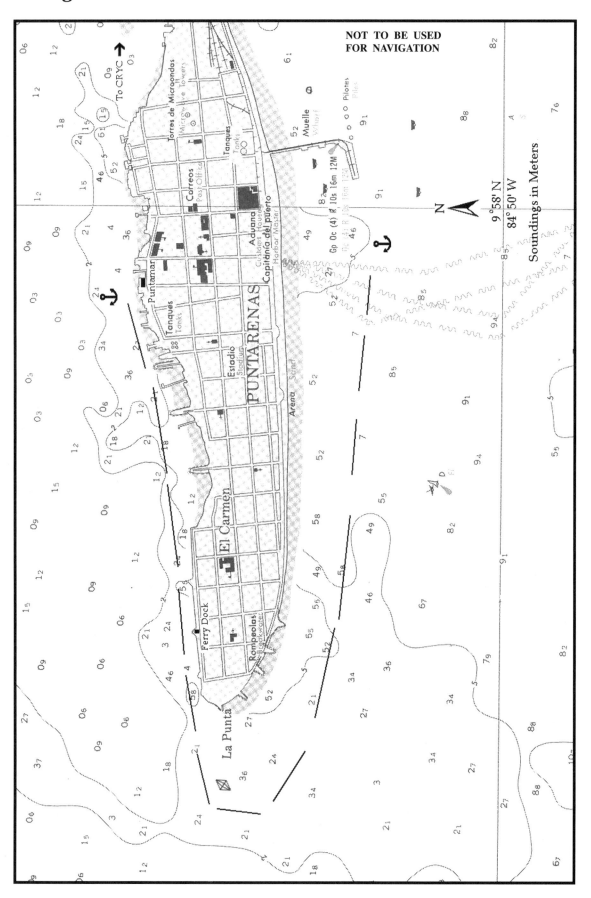

it's not high tide, anchor west of the pier and wait. Depending on wind and tide, this is an exposed, rolly anchorage, but the holding is good.

An hour before high tide, up anchor and head into the inner lagoon. Head west and parallel the beach – staying off about 100 yards. Once you're past the end of the spit you'll see a single white buoy: head directly at it and swing around close aboard, keeping it on your starboard hand. Turn nearly 180° and head directly at the north side of the spit. The water is deepest right along shore, and mud shoals lie off to port. Close along shore are many moored boats; pass just outboard of them, but not too far or you'll hit the unmarked shoals. Continue about 0.9 of a mile. You'll now see moored boats to port. You can anchor among them. The bottom is soft mud. Give yourself swinging room, for when the tide changes. The inner lagoon is very hot and humid with very little breeze.

Port Clearance: The authorities have to come down from the port of Caldera several miles away, so you have to pay $40 for their round-trip taxi ride. Don't go ashore until they come. When the authorities do come on board, you need to have your last port clearance, passports and two photo copies of your vessel's document. Be sure to declare any firearms. Afterward you walk downtown to fill out your tourist cards, which are valid for 90 days. (After that expires, you can stay up to 90 days longer by paying a small daily fine.) After immigration, you go to the Customs office and get a *Certificado de*

Aduana which is like the Mexican temporary import permit; it's good for 90 days and extendible another 90 days. You're now all cleared in.

To clear out, make out another four copies of a crew list. Visit the city hall and pay a small tax, depending on the tonnage of your vessel. Then they'll direct you to a small office near the park where you buy special *timbres,* which are stamps that will be put on your port clearance. Afterward, have immigration stamp out your passports. Now you have to grab another $40 cab to go to the port authorities in Caldera. First visit Customs where you sign their forms. Then go to the Port Captain's office where you show them the Customs form, city tax and *timbres*. They will then give you your *Zarpe*, port clearance, and you are all set to go to sea.

Ship's Agent: Clearance sounds like a piece of cake, right? Well if you don't think so, you can have English-speaking agent Ramon Suarez do all the leg work for you. You can reach Ramon by calling Radio Puntarenas on SSB channel 8A (8.291 Mhz) and leaving a free message as to your intentions to use his services and your ETA. You can also make a schedule

Funky at low tide, Puntamar has the only floating dock in the Puntarenas region.

to talk to him directly, or you can just call him on VHF channel 16 upon arrival.

Local Services: If you arrive during weekday business hours, Ramon may be able to (by prior arrangement with the authorities) get you permission to come straight to the dock at Puntamar (506) 661-2139. They charge $1/foot/day, but it is the only floating dock on the waterfront and therefore a real convenience in a place with +10-foot tides. All the other docks are rough concrete and crowded with fishing boats. If you're taking large quantities of fuel, you can do so directly from a tank truck with a hose leading down Puntamar's dock. If you choose to anchor out, you can land your dinghy at Puntamar's facility for $4/day. They have showers and laundry facilities, also a very rustic lounge area and chiller for cold drinks.

Puntarenas has a municipal dock more suitable for larger commercial vessels. It's located about one third of the way into the back lagoon, adjacent to the main channel. This dock is really just a stationary concrete pier facing (no fendering) without slips, but it provides an excellent place to take fuel or board a big load of provisions. Make arrangements to come here through the Port Captain or your agent. An ice plant operates on the dock, and smaller fishing boats use the back side.

Further up the inner anchorage is the Costa Rica Yacht Club, the only official yacht club in this country. First obtain permission to move there. CRYC has some guest moorings in the shallow water but no alongside berthing. If you intend to be in the region very long, it may be economically feasible to become a member. Ask the club commodore. The club's main disadvantage is that, land wise, it's located several miles away from the center of town. To others, that's an advantage.

Puntarenas has plenty of restaurants and hotels, and even some spare parts stores. Mechanics, electricians, and electronics technicians are available at reasonable prices. A marine railway near the CRYC is capable of hauling even large yachts. The monetary unit is the Colon, and dollars are not generally accepted in stores. Change your money at one of several banks.

Fuel Stop: Puntarenas offers a choice of several fuel piers. The fuel is clean and costs slightly more than in the U.S. You can arrange with the dock to remain alongside the pier for the night after fueling. However shrimpers frequently tie up outboard of you, so fender well to prevent damage. Secure loose items on deck, because their crews will have to use your boat as a gangway to shore.

Provisioning: Puntarenas' downtown is five blocks east of Puntamar. It has a pleasant central plaza, cathedral and park. The best produce in Central America is available at the farmers' market early in the morning, but it is open till siesta. Look for the block-long orange and white building along the shore. Inside are dozens of little shops selling a thousand kinds of fruits and vegetables, plus fresh unwashed eggs and meats. There's also a small cafe that makes "licuado," a smoothie of fresh fruits and either milk or ice. Enterprising locals will help you gather what's on your list, and others have bicycle carts to transport your heavy load back to the dinghy dock or pier – all for a small fee.

Puntarenas has several good grocery stores for staples, but our favorite is on the east side of the street that dead-ends into the middle of the farmers' market, about a half block south. Most everything is displayed on shelves rising to the ceiling behind the counter, easy to see at a glance.

Whole wheat bread from the local bakery is excellent, no preservatives. This store's prices have been very reasonable, and if you have a big order, they can deliver it to your boat. Our only caution about provisioning here or anywhere else in Costa Rica regards fresh milk; it seldom is. Stick to the ultra pasteurized cartons.

Side Trips: Puntarenas is an excellent base from which to explore the interior of Costa Rica. It is such a small country that you can get around it very comfortably and inexpensively by bus. Costa Rica can provide so many interesting side trips that an adventurer could stay busy for months. It has 14 national parks and preserves. For starters, the rain forest and cloud forest around Monteverde contain over a thousand kinds of orchids. There are five volcanoes: Arenal, Barva, Irazu, Poas and Rincon de la Vieja. Lake Arenal is a volcanic lake in the rain forest. There's white-water kayaking, butterfly farms, jungle bird-watching for the fabled Quetzal bird and more. San Jose, the cosmopolitan capital of the country, is about two hours east of Puntarenas by car. The international airport is in Alajuela near San Jose. Rental cars are available, though four-wheel drives are expensive. A typical cab ride from Puntarenas to San Jose is about $60 one way.

Golfo de Nicoya

The Gulf of Nicoya offers many beautiful anchorages scattered among its islands and bays. Boaters visiting Puntarenas often use nearby anchorages to get away from the heat and hustle. They use the ferries to commute into town for their necessities.

Naranjo Anchorage: One of the best getaways is Playa Naranjo, 8 ½ miles west-southwest of Puntarenas. The anchorage is a short distance east of the ferry dock in 18 to 30 feet. This spot is well protected except in north winds. Ashore is the Oasis del Pacifico Resort owned by an English-speaking couple. For a $5 per day charge you may use the facilities of the resort. You can commute to Puntarenas, as the ferry dock is only a short walk away.

Isla Gitana: Another hangout is called Isla Gitana (9°53.0'N by 84°55.6'W). The tiny island (called Muertos on the chart) lies about seven miles southwest of Puntarenas. The anchorage on the south side of the island is well sheltered and has good holding on a sand and mud bottom in 12 to 18 feet. The strongest winds are in the winter and come from the north. However the anchorage is well-shielded from that direction and the wind only helps to dispel the heat of latitude 10 degrees. Ashore you find a palapa bar, swimming pool, showers, cabins, shuttle service to Puntarenas, a telephone and a home-style cafe that's open upon advance notice. Gitana is pronounced "he-TAHN-ah" and it means gypsy.

Nearby you'll find an even quieter anchorage between Isla Jesusita and Cedros. It has a small hotel.

Ballena Bay: Bahia Ballena is a very nice bite into the southwest shore of the Gulf of Nicoya, 20 miles from Puntarenas. Although the chart shows it open to the east, a large handful of boats can get tucked up into the southwest corner behind a reef that gives nearly all around protection. The reef juts out from the southern entrance to the bay and isn't marked on the chart, so swing wide and come into the center of the bay. Anchor in 18 feet of water off the pier. It's good holding, very calm and a quiet, beautiful place to hang out.

Cruising Ports

You'll see a concrete pier and, through the trees, a small village at the head of the pier. A funky restaurant and bar are at the head of the pier. You can land at the pier at half tide and above, but not at low tide. Across the bay is a small resort and a small airstrip with regularly scheduled flights to and from San Jose, the capital.

Ballena is useful to break up the 115-mile haul between Puntarenas and Marina Flamingo.

Carillo Anchorage: Carillo is the next possible stop, 50 miles from Flamingo, but it has a reputation for being rolly – especially during the wet season. Carillo is a small remote bay 10 miles east of Punta Guiones, the southwestern tip of Costa Rica. It has a protected anchorage in all but south winds, no Port Captain and limited support services ashore. Don't over rely on the use of GPS to bring you in here: we found the GPS position inside the harbor to lie 0.42 nautical miles 085 T from the charted positions on Chart # 21543.

For Carillo, a good offshore approach waypoint using GPS is 9°51.00'N and 85°29.46'W. The entrance is ½ mile wide, and a reef extends from the western side toward the southeast. Favor the eastern side to stay clear of the reef, steering 350° M until you're inside. On the eastern shore of the anchorage is a small resort with some palapa roofs. A small fleet of sportfishing boats is anchored in front of the resort, getting protection behind a small island. This would be the best spot to anchor, but there's no room for visitors. Unless you have a south wind and swell, you could anchor anywhere inside in 20 feet of water over a black volcanic sand bottom, which is good holding.

Gulf of Nicoya has extreme tides, which some folks use for careening and doing bottom repairs.

154

Chapter 23
Costa Rica: North Pacific Coast

Along the northern third of Costa Rica's idyllic Pacific coastline, cruisers will find dozens of interesting, uninhabited, undeveloped places to explore. Some of the developed locations are almost legendary in cruising lore, while others are fairly new, and others are just now being built.

Marina Flamingo at Bahia Potrero

Marina Flamingo, Costa Rica (10°28'N, 85°48'W) is the first full-service marina for visiting pleasure boats to be found south of Acapulco – and it's 1,000 miles south. Marina Flamingo is the center of some of the finest sportfishing in the world, located in northwestern Costa Rica – in the southwest corner of a bight called Bahia Potrero.

Marina Flamingo's services and pleasant surroundings make it an ideal cruising port.

Costa Rica is south of the hurricane belt so it's a good place to summer over. Summer does bring rain and occasional wind squalls. During this time, if a hurricane is roaming around off Mexico, swell can make it's way into the anchorage.

Approaches: Just offshore lie the Islas Catalina and an extensive reef area. While these protect the marina from seas coming in from the west and south, they are a navigational hazard to be reckoned with upon approach. If you're coming in from the northwest, use the 2.5-mile-wide

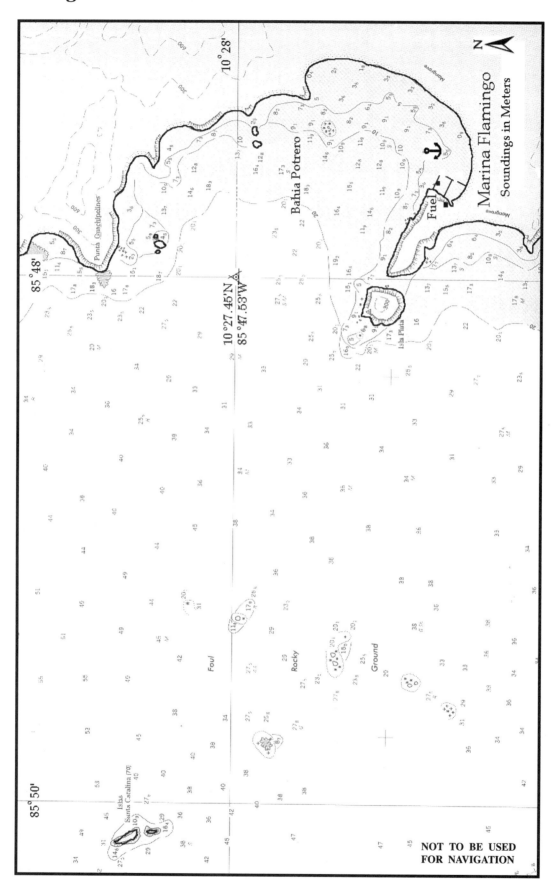

Marina Flamingo
Soundings in Meters

NOT TO BE USED
FOR NAVIGATION

opening on the north side, between Isla Santa Catalina and Islas Brumel. Coming from the south, round Cabo Velas one mile off and then turn northeast between the offshore reef and the mainland.

The marina monitors VHF channel 16. Give them a call to announce your arrival. Owner Jim McKee speaks English, as does Elizabeth on his staff. The marina breakwater has two separate entrances because the basin is divided down the middle; the northeastern entrance is for the fuel dock only, and the slips are in the southwestern basin. You can land your dinghy on their floating docks in front of the marina office in the southwest basin.

Anchorage: Anchor in the southwest corner of Bahia Potrero just east of the breakwaters in about 18 feet. The bottom is firm sand and good holding, and normally there is little swell. The prevailing wind is from the east, so you get good protection. In the winter months, the Papagallo Winds blow strongly from the east and can cause surgey conditions inside the marina itself, even though it's completely surrounded by a breakwater. If you're anchored in these winds, get as close to the lee of the eastern beach as depth will allow, keeping in mind the 10-foot tidal range.

Port Clearance: Port entrance and exit formalities can be handled by going to the Port Captain's office in the village of Playa del Coco, about 17 sea miles north. You can take the bus there to clear in if you like, however if you anchor in Playa, you have to land through the surf on the beach. The drier and more pleasant alternative is to pay bus or cab fare for the port officials to come down 20 miles of road to Flamingo. Port clearance is similar to Mexico's, except that they do ask you for the serial number of you engine(s).

Marina Services: The marina has floating docks for 70 boats, with water and shore power: 110-volt 30 amp and 220-volt 50 amp. They also have repair facilities: a dry dock for 50-foot yachts to 4.5 foot draft; a tide-grid dry dock for up to 60-foot sailboats (max 8-foot draft); and a 20-ton mobile crane. Some sportfishing tackle, outboard parts and boat supplies are in sold a little store attached to the marina office, and the rest can be ordered and shipped direct from Miami via the Lewis catalog. The marina phone and fax is 506-654-4203. The e-mail is: marflam@marflam.com and you can check out their web site at www.marflam.com

Jim McKee, owner and operator of Marina Flamingo is very helpful to visiting boaters.

Fuel Stop: The fuel dock is 120 feet long. Fuel can be paid for by credit card, for which there's an additional 2% fee. When entering this basin, stay close to the fuel dock on your starboard side, because the bottom shoals farther in. If you draw more than seven feet, enter at half tide and rising – then exit before half tide and falling.

Local Services: Flamingo is fairly isolated, so boaters are fortunate that Jim McKee has created and published a special boaters' phone book listing lots of local folks who repair mechanical and nautical items, and the latest edition covers Puntarenas, Quepos and Golfito regions as well. We've had highly specialized O-rings turn up right on the dock, and we've had bus drivers hand-carry items down from San Jose overnight.

The marina is surrounded by hotels and restaurants. Maria's Cafe is the popular watering hole and rendezvous. Closer to the marina and up a hill is a convenience store where you can get limited supplies. During the winter/spring cruising season, a truck comes once a week with fresh vegetables. Brasilito 5 km north has two tiny produce stores. For major provisioning, take a 45-minute taxi or bus ride to Liberia's two larger grocery stores. Santa Cruz, the same distance, has the region's best produce market and an excellent pharmacy, but only one fairly good grocery store. Tamarindo (20 min. ride) has the nearest regular commuter airport, but choppers and private planes from Liberia land at Flamingo. The international airport is at Alajuela, a 5-hour cab or bus ride up into the mountains.

Just up the hill from Marina Flamingo's office, a Belgian restaurant called Amberes has good food, a view of the harbor, and a casino that really swings during the winter/spring dry season. Next door is a car rental agency; it's handy for two couples to rent an air-conditioned car and go touring inland.

In the town of Potrero, which is mostly hidden in jungle foliage, there's an in-home bakery and take-out pizza place, plus several funky cafes and boutiques. Very nice vacation homes climb the hills. We found only three pay phones upon which you can make international calls: outside the marina office, in front of the beach hotel on Playa Brasilito, and on a residential street near the bakery. Howler monkeys and exotic birds and butterflies are common sights in the lush jungle that surrounds Bahia Potrero and Playa Brasilito.

The nearby offshore waters at Flamingo are teeming with every kind of bill fish, dorado, and yellow fin tuna. We've watched rooster fish tear up the waters right inside the marina itself. Just north of Flamingo you'll find several remote anchorages for "get away from it all" cruising. The Islas Murcielagos (Bat Islands) are especially noted for their excellent scuba and snorkel diving.

Playa del Coco

Playa del Coco (10°34'N by 85°43'W) is the Port of Entry for northern Costa Rica. It's one of the major cruising ports in this region, and many boaters spend up to a year gunk-holing around the nearby Culebra area and northern Costa Rica, using "Playa" or "Coco" as their home port.

Approaches and Anchorage: Bahia Playa del Coco is located just 17 miles up the coast from Marina Flamingo. Upon entering the unmistakable bay you'll see the remnants of a small wooden pier in the center of the beach with small fishing vessels anchored to the south of it. Most yacht visitors anchor to the north of the pier, by local custom. Be careful of submerged rocks straight out from this pier; you can't

Coco's tiny "media muelle" or half pier marks the middle of the beach that surrounds this lovely bay. Most yachts anchor in the north end.

see them at high tide when there's no swell. The bay is well protected from prevailing north and east winds. However some swell comes into the bay, especially in the summer months.

You may land a dinghy at the outer end of the rickety wooden pier and walk ashore. At low tide you won't be able to do this and will have to land on the beach. Often a breaking swell makes beach landing difficult.

Port Clearance: The Port Captain's office is just south of the head of the pier, and the Aduana comes from Liberia. Port clearance is easy. See Port Clearance under Marina Flamingo.

Local Services: The tiny rural village of Playa del Coco is a quiet, relaxed community. An open patio restaurant is located near the pier, and two small grocery stores are a couple of blocks away. A paved road connects the town with the regional capital, Liberia, where there's an airport, and with the rest of the country. You can take a comfortable and inexpensive bus to San Jose,

the country's capital. Renting a car here is almost double what it costs in the U.S.

Although boaters often call this simply Coco, that term is also used for Isla del Coco, Costa Rica's island park about 300 miles offshore.

Culebra and Papagallo

Bahia Culebra, located immediately north of Coco, is one of the finest natural harbors in Central America. When the Papagallo winds are blowing, Culebra provides shelter for 14 small but beautiful anchorages with adjacent beaches between Coco and the Nicaraguan border. The coral and soft sand beaches along the coast vary in color from rosy pink to blazing white and even sparkling volcanic black, depending on the geology of the reefs offshore. The terrain is steep and the jungle is lush, but most of it has been logged long ago, so it isn't actually virgin – but it's hard to tell.

Anchorages: Inside Bahia Culebra, anchorage can be found at Playa Hermosa (village), Punta Balena, Playa

159

Panama (village), Monte del Barco (hotel), Playa Iguanita, Playa Manzanillo, Playa Nacascolo, Playa Venado and Playa Blanca. Outside the bay and just to the north, anchorages are at Playa Virador, Playa Prieta, Bahia Palmares, Islas Palmitas and Playa Zapotillal. (Several other anchorages on the north side of Santa Rosa National Park have been used by Navy boats that forced cruising yachts and sportfishing boats to leave immediately, so we don't encourage anyone to go there.) However, diving is excellent along the Murcielago (Bat) Islands chain in that area, and anchoring at the Murcielagos is okay when the Papagallo isn't blowing. Port clearance for all these anchorages is done at Playa del Coco.

Marking the north and south sides of the entrance to Bahia Culebra are two sets of tiny islands; to the south (just outside Playa del Coco) are the Islas Viradores Sur, and to the north are Islas Viradores Norte. One of these "nortes" looks for all the world like the head of King Kong, so it's been dubbed King Kong Rock and is used as a reference landmark.

Chapter 24
Mexico: History & Overview

∼∼∼∼∼∼∼∼∼∼∼∼∼∼∼∼∼∼∼∼∼∼∼∼∼∼∼∼∼∼∼∼∼∼

Before we look at the individual cruising ports of Mexico's Pacific coast and Sea of Cortez, it's important for visiting boaters to have a working knowledge of Mexico's vibrant culture and political landscape.

History

Mexico was inhabited by a very advanced Indian civilization that culminated in the building of the great Aztec city of Tenochtitlan in the country's high central valley in 1325. Hernan Cortes, Spanish conquistador, destroyed that civilization between 1519 and 1521, and three centuries of Spanish rule ensued.

Mexico gained its independence from Spain in 1821. The next century was characterized by revolution, social unrest, foreign intervention and autocracy. The primary conflict was racial; class stature was determined by race. The Spanish-born "Guachupines" were in control. "Creoles" were of Spanish descent but born in Mexico. "Mestizos" were a blend of Spanish and Indian. The pure indigenous people were kept on the lowest rung of this social ladder.

Immediately after Independence, General Agustin Iturbide declared himself Emperor. This lasted until 1823 when a republic was declared. General Antonio Lopez de Santa Ana dominated between 1833 and 1855, but he was defeated during his war with the United States from 1847 to 1848, when Mexico lost more than half of its territory, including Texas and California.

This war is still important in the minds of today's Mexican people. U.S. forces captured Mexico City after engaging in a successful battle at Chapultepec Castle. The castle was then a military school and bravely defended by the young cadets in attendance. According to legend, when their defeat was close at hand, six students wrapped themselves in Mexican flags and jumped to their deaths from the high windows of the castle. Six statues honoring the Child Heroes (Los Ninos Heroes) were erected at the foot of the castle representing Mexico's patriotism and symbolizing the strained relationship with the U.S.

Due to Mexico's unpayable debts to France, Napoleon III appointed Archduke Maximilian of Austria as Emperor in 1865. He was defeated and executed by Benito Juarez. Juarez, a full Zapotec Indian raised as a middle-class liberal, carried out a full number of reforms.

From 1877 to 1911 the country was ruled and exploited by Dictator Porfirio Diaz. Discontent with this exploitation led to fighting by rival forces and a new constitution on February 5th, 1917, which provided for much needed social reform. A stable government finally was able to emerge, because much racial intermixing had created a more uniform people called "La Raza." Since the Revolution Mexico has made much progress with large scale programs of social security, labor protection and school improvement.

Since 1927 the PRI, child of the revolution, has been the dominant political party. Presidents are elected for six-year terms and are prohibited by law from serving another term. The incumbent president often selects his successor who is virtually assured of becoming president, since the PRI has never lost a presidential election, but in recent years it has come close. The balance of power is tilting to include at least two other political parties, especially powerful at state and municipal levels.

Official censorship of the press does not exist, but the government has a monopoly on newsprint. In the face of critical editorials, official pressure is used behind the scenes. What newspaper could exist without rolls of newsprint paper.

However the PRI began to lose its hold on the political system during the 1988 election. Though the PRI's candidate won, it was a hotly contested election with significant gains by parties of both the Left and Right. Public dissatisfaction with the ruling party was created by economic problems brought on by previous administrations, which came to a head during the term of President Miguel de la Madrid (1982 to 1988). The country had to deal with grim fiscal conditions brought on by a collapse in world oil prices, a huge foreign debt and rampant inflation. The peso went through a series of disastrous devaluations, and the period 1982 to 1987 saw an erosion of the average Mexican worker's purchasing power of 56 percent.

President Salinas de Gortari's term expired in 1994, the same year PRI presidential designate Colossio was assassinated in Tijuana, right before the huge peso devaluation at Christmas. Under Salinas' leadership, NAFTA (North American Free Trade Agreement) had begun implementation, linking the economies of Mexico, the U.S. and Canada. Mexico's financial picture started a remarkable turnaround, but later revelations of corruption within the cabinet overshadowed those economic gains.

President Ernesto Zedillo (1994 to July 2000) helped Mexico become more democratic as the PRI began losing its 70-year grip on power. Visitors to Mexico should be aware of the political landscape as they travel through it, but they should steer far clear of politics and never make political statements regarding their host country.

Visitor Friendly

Mexico is very friendly to visitors. Turismo (Tourism) is a branch of the federal, state and municipal governments, and at the federal level Turismo is a complete cabinet, equal to Treasury (Hacienda), of which it formerly was a part. Each state and municipality has its own office of tourism. For example, Baja California's "Green Angels" is a Turismo program to aid stranded motorists. Hotel-based tourism has long been the norm, and RVers have been accommodated for only the past two decades. Taking your recreational boat into Mexican waters makes you a nautical tourist – which is still fairly new. The Chain of Marinas mandate that helped construct more than a dozen tourist marinas and fuel docks during the 1990s is mainly supported by Turismo.

Traveling in Mexico's interior is a real bargain for tourists. Since most of the major ports of Mexico are highly sophisticated areas, prices are much more expensive than in the rest of the country. A recent reorganization of the federal departments of the government gave Turismo more responsibility. Not until recently has Mexico actually turned its attention to developing much of its enormous coastline for yacht marinas and water-oriented diversions. That is changing now – and pronto.

Yacht clearance procedures with local officials has vastly improved over the years, and we can expect it to grow more streamlined and practical in the next two or three years. Incidents of "mordida" (bribes or official extortion) occur much less frequently since tourism took a higher priority, and they occur almost exclusively on the Atlantic coast; in this respect it's almost like a different country. However, the entire port clearance procedure in Mexico is much more accommodating to boaters than that of its southern neighbors. (See Chapter 3, The Paperwork Cha Cha.)

Firearms in Mexico

Having a gun on your boat in Mexico is illegal, and as we go to press, Mexico is warning that it is enforcing these laws even more stringently. Do not take a gun into Mexico on your boat.

Violence involving firearms is an increasing problem in Mexico, and most of those arms have been smuggled into Mexico from the U.S. For that reason, Mexican officials have repeatedly appealed to the U.S. to halt the flow southward. And since 1998, Mexico has been enforcing its gun laws, including visiting vessels, by jailing some boaters for bringing in their guns.

Yet, each year, some foolish recreational boater tries to skirt the rules, often pleading ignorance when they're caught. They have ended up having their vessels confiscated, paying enormous fines and attorney fees, even spending time in Mexican prisons. Having a gun gets you into much more trouble that it could ever get you out of.

(To date, the only way to legally take a firearm into Mexico is by special permit arranged in advance by an officially sanctioned hunting lodge and only for a specific registered guest. Besides a book-full of additional restrictions, a permit is valid only for hunting within the municipality in which the lodge is located, and each municipality requires its own gun/hunting permit. For this reason, hunting lodges provide their guests with hunting arms. Gun or hunting permits are simply not issued for boaters, who, unlike lodge-based guests, move themselves and their firearms between municipalities aboard their boats. Our recommendation is: *no vale la pena* – it's not worth the pain.)

Cruising Ports

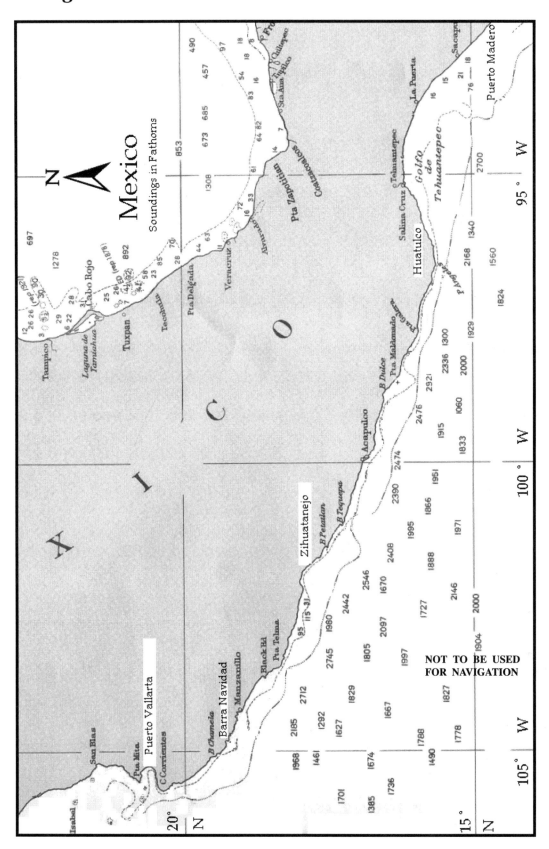

Mainland Mexico - Planning Chart for Chapter 25 through Chapter 34

Chapter 25
Mexico: Weather & Routing

~~~~~~

Until John wrote the book *"MexWX: Mexico Weather for Boaters,"* very little had been written about the weather along Mexico's 3,300-mile coastline or about planning routes based on its seasonal changes. WX is radio shorthand for "weather."

John has written this chapter based on his experience during more than 100 voyages along its full length in all seasons, captaining all kinds of sail and power boats. During college he studied meteorology, but he doesn't pretend to be a professional meteorologist. Before he gets underway, he learns as much as possible about the weather at

sea, because our lives and my livelihoods depend on it. But, of course, with all the space-age technology of this new millennium, nothing remains as unpredictable as the weather. In the end, every captain alone must decide if the weather is right.

Overall Patterns: Most of the weather that boaters experience as they move along the coast of Mexico originates from the northwest and moves southeast.

Use the diurnal land and sea breezes to your advantage.

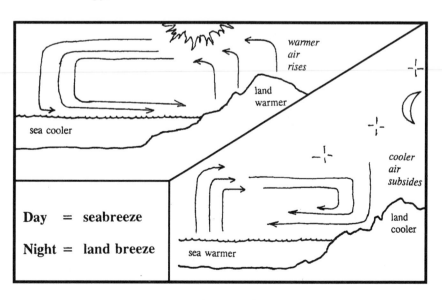

Day = seabreeze

Night = land breeze

Cruising Ports

We can more easily understand what happens where, when and why if we examine the forces at work starting from the top of Baja California working our way southeast along the mainland Gold Coast and Gulf of Tehuantepec, finishing at Puerto Madero. We'll watch how conditions change through an entire year, taking a special look at hurricane season. We'll conclude this chapter with an overview of weather fax and ham radio as it applies to weather wisdom.

Baja California's Pacific Coast

Boaters traversing the northern reaches of the Baja peninsula get the same Prevailing Northwesterlies that affect Southern California, and the same daily cycle of land-sea breezes is in effect close to shore.

Many cruisers don't realize that the Northwesterlies are at their lightest during November, just when the annual migration of cruising boats is heading south from California – the beginning of an annual cruising season. Sail boats often have to motor more than they expect. And in May

when the cruising fleet is returning north toward the border before hurricane season sets in, the prevailing winds are strongest right on their noses. Thus, the notorious beat up this coast is dubbed the Baja bash.

To remedy this problem, boats heading south in the fall often head offshore to find 20-knot winds around the clock, making the Baja in one passage. Fog and overcast skies along the northern portion of the Baja peninsula are common on this stretch, although as you approach Cabo San Lucas, fog and wind both taper off. Boats that are coming around from the East Coast or who have summered over in the south can avoid the Baja bash if they plan to be heading up this coast in fall.

Winter weather here is generated by the southward shift of the Jet Stream and a corresponding breakdown of the Pacific High, which normally resides between Hawaii and the U.S. mainland. Cold fronts can then invade. The strongest cold fronts are preceded by southeast gales and rain, followed by wind shifts to the northwest and clearing. Southeast gales are rarely felt south of mid-Baja.

After the passage of a winter low-

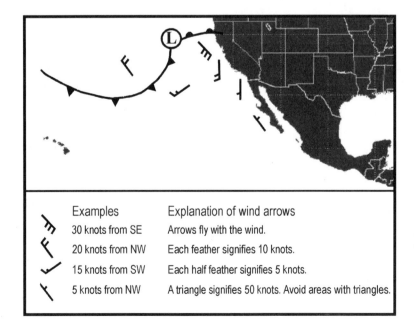

	Examples	Explanation of wind arrows
	30 knots from SE	Arrows fly with the wind.
	20 knots from NW	Each feather signifies 10 knots.
	15 knots from SW	Each half feather signifies 5 knots.
	5 knots from NW	A triangle signifies 50 knots. Avoid areas with triangles.

A winter cold front threatens to invade Baja; light winds are felt in its advance.

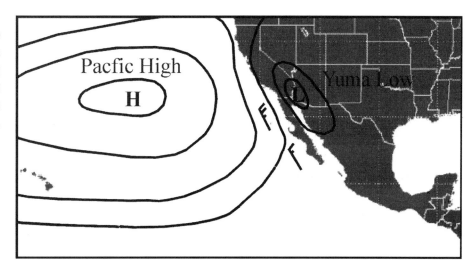

Springtime conditions create strong N'westerlies along Baja's Pacific coast.

pressure system off the Southern California and northern Baja coast, high pressure often moves into the inter-mountain basin near Nevada. This generates north to east offshore winds known as "Santa Ana" winds (or in meteorological circles as "foehns.") They blow strongly near shore and canyon mouths. Turtle Bay and Magdalena Bay get easterly Santa Ana-like winds in early January.

By spring, few low-pressure systems invade Baja, and the Pacific High has resumed its residence between Hawaii and the U.S. mainland. The high's clockwise rotation brings strong and steady Northwesterlies to coastal Baja, making May the most difficult month to head north. Southbound boats get a sleigh ride. Several times I've made the voyage from San Diego to Cabo in May under sail in 4.5 days. In one case we made 400 miles in two days, surfing down huge waves, clenching the wheel, afraid to look over our shoulders at the white-crested monsters that kept trying to crawl over the transom and into the cockpit.

By summer, the prevailing wind has diminished but not disappeared. Occasionally, tropical cyclones threaten as far north as Baja, increasingly as the summer wears on.

All-weather ports of refuge along the Baja coast are Turtle Bay and Magdalena Bay. Good refuge in Prevailing Northwesterlies may be had at Bahia Santa Maria, Cedros, Asuncion and Ensenada.

(For detailed cruising information about Baja California's Pacific coast, see Chapters 36 through 40.)

Sea of Cortez

In the fall and winter, the prevailing wind in the Sea of Cortez is northwest. During winter, the dreaded "Screaming Blue Northers" are the most significant feature. They are caused by conditions similar to those that form Santa Anas in Southern California. After a low passes across the Pacific coast, the ocean air that has quickly pushed in behind it slows down over the land, and the air mass actually gets stranded east of the Sierras and west of the Rockies. This mound of air accumulation is called the Plateau High. When the Plateau High disperses, gravity draws it down either through the Cajon Pass, where it becomes known as a Santa Ana, or it flows down through the Colorado River Valley and into the Sea of Cortez.

Well developed Northers can last for a week or more, and they disrupt fishing and sailing sometimes as far south as La

Paz. Such wind raises a sea chop that is short, steep and notorious in the Sea of Cortez.

During summer, south winds and such long periods of calm dominate the Sea of Cortez that sailboats summering over need auxiliaries to get around. Cruisers hole up in a hurricane hole like Puerto Escondido or find little niches north of Santa Rosalia, which is north of most hurricane tracks. Boats that stay exposed to tropical storms in the southern Sea of Cortez must have the speed and range to scoot to shelter on a moment's notice. More on hurricanes later.

The La Paz area is blessed with a local summer wind known as the Corumuel, a southerly wind that springs up around sunset and dies after sunrise. This gentle but unpredictable breeze is just enough to

The Plateau High creates Santa Anas and Northers.

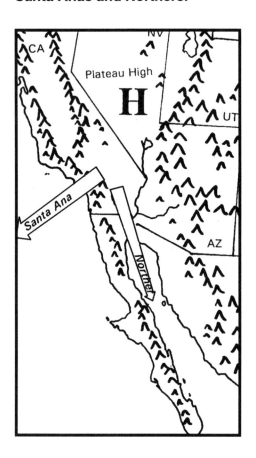

cool the bay, not enough to carry a sail boat across to the mainland.

(For detailed cruising information about both sides of the Sea of Cortez, see Chapter 35 and 36.)

Crossing between the Mainland and Baja

If you're southbound, the passage between Baja and the mainland may be your first major offshore hop. The prevailing north-northwest wind is in your favor, and the only weather hazard may be a far-reaching Norther in the winter or a tropical storm in late summer.

If you're northbound from the Panama Canal, this passage is your last major offshore leg before reaching the U.S. Unfortunately, the prevailing winds are north- northwesterly, but you can lower the "slog" factor as much as possible by altering your jumping off spot on the mainland.

1.) The shortest crossing distance is 160 miles between Mazatlan and Los Frailes on the Baja peninsula. Los Frailes is 45 miles northwest of Cabo, offers a good anchorage in north to northwest winds, and is a handy staging area – before or after this crossing. Because this crossing route is the most northerly of the three I'm suggesting, expect the most influence from northern weather, which may be more significant when you're coming up from farther south.

2.) The second crossing route, from Puerto Vallarta to Cabo San Lucas, is 290 miles of open ocean. On this southeast course the north to northwest winds can give you a nice downwind passage. Note two things on this route. Stay 20 miles away from the forbidden Tres Marias Islands, because the patrol boats guarding this prison colony have

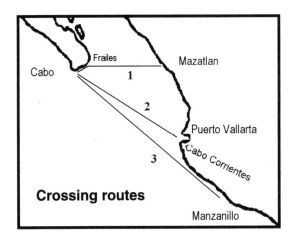

Crossing routes

shot at approaching yachts. The current can set you toward the islands, so be quick to correct your course. Also, you can shorten this passage by 20 miles if you use the anchorage at Punta Mita at the northern entrance to Bahia Banderas. Punta Mita's large anchorage offers good protection from prevailing winds and good holding ground.

3.) The longest route to cross between the mainland and the cape is Manzanillo to Cabo San Lucas (or vice versa), which is 400 miles of open ocean. You can shorten this passage by 30 miles by jumping off or making landfall at Chamela, a good anchorage in prevailing weather. Even so, if you're northbound in a slow boat, you may have the "all clear" upon departure but encounter fresh head winds when you're half way across.

(For detailed cruising information about these mainland areas, see Chapters 32, 33 and 34.)

Manzanillo to Puerto Angel

This region includes the major cruising ports of Ixtapa, Zihuatanejo, Manzanillo and Acapulco, and extends south just to the edge of the Gulf of Tehuantepec.

During winter and spring, this coastline has the most pleasant cruising weather in all of Mexico. Average wind strengths are perfect for relaxed sailing, temperatures are warm but not sweltering, and the sunny skies are wall-to-wall blue every day. For that reason, cruisers who can build their itineraries primarily around the most favorable weather patterns often begin their Mexican season in the south and then move north to the cooler regions when the south begins to heat up.

The land-sea breeze in this region is similar to that of the northern regions, but here the effect is lighter the farther south you are. Boaters can take advantage of this pattern. Winds build to their maximum strengths in the afternoon, usually from the north or northwest. South of Acapulco the afternoon winds can sometimes come from the east, depending on what is happening in the Gulf of Tehuantepec. In the early morning, the gentle offshore breeze known locally as the "Terral" gives sailors a boost when they're moving north or south close in along the coast.

Early summer brings chubascos, which are locally generated thunderstorms of occasionally intense strength – but normally of short duration. The farther south you are, the earlier in the summer the chubascos begin.

During summer hurricane season, this region is extremely dangerous, it often takes direct hits from hurricanes, and it offers no all-weather protection or hurricane-safe harbors. In the worst-case scenario, some very minor survival protection might be found by running a boat up into the mangrove swamps inside the lagoon at Barra Navidad, in the west basin at Ixtapa, or into Puerto Lazaro Cardenas.

(For more detailed cruising information about these areas, see Chapters 28 through 31.)

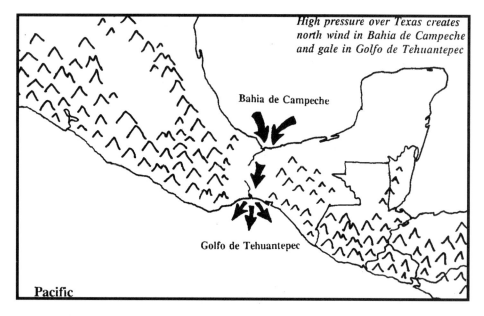

High pressure over Texas creates north wind in Bahia de Campeche and gale in Golfo de Tehuantepec

Bahia de Campeche

Golfo de Tehuantepec

Pacific

Gulf of Tehuantepec

"Gale in the Gulf of Tehuantepec" is the phrase most commonly heard over voice-radio weather forecasts for this region. The almost constant windy conditions are caused by its geography and by weather in the Gulf of Mexico. The valley of the Isthmus of Tehuantepec runs between two tall mountain ranges and crosses Mexico's land mass at its narrowest location. (This isthmus is such a good link between the Pacific and the Gulf of Mexico that it was once proposed for a trans-oceanic canal.) The mountains on each side form a funnel that intensifies any wind, exactly like a venturi tube.

When intense high pressure is centered over Texas, winds channel through the valley of the Isthmus of Tehuantepec, intensify and sweep out into the Pacific for 300 to 500 miles. Force 8 winds occur in January, but the gale season runs from October through April.

Any gale in this gulf is known as a Tehuantepecker, and it can last from several hours to several days, depending on the distant conditions that generate it. Onboard barometers or observations cannot predict the approach of a Tehuantepecker, and

Pacific weather stations NMC and WWV can only tell you that one is presently occurring. You'll have to become your own best forecaster.

To predict a gale here, listen to NMN and NMG weather reports of a cold front moving into the Gulf of Mexico from the northwest. In advance of that front, the prevailing easterly wind will shift to the southeast and south. As the cold front passes, high pressure builds behind it. When this high moves over Texas, wind in the Gulf of Mexico clocks around to the north, and bingo, a Tehuantepecker begins and quickly scours the Pacific.

When is it safe to pass? Monitor weather for the southwest Gulf of Mexico. In advance of a cold front, if the wind is from the south, you have a small weather-window, an immediate opportunity to scoot across the Gulf of Tehuantepec. If the cold front stalls out over the Gulf of Mexico and alters course to the northeast as a warm front, the south wind will endure, giving you a slightly longer window across Tehuantepec. It won't bring you southerlies, but it's the best it can get.

Cross the Gulf of Tehuantepec by hugging the coast.

By using the lee of the beach and shoreline, I have run this gulf in 50-knot winds but in flat water, because there was no fetch. The beach berm along the western

The weather window for crossing the Gulf of Tehuantepec is CLOSED.

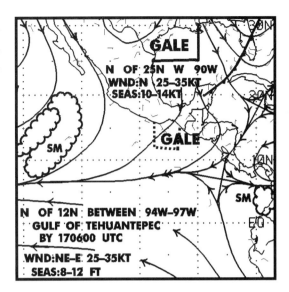

two thirds of the gulf is level and regular, and when you're close in, it makes a good radar image. You can get right in close, about five fathoms, because the bottom is level and regular, too. If you're overpowered by the wind, set a good storm anchor close to the beach and ride it out.

However, when you approach the two lagoon entrances, cut out to 60 feet in order to pass their shoals, then scoot back in toward the beach. Their shoals extend farther offshore than the charts indicate. The lagoon entrances will be breaking wildly if the wind is blowing, making good radar images of their own. Bite the bullet for a short time, because the wind often increases in strength at the lagoon entrances.

Running inshore adds only 30 miles to the entire distance between Puerto Angel and Puerto Madero. That's not bad when you consider that trying to avoid a Tehuantepec gale by running offshore could take you up to 500 miles offshore. The best times to transit Tehuantepec are the first of November and the middle of May, but it should still be done close to the beach.

Routing through Tehuantepec: If you're coming from Puerto Madero toward Puerto Angel, it's easy to stay in the lee the whole way until you're past Salina Cruz.

The weather window for crossing the Gulf of Tehuantepec is now OPEN, but keep one foot on the beach.

You'll notice a big swell after Puerto Madero, and the show will begin as you pass the village of Solo Dios. Handle the lagoon entrances as indicated above. Once past Salina Cruz, turn southwest to put the wind on your stern, and stay a mile off the coast until the wind subsides, usually around Morro Ayutla.

If you're southbound from Acapulco, then Puerto Angel or Huatulco offer shelter when the wind is hooting. Hole up here to await your weather window. When you enter the Gulf of Tehuantepec from this direction, you can't hug the rocky shoreline too closely until you're past Salina Cruz and Bahia Ventuosa (Windy Bay). But about two miles of shore, you can still find welcome shelter in the lee of the high land. The wind will be on your nose along Salina

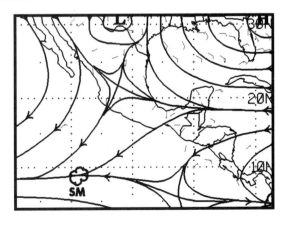

Cruz, and on your beam while crossing Windy Bay. Then from there to Puerto Madero you can run safely in 30 feet of water, which is only a couple hundred yards off the sandy beach. Again, move out to the 10-fathom curve with great caution at the lagoon entrances, because their shoals are farther offshore than the charts indicate. Bite the bullet for a short time, because the wind often increases in strength at the lagoon entrances.

Hurricane Season in Mexican Waters

Hurricanes are nature's most destructive phenomena. The English word "hurricane" came from the Carib Indian's name for their god of winds. In Spanish it's pronounced "oo-rick-CAHN-oh." However you will more often hear it called "ciclon,"

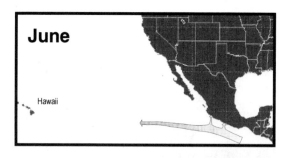

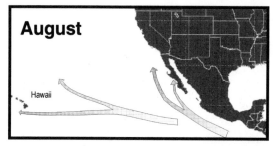

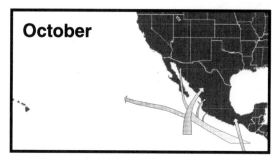

pronounced "see-CLONE." The term chubasco is not synonymous with hurricane, but many gringos make that mistake. A hurricane is the most severe level of tropical storm

Mexico is subject to these hurricanes from late May through the beginning of November. Hurricane season begins when the Intertropical Convergence Zone (ITCZ) moves north from the Equator with the seasonal warming of the sea and air. Inside the ITCZ you'll encounter moist unstable air rising, cooling, condensing and falling as intense rain and thunderstorms with lightning.

Hurricanes draw their tremendous energy from warm ocean water and its released heat of condensation (598 calories per gram). As long as a hurricane's center remains over warm water, its energy supply remains almost limitless.

Here are the prerequisites for hurricane development:

1. An existing Tropical Depression traveling on the surface at less than 13 knots.

2. Barometric pressure below 1004 millibars in the low latitudes.

3. Sea-surface temperature of 78.8°F or higher.

4. Easterly winds at least 30,000 feet aloft, but diminishing with lower altitude.

5. Vigorous rain showers in the vicinity.

Mexican hurricanes are often born in the Gulf of Tehuantepec at about 15 degrees north, and they don't normally travel north of latitude 30 degrees north due to the presence of the cold California Current, which cuts off their energy supply. However, some weakened storms have brought flooding and wind damage to Southern California and Arizona.

Some early-season tropical disturbances recurve and hit the coast near

Acapulco, but most continue west-northwest offshore, where they die half way to Hawaii.

As the season progresses, the storms travel farther north and may hit coastal regions during August and September. During this period, an average of 4.3 tropical disturbances form each month, 2.2 of them become hurricanes. But this is when they have their greatest forward speeds, averaging seven to 12 knots – occasionally reaching an astonishing 25 knots of forward speed.

October hurricanes are the most dangerous to boaters, because they are particularly erratic in their courses, they can intensify very quickly, and they most frequently recurve and hit the Mexican coast. The first 15 days of October are marked by what is usually the final blast of hurricane season.

Nothing magic happens on November 1. If conditions remain ripe for hurricane formation during November, they form. Statistically, cyclonic activity this late generates relatively weak hurricanes and they are short-lived, because the cold California Current penetrates further south in November. El Nino is responsible for keeping coastal waters warmer than normal, thus providing tropical storms with extra energy to grow into full-blown hurricanes.

Sailboats without powerful, reliable engines are out of place in central or southern Mexico after July 15. Power boats that carry enough fuel to be considered long-range cruisers

and that can move very fast (at least 10 knots) for several hundred miles without exhausting their fuel reserves may possibly be able to travel through Mexico during hurricane season, but this would all depend on the hurricane savvy of their captains.

For years I turned down yacht deliveries that involved going through Panama later than July, because, even though I had studied tropical weather patterns for more than a decade, I didn't feel I could get enough timely data to predict when conditions were ripe for hurricane formation in the Pacific. I had a good handle on the easterly waves crossing the Caribbean, but the Pacific remained an enigma. NMC weather faxes showed tropical problems only after they had formed, so I often found myself traveling on the fringe of a tropical depression 24 hours or more before it showed up on the weather fax.

However, I later discovered the 36-hour Prognosis Blend from NMG in New Orleans, Louisiana at 0030 and 1230 Zulu on frequencies 4317.9, 8503.9 and 12789.9. Although most of this chart is the North Atlantic and Caribbean, a small portion covers the Eastern Pacific as far west as Acapulco, including easterly waves. I was very glad to find this chart.

Easterly Waves: Any of them could generate a tropical storm in the Gulf of Tehuantepec.

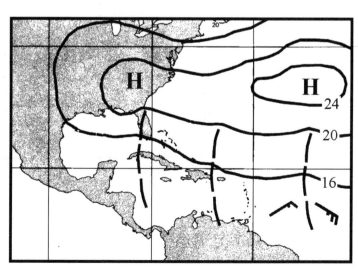

An easterly wave occurring in the Trade Wind belt is a northward bulge in the isobar lines. When upper-level conditions are right, an easterly wave develops a closed circulation of its own and can develop into a tropical depression, tropical storm or hurricane. Ahead of a wave, the weather is partly cloudy and winds are from the northeast. As it passes over you, cloud cover increases, rain comes more frequently in squalls, and the wind shifts to the southeast. This gradual transition zone is from 30 to 100 miles in width. A period of several days may separate the passage of one wave and the next. They travel at between 10 and 13 knots.

The trick of course is to travel between easterly waves and be safely in port when one passes over your location. Since these waves travel from east to west, fast boats traveling northeast up Mexico's coastline have a better chance of staying between waves. Better that is than boats moving southeast down the coast, which puts them on a closing course with the oncoming easterly waves.

Cruisers should use the above information judiciously. Remember, as a yacht delivery captain, I'm paid to handle large, fast, well equipped, long-range vessels, and most of my crew members are U.S. Coast Guard licensed professionals. I would never attempt this type of voyage with anything less. In spite of all the theories, satellite charts and local knowledge, luck still plays a factor. Please don't take chances with your lives.

In the case of a direct hit by a hurricane, no boat has much chance for survival. Some cruisers do summer over in various Mexican ports, more so each year. In the middle reaches of the Sea of Cortez, Puerto Escondido is a popular hurricane hole, but if all the boats in the region were to try to take refuge in the face of a direct hit, they would probably drag each other to splinters against the concrete seawalls. Across the Sea of Cortez, San Carlos near Guaymas suffered a direct hit by the reborn Hurricane Lester in 1992, and many anchored and unattended boats perished after being dragged in mass onto shore in the outer bay. Summering over in the northern Sea of Cortez, such as near L.A. Bay, is feasible because it's so much farther north. In the southern end of the Sea of Cortez, the commercial port of Pichilingue near La Paz also is a hurricane hole, larger than Puerto Escondido, but even more boats summer over in La Paz, so as a hurricane approaches, crowding would also be a problem.

Puerto Vallarta is probably the best place to summer over in Mexico, because the mountains running out to Cabo Corrientes form an effective barrier to the typical forward motion of Mexican hurricanes.

Weather Fax and Ham Radio

Weather facsimile devices (WXfax) are frequently used on the larger or better equipped cruising yachts. NMC is best for all of Mexico, but NMG is best for the coast south of Acapulco.

If you already have an all-band receiver built into your radio and have an onboard computer, you can also have weather fax capabilities fairly inexpensively. A $100 software package includes a modem that links your radio and computer to receive weather fax. One we know of comes from Software Systems Consulting, 615 S. El Camino Real, San Clemente, CA 92672. Or check out another good software package at http://www.xaxero.com

The very best information about weather in Mexican waters is heard on the

California-Baja Amateur Radio (ham) Network. This net convenes at 0745 San Diego time on 7.238 Mhz lower sideband. During the first 15 minutes, licensed hams located throughout Baja, the Sea of Cortez and sometimes in Puerto Vallarta are asked to call in and share their on-site information. By 0815 the net's volunteer weather forecaster has combined the on-site reports with that day's National Weather Service satellite reports, creating the most timely weather picture available. Afterward, the forecaster calls for questions.

You don't have to be a licensed ham to monitor, but you do if you want to ask questions or contribute your weather report. This is a free public service, and the net gives its valuable weather reports with the disclaimer that it is in no way responsible for the consequences of the report or how any skipper uses the information.

Mexican weather is given in Spanish at 0930, 1530 and 2130 Central Standard Time over the national marine-safety system called Radio Costera on SSB frequency 8242.8 Khz. The weather is for the entire Mexican coast by sections, and it's given by the various Port Captains throughout the country. They deliver it slowly and clearly, so even with a modicum of Spanish, most boaters should be able to understand it. Because all the Port Captains are listening in, it makes a great emergency-calling frequency.

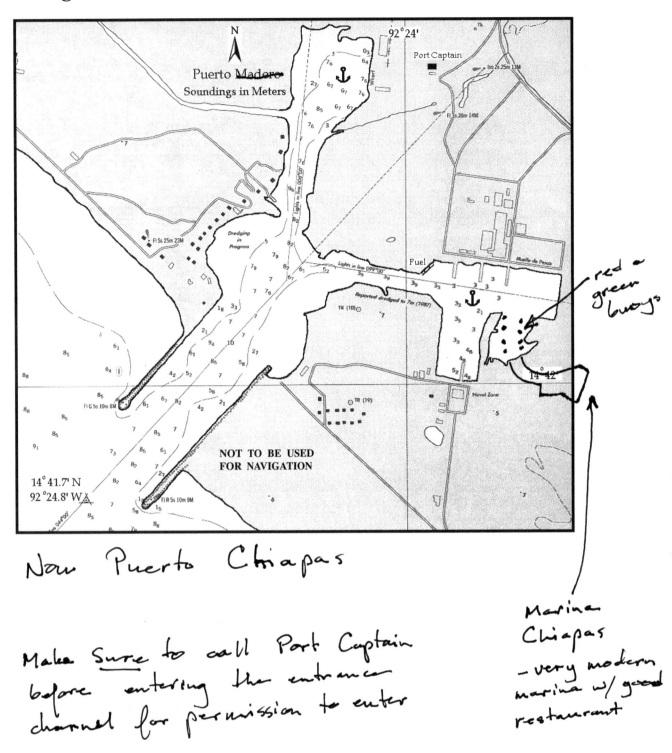

Now Puerto Chiapas

Make Sure to call Port Captain
before entering the entrance
channel for permission to enter

red &
green
buoys

Marina
Chiapas
- very modern
marina w/ good
restaurant

Antonio Luttmann is marina owner

Chapter 26
Puerto Madero & Tehuantepec
Chiapas

Chiapas

In this chapter, we'll look at Puerto Madero, the first (or last) Mexican port (depending on which direction you're traveling) and also at the infamous Gulf of Tehuantepec. (For more information on weather and routing through the Gulf of Tehuantepec, see the end of the previous chapter.)

Puerto Madero *Chiapas*

Puerto Madero (14°42'N by 92°27'W) is a little-known man-made harbor in southern Mexico near the Guatemalan border. Small freighters load bananas and cotton, and the local fleet of shrimpers and shark fishermen come in for service. Though filthy and hot, this port stop is often a necessary evil for boaters, because it's the last Mexican port before they jump off into Central America – or the first Port of Entry for northbound boats.

Approaches: Puerto Madero *Chiapas* can be difficult to find, because the surrounding terrain in both directions is very flat, the coastline is straight, the bottom contours are smooth and regular, and very few of the light houses in southern Mexico operate consistently. When you think you are near, you can close with the shore and run along the beach about a mile off, to avoid missing Puerto Madero Light, a tower just north of the small rock jetties that mark the harbor entrance. The only hazards in the vicinity are the mouths of a river and a lagoon, which lie well within the one-mile line.

The entrance channel into the port of Puerto Madero has to be dredged continually to keep it from silting closed. Silt is swept in on huge swells generated by tropical storms that roam around offshore in the summer months. Because of the constant dredging, we're never quite sure what we'll find from one visit to the next. As you enter the channel going northeast, watch out for dredge barges and buoyed pipelines. The worst area for shoaling is at the landward end of east breakwater. Never try a night entrance.

Inside the northeast-running entrance channel, many shark-fishing pangas and a few palapas line the port shoreline. Then there are two narrower

Cruising Ports

East Basin: Fuel truck comes to pier, viewed from wrecked shrimpers.

channels leading to two separate basins, one to the north and one to the east.

East Basin: Yachts generally use the east basin. Its narrower channel has range markers. Once you enter the east basin, at the east end of the channel and on the north bank is a concrete fuel dock. It has two Pemex (Petroleos Mexicanos) diesel pumps on it, but don't be deceived – they don't work. Yachts should anchor in the area immediately south of the concrete piers. The pier at the nearby Navy base is off limits to civilians.

Anchoring is easy and safe. The bottom is a combination of sand and mud in 12 feet of water. This anchorage is very secure from wind and surge. Go alongside the pier ONLY to obtain fuel and water. Remaining alongside this pier more than a few hours is to invite damage from the shrimpers' less-than-gentle docking maneuvers.

Water is available on the pier for a small service charge, but you must somehow reduce the size of their hose to fit your deck fill. If you're jerry-jugging water, the Navy base may be able to give you small quantities.

North basin: A string of palapas lines the port side of the entrance channel. The villagers use these palapas for drying shark meat. The smell is horrible; buzzards and flies are everywhere. We've anchored here even during a hurricane watch. Though the land is flat here, a brush covered pile of dredging spoil blocks the wind from the southeast, the primary storm direction. The basin is small, without much swinging room.

Getting up on the high concrete pier from the boat is a problem, but you can just manage to scramble ashore on the muddy bank close by the north end of pier. The north basin pier is much closer to the Port Captain's office than is the east basin.

Port Clearance: No matter where you dock or anchor, you can expect an armed naval boarding party to give you an *inspecion rutina*. The Port Captain's office is right across a large lot from the north pier. If you're arriving from the south, you need your *Zarpe* (port clearance from the last foreign port) and your crew list in order to obtain your exit papers. You must then visit *Migracion* which is located at the Tapachula airport several miles inland. Getting there can be an adventure, because taxis are very scarce. Instead, you have to stand out on the highway and stick out your thumb. You'll shortly be picked up by a *pirata,* an unlicensed taxi, and then work out your own deal for a round trip. If you're coming from the south, this immigration office supplies the tourist cards. Daily jet flights from this airport connect you to the rest of the world via Mexico City.

Fuel Stop: Upon entering the breakwaters, the diminutive, smiling and enterprising Catalan brothers are likely to greet you by paddling out in a dugout canoe. They speak rudimentary English and will ask if you want fuel. They'll arrange a truck for larger quantities than you can carry in jerry jugs. It's expensive and they'll want cash up front. U.S. dollars are very welcome, but the negotiated exchange rate may not be to your liking.

Port Captain's office ↓

North Basin: High concrete pier is used mostly for ships.

Tie up to the stationary concrete fuel dock in the east basin (The Port Captain collects a moderate charge.) and wait for the fuel truck. Large tractor tires line the pier for fendering, and you'll have to watch your lines to account for rise and fall of the tide. The pier has no potable water. The truck supplies you by gravity, and there is no meter and no official way to know how much fuel you're getting (or not getting).

TIP: In the past, all vessels had to use only the north basin, and this still happens occasionally when the narrow channel into the east basin shoals closed due to southerly surge or dredge failure. So be prepared for this possibility when entering Puerto Madero.

Local Services: The village of Puerto Madero lies on the northwest side of the main entrance channel, which is several miles by road but a simple launch trip to the area of the fishing palapas on the west bank. This town is a casual beach getaway for folks in the city of Tapachula (see below). Puerto Madero does has the San Rafael hotel and restaurant, a small grocery store and, as you will find throughout Mexico, a distributor who sells beer and soft drinks in bulk. The hotel has a public telephone, and on the north edge of town is a Pemex station. If you need only a small quantity of diesel you can sometimes get it here. But it's one of those gas stations where the pump is often broken, and a remote village where the electricity goes off all over town.

For banking, provisioning, parts or supplies you'll have to go to Tapachula, 15 miles inland. It's a clean, prosperous city of 135,000 serving this rich agricultural region. Unlike in the average Mexican city, many Mayan Indians here still wear native costume and follow the old ways. They come to town from the highlands of Chiapas and neighboring Guatemala.

In Tapachula, you can do a complete re-provisioning in the well-stocked grocery stores, and eat at the outdoor cafes on the central Hidalgo Plaza. Tapachula's huge central market is a maze of fresh produce stalls. Because farm machinery is common, you can find a wide variety of machinery parts. Hotel Loma Real or Hotel Kamico have nice rooms and restaurants.

Gulf of Tehuantepec

As you leave Puerto Madero heading northwest, you will enter the dangerous Gulf of Tehuantepec. Review the tactics described in Chapter 25, Weather and Routing in Mexico, regarding crossing this gulf. Although northbound is the easier direction of travel, you still need to stay within one mile of the beach or closer. The wind usually won't start blowing until you get 80 miles northwest of Puerto Madero.

The older navigation lights along this stretch of coast, as in most of Mexico, are unreliable. New solar-powered lights are still being installed here and there, but because the solar panels are often stolen, it's more safe to assume the light is not working – rather than that it isn't there. The coastline is low and regular, so it offers only a few definable features from which to take bearings.

During the daylight, you should check off each light tower as you pass it. Likewise at night if these lights are working. You may encounter hundreds of shrimp boats working in the area.

At various intervals you will see isolated villages of thatch-roofed huts, inhabited by primitive indigenous folks whose sole income is from shark fishing.

Eight miles east of Barra Tonala lies the village of Puerto Arista (15°56'N by 93°50'W), the only semblance of civilization on the 190-mile coast between Salina Cruz and Puerto Madero. Puerto Arista could provide some emergency aid, since it's connected to the rest of the world by road. You'll often see shrimp boats anchored in the open roadstead off Puerto Arista's brightly painted beach palapas.

Just west of Tonala is Barra Tonala and Boca de San Francisco (16°13'N 14°45'W), two major lagoon entrances. Pass them with great caution, because shoaling may occur at a greater distance offshore than is charted.

During the day and at low tide, the breakers are highly visible – shooting huge plumes of white water high into the air, so passing outside of them is relatively easy. At night, both of these lagoon entrances are more dangerous because even your radar may not detect them – depending on the state of the tide. If the wind is blowing at all, it will howl with increased fury at these entrances. When you move offshore to pass them, you will temporarily be exposed to greater wind and wave action. Once you are past them, move back close to the beach for protection.

Chapter 27
Oaxacan Ports

Mexico's under-developed state of Oaxaca (pronounced "wah-HOCK-ah") has some beautiful and rarely visited anchorages that make excellent destinations for pleasure boaters, plus emergency and commercial services elsewhere. We'll look at

1.) Salina Cruz (emergency)
2.) Huatulco and its anchorages
3.) Puerto Angel
4.) Puerto Escondido

Salina Cruz

Salina Cruz (16°09'N by 95°11.6'W) is a petroleum service port, not a pretty destination spot for pleasure boats. But because Salina Cruz lies almost in the middle of the notorious Golfo de Tehuantepec, its anchorage and inner harbor can be useful to any boat traversing this dangerously windy stretch. And like any commercial port, Salina Cruz has general marine parts and repair services in case you have an emergency.

The temptation is to seek shelter from the wind here, because it lies in the very vortex of the wind – which blows at gale force 140 days a year. However, traveling in either direction, if you've made it through the Gulf of Tehuantepec as far as Salina Cruz, you have the worst behind you. If you're bound for Acapulco, you can run out of the affected area with the wind astern. Bound the other direction, you're able to continue close to the beach and in the lee of the land. Therefore, consider Salina Cruz an emergency stop only.

Anchorage: The Salina Cruz Port Captain established the rule that no boats can anchor inside either the inner or outer harbor, both of which lie inside the enormous rock breakwaters. Don't try to plead ignorance; all that area is reserved for ship maneuvering.

So to seek refuge from prevailing Tehuantepec winds, you can anchor outside the eastern breakwater in Bahia Salina Cruz, in the lee of the sandy beach that forms the northern side of this bay. Remember to call "Port Control," the port's marine traffic control on VHF channel 16 long before you make motions to anchor. They're inside the

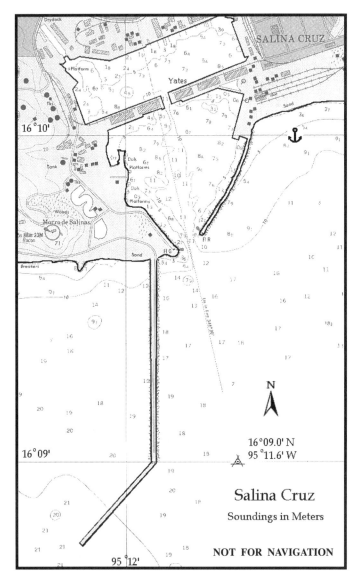

Salina Cruz

Soundings in Meters

16°09.0' N
95°11.6' W

N

NOT FOR NAVIGATION

the beach or into town. But leave a crew member guarding the dinghy.

Docking inside Salina Cruz: If shorebreak is rough, the only alternative is to enter the port.

PORT CAPTAIN'S RULES

To enter the harbor, the Port Captain requires that you bring your skiff through the outer breakwaters and continue immediately through the inner channel to the inner harbor, called the "darsena," and you must immediately clear in with the Capitania. To do this, (1) you can land your skiff on the small dirty beach at the south end of the east wall of the inner harbor, which means behind where the shrimpers are rafted four deep. Be sure to leave one of your crew with your dinghy. (2) Otherwise, you might try to tie your dinghy very close into the eastern corner of the high seawall, which is the corner nearest to the Port Captain's office. If you do tie to this corner of the seawall, absolutely do NOT block any space that a shrimper might otherwise fit into (or they will), and be ready to move your dinghy at the Port Captain's orders. That means, don't leave it untended and go off to town.

If you have a time-critical emergency (sinking, med-evac) and simply must bring a yacht inside the darsena immediately, you must first call Salina Cruz marine traffic control on VHF channel 16. Ships have priority, so you may have to wait for a giant to turn around with its tugs, or you may be asked to come in quickly right away. Enter the outer harbor between the red and green lights of the outer entrance. The range markers (157°M to enter) lead you only

control tower just west of the harbor entrance. They'll tell you what to do, because ships you can't see may be about to cross your path to the anchorage. Then drop the hook east of the breakwater, about 200 yards off the beach in about 30 feet of water over hard sand. (A traffic separation scheme is in effect to bring ships up to and depart from the three oil-loading buoys, the farthest located two miles offshore. Small craft may transit the area, but they are requested to stay clear of all vessels maneuvering in this scheme.)

If shorebreak doesn't prevent landing a dinghy here, you can walk to the cafes on through the outer breakwater entrance, not into the "darsena." If you stayed on that first heading, you'd run directly into the older stone wharf. There's no anchoring allowed in the outer harbor. While you're moving through the outer harbor, everything on the western half is prohibited; don't even check it out. The entrance to the "darsena" or inner harbor is a 50-yard wide slot to the right of the older stone warehouses, between them and the newer white-and-blue buildings that stand on the northeast wall.

Yachts must tie up along the high concrete sea wall that runs to the immediate starboard after you enter the "darsena." Have all your largest fenders and fender boards ready. The prevailing winds, which frequently gust to gale force even within the harbor, pin you onto this wall. An occasional giant tire/fender is slung halfway down with chain. The maximum tidal range in Salina Cruz is about six feet, and the giant yellow bollards are ship-sized and are placed at distances more comfortable to ships. So have your longest lines ready. Because this dock is very high, getting to shore may require a ladder. If you don't carry a boarding ladder, mention to your ships agent in advance (see below) that you will probably need one. He may be able to provide longer lines as well.

Ship's Agent Required: Even for small private yachts, the use of a ship's agent is mandatory in order to enter and clear Salina Cruz. The most common reasons are to get fuel or to disembark crew. Several agencies are located up and down the street that runs along the east side of the inner harbor. They normally handle large tankers, freighters, and commercial fishing boats for the national or international corporations that own the vessels.

However, one agency that also handles the occasional yacht is Operistmo (pronounced "oh-pear-IST-moh"). They

speak English, are a Lloyd's affiliate, and they know how to fend for the special needs of pleasure boats in a busy commercial harbor. The general manager of Operistmo is a pleasant gentleman named Mario Ramon Cisneros L. His father began the agency many years ago. (Their phone is 011-52 (971) 4-02-33 or 4-18-36, or fax 4-33-59.)

Call "Operistmo" on VHF channel 16 when you're within range of Salina Cruz, switch to working channel 67 and tell them exactly what you need. The last time we stopped here, their price for the basic service of clearing in and out was $300, and taking fuel and water was more. If you need an electronics specialist, a diesel mechanic, an electrician, parts expressed in, people expressed out, an emergency haul-out or medical help, Salina Cruz has it.

Fuel Stop: Plans call for bigger yachts to take centrifuged fuel from a large Pemex tank in the inner harbor, so they would pay only the commercial fuel price. At present they take it either from a fuel truck that drives to the seawall, or from the crowded shrimper fuel dock on the north wall. For jerry-jug quantities, the Pemex is about four blocks north of the Capitania

If all of this sounds inconvenient for pleasure boaters, you're right. The preferred stop for sailboats is Huatulco, 60 miles away. Salina Cruz is useful in emergencies.

Huatulco
The ancient port of Huatulco (15°43'N by 96°08'W), located 235 miles southeast of Acapulco, is the center of a 20-mile-long cruising ground that includes 12 nearby anchorages, each one lovelier than the last, but most suitable mainly for settled weather. Even though Huatulco is located on the western side of the infamous Gulf of Tehuantepec, this narrow little bay is very seldom affected by gulf winds.

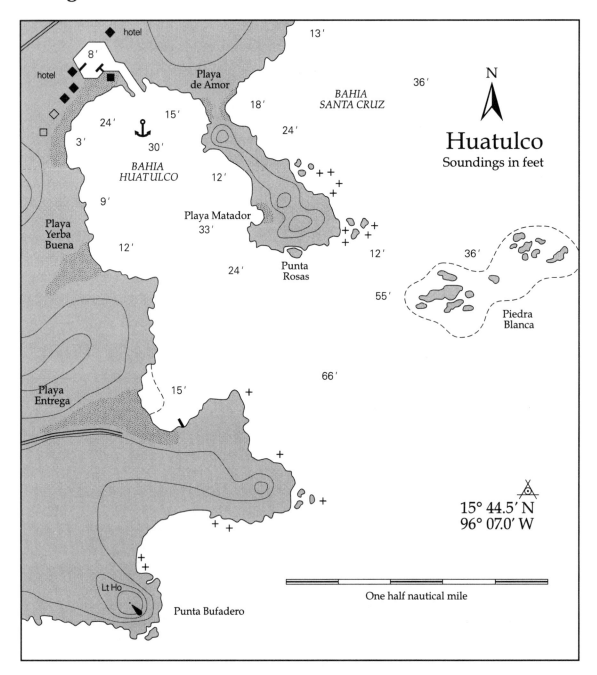

For that reason, Huatulco (pronounced "wah-TOOL-coh") bay is a very convenient refuge in which to wait out bad weather – and to be in a good position to scoot across the Gulf of Tehuantepec when the wind drops. Although it's not a convenient fuel stop for larger quantities than you can jerry jug, Huatulco is a Port of Entry, so vessels bound to and from Costa Rica are more frequently using the harbor as a staging area for exiting and entering Mexico. Thanks to the beauty of its nearby coves and anchorages (see below), the Huatulco area is becoming a popular stop for long-range cruising and sportfishing boats.

Huatulco is located well within the hurricane formation latitudes, and it is open to any southerly weather – so it's not a place to be during summer's frequent tropical storms.

History: First inhabited by the Olmecs, Huatulco was later colonized by the Zapotecas, and their descendants still live here. Hernan Cortez anchored here and later Sir Francis Drake attacked it during his circumnavigation. Until 1983, Huatulco remained virtually unchanged – a collection of small thatch-roofed huts on the edge of a small but well protected bay. Then Fonatur, Mexico's tourist development agency, began building an infrastructure (airport, roads, hotels and – eventually – marinas) intended to make Huatulco the largest tourist area in Mexico. Economic downturns in the late 1990s squashed some of those expansive plans. Tourism is still the main industry, and most hotel-based visitors are from Mexico City and Europe. So visiting yachts are held in some awe.

Approach: The coast along here is an endless succession of forested hills that come right down to the water, forming an irregular coastline. In winter cruising season, it's often the local dry season, so the hills may appear brown from sea. Bufadero Light stands on the high point of land about half a mile southwest the opening into Huatulco Bay. In the outer part of your approach, be careful of the off lying reef to starboard called Piedra Blanca. Come to GPS approach waypoint (15°44.5'N 96°07.0'W) and head into the harbor on a northwest heading.

Huatulco Bay: Most cruising boats prefer to anchor in Huatulco's outer bay, rather than enter the darsena. You can anchor anywhere outside the buoyed-off swimming beach. The preferred spot to drop the hook is in the north end of Huatulco Bay, just south of the riprap jetties that lead into the darsena. Anchor here in from 15 to 30 feet over sand and gravel. There's room for two dozen boats to swing freely. In case a large fleet of cruising boats builds up, we would also anchor along the base of the arm of Punta Rosas. Another place is off Playa Yerba Buena on the southeast side of Huatulco Bay, which still has protection from the east due to the tip of Punta Rosas.

This anchorage is very sheltered, open only to the southeast, and winds are rare from that direction during the winter cruising season. Within Huatulco Bay are several beautiful beaches, some only reachable by dinghy. Playa Entrega is the largest, and the scuba diving and snorkeling is fantastic amid the coral heads.

You can land your dinghy at a small floating dock just inside the inner harbor in front of the Port Captain's office. You can embark and disembark crew members at this dock, but move your dinghy to one side before leaving it unattended.

Huatulco's inner harbor contains a dinghy landing. The seawalls are crowded with local fishing and diving boats.

Inner Harbor: An inner harbor (darsena) has been dredged from a former lagoon, and a sea wall surrounds the darsena. Two riprap jetties in the north end of Huatulco Bay lead you into the darsena. The Port Captain's office is conveniently located near the entrance to the inner harbor, viewing the outer bay as well. Vessels drawing no more than eight feet can enter and Med-moor to the sea wall, with prior permission of the port authorities, but it's crowded with tour boats.

Fuel Stop: Fuel can be ordered and trucked down in barrels from the Pemex station (three barrels at a time) to the boat moored in the inner harbor, or you can jerry jug it by taxi. Ask the Port Captain to refer you to whomever is presently delivering fuel to private boats. Huatulco's darsena is so small and crowded, and its fueling methods are so awkward that it can only be considered a fuel stop for smaller boats, not larger boats or big sportfisher.

Port Clearance: This is a Port of Entry, so normal port clearance procedures are in effect. Start at the Capitania, located along the entrance to the inner harbor, and Migracion and Aduana will follow. A ship's agent isn't necessary, but a fuel permit may be needed.

Local Services: Several restaurants and hotels surround the bay. The town of Crucecitas lies about two miles inland. This attractive, planned community is the area's service center, providing boaters with a central market, several fairly good grocery stores, at least two banks, two gasoline/diesel stations and many English-speaking doctors. An international airport about 10 miles away has daily flights to Mexico City.

New marina basins for small local boats (covered pangas for local diving and sportfishing) are still under construction in the nearby bays of Santa Cruz and Tangolunda.

Anchorages: Increasingly, cruising boats are thinking of Huatulco and its 12 adjacent yet remote anchorages as a destination in its own, not just a place to wait out a Tehuantepecker. More often, Huatulco and its surrounds are replacing Acapulco as the southerly turning point in their Mexico cruise from the U.S. West Coast.

Listed from southwest to northeast as you encounter them when cruising down from Acapulco: Bahia Sacraficios, Jicaral Cove, Riscalillo Cove, Manglillo Cove, Chachacual Bay, Isla Cacaluta, Maguey Cove, Organo Cove, Huatulco Bay, Chahue or Santa Cruz Bay, Tangolunda Bay, tiny little Conejo Cove.

Take your pick from the boogy-woogy atmosphere off the Club Med in Tangolunda to the tranquillity of La India, a remote beach located in the northeast corner of the bay behind Isla Chachacual. Our favorite anchorage is snuggled up in two fathoms of water in the northeast corner of Maguey, where there's an excellent dinghy-landing beach free of surf or even breaking waves. The popular Mexican movie "La Cubana" was filmed here.

Southbound: If you're moving southwest along the coast of Mexico toward Costa Rica, Huatulco will be the last well-sheltered port before you turn northeast into the Gulf of Tehuantepec. As such it is important to keep in mind. If wind is blowing in the gulf, put into Huatulco to wait until the gale warnings drop. When they do, depart immediately, because it's usually a matter of only hours until the wind starts blowing again. We've had to spend several days here waiting for the right weather window when bound toward the Panama Canal.

Puerto Angel

It's hardly a port, but it is angelic. Tiny Puerto Angel (15°39'N by 96°31'W) is a well sheltered bay during the cruising season. Thanks to its pleasant town and friendly

**Puerto Angel:
A nice stop
in dry season; two
tiny anchorages
and a stairway
on the pier.**

people, its choice of two anchorages and its proximity to the coastal highway, Puerto Angel makes a nice destination – and a good stopover whenever high winds are blowing in the Gulf of Tehuantepec.

Approaches: Coming from the west, the approaches to Puerto Angel are clearly defined by two rocks, one black and one white, appropriately called Roca Negra and Roca Blanca. A small "bufadero" or surge geyser is sometimes seen spouting near an arch rock on the western approach to this small bay. The bay itself has an entrance 200 yards wide. Two range markers atop orange and white poles in the north end of the bay mark the entrance bearing at 003° M.

Anchorage: The small bay will accommodate only about a couple dozen small craft at anchor. That is sometimes a problem, as visitors to the port are increasing. The sand bottom is good holding ground. The main part of the bay is ringed by two white sandy beaches. A huge concrete pier juts out from the beach in the northeast corner of the bay. The larger anchorage is off this main town beach, kiddingly called the downtown beach. A rocky prominence separates a smaller western beach from the main town beach, and a unique stone-walled walkway or *paseo* carved into this steep hill connects pedestrian

traffic. A smaller anchorage is found off this western beach, called Playa Panteon, which has palapa cafes with tables on the beach. We prefer this smaller anchorage. Actually, you can anchor just about anywhere inside Puerto Angel, as long as you don't encumber the Navy's big mooring buoy in the center of the bay.

Port Clearance: The office of the Port Captain and Aduana is just east of the head of the pier, but surge usually prevents boats from coming alongside this pier. Landing a dinghy can be wet due to the swell that occasionally sweeps into the bay. If the tide is high, it may be better to disembark passengers on the pier's concrete stairs, located on the pier's northwest corner near the beach. If the tide is low, land on the beach east of the pier. A Navy base in the north end of the bay is where the range markers are located.

Local Services: Puerto Angel is a delightful cruising stop because of its natural beauty, friendly people and casual ambiance. It's too far from Mexico City for weekenders, but it's been discovered and is getting slightly trendy – in a Mom and Pop sort of way. Similar to its neighbor Puerto Escondido, Puerto Angel has vegetarian restaurants, Italian eateries, cappuccino cafes and fresh

Cruising Ports

juice bars. Our favorite watering hole is the Villa Florencia hotel's restaurant, right on the cobble-stone malecon circling the downtown beach. But there are a dozen other good choices in this vicinity, among the quaint houses and verandas laced with bougainvillea. Playa Zopilote, the beach village two miles west of this bay, is worth exploring too.

Puerto Angel has a bank and telephone service, but Pochutla, about 10 miles up into the foothills (daily bus service), is the nearest service town of any consequence. The farming countryside is interesting, and the hot, dusty town looks like a set for western movies.

Fuel Stop: Puerto Angel is not a convenient or dependable fuel stop, so we don't recommend it. However, if you must get fuel here, ask the Port Captain how to go about it. You may have to buy a tank-truck load of diesel in Pochutla, or hire a local truck from the fishing cooperative and round up barrels to fill at the town Pemex. Either way, you'd probably have to Med-moor off the surgey pier and take your fuel by gravity flow, i.e. very slowly. For small quantities, ask a taxi driver if he'll carry jugs back from the Pemex station on the highway.

Puerto Escondido

Puerto Escondido (15°50'N by 97°04'W) is 35 miles northwest of Puerto Angel and 175 miles southeast of Acapulco. Don't confuse this southern Puerto Escondido with the northern one, which is a hurricane hole in Baja's Sea of Cortez. (For the other Puerto Escondido, see Chapter 35.)

This Puerto Escondido is dedicated to surfing and small-scale tourism. It's not really a port, merely a small, not deeply indented bay that is wide open to the south and southwest, so anchoring here is possible only during the dry season, winter and spring

cruising season. During summer and fall hurricane season, this region of Mexico's West Coast is swept by tropical storms and huge surf, so the open bays cannot sustain large breakwaters or boat docks.

Approaches: Puerto Escondido Light stands on a prominent cliff overlooking the town and marks the northwestern side of the bay, and another light marks the southeastern point, easily visible as a long white beach. When approaching from the northwest, don't mistake the small rocky swimming cove of Angelito (1/4 mile west of the real bay) for the main anchorage. It is an easy port to enter at night, because house lights cover the prominent cliff overlooking the northwest side of the bay.

Anchorage: After you enter the bay, a stubby little breakwater on a rocky peninsula is visible to port. The best place to anchor is on a 15-foot shelf in the lee of this breakwater, close to the dinghy landing beach and Port Captain's office, but this corner is often filled with private mooring buoys for local boats. Next choice is along the adjacent palapa beach, or farther down the beach to the east. Larger boats might anchor over a small seamount (47 to 57 feet of water) located a few hundred yards southeast of the breakwater. The bottom is good holding sand, but even in calm weather a slight swell enters the bay, making the anchorage rolly.

Port Clearance: The Capitania and Navy buildings are right above the dinghy landing beach, which lies in the cramped northwest corner of the bay behind the little breakwater. There is no dock or pier for landing, but since this is the only beach without breaking swell, it's the only place for landing and loading. Watch out for swimmers off this beach, and cover anything in your dingy from playful children and dogs.

Puerto Escondido has a simple check in, but if you don't do it pretty soon after you get settled from anchoring, a boat load of Navy guys with guns is likely to come out to your boat and ask you to do it right then.

Local Services: Fuel and water must be hand-carried in jerry jugs from the Pemex on the highway, then loaded into a panga or your dinghy. The beach area has half a dozen small hotels, two long-distance phone booths, two banks and a laundromat. Any marine products you find at the two hardware stores north of Highway 200 are designed to keep the local excursion pangas running. The airport is five miles west of town, and there's regular bus service.

Because Puerto Escondido lacks a dock, loading provisions is not convenient. However, it has two larger grocery stores, both north of the east-west running Highway 200, and several smaller groceries. Taxis are plentiful. Fruit and vegetable stands are found on almost every corner.

New Age eateries and health food stores are sprinkled throughout the beach area. The best seafood is in the nicer beach palapas off the paseo or pedestrian walkway. Early mornings, the fragrance of wood smoke, espresso and toasted corn tortillas fills the still air. Mayan Indians from the mountains sell their colorful handicrafts along the paseo. Tie dye still lives here, as do many hippie-era holdouts.

TIP: A note of caution; the state of Oaxaca is famous for its rich coffee and its potent "mota" (marijuana). Pangueros may come alongside and try to sell you some mota in plain view of the Navy and Port Captain. This may occur in Puerto Angel as well. Do not touch the stuff unless permanent residence in a Mexican prison sounds like fun.

Dinghy landing beach is in front of Puerto Escondido's Capitania.

Cruising Ports

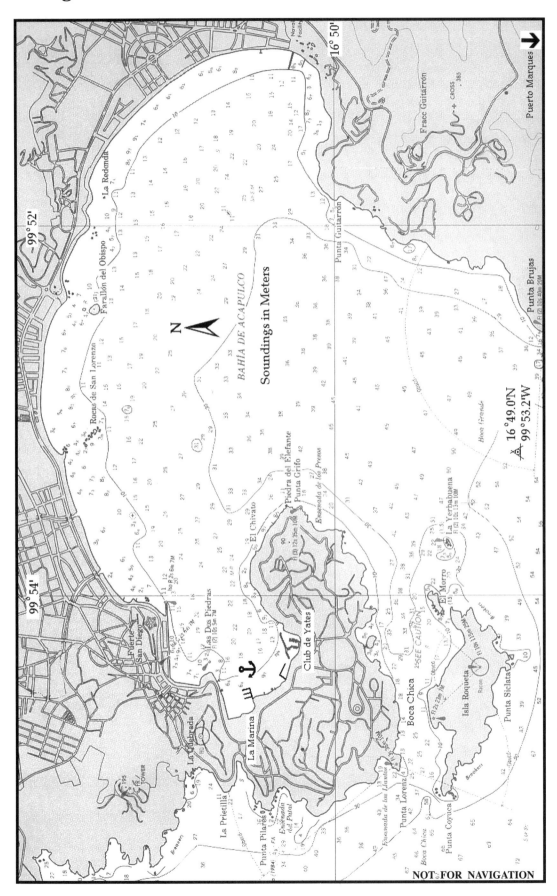

NOT FOR NAVIGATION

Chapter 28
Acapulco

∿∿∿∿∿∿∿∿∿∿∿∿∿∿∿∿∿∿∿∿∿∿∿∿∿∿∿∿∿∿∿∿∿∿

In this chapter, we'll look first at Acapulco; then we'll examine two intermediate stops you may want to make on your way to Acapulco: Punta Galera to the south, and Papanoa to the north.

Acapulco

For cruising boaters, a stop at Acapulco is both functional and fun. The large city of Acapulco climbs the hills surrounding one of the finest natural harbors in the world. It was the western terminus for voyages of the Manila galleons that plied the Pacific from 1565 to 1815 – for three centuries. Mexican silver and other treasures were loaded in Acapulco and exchanged in the Philippines for Asian silk, porcelain and gold work. They were carried back to Acapulco, where some were later transshipped to Lima, Peru and to Spain.

For nearly 50 years, Acapulco has been an international jet-set resort, and it's still a major destination for most Mexico tourists – including yacht-based tourists. Compared to some of the newer coastal tourist areas like Cancun, Ixtapa and Cabo San Lucas, a stop at Acapulco can be a real bargain as long as you don't spend too much time in "Gringo Landia" (the dazzling high-rise hotel district lining the northeast shores of the bay). In the rest of town (notably, the west end of the bay), you'll find that prices for food, restaurants and hotels are well below the newer resorts.

Acapulco has two excellent marinas, and it's a major port for cruise ships, small commercial shipping and the local fishing industry. So it's possible to find marine supplies.

For most long-range cruising boats from the U.S. West Coast, Acapulco is their last major port call before jumping down across Central America toward northern Costa Rica. So it's their place of preparation. For anyone making a Mexico-only itinerary, either Acapulco or Huatulco can be their southern terminus – before turning around and heading north. For those boaters arriving from the U.S. East Coast, Acapulco is their first big taste of Pacifico Mexico.

However, Acapulco lies well within the summer hurricane alley of the eastern

Cruising Ports

Acapulco YC is nestled into the lower left corner, and La Marina is above and to the right.

Pacific, so unless you're a very fast long-range power vessel, you should plan to not hang out in or near Acapulco during hurricane season.

Approaches: Our GPS approach waypoint right in the middle of the Boca Grande entrance to Acapulco harbor is 16°49'N by 99°53.2'W.

If you're arriving from the south (see Punta Galera below), you can enter Acapulco Bay through Boca Grande (large mouth) which is the wide passage between Isla Roqueta and Punta Brujas. Boca Grande is wide open except for the lighted rock called La Yerbabuena. Boca Grande is the safer entrance, especially if you're arriving during the night from the north.

If you arrive from the north (see Papanoa below) during the daylight hours, you can enter through Boca Chica (small mouth), the narrower but deep passage between Isla Roqueta and Punta Lorenzo. Even some cruise ships enter Acapulco Bay through Boca Chica, so it's not all that small. Besides, the Mediterranean-style villas that cling to Boca Chica's rocky cliffs create a very dramatic introduction to Acapulco. To enter through Boca Grande, swing south of Isla Roqueta.

Both of the modern facilities that have slips and services for yachts are located in the nearly enclosed west end of Acapulco Bay.

Acapulco Yacht Club: The older place is the venerable Club de Yates de Acapulco (Acapulco Yacht Club). Most of the AYC's members are gracious, wealthy Mexicans who live in Mexico City, a short jet flight away. Reciprocal privileges from yacht clubs around the world are recognized here, and you'll get a discount on slip fees. But it's not necessary to be a member of any yacht club to stay there, if there's room. Swimming pool under the palms, nice patio dining, hot showers, new laundry, phone and fax in the office, paper clearance service, helpful uniformed staffers and the only yacht fuel dock in town make "the club" hard to pass up. The AYC's phone numbers are 011-52 (748) 2-38-60 and 2-38-70 and its fax number is 2-28-36.

Upon approaching the club docks, you call "Club de Yates" on VHF channel 16 during business hours (0900 to 2100) and ask for a berthing assignment. You can choose between laying alongside or Med-mooring to the newer floating guest dock west of the older docks (depending on how crowded it is), or using an offshore mooring, or anchoring and using the club's dinghy dock, or Med-mooring to the older non-floating concrete piers on the north edge of the club. The newer dock is much nicer than the older piers, but it's a longer walk to the club. The older docks are surfaced with white plastic planking. Before deciding, swing by and look, then find a uniformed staffer who should check with the office via

* Great place!

192

hand-held VHF before pointing you to an open spot.

If you choose to Med-moor to either the older non-floating concrete piers or the newer floating dock, allow for plenty of scope in this depth of 35 feet. These slots are often tight, and putting down an anchor without crossing others can be difficult when the afternoon sea breeze blows strongly on the beam. Try this maneuver in the morning before the wind comes up. After the hook is down, back toward the dock and secure two stern lines crossing one another. Dock workers will be on hand to take your lines. It is also helpful to secure two spring lines from the pier (on both sides to a spot forward of the beam) to prevent lateral movement.

The club's floating dock to the west is heavily anchored, as opposed to being secured to deep pilings. So far, it's survived tropical storms. Though Acapulco Bay is well protected during winter and spring cruising season, a troublesome surge sweeps the harbor, so I'd recommend sturdy dock lines with chafe protection. The large gap between your well-fendered stern and the dock is going to require a gang plank; ask a staffer to borrow one for you to use for the length of your stay. (If you're on the older concrete pier, secure the plank so it can rise and fall with the tide.)

La Marina de Acapulco: Located only a few hundred yards west of the yacht club, this newer marina was built on the grounds of the former Club de Pesca. That's what still shows on some older charts. La Marina's attractive floating docks have water and good electricity, but the long outer dock for 60- to 100-footers was damaged in tropical storms and, as we go to press, some of their big-boat spots aren't available.

The maximum individual slip size is 60 feet. Security is good here, and the office can clear your papers. The marina's docks all float, and it has a swimming pool under the sun. But the walk up the hill to the street level is long and hot, and there's no eatery on the premises. Street wise, the marina is only three blocks closer to downtown than is the club. To get a slip here, call "La Marina" on VHF channel 16 on your approach. La Marina de Acapulco's phone numbers are 011-52 (74) 83-75-05, and 83-74-61, and 83-10-26 and 83-74-98. The fax machine is usually on their first number.

Anchorage: Puerto Marques (pronounced "mar-KEZ") is a separate smaller bay that lies southeast of Acapulco Bay; you enter it between Punta Diamante and Punta Brujas. Marques is nicely protected from the south, east and north, but when prevailing westerlies build up, they can make the main anchorage in the

La Marina is the newer place in town.

eastern part of this small bay too rolly for comfort. So the preferred spot is in the north cove of Puerto Marques, in 30 feet of water over good holding sand and gravel. (16°48.53'N by 99°50.85'W) Ashore are private homes, hotels, beach cafes, taxis and a sportfishing dock. It's about 4.5 miles by dinghy to the marina end of Acapulco Bay. If you're picking up folks at the airport, Puerto Marques is much closer.

Inside Acapulco Bay, the protected anchorage area is off the club and marina, and between them. The bottom is soft mud, not very good holding, and we've had anchors fouled by lost fishing nets and a sunken mooring float. If you opt to use a mooring, dive on it to check the condition of the ground tackle because some are in bad condition. Be sure it's not being rented by a local boat that's out of port for a few hours. The best spots in the anchorage (between AYC and La Marina, 20 to 30 feet of water) are often crowded, so you may need to anchor farther out in deep water.

TIP: Acapulco is a favorite target for hurricanes in the summer and fall. Local boats survive only if they are heavily moored, and visitors sometimes come adrift and bang into one another. I recommend anchoring away from the club if a storm is approaching. Often the Port Captain will close the port for several days at a time when a storm approaches, keeping all vessels inside.

Port Clearance: You can handle your own port clearance papers through the Port Captain, Aduana and Migracion. Or port clearance services are available at the club and the marina. After securing your boat, take all the boat papers to the office. It may take half a day, but usually no officials even board the boat. The office will also, for a moderate charge, take care of your exit papers. It is well worth the price.

Fuel Stop: Only the yacht club has a fuel pier, but the marina has plans for one. To get fuel, you must make prior arrangements in the club office. If you need very large quantities you'll have to order it, and the wait is often a couple of days because the club's tanks are very small. Prices have varied widely over the years, but recently the price has been more expensive than in the U.S. We've always found this fuel to be clean.

Come along side the non-floating concrete fuel dock, which is about 120 feet long. Use large fenders because of the surge, and watch your lines for chafe. Even if you have a reservation for fuel, some boats try to sneak in and grab your fuel first.

Fuel and all other club bills can be paid with American Express, Master Charge, Visa or travelers checks. Both the club and marina may cash small denomination travelers checks or exchange dollars for pesos. The club has an ATM cash machine behind the bar. A bank is two blocks away from the either facility.

Local Services: City water is plumbed to the club's fuel pier and all the docks at both facilities, but don't drink the water until you've treated it. Acapulco's water-delivery system is so overworked that bad things find their way into the public water supply, especially after heavy rains. You can buy safe drinking water in many sizes of plastic gallon bottles in every grocery store.

A sling travel lift for haul-outs is available at the Acapulco Yacht Club. You can make long-distance collect calls 24 hours a day at both places.

Some dock workers are available to do everything from general cleaning (inside and out) to engine work (from precision work to cleaning the bilge). The quality and price of the work varies greatly; you have

Acapulco Yacht Club has a Travelift and dry storage yard.

to be sure the worker knows what needs to be done and how to do it. Agree on a price in advance. The club is not responsible for any of the workers' actions. To help you find a reliable service or person, we highly recommend our friend Jesus Moreno, who is the captain of a local power boat kept at the yacht club.

Acapulco is one of the few places outside of the U.S. where you can get electronics work done. We highly recommend Pablo Nuevo at 87-64-64 or 5-06-49. He speaks English and is very knowledgeable, but getting replacement parts sometimes takes time.

To have boat parts flown down and cleared through Customs or Aduana, we recommend the services of Joe Neale. His assistant Chica is the captain of a boat in the yacht club, so if Joe isn't in town, you can ask for her. Joe Neale's telephone number in San Diego is (619) 224-4495. We've had parts drop-shipped to Joe's office in San Diego, then he's carried them down and cleared them through the Aduana in Tijuana, and we've picked them up at the airport – *no problema*. It's a reliable, valuable and relatively inexpensive service.

The Port Captain or Navy broadcast the local weather forecast at 1200 each day on VHF channel 16 in Spanish. It's given slowly and distinctly. Both the club and marina post the daily weatherfax charts, especially if trouble is brewing and during hurricane season.

Provisioning: Of all the places mentioned in this guidebook, Acapulco is one of the best places for reprovisioning. We've found that the best prices and selection are at the WalMart Super Tienda located in the east end of town. It's a long taxi ride but worth it. It's air-conditioned and has several specialty shops: an excellent carniceria, a cheese shop, a delicatessen, a sausage shop, and a huge produce section. Other departments out front have clothing, housewares and books. Unlike other grocery stores, WalMart always seems to have plenty of carts, also young baggers carry your stuff outside and to help you corral a taxi. (Tip: the VW taxis charge less for the long trip back to the marina area; make sure all your groceries fit inside.)

Closer downtown you'll find three large well-stocked grocery stores along the "costera," the coast road. There's a good farmers' market a few blocks inland. Sometimes coastal cargo boats sell their fruits and coconuts along the seawall downtown near the Zocalo, the central plaza.

Several reasonably priced restaurants are within walking distance in the marina area. Between the two is the La Jolla, an air-conditioned round top with good food and service. Two blocks south of the yacht club you'll find a beautiful swimming beach called La Caleta. We especially like the Las Cabanas restaurant on this beach, but it closes fairly early. The bull ring is a short walk from the club. If you are in town on a Sunday during the season, you can soak up some traditional culture by taking in a corrida.

Frequent flights connect Acapulco with virtually every major airport in the world. But the airport is an hour east from the marinas by taxi. Acapulco is a good jumping-off point to explore the interior of Mexico. Arrangements can be made to leave your boat safe and secure. A new toll road connects Acapulco with Mexico City, now less than three hours away.

Acapulco Ambiance: The climate in Acapulco is very hot year round. The sea breeze is cut off by the surrounding topography. To help alleviate this problem centuries ago, the Spanish had the local Indians cut a slot through the hills, and they called it "La Ventana," the window. This slot is right above La Marina de Acapulco, and it keeps these docks ventilated.

One way to beat the heat is to relax around one of the pools in a lounge chair, reading or talking to the numerous visitors of the international yachting community, while sipping cool drinks served by the uniformed waiters. When the heat builds up sufficiently, slide into the pool to cool off. It beats working eight hours a day in an office.

Another way to beat the heat is to go snorkeling to see the Virgin of Guadalupe statue that looks up from bottom, between Isla Roqueta and La Yerbabuena Rock. Or scuba dive on the two wrecks right in the bay. The 300-foot Rio de la Plata cruise ship that sank in 1944, and the freighter Corsana that sank near Punta Grifo Light. Acapulco Bay has an exemplary waterfront clean-up program, and it has paid off in much cleaner water.

To get downtown, take a taxi or climb aboard any of the white mini-buses that frequently run downtown from Caleta. Get off at the Zocalo or "centro," the town's center with a plaza, shady benches, a nice fountain, big church, inexpensive cafes, restaurants and shops. Farther east is the Fuerte San Diego, an ancient fort that

defended the harbor against pirates. It was destroyed in an earthquake in 1776 but has been rebuilt and now houses a neat little museum.

Several times a day, the famous Quebrada Divers leap from the cliffs into a narrow cove, called La Quebrada, located just outside Acapulco Bay and to the northwest. You can watch them from the patio of the Plaza las Glorias hotel, or, for a better view, stand off in your boat to watch. But don't try to get in too close; uncharted rocks are reported.

Punta Galera

The east side of Punta Galera is the only possible place to anchor in between Puerto Escondido (35 miles to the southeast) and Acapulco (138 miles to the northwest). But as an anchorage, even in the best of cruising season weather, Punta Galera is definitely rated "marginal" to "emergency only."

Punta Galera Light (15°57.85'N by 97°40.74'W) stands on atop a three-lobed rounded peak. As you approach, the hill may at first look like a small island just off shore of the long stretch of sandy beaches and mangrove lagoons. Beware of Rocas Ahogadas (drowned rocks), which is the submerged reef that lies within ¼ mile south of the tip of Punta Galera. Don't confuse it with two visible detached rocks about ¼ mile due east of the tip of the point. To make this anchorage, you must come in close behind (¼ mile northeast of) both these obstacles, and anchor northeast of the point in 18 to 40 feet of water off the sand dunes.

The safest place to land a dinghy through the heavy shorebreak is usually wherever the local pangas are pulled up on the beach. In this case, it's usually close behind the rocks at the base of Cerro Galera.

The entrance to Chacahua Lagoon that still shows on some charts is in error.

The lagoon entrance has been closed for a decade, so the only anchorage is outside. There's a dirt road just west of Cerro Galera that leads to a very small fishing village about two miles inland. The village has one unreliable telephone, no services and no public transportation inland. (Chacahua Lagoon is polluted, so avoid eating or drinking anything here. The villages around the lagoon have a history of cholera outbreaks.)

For emergencies, the lighthouse keeper has a generator-powered SSB for communicating with the Port Captain and Navy at Puerto Escondido.

Papanoa

The little harbor called Papanoa is a possible stepping stone between Acapulco (70 miles to the south) and Zihautanejo (35 miles to the northwest). Located on the north side of Morro de Papanoa at the south end of Tequepa Bay, this tiny anchorage offers great shelter from the west, south and east, but swell from the north and northeast comes in. It has a tiny fishing village, a small Navy base, a launch ramp, two places to anchor and two places to tie alongside a concrete pier.

The harbor is defined by two lighted riprap breakwaters, and the entire harbor is lined in tall light posts – looking like a fleet of sailboat masts when you approach from the north.

Outer Basin: The straight outer breakwater (red light) shelters a large non-floating concrete dock that's favored by shrimpers and commercial fishing boats. You can come alongside with plenty of water, but fender well. There's a concrete launch ramp in the south end, and a huge bollard nearby; the preferred anchorage is just north of the ramp and bollard, in 22 feet of water, just so you're not impeding panga traffic into the inner bay. Or you can anchor out in the middle of this outer basin in 30 to 39 feet of water.

The palapa-roofed cafes (bars) behind the pier normally serve the commercial fishermen. A taxi from the village may show up on the road leading south from the pier.

Inner Basin: The curved inner breakwater (green light) shelters a smaller inner bay, and the entire perimeter beach is often lined with pangas. A reef in the south end of this inner bay makes anchoring difficult. You might ask permission to come alongside one of the two concrete fingers that jut south from the head of this curved breakwater. We found nine to 12 feet of water at their outer ends.

The village surrounds this bay, and the Navy base looks down from the saddle between the village and Cerro Papanoa. We know of no easy way to get fuel here, because the locals all get their through the fishing cooperative. There's a nice little motel with a telephone, restaurant and pool, located on the highway one mile north of the village of Papanoa.

"What's the name of this place? I keep forgetting it."

"Think of the father of the guy who built the ark."

"Papa of Noah? Oh, yah – Papanoa!"

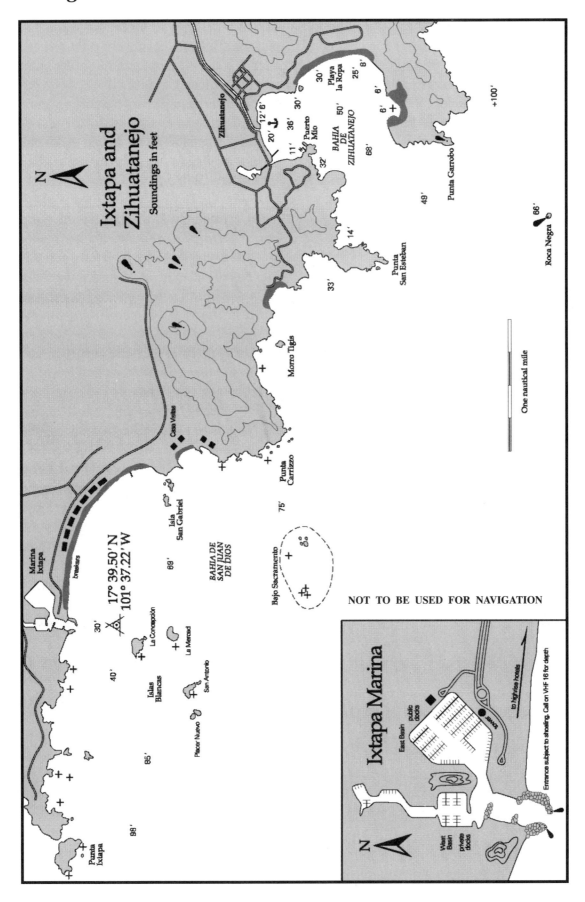

N

Ixtapa and Zihuatanejo
Soundings in feet

Zihuatanejo

12' 6'
20'
11'
36'
30'
30'
Puerto Mio
8'
8'
25'
Playa la Ropa
6'
6'
BAHIA DE ZIHUATANEJO
50'
68'
6'
+100'
14'
Punta Garrobo
49'
33'
Punta San Esteban
66'
Roca Negra

Morro Tigis

Casa Vieitas
Punta Carrizzo
75'

Marina Ixtapa
breakers
30'
17° 39.50' N
101° 37.22' W
40'
La Concepción
68'
Isla San Gabriel
La Merced
BAHIA DE SAN JUAN DE DIOS
Bajo Sacramento
Islas Blancas
San Antonio
85'
Placer Nuevo
98'
Punta Ixtapa

One nautical mile

NOT TO BE USED FOR NAVIGATION

Ixtapa Marina

N

East Basin public docks
RAMP
to highrise hotels
West Basin private docks
Entrance subject to shoaling. Call on VHF 16 for depth.

Chapter 29
Zihuatanejo
Ixtapa & Isla Grande

〜〜〜〜〜〜〜〜〜〜〜〜〜〜〜〜〜〜〜〜〜〜〜〜〜〜〜〜〜〜〜

In this chapter, we'll focus on the major boating destination of Zihuatanejo Bay, then we'll look into three adjacent stops: Barra de Potosi about 11 miles to the south of Zihuatanejo, and then Isla Grande and Marina Ixtapa a few miles to the north of Zihuatanejo.

Zihuatanejo Bay

Zihuatanejo (17°37'N by 101°33'W) is a town and small bay 110 miles northwest of Acapulco, in the state of Guerrero. This attractive bay enjoys protection from prevailing wind in winter and spring cruising season, but it's open to the southerly swell that enters during the summer and fall storm season. The pleasant little city of Zihuatanejo (pronounced "see-wah-tah-NAY-ho") has much of interest to long-range cruising boaters and avid sportfishers, many of whom stay for months before heading on. It has a small marina and fuel dock, several places to anchor, a Port Captain and Navy base, an airport, okay provisioning, and plenty of entertainment ashore.

History: The Cuitlateca and Panteca people who lived here for thousands of years were conquered in 1480 by the Aztecs. They called this region "Cihuatlan" – "cihuatl" for woman and "tlan" for place of – the place of women, but the more mystical meaning was the place of the goddess women. In 1522, the first explorers to the Philippines embarked from Bahia Zihuatanejo, but Acapulco soon took over as home port of the famous Manila galleons that followed. After nearly 500 years of slumber, Zihuatanejo was linked to the world of the 1960s by a paved road to Acapulco. Thanks to an international airport, the dazzling white beach at nearby Ixtapa was plastered with high-rise hotels, and then Marina Ixtapa was carved from the mangrove lagoon.

Today Zihuatanejo has nearly 80,000 residents and year-round tourism, but it retains a charming laid-back atmosphere – especially compared with the neon and disco beat of Ixtapa. We know of more than a few single yachtie guys who come to "See-what" and "Stoppa" in pursuit of the legendary goddess women.

Cruising Ports

Zihuatanejo's municipal pier is the landmark in this popular cruising and sportfishing harbor.

Approaches: When arriving from the north, stay outside Isla Grande, Punta Ixtapa, Isla Placer Nuevo, Sacramento Reef and Punta Carrizo. Head in toward Roca Negra Light (GPS: 17°53.57'N by 101°34.00'W), which lies one mile due south of the harbor entrance to Zihuatanejo. Punta Garrobo Lighthouse stands out white and blocky on the cliff at the east side of the mile-wide entrance. It narrows down to half a mile wide, then opens and elongates.

Puerto Mio: The only marina inside Bahia Zihuatanejo is called Puerto Mio. It's located on the western corner of the bay just to port after you enter the bay proper, tucked in south of the big municipal pier. This tiny corner (Playa del Almacen) gets good protection from all sides.

Although there are plans for additional slips and moorings, the marina currently has only 15 slips, the largest being a 100-foot end tie, all with 110-volt and 220-volt power and city water. Some are leased to local excursion and sportfishing boats, so get a reservation long before you show up here. The weekly and monthly rates are a good deal. Or take a chance on a temporary opening. Puerto Mio has a few mooring buoys for rent near the slips. Call "Marina Puerto Mio" on VHF channel 11, or phone toll free (888) 633-3295. Their web page is www.puertomio.com.mx

Puerto Mio's marina has a mini-super, a scuba dive shop, a casual marina cafe and, overlooking Caleta Morro Viejo, one of the finest restaurants in town. Puerto Mio also is a small but very nice hotel, and some suites have private jacuzzis. This would make a nice treat for weary voyagers.

Puerto Mio: Marina and fuel dock are tucked into the sheltered corner of Bahia Zihuatanejo.

Fuel Stop: Puerto Mio has the only fuel dock between Acapulco and Lazaro Cardenas. It's a Pemex fuel dock, but large quantities of fuel need to be ordered in advance, then an appointment is set. Call "Puerto Mio Gas Station" on VHF channel 09. They'll direct you to come alongside the 150-foot dock or whichever end-tie or slip is currently being used for fueling.

Anchorages: The bottom of Zihuatanejo Bay is generally sand and mud with good holding capability. The wind seldom blows during cruising season, but during hurricane season the bay is not protected. The anchorage with the best shelter is on either side of Zihuatanejo's big municipal pier, painted black and white stripes. The best spot to land a dinghy on the town beach is usually just northeast of the pier, which is closest to the center of town.

Other anchorages are in the north end of the bay, west of the little river mouth, or across the bay on the southeast side, off the north end of the big beach called Playa la Ropa. You can land a dinghy almost anywhere along this beach, which has plenty of palapa cafes. Taxis come down from the paved road back to town.

Port Clearance: Puerto Mio marina has the port clearance service for boaters. Or you can handle your own papers fairly easily, because nothing is very far away.

The Port Captain's office and the Aduana's office are just east of the head of the municipal pier. (In the past, so many private dinghies clogged this pier that they prevented local boats from embarking and disembarking passengers, so dinghies were prohibited. We hope this will change soon, but meanwhile, land on the beach adjacent to the pier.) The Navy office is here too.

Zihuatanejo is one of those places where, if you don't check in fairly soon after you anchor, the Port Captain sends out a Navy patrol boat to invite you to do so, pronto. In order to keep this busy bay clean, all visiting yachts are expected to up anchor and go out past Roca Negra every 10 days or so – to pump holding tanks.

Local Services: Zihuatanejo has mechanics for Detroit, Kohler, Volvo and ZF; ask at Puerto Mio. The town has a couple decent grocery stores, and fresh produce from the central market is a few block away. There's a Pemex for jerry jugging closer to the north anchorage. In the center of town the streets are blocked off, allowing pedestrians to stroll freely from one shop to the next. The stretch of beach along the waterfront contains some inexpensive hotels and seafood restaurants.

Barra de Potosi

If you're approaching the Zihuatanejo area from the south, you'll be interested in the marginal anchorage at Barra de Potosi, which lies 11 miles south of Zihuatanejo Bay. The anchorage is open to the north and northwest, and there's just a small village ashore. For boaters spending a lot of time in Zihuatanejo, a day trip down to Potosi makes a good getaway.

Approaches: Barra de Potosi lies at the south end of Bahia Petatlan, which isn't a very deep indentation; it's north end is defined by Roca Negra, the landmark outside Bahia Zihuatanejo, and it's south end is marked by Morro Petatlan and Rocas Potosi. From either direction, these prominent Potosi Rocks look like six giant white elephants frolicking a mile offshore of the green hill of Morro Petatlan. Punta Gorda Light stands on shore, atop Morro Petatlan. You can pass through between

Rocas Potosi and Punta Gorda, because there's deep water all around the elephants. The north side of that pass lies at GPS position 17°32.5'N by 101°28'W.

Anchorage: The anchorage is snuggled in behind the northeast flank of Morro Petatlan. Anchor off the south end of the beach in 20 to 25 feet of water. If you're tucked in close, you can't see the elephants. Otherwise, in very settled weather, this whole long beach backed by coconut groves provides a roadstead. This beach is affected by daily changes of wind and swell direction, so come ashore wherever the pangas do. Most often, it's just south of the old lagoon entrance.

Ashore: This anchorage and the tiny fishing village ashore are named for Rio Potosi and the river bar that at one time gave pangas entrance into Potosi Lagoon, just east of the beach berm. The lagoon entrance is silted closed, but during summer storms and flash flooding the river and lagoon waters overflow here.

The beach contains a hand full of small hotels, and the village offers very few services. A paved road north of the lagoon leads to coastal Highway 200, which has daily bus service into Zihuatanejo.

Barra de Potosi beach is a natural flotsam catch basin, so shelling is good. The beach cafes have been friendly. Fishing and diving are good among the Rocas Potosi. Their name means white friars, but they smell more like elephants due to the white bird droppings.

Isla Grande

If you're approaching the Zihuatanejo area from the north, Isla Grande (17°40'N by 101°40'W) is on your way in. Also known as Isla Ixtapa, it lies a

**Isla Grande & Ixtapa:
The tiny island in the upper center is Isla Grande, and the jetty entrance to Marina Ixtapa is found on the west end of beautiful Ixtapa beach.**

half mile northwest of Punta Ixtapa, about three miles northwest of Marina Ixtapa entrance, and about nine miles northwest of Zihuatanejo.

This tiny island measures only about half a mile wide at the most, but it's a beautiful and protected spot to anchor. If you don't want to hassle with formal port clearance at Zihuatanejo and your stop is a very short one, you can break up your run between Acapulco and Manzanillo by stopping overnight here instead.

Approach: Isla Grande is difficult to see from well out to sea, because it blends in with the nearby mainland. Approach the island from the north, but do not pass between Punta Ixtapa and the island because of rocks.

Anchorages: The island is made up of three small beach-bays: two on the north side and one on the south. You'll want to anchor in either one on the north side. The bottom is good holding ground, and these are fairly protected from the prevailing wind, though a current reaches through. Isla Grande is considered one of the most beautiful anchorages in Mexico. The narrow cove on the south side of Isla Grande contains delicate coral heads, so we don't encourage anchoring there. Instead, come around in the dink to snorkel over the corals.

Local Services: The only service here is food and drink at the beach cafes, and an awkward bus

link to Marina Ixtapa and Zihuatanejo. During the day, hotel-based tourists come out to this island in launches to hike, swim and eat fresh seafood in the palapa restaurants. Fortunately for us boaters, the island has no overnight accommodations, and no one lives on it. A few caretakers and dogs guard the palapas at night. Everyone else departs before dark, leaving the anchored vessels in peace until the thundering herd returns the following morning.

Ashore, a meandering path connects the island's three beaches. The island is partially split by a brilliant coral sand beach with ocean on both sides. The atmosphere of the island is more Caribbean than Pacific. You may resupply from the island by landing your dinghy at the Club Med or at the excursion docks in Playa Quita. Then take a bus or taxi into Marina Ixtapa or Zihuatanejo.

Marina Ixtapa

Marina Ixtapa is a 500-slip full-service marina located about eight miles northwest of Bahia Zihuatanejo. The marina lies inside a man-made basin or "darsena" that was carved into a former lagoon during the early 1990s. Many slips on one or two docks are kept open for marina visitors, but the rest are locally owned. The marina can clear port papers for its guests. The darsena is surrounded by residential villas, cafes,

Marina Ixtapa's landmark lighthouse is visible off shore, marking the east basin. West basin has slips for private villas and small hotels.

boutiques and a golf course. Ixtapa's high-rise hotels and all-night clubs are within walking distance. As we go to press, the fuel dock inside Marina Ixtapa is not working.

Approaches: Marina Ixtapa's entrance jetty (GPS: 17°39.7'N by 101°37.2'W) lies eight miles northwest of Zihuatanejo Bay. From seaward you can see the high-rise hotels of Ixtapa, and the entrance to the marina lies to the left of them, at the foot of a chain of hills that leads west to Punta Ixtapa. (You may see the landmark decorative light tower in the back of the marina.) When coming in from the northwest, beware of one submerged rock within the 20-fathom curve west toward Punta Ixtapa. An approach from the southeast needs to avoid a dangerous reef area called Bajo Sacramento.

The safest approach is from the southwest. Head for Punta Ixtapa, being aware of the submerged rock within the 20-fathom curve. You'll see four small islands called Islas Blancas. Turn between Punta Ixtapa and the inner island of La Concepcion, which lies a half mile due south of the breakwater entrance.

TIP: This breakwater entrance is subject to seasonal shoaling, sometimes as shallow as five feet in spots. A sand shovel dredge sometimes is working here, so be sure to call first to find out the status of the entrance channel. Call "Officina de Marina Ixtapa" on VHF channel 16.

If all's well, just inside the breakwaters there may be several sets of red and green buoys. Head in with red to the right, which should be logical, but it's not always so in some parts of the world. The channel bifurcates a short distance inside the breakwaters. To get to Marina Ixtapa, turn to the right.

The marina monitors VHF channel 16, and the staff members wear blue and white uniforms. Let a staffer direct you to an available slip, usually in the more protected north end of the basin. The docks are well-built in the style of Southern California marinas with substantial floating docks and individual slips. They do have good 220-volt, 50-amp power and potable water. In the clubhouse, the marina office has telephone and fax service for marina guests, plus showers are a washer. A bar and cafe are located inside the lighthouse, and a golf course lies behind the clubhouse.

TIP: At the bifurcation, don't enter the narrower basin to port, because it's a private residential development guarded by armed sentries. We hope that in the future some of those slips may become available as long-term guest slips, but for now it's strictly off limits.

TIP: Don't swim in the marina; it has a few crocodiles, the kind with big pointy teeth and snapping jaws. The "cocodrile" that Pat saw was five feet long and looked well fed. It had its hungry eye on someone's little poodle prancing down the dock. These wild creatures may have been born in this basin when it was a mangrove lagoon. Locals take the cocodriles very seriously; local divers won't clean bottoms inside Marina Ixtapa, so we suggest that you anchor outside the marina before cleaning your bottom.

Local Services: Not everything around Marina Ixtapa is glitzy; if you look hard, you'll find a few modest cafes and a gringo-type convenience store. Most boating services are found in neighboring Zihuatanejo, which is easily accessible by local bus. Catch the bus to "Zihuat" outside the marina, near the traffic circle.

Chapter 30
Marginal Michoacan

〜〜〜〜〜〜〜〜〜〜〜〜〜〜〜〜〜〜〜〜〜〜〜〜〜〜〜

Between the two comfortable and popular cruising ports of Manzanillo and Zihuatanejo, you'll find 187 miles of very rugged coastline – mostly in the state of Michoacan. It's mostly wild jungle cascading down the steep cliffs and vast uncharted lagoons. The best plan is to pass this stretch about five miles off shore.

Along this entire 187-mile stretch, pleasure boaters will find only four very marginal anchorages and one port of limited significance – but NO true cruising ports.

We mention these five locations only to give visiting pleasure boaters some possible "port of refuge" in case of emergencies along this very remote and unforgiving shoreline. Starting from the south, the five Marginal Michoacan locations are:

1.) Lazaro Cardenas, a commercial port and possible emergency hurricane hole.

2.) Caleta de Campos, a marginal anchorage in a small bay and town.

3.) Pechilinguillo or Lizard Bay, a very marginal anchorage, uninhabited, but near a highway.

4.) Muruata, a marginal anchorage in a small bay near a village and highway.

5.) Cabeza Negra, two possible marginal anchorages, near a private club.

Lazaro Cardenas

Pronounced "LA-sah-row, CAR-day-nez," this busy commercial port was named for a beloved president. Lazaro Cardenas lies about 40 miles north of Zihuatanejo. It is a maze of sooty, oily canals and has no facilities for pleasure boats. It's primary purposes are the steel refinery loading docks, the electricity generating plant on the Rio Balsa and the Navy base. Like at Salina Cruz, any vessel that approaches within two miles has to call the traffic control tower on VHF channel 16 and request permission to pass through the deep-water shipping channels or to enter the port. The sea buoy is located at GPS position 17°53.20'N by 102°09.09'W.

Cruisers used to try to sneak into Pesquero Basin, a tiny cove located on the northeast side of the outer entrance channel, about 300 yards inside, but it's now developed into a busy commercial facility, and pleasure

205

boats are not allowed in – except of course if your boat is truly sinking or on fire or you're having a real medical emergency.

Hurricane hole: If you're somehow unwittingly caught in this region during hurricane season, and if a hurricane is approaching, you can call on VHF channel 16 and ask the Port Captain for emergency refuge. You'll probably be directed to enter the outer channel on a heading of 302° and go 1.2 miles to the main turning basin, then turn starboard and go 1.4 miles up the Canal Secondario Industrial Oriente, then turn starboard again and go about another 0.3 of a mile. Once you enter this tertiary channel, you can anchor in 47 to 50 feet of brackish water over soft mud. Mangroves to the north and east, seawall to south and west.

This narrow dead-end canal may well be the safest hurricane hole south of Puerto Vallarta. We've been in here only during calm weather, but a boat would have a half mile of flat land between itself and the stormy seas. Note: whenever the flood gates on the Rio Balsa dam are opened, the water level inside the entire port rises quickly.

Caleta de Campos

Located about 33 miles north of Lazaro Cardenas, the little cove of Caleta de Campos is so difficult to find that most boats go right past – even when they're looking for it. Marginal and rolly as this anchorage may

be, we really like the little town of Caleta de Campos.

You may see town buildings atop the rocky bluff west of the ½-mile-wide cove, which is wide open to the south and southwest. Bufadero Bluff Light (18°04.32'N by 102°45.42'W) stands atop the town bluff. On the east side of that rocky point and about a half mile farther east is the nearly invisible breakwater made of gray concrete and stone. Punta Corolon juts ¼ mile farther south on the cove's eastern side. Palms and a nice sandy beach line the north shore of the cove, and a triangle shaped bolder splits the beach almost in half. (This beach has the most romantic name, Huerta de Luna, orchard of the moon, but it was named that because it used to be an orchard owned by a family named Luna.)

Anchor in 15 to 20 feet of clear water over sand as far behind the stubby breakwater as you can get, but beware of the steep shelf that forms shorebreak. Pangas pull up on the sandy beach behind the breakwater. There's a long flight of stairs leading up to the town, and a sand road behind the palapas goes up.

The Centro de Salud emergency clinic is topside, two blocks west of the Bahia Cafe. A dentist and long-distance telephone office are also found in Caleta de Campos. The locals are very friendly, and if you stay here long enough, they'll show you Cara de Nixon. Life moves very slowly in this remote and isolated town.

If the breakwater is ever extended, we think Caleta de Campos would certainly qualify as a regular "cruising port."

Caleta de Campos: Although a marginal anchorage, the town is pleasant. The small breakwater, shown on the right side here, is hard to see from off shore.

Pechilinguillo Bay

Also known as Lizard Bay or Bahia Lizardo, this tiny spot is easy to miss and probably the most marginal of the Michoacan locations we've mentioned. Located 23 miles north of Caleta de Campos, this bight is open to the south, and the only thing that gives it more shelter than a totally open roadstead is Morro Chino, a large rock off the west end of the beach. If you come to 18°11.5'N by 103°07.5'W, you'll be about between Punta Lizardo and Morro Chino, and about ¾ of a mile off the beach. Anchor in the lee of Morro Chino in about 30 feet of water. Don't try to pass behind Morro Chino with anything larger than a kayak, as that area is foul ground.

Shorebreak can be heavy, and the uninhabited beach is composed of baseball-sized boulders, not easy walking. However, the two-lane coastal Highway 200 passes close behind the east end of this beach, so if you have an emergency, you could thumb a ride south to Caleta de Campos.

TIP: Highway 200 north and south of here has been known for frequent bandito ambushes; even the bus gets held up while all passengers are robbed.

Muruata

Located 14 miles north of Pechilinguillo, the indentation and village of Muruata is only a little less marginal. Stay well outside Piedra Blanca and the vertically fractured rock facade at the GPS position of 18°16.0'N by 103°20.7'W. East of this facade, a long sandy beach and a highway are visible. That's called Muruata Bay, but it's not much more than an open roadstead. The anchorage is off the west end of this beach, tucked in behind the up-ended rocks.

Palms and river willows are visible behind the anchorage, and a small river usually breaches the beach berm. When it's flowing, the pangueros bravely drive their pangas up inside the lagoon. Otherwise, they pull up on the protected corner of the beach. Either way, it's usually a wet landing. Behind the beach, a tiny collection of huts and burro ramadas is scattered among the trees. The only electricity we saw was one lightbulb outside the village's only store, a small Conasupo, which sells rice and beans.

From offshore you may see that an old airstrip lies below the bend in the highway, and some Marine and Navy buildings stand guard over the east end of the airstrip. If you have an emergency, ask the soldiers for help.

Cabeza Negra

Cabeza Negra is a rather significant point of land about 48 miles southeast of Manzanillo, about 29 miles northwest of Muruata.

Punta Cabeza Negra Light stands on the rocky point, and both the northeast and southeast sides of this point have a place for marginal anchoring. The northeast side is much tighter and is developed by a very private club that posts guards and "no trespassing" signs. Look out for their not very well buoyed "shark fence" a few hundred yards off the beach, intended to insure shark-free swimming. By contrast, the southeast side of Cabeza Negra has a 3-mile long undeveloped beach. But from either side, it's a two-mile hike east to the Highway 200.

In northerly weather, pass ¼ mile south of the rock reef on the south side of Cabeza Negra. An old red-brick ruins sits above the anchorage. Anchor off the southeast beach in about 30 feet of water. Our GPS approach waypoint for this anchorage is 18°35'N by 103°42'W.

In southerly weather, pass ½ mile north of the detached rocks off the north side of Cabeza Negra, and anchor in about 30 feet of water off the beach. Emergency access may be granted at a gate on the north end of the beach.

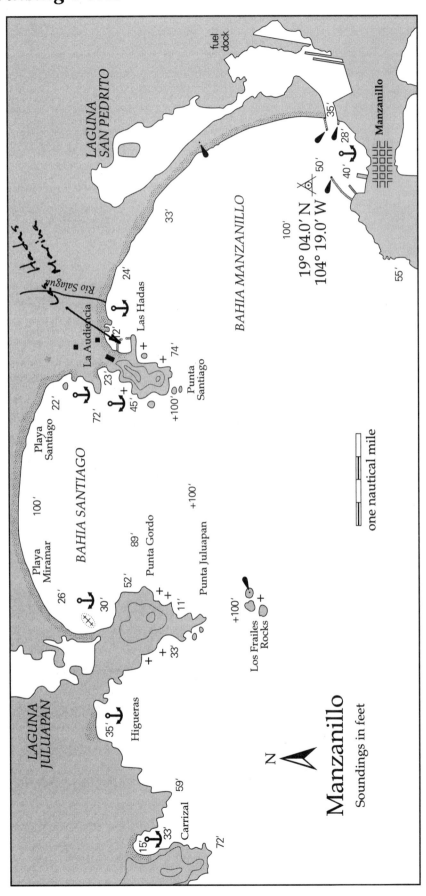

LAGUNA
SAN PEDRITO

fuel
dock

35'

28'

40' 50'

Manzanillo

33'

Rio Salagua

24'

Las Hadas

12'

La Audiencia

+ 74'

+

23'

Punta
Santiago

22'

72' 45' +

+100'

BAHIA MANZANILLO

19° 04.0' N
104° 19.0' W

100'

55'

Playa
Santiago

BAHIA SANTIAGO

100'

89'

Punta Gordo

+100'

Playa
Miramar

52'

26' 30'

11'

+ +

Punta Juluapan

+100'

33'

+ +

Los Frailes
Rocks

+

LAGUNA
JULUAPAN

Higueras

35'

N

59'

Carrizal

15' 33'

72'

Manzanillo
Soundings in feet

one nautical mile

Chapter 31
Manzanillo

〰〰〰〰〰〰〰〰〰〰〰〰〰〰〰〰〰〰〰〰〰〰〰〰〰〰〰〰〰〰〰〰〰〰〰〰〰

In this chapter, we'll focus first on the major cruising port of Manzanillo. In the next chapter, we'll work our way northward through the smaller Gold Coast nuggets.

Manzanillo

The pretty town and port of Manzanillo lies about 120 miles southeast of Cabo Corrientes, is one of the original cruising ports, because it contains the venerable Las Hadas Marina, which was the first marina built for pleasure boats in Mexico. Manzanillo is in the small state of Colima. Several little anchorages lie within the twin-lobed Bahia Manzanillo, and the mid-sized town of Manzanillo has an older and newer inner harbor, both commercial ports, and a Navy base. Manzanillo is a good place to spend some time, to take on fuel and provisions, to pick up or drop off guests, or possibly to leave your boat for a little inland exploration.

Approaches: If you're moving south, the 120-mile stretch southeast from

Cabo Corrientes is loaded with nice stops (See below.), and about 15 miles southeast of Punta Graham you'll find Punta Carrizal, the point of land that forms the eastern edge of the greater Manzanillo area. The next major point is Punta Juluapan, forming Santiago Bay, and ½ mile south of that are three high offshore rocks called Los Frailes. Southeast of Punta Santiago is Bahia Manzanillo proper.

If you're moving north from Zihuatanejo or the Michoacan region, the 40 miles of coastline northwest of Cabeza Negra are flat beach backed by mangrove lagoons and foothills of the Sierra Madre mountains. The first prominent headland is Punta Campos, the point of land that forms the southwestern edge of Bahia Manzanillo. About four miles northwest of Punta Campos you'll see some tall rocks in the north part of Manzanillo Bay, and they're called Los Frailes rocks.

Most boats enter the large and lovely Manzanillo Bay just south of Los Frailes rocks. Our GPS approach waypoint just south of Los Frailes is 19°04'N by 104°24'W.

[handwritten marginalia:] Great Stop
Roberto:
excellent
mechanic from
Colima

209

Las Hadas Marina: The tiny marina at Las Hadas resort hotel is the yachting center of Manzanillo. It's located inside two encircling breakwaters on the east side of Punta Santiago, the next point of land east of Punta Juluapan. The fantastic Moorish-style architecture of towering spires and rabbit warrens climbing the steep hillside was designed by Spaniard Jose Luis Ezquerra and developed by Antenor Patino, a wealthy tin magnate. "Las Hadas" means the fairies, and it refers to an ancient Moorish fairly tale long told to Spanish children. This fairy tale setting of lavish restaurants and swimming pools with swings and swim up bars normally caters to jet setters, not their children. The movie "10" was filmed here.

Las Hadas docks have 110-volt and 220-volt power, city water for wash downs and filtered water for drinking. Showers and laundry are available through the marina office, located in the opposite corner of the basin from the entrance. Ask about fees for using certain hotel facilities. Although Las Hadas marina lies only about three miles northwest of Manzanillo's commercial harbors, the cab ride around the bay to town is about eight miles. (The fuel dock near the marina entrance is not in operation as we go to press.)

Anchorages and Moorings: You can swing from one of the marina's 20 moorings just west of the entrance jetties and use the marina's protected dinghy dock.

Pool @ resort w/ Bar in pool ! ≠ ✗

Las Hadas: Fairytale architecture and a breakwater surround this small marina. Manzanillo lies across the bay.

If you have trouble finding the marina, call "Las Hadas Marina" on VHF channels 09, 69 or 16. The outer end of the north jetty into Las Hadas marina lies at GPS position 19°05.97'N by 104°20.68'W. Inside you'll find low floating docks circling the small basin, but you must Med-moor (25 feet depth in center of basin) to them and use stern fenders and spring lines against the surge that makes its way inside. There's room for a good 45 long-range sportfishers and cruising boats, and it gets filled up during cruising season, especially if race boats are in town.

Call "Marina Las Hadas" on VHF channel 09 or 69 to request an available mooring.

Or six places to anchor provide lots of alternatives.

Starting from the northwest, the first place to anchor is a narrow cut inside steep-sided Caleta Carrizal. Punta Carrizal forms the west wall of this cove. Anchor in 15 to 33 feet off the small beach in the head of the cove. This is well protected from the southwest, north and northeast. This place is best for boats with good sized dinghies, because it's a 3.5-mile ride to the marina or a 6.5-mile ride to Manzanillo proper.

Bahia Higueras is the next little bay east, but it's wide open to the south. Our favorite anchorage is off the small beach at the low head of this bay. Anchor in about 35 feet of water.

Next east, Bahia Santiago is the twin bay to Manzanillo Bay. Santiago Bay has at least three places to anchor: the first is north of Punta Gorda and off the entrance to Laguna Juluapan. Two more places in the east end of Santiago Bay are south of La Audiencia beach (big hotel), also west of the little beach-hotel community of Playa Santiago.

Bahia Manzanillo is a pleasant place for wind surfing, especially during the afternoons near the headlands of the bay entrance. Try anchoring off any one of the bay's beaches and enjoy a swim in the clear water. Landing a dinghy presents challenges in the ever-present surf.

The last, but not least, place to anchor is inside the old port of Manzanillo. It's located in the southeast corner of Bahia Manzanillo, protected by a tall rock breakwater. It's slightly open only to the north but still gets some protection from Playa Las Brisas beach to the north. Anchor in about 20 feet of water east of the high concrete pier, but stay clear of the ship maneuvering areas. The holding seems pretty good, because we rode out a hurricane watch here. You can land your dinghy at the concrete quay at the foot of the town plaza or at a any of several waterfront restaurants much closer to the anchorage. The old port anchorage is closest to the Port Captain's office and all town services, but it's subject to ship wakes, car noise and shore lights. Someday, pleasure boats may not be allowed to anchor here.

Old and New Ports: The original or old port (above) was formed south of the town breakwater, and it's a small and busy basin on the north side of the town of Manzanillo, which covers Punta Campos north of Cuyutlan Lagoon and spreads east and northeast, behind San Pedrito. Some local sportfishing docks are located along the east side of the old port. Manzanillo does not depend principally on tourism; it's a picturesque but businesslike Mexican port.

The new port was carved into the huge San Pedrito Lagoon, and its wide jetty lined opening is just east of the old port. This lagoon runs behind Playa Las Brisas for about three miles northeast of the town, but the shallow upper end is still being dredged. The fuel dock for pleasure boats is now located inside San Pedrito Lagoon. Across from the Port Captain's office is the Manzanillo Oceanographic Institute and the Navy base. Large ships use the container off-loading facilities in San Pedrito, too.

Port Clearance: Las Hadas marina office can clear papers for their guests, or you can do your own. On the south side of the entrance to the lagoon is a large concrete building containing all the offices necessary for port clearance: Capitania, Migracion, Aduana. Because all of the offices are in one place, this is perhaps the easiest port in Mexico to clear. The port charges a small amount for harbor use, which you pay at an office just across the street. Ask the Port Captain for permission to take fuel.

Fuel Stop: Manzanillo's fuel prices are the cheapest in all of Mexico, especially for larger quantities. On a recent port call, we paid 80 cents per gallon.

The nice new concrete fuel dock is located in the northwest end of the huge San Pedrito Lagoon, most of which has been dredged out for ships. This is really the new port of Manzanillo. Enter through

Cruising Ports

Anchorage area at Las Hadas is just outside the breakwater.

the wide channel lined by riprap jetties. You'll pass the Capitania, the Navy docks and many commercial piers. The concrete dock used for fueling yachts and small ships lies more than a mile up in the northwest corner, and it has black and white stripes. Depths go from 30 to 12 feet at the white mid-channel buoy 200 yards from the fuel dock. The fuel dock has two pumps, large black rubber fenders and big bollards far apart. Have your largest fenders and longest lines ready. At low tide, some low freeboards may be below the concrete.

Town Services: For an emergency haul-out, there's a 200-ton crane in San Pedrito Lagoon. For simple marine stuff, like cordage, anchors and chain, diesel and water pumps, refrigeration parts, you'll find most of the small "ferreterias" or hardware stores in the vicinity of the Port Captain's office, on south Madrid, and in the downtown area. Banks, laundromats and phone offices are not hard to find, either. The local propane is called Impulsora de Gas Pemex.

Manzanillo has one of the nicest plazas we've seen, full of shade trees, flower gardens and lacy iron benches. Near the dinghy landing on the east side of the plaza you'll find an ice cream parlor were you can make long-distance phone calls. Avenida Mexico, the main drag, runs south from the southwest corner of the plaza.

Along this street you will find more shops, pharmacies, parts stores and repair shops. The Hotel Colonial on this same street and not far from the plaza has a good restaurant and is a moderately priced place to stay.

The Comercial Mexicana grocery store on Madrid road between Las Hadas and Manzanillo is the best place to provision, because it has good selection and prices for staples, produce and miscellaneous housewares. It's located in a small shopping center on the west side of the road. Otherwise, the mercado central farmers' market on Calle Cinco de Mayo is the next best place to provision, open 6 a.m. to 1 p.m. From the plaza, it's four blocks south on Avenida Mexico and about four blocks east. For smaller orders, immediately outside the entrance to Las Hadas' main gate is the Servi Super Mercado. It's clean and well stocked including good meats, fresh produce, an excellent selection of fruits and some wines. They usually deliver to the marina.

History: Noted and charted by Hernan Cortes in the early 1500s, Bahia Manzanillo played an important part in early explorations. Juan Rodriguez Cabrillo set sail from Navidad, just north of Manzanillo, in a fleet of ships that were the first European vessels built in the Pacific. He went on to discover San Diego in 1542. Lopez de Legaspi departed Manzanillo westbound in 1549 with part of the same original fleet. He discovered the Philippines and opened up the Oriental trade route between Manila and Acapulco.

The bay was named for the manzanillo fruit trees that at one time grew wild here. In some farms, the small red and yellow fruit (like "manzana" – apple) was cultivated as feed for goats, but was poisonous to humans. True apples don't grow at this latitude at sea level.

Chapter 32
Gold Coast Nuggets

In this chapter, we'll be working our way northward and looking at
1.) Navidad
2.) Tenacatita
3.) Careyes
4.) Chamela
5.) Ipala
We'll end this chapter just south of Cabo Corrientes.

What is the Gold Coast? The entire 55-mile coastline from Chamela southeast to Manzanillo is usually considered the Mexican "Gold Coast" cruising ground. The weather during winter and spring cruising season is usually the most pleasant and benign of all the places mentioned in this book. Dozens of little nuggets, idyllic spots to drop the hook and spend some time, superb sportfishing and scuba and snorkel diving opportunities, are what make visiting boaters give this stretch its Gold Coast reputation. Most of the tourist development has been small and mid sized, so the Madre y Padre hotels and shore services are still the norm.

Since the marinas at Puerto Vallarta and Zihuatanejo were built, many long-range boaters consider everything from Banderas Bay down to Zihuatanejo to be part of their Gold Coast cruising grounds.

Weather: As you head northwest from Manzanillo, the wind can pick up from the northwest, but it doesn't blow strongly until you round Cabo Corrientes (20°24'N by 105°43'W). All these are well-protected anchorages in the winter and spring. But, with the exception of the lagoon at Navidad, all these places are exposed to southerly wind and swell in the summer and fall. Laguna Navidad is the most protected, then the inner anchorage of Tenacatita. Careyes becomes very rolly inside from the swell generated by northwesterlies. The Gold Coast is not a place to visit during hurricane season.

Navidad

Located 25 miles northwest of Manzanillo, this Navidad cruising port includes the outer bay of Bahia Navidad, the little sand-spit town of Barra Navidad,

Cruising Ports

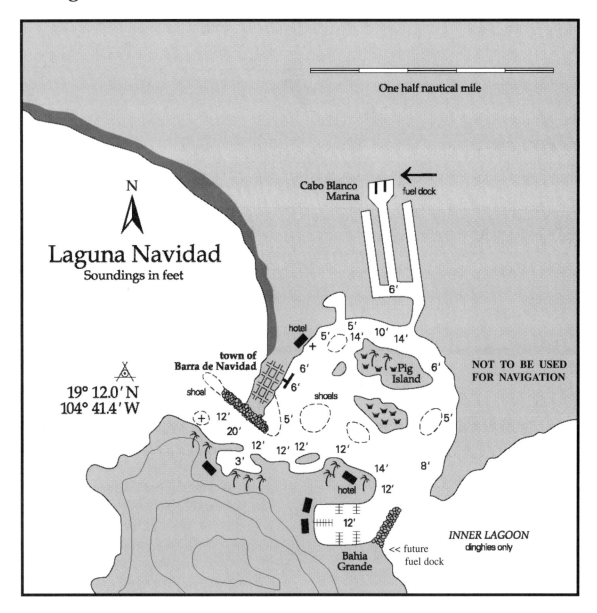

which has a Port Captain, and the inner lagoon called Laguna Navidad, which has two small marinas. Navidad is pronounced "nah-vee-DAHD."

Bahia Navidad is a 7-mile-wide indentation between tall Punta Graham on the southeast and Cabeza de Navidad on the northwest, but the best place for all-around overnight anchoring is inside the beach-lined eastern portion, tucked in north of Bahia Point (19°13'N by 104°43'W). On the north shore, the village of Melaque (pronounced "may-LAH-kay") celebrates Saint Patrick's Day (their patron saint) big

time, and visiting boaters are welcome – some folks even plan their itinerary to be in Navidad by March 17th for the fiestas.

Approaches: Barra Navidad, the town on the eastern shore of this bay, covers the narrow sand-spit that divides the bay from the lagoons to the east, and also climbs the foothills to the north. Visit the Port Captain here for a paper stamp. On the sand-spit, you'll find one small marine hardware store, phone booths, a small grocery store and several nice cafes. Shorebreak sometimes hits the outer or west side of the

214

Dinghies land here, in the middle of downtown Barra Navidad.

sand-spit. The easiest way to get ashore to explore the town is by coming through the main entrance (12-foot least depth, but there's a migrating 6-foot spot, so ask the Port Captain first) and landing a dinghy on the protected east side of the sand-spit. Our GPS approach waypoint just outside this entrance channel is 19°12'N by 104°41.4'W.

Laguna Navidad: Laguna Navidad, for our definition, is everything between the entrance channel eastward to the next entrance into the shallow back lagoon. In the very first lagoon you enter, its whole south and north sides are developed, but there are several shoals and brush-covered islands. The back side of the town of Barra Navidad is easily reached by some concrete stairs in the northwest corner of this lagoon, and, combined with the dinghy tie up, this makes a good meeting place for groups of boaters going ashore.

You'll find two marinas reached off this lagoon. The older and smaller Cabo Blanco Marina lies off the north side of this lagoon, up a series of narrow man-made channels (6-foot least

depth) between vacation homes. The first channel lead north behind the east end of Pig Island. When this channel splits, bear left, then take the next right to reach Marina Cabo Blanco. You can see the roof of the shore building. It's a private club for smaller local power boats, but it has a diesel dock. (Another smaller basin northwest of Pig Island is slated for a future marina.)

The larger newer marina for visiting cruising yachts, called Isla Navidad or Marina Puerto de la Navidad, lies in front of the Hotel Bahia Grande (Grand Bay Hotel) on the south side of Navidad's 1st lagoon. A buoyed channel leads you to their palm-fringed darsena. This marina has 207 full-service slips, 30-, 50- and 100-amp shore power, phone and cable on the docks. Least depth is 12 feet. Call "Marina Puerto

Marina Cabo Blanco, up the canals in the north end of the lagoon, has a fuel dock.

Bahia Grande's nice new marina has end ties for 150-footers, and their fuel dock will be just outside the marina.

de la Navidad" on VHF channel 16 to check slip availability. Even some 150-foot megayachts use these end ties. For daily and monthly rates, call toll free in the U.S. (888) 804-7263. Or the marina's number is 011-52 (335) 5-59-50. As we go to press, their diesel dock just beyond the marina hadn't opened yet.

The next lagoon east is shallow, but pangas and dinghies can follow the south shoreline to a dozen palapa eateries. This back lagoon is great for shallow-draft multihulls, kayaking and bird watching.

Tenacatita

Located about 30 miles north of Manzanillo, 80 miles south of Cabo Corrientes, and 17 miles south of Careyes, the 4-mile-wide Bahia Tenacatita is a fine deep indentation into this lush and hilly coastline. Cabeza Navidad is the southeast edge and Punta Hermanos is the northwest edge.

Tenacatita is becoming famous for its Jungle River Ride, a pleasant little dinghy adventure up the Rio Boca las Iguanas, which meanders beneath a canopy of mangrove trees beyond the north end of the bay. We had fun charting the main channel of this Rio Boca las Iguanas with a recording GPS.

Approach and Anchorages: Our GPS waypoint in the middle of the Tenacatita Bay is 19°16'N by 104°50'W. The best all-around overnight anchorage (call it "A") is about ½ mile northeast of Punta Chubasco, the taller point of land about 2.2 miles east of Punta Hermanos. (Roca Central is quite obvious and has deep water all around.) Here, you can anchor right off the entrance to Rio Boca las Iguanas, in 12 to 30 feet of water, being aware of the little reef or bar off the river. The palm oasis ashore is a pleasant campground.

Other anchorages are off the sandy beach behind (northeast of) Punta Hermanos and its detached rock formation called Las Escolleras, in 20 to 30 feet of water. The beach has palms and a string of friendly palapa cafes. This "B" anchorage is more open to any south swell.

In front of the town of Tenacatita, you can anchor in 30 feet of water and land on the beach for going ashore. This location and farther south along the Tamarindo shore are better in southerly weather than across the bay. The pretty town climbing the hills has a few groceries and lots of restaurants that cater to the dozen or so small and mid-sized hotels scattered around the bay. But there're no port authorities to check in with.

Jungle River Ride: The Jungle River Ride is fun for two or three dinghy loads. Start in the morning with the tide half and rising. It can be done in as little as three hours, and you can't really get lost, (but do be out before dark). Larger dinghies may need to be helped over the bar, though inside depths are 4- to 15-feet. Colorful birds, butterflies and iguanas dart through the lush foliage, and tendrils of aerial roots dangle down from the green canopy overhead, creating a cool twilight, touching the mirror clear water. Lots of side loops and dead-end channels may encourage friendly ambushes by others in your dinghy party. Two miles upstream, the main channel Ts. If you turn right, the lagoon shallows out after another mile or so. If you turn left, at the south end of the lagoon you'll see palms and a beach – the same beach that backs "B" anchorage. It makes a great cerveza stop and turn around point.

Careyes

Pronounced "kah-RAY-yayz," this intimate little anchorage is located 42 miles north of Manzanillo, about a mile north of Punta Farralon, and about 75 miles south of Cabo Corrientes.

This little nugget is the crown jewel in the Gold Coast – visually at least. Its two little pocket anchorages provide decent protection from north and northwest wind, but any swell from the west and south makes its way inside. And it's tight – room for five or six good-sized cruising boats plus a local boat or two.

Approach and Anchorages: Our approach GPS waypoint (19°26.4'N by 105°02.5'W) lets you see the buoyed rock, the 053°M range markers, the offshore islet and all three lobes of Careyes. First time, jog in place until you get the lay of the land. The former Club Med in the north lobe may get renovated, but for now they don't welcome visitors to their dock.

Our favorite place is off Playa Rosa, the next lobe east; it contains palms trees, a stunning beach and a friendly restaurant. Anchor off this beach in 18 to 26 feet of crystal water.

A third choice is just south of the range marker, off the beach of the Hotel Bel Air in 20 to 29 feet of water. From here you can swim over and snorkel the little reef adjacent to the hotel's roped-off swimming beach. (For a day fee, visiting yachters can use the hotel's pools overlooking the whole anchorage, two restaurants, air-conditioned child care, spa, gym, etc. Just be sure to cut your dinghy motor before you enter their swimming beach.)

Endangered Sea Turtles: Playa Careyito a mile south of the Bel Air is where the endangered Careyes sea turtles return to lay their eggs. Landing ashore is strictly prohibited, but sometimes you can visit or help the naturalists who work here by going with a hotel staffer. Playa Careyito is on the west flank of Punta Farralon.

Chamela

Northernmost of the four smaller Gold Coast nuggets, Chamela is located about 60 miles south of Cabo Corrientes, 52 miles north of Manzanillo, so it's the first Gold Coast nugget you'll encounter when coasting south. Bahia Chamela (pronounced "chah-MAY-lah") is the 4-mile-wide indentation immediately southeast of Punta Rivas – easily identified on all charts.

Approach and Anchorages: During the winter-spring cruising season, the best all-around overnight anchorage at Chamela is tucked in behind (northeast of) Punta Perula, a lesser chunk of Punta Rivas. Our GPS approach waypoint is 19°33'N by 105°07'W. Give the headland a half mile berth as you round it, then come north to the west end of the sandy beach. You can drop the hook in 24 to 36 feet of crystal clear water. In summer rainy season, a stream cuts across the berm here. This anchorage offers only mediocre shelter from southwest swell that might develop in summer.

Seven small islands are scattered along the middle and south half of Bahia Chamela. The two larger islands in the center of the bay are Isla Pasavera and Isla Colorado. On the more protected east and south sides of these two islands, you'll find three small beaches, each providing a possible anchorage for a boat under 60 feet in length. Pick your way in from the southwest, between these two islands.

Even if you anchor in the north end of Chamela Bay, the Pasavera and Colorado islands provide excellent small-boat fishing among the 20- to 60-foot-deep, rocky bottomed passages between the islands. Sailfish and other warm-water species are the attraction here, because right outside the bay you're only 3 miles from deep coastal waters that run northward with the warm Equatorial current.

Scuba and snorkel divers floating on crystal-clear water are usually enchanted by the volcanic and coral formations surrounding not only Pasavera and Colorado, but also the lesser islands in the south end of the bay: Islas Cocina, Augustin, Pedro, Andres and Negrita.

You'll see a few houses and palm-roofed cafes (palapas) on the shore behind the lesser island, and a gravel road leads to the village of Chamela a few miles inland. There's no Port Captain here. Don't look for any marine services in this remote outpost; for simple parts or hardware, head down to Barra Navidad, and the nearest diesel dock for big boats or sail boats is in Manzanillo.

Ipala

Northernmost of the places mentioned in this chapter, the small anchorage at Ipala (pronounced "ee-PAH-lah") is merely a possible stepping stone north or south, not a cruising port in its own right. Located 48 miles north of Chamela and only 13 miles south of Cabo Corrientes, the shelter from northwest winds that Ipala offers may help northbound boaters who are

waiting to round that blustery cape during the pre-dawn hours. And a stop at Chamela breaks up the southbound run to the Gold Coast destinations mentioned above.

If you're northbound, the only feature between Chamela and Ipala that requires attention is Roca Negra, which lies one mile off shore about 18 miles north of Chamela. The south-facing bight of Ipala is marked by Ipala Light on a 315-foot headland and then a village, road scar and dark tan beach to the east of the headland.

If you're southbound, Cerro Ipala with the navigation light makes a good radar target. Come around to the south and east of the point to enter the lee. Our GPS waypoint just 0.2 of a mile east of Ipala Light is 20°14.1'N by 105°34.3'W.

TIP: A dangerous unmarked submerged rock pinnacle lies at GPS position 20°14.23'N by 105°43.31'W, which is about 75 yards off a small rock pile in the east wall. It's covered by only two feet of water at low tide, but has 24 feet all around it. We named it "Roca Heddy" in memory of a friend's boat that "discovered" it 20 years ago.

You can anchor in 20 to 30 feet of water off the stone ruins of the old pier. This is where the pangas pull out. Otherwise, we found a 15-foot spot off the two "A" shaped rocks farther out on the east wall, which is okay in very settled weather and farther from the village.

Ipala has no services for visiting boats; it's an 8-hour drive on rugged dirt roads to the nearest town, Yelapa in Banderas Bay. That road starts at the panga beach. The village of Ipala is so isolated that it's one of those places where we try to drop off school supplies for the children.

Chapter 33
Banderas Bay

In this chapter, we'll look at the points of interest around the large and important bay called Banderas Bay. (Puerto Vallarta is covered in the next chapter.)

Banderas Bay

Bahia Banderas is the large bay in which Puerto Vallarta lies, and it is lined with interesting villages and anchorages enjoyed by visiting yachts. For sportfishing, the season is year round. The opening of Banderas Bay is 20 miles from Punta Mita in the north to Cabo Corrientes in the southwest. From the Tres Mariettas islands to Puerto Vallarta is 17 miles east to west.

Approaches: From Cabo San Lucas on the Baja peninsula to Punta Mita on Banderas Bay is 276 nautical miles of unprotected water. From Cabo, boaters can lay a course of 108°M for passage into Banderas Bay between Punta Mita and the small Islas Tres Mariettas (Three Mariettas), which stays the minimum 20-mile distance off the larger prison-colony islands en route, called the Islas Marias

(Maria Islands); it also keeps them four miles north of Roca Corbetena and its smaller brother. Beware of getting set south. Our GPS approach waypoint for this passage is 20°45'N by 105°40'W.

Because many boaters entering Banderas Bay from the north or northwest will come between Punta Mita and the small Tres Mariettas Islands, they should be aware of two dangerous submerged (about three feet; break only occasionally) pinnacle rocks that lie within that passage. Favor the Mariettas side of the channel to miss them.

    1.) 20°45.61'N by 105°32.89'W
    2.) 20°45.64'N by 105°33.16'W

If you're approaching Banderas Bay from the south by rounding Cabo Corrientes, be aware that this major headland can be affected by "cape effect" wind. You may want to use Ipala (See Chapter 32.) as a staging ground to round Cabo Corrientes in the pre-dawn hours – when the cape winds are generally less strong. Mixing currents off Corrientes can create turbulent seas even when there's no wind.

Points of Interest: Moving clockwise around the jungle-clad shoreline of Banderas Bay, the primary points of interest for visiting boaters are:

Las Mariettas Islands
Punta Mita
La Cruz
Nuevo Vallarta
Rio Ameca
Puerto Vallarta harbor entrance
Los Arcos
Mismaloya
Tomatlan
Las Animas
Quimixto
Yelapa
Cabo Corrientes

Las Mariettas Islands

These small barren islands are most notable for their great scuba diving and hiking, but they don't provide good overnight anchorages if the weather is anything less than very settled. Navigation lights stand atop both of the two larger Mariettas.

Located about four miles southwest of Punta Mita, the larger and southwesternmost of the two big islands has the easiest access ashore for hiking, but it has only a marginal anchorage because it's deep so close to shore. You can anchor off the series of caves and arches on the southeast face of this island, about 50 yards off shore in 35 feet of water. Although a wide variety of sea-bird nesting grounds are easily accessible here, it's best not to walk among them; use only your binoculars and long camera lenses. Eggs and nestlings touched by humans are abandoned and die.

The smaller Marietta is closer to Punta Mita. It's favored by scuba divers as a good spot for drift diving along the sheer walls on the east side. Sportfishermen find the entire area productive. The smallest Marietta island lies 3.8 miles west of the largest island, and between the two lies a rock pile.

Punta Mita

This low narrow headland 20 miles northwest of Puerto Vallarta forms the northwest arm of Banderas Bay is called Punta Mita (pronounced "MEE-tah"), and it carries Punta Mita Light. In the lee south of its 454-foot-high elongated cone-shaped hills, the large and popular anchorage at Punta Mita enjoys excellent protection from prevailing northwest and north winds of the winter and spring seasons. However, Punta Mita anchorage is open to the southwest and south.

Punta Mita's 2-mile sandy beach has scads of little seafood cafes and bikini bars under palm-frond roofs, plus several newer resort hotels. You can anchor almost anywhere off this tourist beach in from 15 to 36 feet of water over good-holding sand and shell.

Playa Punta Mita is a very popular sunbathing and swimming beach, and we've had swimmers hang onto our anchor chain for a few minutes, to catch their breath before swimming back to shore. Anchor farther out on weekends or holidays if jet boats become troublesome. Shore services are limited to a few convenience stores. Punta Mita offers no real boating services, except perhaps an emergency ration of cold beverages. Beach games are popular.

Many boats hang out at Punta Mita, keeping in touch with their brethren inside Puerto Vallarta marinas via cell phones or the weekday VHF net. For the Punta Mita section of the net, usually one or two boats with strong signals can relay messages from their neighbors. A daily bus makes the 20-mile run east to Puerto Vallarta, and it stops at La Cruz de Huanacaxtle, the next anchorage east.

Nuevo Vallarta or El Norte or Marina Vallarta North is a smaller harbor, not actually in Puerto Vallarta.

La Cruz

Located about half way between Punta Mita and Puerto Vallarta, the small fishing village of La Cruz de Huanacaxtle has another popular anchorage outside its small breakwater, but most of the inner bay behind the breakwater is either shoal or crowded with local boat and their moorings. Our GPS position for the seaward end of La Cruz's breakwater is 20°44.93'N by 105°22.80'W.

You can anchor just east of the tip of the breakwater in 15 to 20 feet of water. If rain or darkness obscure your approach to this anchorage area, be aware of the partially submerged wreck about ¾ of a mile southeast of the tip of the breakwater.

Concrete piers inside the inner bay are usually reserved for local fishing boats to pick up and drop off passengers from the hotels. A panga haul-out ramp crosses the west end of the inner bay; dinghies are pulled up all along the sandy shoreline to the north and east of there. A few beach cafes, grocery stores and telephones are the main attraction ashore. The daily bus between Punta Mita and Puerto Vallarta stops at La Cruz.

For smaller boats, two other anchorages are available west of La Cruz. A sandy beach lines this whole region east of Punta Piedra Blanca, and you can anchor in 10 to 15 feet of water over good holding sand in either of the two scallop shaped beaches west of La Cruz breakwater.

Nuevo Vallarta

Located about 3.5 miles northwest of Puerto Vallarta, this smaller man-made harbor contains a smaller Marina Vallarta Norte (dubbed "El Norte" to avoid confusion with the larger Marina Vallarta inside Puerto Vallarta's municipal harbor). Nuevo Vallarta contains 70 slips for boats up to 43 feet in length. The concrete diesel dock inside this harbor is still not operational as we go to press.

With only a verbal description, first timers often mistake this entrance, and to go east of it puts you onto the shoal at Rio Ameca. Our GPS approach waypoint for entering the riprap jetties into this smaller harbor is 20°41.2'N by 105°17.9'W.

If the short entrance channel has recently been dredged, it has a 10-foot least depth, but silting after any heavy rain is a long term problem here, often building up a 5-foot mud bar across the entrance channel. Inside depths range from six to 14 feet.

Once you're inside, the channel bends north and aims you at the newer floating dock for PWCs, sail cats, water-ski boats and charter dive-fish boats for their hotel guests. The harbor opens up north end east from the entrance channel. Marina Vallarta Norte's docks lie to starboard, and the office is in the building at the head of the concrete pier. The dockmaster monitors VHF channel 16 and can help clear your papers, or you can get a taxi and handle your own clearance procedures. Because this harbor lies within the state of Nayarit, it has a different Port Captain than does Puerto Vallarta, which is in Jalisco. It's also a different time zone. If you're also visiting Puerto Vallarta, you'll have to clear in there too.

Rio Ameca Shoal: This hazard to navigation extends up to one mile off shore starting less than ¼ mile east of the entrance to "El Norte" or Marina Vallarta Norte. It's created by the silty outflow of the Rio Ameca, the Ameca River, which washed down from the high hills surrounding the north side of Banderas Bay.

Puerto Vallarta's municipal harbor entrance

A racon "K" guides you to the jetty lined entrance channel into the big municipal harbor that is home to the major marina, fuel dock, haul-out yard, etc. Our GPS approach waypoint about ¼ mile offshore of this large entrance is 20°39'N by 105°15'W.

See Chapter 34 on Puerto Vallarta for the complete description.

Los Arcos

Named for the many arches and caves that lie above and below sea level, Los Arcos is an underwater park. Located 6.5 miles south of Puerto Vallarta on the south side of Banderas Bay, this collection of five giant boulders provides two small anchorages for daytime play in settled weather, not overnighting.

If you're careful to approach when no scuba divers are down here, you could anchor northeast of the largest rock in about 43 feet of crystal clear water over white sand and rocks. The other place we've anchored is in 40 feet of water over rock, east of the navigable slot between the biggest rock and the next smaller one, which lies closer to shore. If you block this slot, excursion boats blasting through will probably make you uncomfortable – and vice versa.

Don't pass between shore and Los Arcos in anything but a kayak or dinghy. The rocky bottom is great for scuba diving and snorkeling toward the beach. Strong swimmers can make it to the nearby shore from the anchored boats – and vice versa.

Mismaloya

Pronounced "meez-mah-LOY-ah," this pretty little beach cove seven miles south of Puerto Vallarta became famous when Liz Taylor and Richard Burton filmed the steamy classic "Night of the Iguana" here for director John Houston, who had a vacation home nearby. The stone ruins and stairs of their fictional hotel scenes are still visible among the weeds on the south arm of this bay. Hollywood celebrities still show up from time to time, at the big hotels and giant archway that mark this popular crescent-shaped swimming beach.

As an anchorage, Mismaloya ranges from marginal to miserable. We've always anchored here stern in, bow out from the short sandy shelf close to the shorebreak, because the bottom drops off steeply. The west side is more protected. Our GPS waypoint for this anchorage is 20°31.99'N by 105°17.61'W. This may serve as a photogenic place to bring guests, and it's within sight of Los Arcos (above), but with all the shore activity, it's not a quiet anchorage.

Tomatlan

Bahia Tomatlan is located only about 2.5 miles west of Mismaloya, about eight miles southwest across Banderas Bay from Puerto Vallarta. This idyllic little bay is a ¼-mile deep indentation into the south side of the larger Banderas Bay, the next best bay to Yelapa (below). Backed by steep green hills and a small beach, the eastern side of this 100-meter wide entrance is flanked by a split-level hotel climbing the boulders. Again, the anchorage is as steep and deep as Mismaloya, but the bay's protection is much better.

You can anchor is about 50 feet of water off the middle of the beach. Several small hotels at Tomatlan use pangas and other small boats catering to sportfishers.

Las Animas

John Houston kept a tropical retreat at Las Animas, a fine stone and brick home. Las Animas translates to "the spirits," but it has a slightly pagan overtone, as in restless spirits or ghosts.

In truth, Las Animas is not much better than an open roadstead with a narrow anchoring shelf next to really deep water. But that's why the fishing is so spectacular here. The small fishing piers along the beach occasionally have room for visiting yachts. Otherwise, you'll have to find room to anchor between the private moorings – or ask about renting one for a week or so. We've anchored in about 50 feet of water at a

Dinghy landing helps inside Yelapa bay, which can get surge from the north.

GPS position of 20°30.55'N by 105°20.68'W.

Quimixto

Located about 2.25 miles farther west than Las Animas on the south side of Banderas Bay, the little dent known as Quimixto is even smaller than Las Animas, but its anchoring shelf is slightly wider and less crowded with tourist boats. The village wedged between hills at the back of the little bay is quite remote.

We've anchored in 25 to 30 feet of clear water (winter cruising season) off Quimixto beach, at a GPS position of 20°30.36'N by 105°22.19'W. If a north wind is blowing, this anchorage isn't great. In summer rainy season, the river fills the lagoon behind this beach and breaches the berm out to sea, clouding the waters and carrying lots of debris from the jungle inland.

Several more indentations dot the south side of Banderas Bay between Quimixto and Yelapa, but as anchorages they're too marginal to mention.

Yelapa

The old saying goes, "A palapa in Yelapa beats a condo in Redondo," referring to the contrast between this laid-back hippie hang-out (no road or electricity until recently) and the jiving jet set scene of Redondo Beach, California.

Pronounced "yah-LAH-pah," this exquisitely green and turquoise bay is the largest indentation in the south side of Banderas Bay. It's located about 14.5 miles southwest of Puerto Vallarta and 16 miles northeast of Cabo Corrientes. Our GPS approach waypoint to enter Yelapa Bay is 20°30.0'N by 105°27.0'W.

Unfortunately, Yelapa's mile-wide U-shaped bay is open to the northwest, not as sheltered by Punta Mita as are some of the locations east of here. So as an anchorage, it's a rather indifferent day stop in settled weather. The middle of the bay is very deep. In winter cruising season, the best place to anchor is tucked down into the southeast corner of the bay, off the east end of the main beach, in 25 to 30 feet of clear water over rock and white sand. Ashore you'll see the concrete dinghy landing pier among the trees and a string of cabanas.

Other places to anchor in Yelapa Bay are off the village in the southwest corner of the bay, beyond the moorings for local pangas, and out along the steep west wall.

The beach is not fine sand, so take foot-gear ashore. This beach is where all the action is – from American-style pies to tie-dyed T-shirts – all hoping to sell something to the boat loads of tourists that come out from Puerto Vallarta and disembark ungracefully across the beach.

A seasonal lagoon lies behind the beach berm, and in rainy season it gushes out across the south end of the beach. Right there you'll see the children's diving rock, dividing the beach from the village shoreline. Behind the village there's a trail that leads up to a couple waterfalls in a jungle setting. These river banks afford one of the most idyllic, primitive scenes in Latin America.

Cabo Corrientes

This major headland marks the southwest approach into Banderas Bay and carries the Cabo Corrientes Light. "Corrientes" means currents, and it's where local wind and sea currents get amplified and mixed. So it's not a place you'd want to hang out. Generally pleasure boats want to stay at least a half mile off when rounding this cape.

However, Cabo Corrientes does contain a tiny cove that might serve as an emergency anchorage in summer rainy season. Corrientes Cove is located just east-northeast of the lighthouse, and it has a narrow opening – albeit open to the north. Sometimes a few pangas haul up on the rocky shingle at the back of this cove. The sides of this narrow cove are steep rock cliffs, and we don't know of any road out from here.

Chapter 34
Puerto Vallarta

Thanks to its sheltered marinas, fuel dock, haul-out yard, annual boat show, fishing tournaments, hurricane protection, pleasant year-round temperatures and myriad boating services, the town of Puerto Vallarta (20°37'N by 105°16'W) has become the largest vortex of boating activity on the Pacific side of Mexico. It has long been a romantic destination for land-based fly-in tourists. The reasons are obvious: brilliant white beaches, sparkling blue waters, waving coconut palms, burros on rustic cobblestone streets, white adobe colonial architecture with red tile-roofs, and a backdrop of lush jungle-covered mountains.

Puerto Vallarta is located on the Mexican mainland about 1,100 miles south of San Diego in a large bay called Bahia Banderas (See Chapter 33.), which is itself studded with pleasant anchorages within a day's sail of town.

Hurricane Hole: Puerto Vallarta's land-locked marinas are often used by yachts waiting out the hurricane season. For this purpose, PV is the best spot on the Mexican mainland, and you'll find no ports as well protected to the south. The high mountain range running east to west out to Cabo Corrientes presents a natural barrier to these killer storms. At least, Puerto Vallarta has a 155-year history of protection from direct hits from hurricanes.

Approaches: If you're approaching Banderas Bay from the south, round Cabo Corrientes well off and be prepared for the wind to funnel and intensify somewhat. Puerto Vallarta is a safe and easy shot from there.

If you're approaching Puerto Vallarta from the north or from Cabo San Lucas, be aware of several things. We often encounter a definite current flowing from south to north as we depart Cabo San Lucas for Puerto Vallarta, and it's enough to set you off course if you don't make allowance for it. The rhumb line is 290 miles long and takes you within sight of the Islas Tres Marias – excellent landmarks for obtaining bearings when you're several hours out of Puerto Vallarta. The islands are a prison

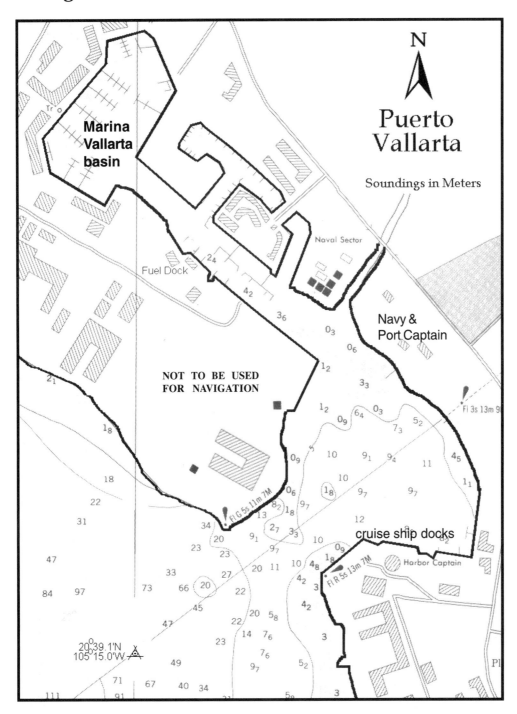

colony, and Mexican regulations require that you stay at least 20 miles off. A patrol boat ensures compliance.

The next landmark is Roca Corvetena but the light on it seldom works. You must decide whether to pass between Punta Mita (20°46'N by 105°33'W) and the Tres Mariettas, or to pass farther to the south. We would use the south entrance if we didn't have radar and GPS. Punta Mita is a calm anchorage in prevailing weather (See Chapter 33.).

Weather for Crossing: The weather during this crossing from Baja is usually moderate, and the strongest winds blow from Cabo San Lucas to about 100 miles southeast. The prevailing wind is northwest, and it occasionally kicks up, making for either a nice southbound passage or a wet crossing north. In the summer months, intense rain squalls may occur.

Municipal Harbor: All of Puerto Vallarta's nautical-tourism interests lies inside its busy municipal. Although Navy boats and big cruise ships dock in the larger outer basin of this harbor, the more sheltered north end contains all the marina slips, the fuel dock and haul-out yard, a few private docks and many excursion boat docks. (Do not confuse this harbor with the smaller one 3.5 miles to the northwest. See "El Norte" in Chapter 32.)

Just outside the rock jetties that form the entrance to the harbor one may

Puerto Vallarta's municipal harbor contains Marina Vallarta, Opequimar fuel dock & yard.

encounter speed boats towing parachutists. Be sure to look skyward. We once nearly impaled a chutist on the mast of a 77-foot motorsailor. The guy was being towed across my port bow, but my sail blinded my view of the sky, where he hung.

The single entrance for Puerto Vallarta's municipal harbor lies about 1-½ miles north of the distinctive crown on the cathedral in the heart of downtown. Marked by a racon "K," the wide entrance is easily distinguishable. Our GPS approach waypoint ¼ mile outside the harbor's entrance jetties is 20°39.1'N by 105°15'W.

Once you enter the outer basin, you'll see where cruise ships dock to starboard, the Navy docks straight ahead in front of the new Port Captain's office, and to port are newer Med-moorings for local excursion boats. A busy 50-foot-wide channel leads to port, northwest, and at the far end you'll see a 200-foot tall Moorish-style lighthouse. This narrow channel calls for careful boat-handling for skippers of large vessels when the strong afternoon

seabreeze sets strongly on the beam and the boat traffic is heavy because of all the returning charter boats. Although two smaller side channels turn off to starboard, they dead-end in private villas; this harbor has only one entrance. The north end is so nearly landlocked that it affords excellent shelter from storm winds.

Stay in the main channel, and you'll pass Opequimar's Pemex fuel dock and haul-out yard on your port side, and then you'll enter the larger basin filled with Marina Vallarta's slips.

Marina Vallarta: The marina office is immediately to port as you enter this large basin, behind the swimming pool, in the 2-story white building on the outer corner. Marina Vallarta has 470 slips up to 140 feet in length on floating docks with 30-amp, 50-amp, 3-phase power, filtered water, cable TV, ATT phones, trash pickup, swimming pool access and 24-hour security. The office provides fax message services and golf-cart transportation. To ask Dockmaster Karl Raggio about slip availability, call "Marina Vallarta" of VHF channels 16 and 18 when you're in range. He will direct you to a slip and have a uniformed guard waiting to take your lines. Then, marvel of marvel, plug into 50- amp, 240-volt shore power without having to hot wire into it. The phone number is 011-52-322-10275, or fax 10722. Marina Vallarta's prices are moderate compared to Cabo and stateside prices. Many surrounding buildings house cafes, shops, delis and mini-supermarkets.

Port Clearance: You can do your own papers, or have the marina do them for you, or you can call Juan Arias, the ship's agent used by the marina. He has the least expensive and most efficient port clearance service of anywhere mentioned

in this book. He'll come to your boat, pick up your papers, run around to all the offices, and then deliver the papers back to you on board in just a few hours. If you did all that yourself, the cab fare alone would be more than his charges.

If you opt to do your own papers, start by visiting the Port Captain's office, located next to the Navy building on the outer basin of the municipal harbor. By land, it's located on the highway going toward downtown Puerto Vallarta.

Fuel Stop: The fuel dock and shipyard (with travel hoist, no less) and marine hardware store is called Opequimar. They monitor VHF channel 16. Vessels taking more than 2,500 gallons of fuel can lay easily alongside the long pier on the north end of the fuel facility and a fuel truck comes down to fuel you through plumbing already on the dock.

However vessels requiring lesser quantities will have to use the smaller docks with pumps at the south end. The maneuvering area around the small dock is very tight for large boats, so their bows may stick out into the main channel and block navigation. With a 78-footer twin screw boat we found it difficult but not impossible to get in. With a 110-footer, we had to lay it across the ends of two smaller docks. It is not a very well planned fuel dock.

Puerto Vallarta Port Call: The marina is a few miles from the center of town. A taxi ride is fairly inexpensive. Much cheaper still are the buses that pass right by. Marina Vallarta is near the airport where you'll find daily flights with connections to Los Angeles, San Diego, Miami and New York.

The center of town is colorful, exotic and not very expensive. One reasonably priced treat is breakfast on the open-air balcony of the Hotel Oceano, overlooking Bahia Banderas and the red-tiled roof tops of the city. The colonial style rooms offer louvered windows that open to an ocean view. Slow motion overhead fans keep you cool enough even in the steamy heat of summer.

Puerto Vallarta is a jet-set capital and its nightlife shows it. The action begins at sundown and goes until dawn.

Provisioning: Puerto Vallarta is a pretty good place to reprovision before or after visiting the Sea of Cortez – where good groceries are few and far between. Across the street from the marina is a large shopping center with an okay hardware store and an excellent air-conditioned grocery store.

Two other large grocery stores are located in town, and there's a good "mercado municipal" on Cuale Island in the downtown district. Panaderias are everywhere in town; you'll see fewer of the "boleo" breads in Puerto Vallarta than in Baja California, but more of the home made "barras" or loaves for slicing. During the winter and spring cruising season, fruits and vegetables here are very good, and during long hot summers, they're still fresher and more plentiful than elsewhere in Mexico.

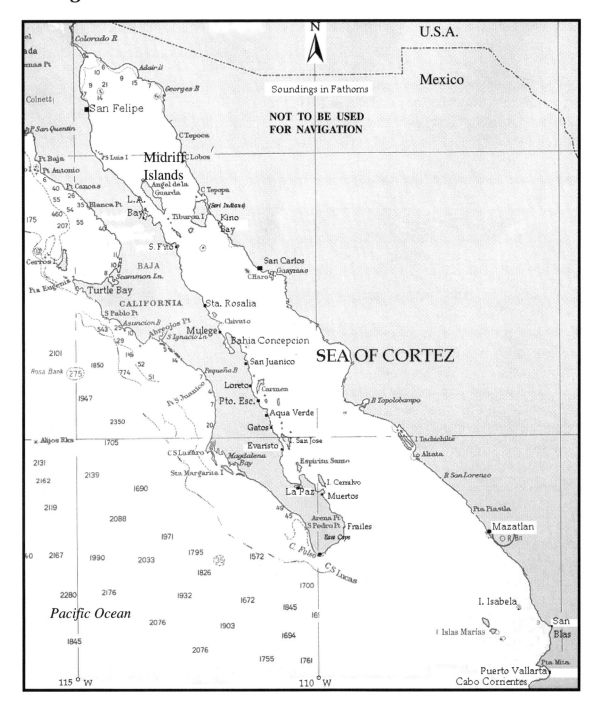

Sea of Cortez
**Use this Planning Chart for
Chapters 35 and 36
covering the mainland side
and the Baja side
of the Sea of Cortez.**

Chapter 35
Sea of Cortez: Mainland Side

In this chapter, we'll begin looking at the Sea of Cortez, starting with the mainland side. The shoreline of the Sea of Cortez touches on the states of Sonora and Nayarit. We'll look at this side's four most popular boating destinations - from south to north.

1.) San Blas and Matenchen Bay
2.) Isla Isabela
3.) Mazatlan
4.) San Carlos and Guaymas

For an Overview of the Sea of Cortez, see the last pages in this chapter. For the Baja side of the Sea of Cortez, see Chapter 36.

San Blas & Matenchen Bay

"Oh bells of San Blas, in vain ye call back the past again." Henry David Longfellow's final poem, "The Bells of San Blas," refers to this tiny fishing village, and you can still see the ruins of Cerro San Basilio, the church he immortalized. San Blas is the last cruising destination in our circuit of the mainland side of the Sea of Cortez (or the first, if you're going the other direction).

San Blas lies on the Mexican mainland only 48 north of Punta Mita near Puerto Vallarta, about 120 miles south of Mazatlan. The port town of San Blas lies mostly inside the mouth of the Pozo River, and it has a Port Captain, fuel, and some services ashore; its neighboring Matenchen ("mah-tayn-CHAYN") Bay provides more anchoring room. But neither location is tenable during summer hurricane season, when they're often swept by high surf.

Approaches: If you're arriving from the south, you may want to visit the intermediate anchorage at Bahia Chacala, a very pleasant little overnight anchorage about 30 miles northeast of Punta Mita (north arm of Banderas Bay) or about 20 miles southeast of San Blas.

⚓ Chacala offers shelter from the north, and coconut palms and seafood cafes line the beach, but this village is small. A new hotel has sprouted along the hillside north of the anchorage, but you can still land a dinghy on the concrete mole used by pangas and small fishing boats for hotel guests. Chacala is our favorite anchorages in this region.

231

Chacala: Anchorage and dinghy pier in north end of bay.

If you're arriving from the north, you'll see a 145-foot-tall white rock called Piedra Blanca del Mar about 12 miles northwest of San Blas Light marking the lighted harbor entrance. Pass this rock to port about 2.5 miles off. Then a shorter white rock called Piedra Blanca del Tierra lies only one mile southwest of the harbor entrance, and you give this one a ¼-mile berth, either side.

As you reach the San Blas area, you'll enter the wide open south side of Matenchen Bay and then need to round Punta Camaron about ¼ mile off, due to its adjacent reef. The first estuary mouth immediately behind Punta Camaron is not the harbor. The entrance to San Blas harbor is two miles northwest of Punta Camaron.

San Blas Light, a striped light tower, stands on the west bank of the Rio Pozo. The south-opening entrance lies between two riprap jetties, lighted red and green, and the narrow entrance channel is well buoyed. Our GPS approach waypoint just off the seaward end of the west breakwater is 21°31.5'N by 105°17.5'W. Range markers (335°M) lead you to the foot of the Port Captain's office, so there you have to angle northwest.

Anchorages: About half a mile inland from the harbor entrance, you'll see a dinghy landing and panga beach on your right, and the harbor anchorage and fuel dock basin are another 0.2 of a mile up this channel. You can anchor in the buoyed area anywhere past the concrete lined turning, in 10 to 12 feet of water over good holding mud. To clear in with the Port Captain, this anchorage is closest, but the teensy biting flies called "no-see-ums" may swarm around sundown. They're so small, some mosquito netting won't keep them out.

TIP: Try burning the fibrous husks of coconuts like incense to drive away no-see-ums. It's non toxic and smells nice.

Oh Bells of San Blas: Longfellow wrote of San Basilio ruins.

Rio Pozo leads beyond this anchorage for a good dinghy or kayak trek.

Matenchen Bay is a larger and better anchorage for longer visits, and a bus connects it to town. Anchor about 100 yards east of Punta Camaron in about 20 feet of water. Some cafes, cabanas and services ashore cater to visiting yachties.

Port Clearance: San Blas has a Port Captain, Aduana and Migracion office, but you start your rounds at the office of Puertos Mexicano, next door to the Aduana's office on Calle Campeche, all near the range markers and dinghy landing in San Blas harbor.

Fuel Stop: Make arrangements with the Port Captain and Puertos offices, to order the fuel and have it delivered in a small tank truck to the commercial basin in the harbor, and then for your dock space alongside this busy little seawall frequented by shrimpers. Small quantities of diesel may be brought by taxi or pickup truck to the fuel basin from a Pemex station on the north side of town, corner of Juarez and Mercado, but ask the Port Captain first.

Local Services: The very pleasant central plaza or zocalo of San Blas is only about four blocks north of the dinghy landing, and it makes a good reference and rendezvous spot. A good pharmacy is across the street from the plaza on Mercado Street. For dry groceries, a small but very good Grucoso tienda is on the corner of Mercado and Paredes. For fresh produce, the best big place is San Blas's mercado central, one block north of the plaza on Sonora. Out at Matenchen Bay, several of the cafes ashore have set up cruisers' services, such as referrals for local mechanics and repair services, rides to town and use of phones and faxes.

History and Side Trips: In the 1500s and 1600s, this tiny estuary saw more than its share of Spanish galleons and flagless pirates. The Fuerte San Basilio atop the cerro was the original town, and Father Junipero Serra set sail from San Blas to begin his chain of missions. During the War of Independence from Spain, insurgents captured the fort and moved its 43 cannon to Guadalajara, where they helped defeat loyalists. This harbor's decline began soon after independence, so by the 1870s when Longfellow visited San Blas, the church (Iglesia de Nuestra Senora del Rosario) on the side of Cerro San Basilio was already a ruin pining for its glory days.

You can visit the ruins of both the church and fort by climbing (or taking a taxi) up the paved road to the top of Cerro San Basilio, to view the surrounding flat countryside and mangrove lagoons. Many pangas take visitors to Tovara Estuary for waterfalls, swimming holes and picnics. "Huichol" folk art of colorful string painting is the primary local handicraft.

Isla Isabela

This small, remote island named for Queen Isabela of Spain makes a good stepping stone between San Blas and Mazatlan, especially during northwesterly weather, because its anchorages are on the south and east sides. The Mexican Navy brings propane and water to the tiny panguero village on the south side, and students from Guadalajara occasionally arrive to record the mating and nesting habits in the adjacent frigate-bird rookery. There are no services on this virtually uninhabited chunk of rock.

Isla Isabela is located about 82 miles south-southeast of Mazatlan and 40 miles northwest of San Blas. The entire north end is foul with off-lying rocks, so we consider

The Spires: Isla Isabela's east side has the better anchorage.

it unapproachable. The land rises to a crest on the south end, dropping off into a very small two-lobed cove that is approachable – with care. Our GPS approach waypoint about a tenth of a mile south of this cove is 21°50.4'N by 105°53'W.

Anchorages: The south cove is pretty tight, but the best place to anchor here (with prevailing north winds) is in the center of the larger eastern lobe, in 12 to 23 feet of water. There's room for only one boat, and you may want to anchor bow in, stern out.

As you pick your way in, beware of a rock pinnacle (about 5-foot depth) that lies about 100 yards off the southeast tip of the small peninsula dividing the two lobes, and also stay clear of the breaking rock off the southeast tip of the island. The steep volcanic facade along the north side of this cove provides good shelter in prevailing winds.

From here you can land a dinghy on the west end of the panguero beach in the smaller western lobe, then hike up to Frigate Conservation building. The path leads you among stubby bushes housing many frigate nests, each numbered and tagged. This is an ecological preserve. Walk very slowly so you don't disturb the easily agitated frigates. Enormous adult birds and or their fuzzy white nestlings will be about

head level above the ground. From the top of the roof of the observation building, you get a good view of the island.

If the south cove feels too tight, or if you're here when southerly weather is brewing, move over to the island's southeast side where there's much more swinging room. We prefer the anchorage just south of the two 150-foot-tall twisted rock spires that rise about 200 yards off the island's eastern side. We call these Isabela's Spires. The spires are steep to and provide good snorkeling even between them. In northwesterly weather the best protection is just south or southwest of the spires in 20 to 24 feet over coral rocks and mud. A shoal shelf juts out just south of the nearby beach, but you can land a dinghy on that beach, then hike over the island to the frigate sanctuary.

TIP: Don't go near either "lagoon" on Isla Isabela because they're used as latrines.

Mazatlan

Mazatlan lies on the same latitude as Cabo San Lucas, except that it's on the Mexican mainland. Similar to Cabo, Mazatlan has full-service marinas, a free-anchorage harbor, marlin madness by day and disco dancing by night. Unlike Cabo, Mazatlan is much more tropical in climate, friendlier in nature – and less expensive all around.

Mazatlan is located about 390 miles southeast of Guaymas, about 200 miles east of Cabo San Lucas (across the lower Sea of Cortez), 120 miles northwest of San Blas, and 145 miles northwest of Punta Mita, near Puerto Vallarta.

The genteel old port of Mazatlan (pronounced "mahs-aht-LAHN") handles cruise ships, shrimpers and cruising yachts in various locations along its city seawalls. It's quite a contrast to Mazatlan's new marina district, located seven miles up the coastline, surrounded by time-share villas and big hotels that sponsor big-bucks billfish tournaments.

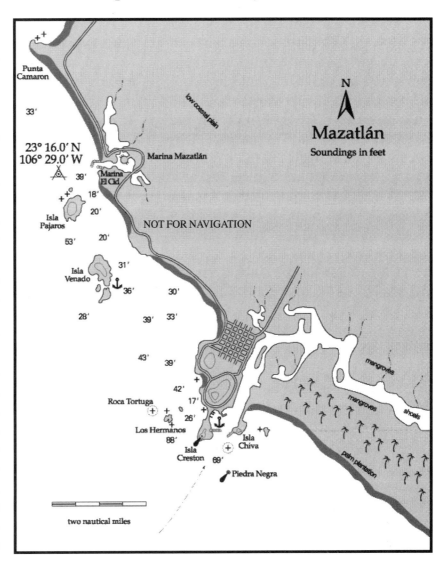

Approaches: From the north, the 213-mile leg south of Topolobampo is flanked by shoals and shallow mangrove lagoons accessible only by panga. (Topolobampo is a sleepy commercial harbor, but it has several anchorages in case of emergency.) Punta Piaxtla Light 35 miles north of Mazatlan isn't always working. Nine miles north of Mazatlan, Punta Camaron and Isla Pajaro are the landmarks for Mazatlan's marina district, which lies inside what the older charts call Laguna Sabalo, just south of Punta Camaron. Our GPS approach waypoint between Punta

Camaron and Isla Pajaro is 23°16'N by 106°29'W. This is close to the marina district north of the old port.

Enter the lighted jetty-lined breakwaters, and El Cid Hotel's excursion boats and then its marina slips are on your right. For Marina Mazatlan, continue straight ahead about 100 yards and the inland yacht basin for Marina Mazatlan opens up to your left.

From the south, you approach the old port of Mazatlan first. All vessels enter the breakwaters between the easily identifiable Isla Creston (point leaning to left) on the left and the smaller Isla Chiva (point leaning to right) on the right. But two hard spots on your approach are: the lighted Piedra Negra rock that lies ¾ of a mile due south of the entrance, and the unmarked rock awash lies only ¼ of a mile due south of the entrance. To avoid this dangerous rock, keep both Piedra Negra and the eastern breakwater well to starboard (east of you) as you approach.

Between the old port and the new marina area, first timers should stay ¾ of a mile outside Islas Hermanos, the two small white islands west of Isla Creston, due to a dangerous rock awash, Roca Tortuga. But it's okay to come inside both Isla Venado and Isla Pajaro where you're closer to the marina jetties.

To approach the old port of Mazatlan from the south, come to our GPS approach waypoint of 23°10'N by 106°25.25'W, which is about ¼ mile west of Piedra Negra Light. Due to a dangerous unmarked rock awash (located ½ mile due north of Piedra Negra and ¼ mile due south of the seaward tip of the eastern breakwater), keep Piedra Negra and the eastern breakwater well off to starboard. Never enter between them. Instead, from the above waypoint, aim for the western breakwater, then bear into the harbor once you're clear of the eastern breakwater.

TIP: Never enter between Piedra Negra and the eastern breakwater, due to a dangerous rock awash.

Port Clearance: Start your port clearance procedures by visiting Mazatlan's Port Captain's office, located on the east side of the downtown district, overlooking the old port. VHF channels 06 and 09 are reserved for port operations. Besides the usual Port Captain, Aduana and Migracion offices, Mazatlan also has a Ports and Harbor's office. Alternately, you can have either of the marinas handle your port clearance for you, for a small fee.

Marina El Cid: Most of Marina El Cid's 100 slips for boats up to 120-feet in length are located in the south end of the inner lagoon (although its diesel dock and sportfishing fleet are in the outer channel). To reach the marina slips for visiting yachts, go through the 15-foot-deep outer entrance channel, past the fuel dock and excursion boat docks, and about ½ a mile on your right is the marina.

The floating concrete slips come with 30-, 50- and 100-amp shore power, dock carts and boxes, potable water and 24-hour security; cable TV and cell phones are extra. The marina's showers and laundry are near the office, and many niceties of the El Cid Mega Resort, with which the marina is associated, are available to marina guests, such as the waterfall pool, room service onboard, a visit to the health spa, tennis courts and 27-hole golf course.

When within VHF range, call "Marina El Cid" on VHF channel 12 or 16 to ask about slip availability and directions. At various times of the year, Marina El Cid hosts some big-bucks big-boat bill-fishing tournaments, and the guest slips can get filled up. To call ahead for reservations, the marina's phone is 011-52 (69) 16-34-68, and fax is 16-62-94.

Marina Mazatlan: Located in the new marina district, inside the large inner lagoon, this development was halted amid construction, and only a few of the planned floating docks were completed, some with electricity or water, others without. Those without are offered at reduced rates. Many boaters have found this a convenient anchorage.

To reach Marina Mazatlan, enter the 15-foot deep outer channel, go past El Cid's fuel dock and outer marina slips (above), and follow the channel east into the larger inner lagoon. To your left (north) is a circular man-made island inside a circular basin. Marina Mazatlan's slips are along the north end of the island developed with a hotel complex and villas. Some slips are reached by going around the west side, others via the east side. Call "Marina Mazatlan" on VHF channel 16 to ask for slip availability and directions around the island. For more information, Marina Mazatlan's phone and fax is 011-52 (69) 16-36-14.

Anchorages: The municipal anchorage for visiting yachts is inside the old port, which is very handy for visiting downtown. After you clear the western breakwater heading north, the anchorage is on your left-hand side. The boundaries are from the northeast foot of Isla Creston, along the causeway connecting it to town, up to the commercial and cruise ship docks and out to the green buoys marking the ship channel, which continues northward from here. If there's any wind from the west or northwest, it can bridge the causeway and stir up chop, so the best shelter is in the southwest corner (10 to 12 feet of water) at the foot of Isla Creston. For easiest shore access, try the west side or northwest corner (nine to 12 feet of water). The bottom throughout this anchorage is soft mud, not good holding. You can land at the Club Nautico or one of the sport fishing docks north of there for a small fee.

Day anchorages are found at the islands just off shore of Mazatlan, but the excursion and diving boats are there during the daytimes, too.

Some boats anchor in the side lobes of the lush Mazatlan Estuary that stretches for several miles behind of the old port. First time, scout it out in your dinghy. Follow the main ship channel north, around the center shoal, then the main channel angles right (east and southeast) and winds through a mangrove forest. The deep-water passage is fairly well staked, showing a few shoals on the turns. You can follow one of the big shrimp boats as far as their dock, about a mile south.

Fuel Stop: Both parts of Mazatlan have a fuel dock. For long-range cruising boats and sport fishers, probably the easiest is Marina El Cid's diesel dock, located on the right hand (south) side, just inside the lighted entrance jetties leading to the new marina district. The depth is 15 feet, and the facilities are modern and efficient, including the pump out station. You can pay by credit card.

In the old port, smaller craft can take fuel from the Club Nautico, next to the launch ramp at the south end of the causeway connecting Isla Creston to the town. This is not a slick operation, and we've had to Med-moor to a floating raft to take diesel, getting bounced by wakes and wind.

Local Services:

The local cruisers net operates on VHF channel 68 on weekdays, sometimes also on Saturdays.

One of our favorite things about Mazatlan is the local "pulmonia," a unique kind of taxi. They're a cross between a golf cart and a VW bug, and except for a little bimini top, they're wide open to the breezes (or raindrops). Usually about half the price of a regular taxi, they're a bit slower and smaller – room for three people, the driver and a few groceries. Flag down a pulmonia (pronounced "pool-mohn-EE-yah") to get around town.

Mazatlan is first and foremost sportfishing town, so basic parts and repair services for power boats and marine engines are plentiful. Sailboat rigging repairs are less likely. Ask for particular recommendations from the Port Captain or the dockmaster in either of the marinas.

For hauling out a yacht, contact the Industrial Navales de Mazatlan ship yard, located 1.5 miles north of the municipal anchorage in the old port. INM has cranes and ways for vessels from 30 to 175 feet in length, up to 750 tons.

Carnival is the biggest celebration of the year in Mazatlan, and it's reported to be the third largest Carnival in the northern hemisphere. If you plan to be here during Carnival (pronounced "kar-nee-VAHL"), plan on seven days of non-stop parades, food festivals and dancing.

San Carlos Bay & Guaymas

On the Mexican mainland, these two dissimilar harbors are usually thought of as one happy cruising ground; the modern recreational Marina San Carlos is sheltered inside little San Carlos Bay (and a smaller marina is nearby) – and about 20 sea miles west of San Carlos is the busy commercial port city of Guaymas (pronounced "WHY-mahs"). Combined, the San Carlos-Guaymas area is the only major cruising port on the mainland side of the upper Sea of Cortez.

San Carlos is located about 76 miles east-northeast of Santa Rosalia, 175 miles northwest of Topolobampo and 385 miles northwest of Mazatlan. Bahia San Carlos is a favorite summering over spot and hurricane hole for many long-range cruisers – and a popular base camp for several hundred Arizona trailer boaters.

Approaches: The main landmark for the San Carlos region is a distinctive set of red-rock peaks called Tetas de Cabra (goat teats) that looks like, evidently, an upside-down udder. The narrow, blade-like

Punta Doble lies just east of Tetas, and the entrance to San Carlos Bay lies just northeast of the south tip of Punta Doble. If you're coming from the south or from Guaymas, pass Punta Haro and Punta Arco to starboard, then cross Bahia San Francisco and aim for the Tetas to reach the entrance to San Carlos Bay.

The ¼-mile-wide entrance to San Carlos Bay is slightly tricky, between the red and green lighted Punta San Guillermo and Punta Paradores. Keep tiny Isla San Nicolas to starboard as you come to our GPS position in the middle of the entrance channel: 27°56.1'N by 111°03.3'W. Proceed northwest until a small beach and anchorage lies close on your starboard beam. From here the bulk of Bahia San Carlos lies ahead and to port.

To reach Marina San Carlos, continue north and go around the steep-sided hill on your right side (east side of bay). The marina's fuel dock and slips soon become visible inside this sheltered side lobe. The least depth to enter this side lobe is 10 feet, and the least depth in Marina San Carlos's center is 7.5 feet.

Marina San Carlos: The first marina built in the Sea of Cortez, Marina San Carlos contains 331 slips for up to 80-footers on floating docks with filtered water, shorepower (110-volt 30-amp and 220-volt 50-amp), dock boxes and carts, 24-hour security, etc. For slip availability, call ahead for reservations; phone 011-52 (622) 6-12-30 or fax 6-05-65. Marina San Carlos is owned by Ed and Tere Grossman.

Ed Grossman's "cama baja" is a unique low-bed trailer with hydraulic arms that allows boats (maximum 60 feet, 60 tons) to be carefully hauled out at the marina's grooved concrete launch ramp and transported to its nearby dry storage yard or adjacent work yard. Boats up to 45 feet or 30 tons can be hauled across the U.S. border at Nogales and transported to Tucson, Arizona.

San Carlos Yacht Club, which is very informal, has a new clubhouse on the north seawall of the marina basin. Their double-wide grooved concrete launch ramp and 10-ton crane are also on this north side. The much appreciated swimming pool of the Plaza las Glorias hotel overlooks the marina's east. The marina office and a few cafe bars and boutique shops line the marina's northeast corner.

Marina Real: Located a few miles north of Bahia San Carlos, the jetty lined entrance channel into this more remote marina lies at the south end of the beach of Bahia Algodones. The seaward end of the south jetty lies at GPS position 27°56.72'N by 111°05.70'W. Marina Real (pronounced "ray-AHL") contains 250 slips for boats 25 to 48 feet, floating docks, 110-volt 30-amp shore power and non-filtered water (use chlorine). Marina Real has its own fuel dock and launch ramps. The fuel dock is just inside the entrance channel, to starboard. The launch ramps and parking

are in the far north end of the marina basin.

Most of the slips here are owned by the residents of the vacation villas on Algodones beach, but to inquire about slip availability, phone or phone 011-52 (622) 7-01-10.

Anchorages: The primary anchorages in San Carlos Bay are in the west end (18 to 36 feet) and south end (12 to 29 feet). For a small fee, owners of

Tetas de Cabra

Cama Baja:
Hauling out
at San Carlos
for the
highway to Tucson.

larger Bahia San Carlos. Call the marina to order large quantities.

anchored boats can use the marina's dinghy docks and shore facilities. Dinghies left on the beach at the north end of Bahia San Carlos need to have everything locked down and covered, because it's so close to the highway and not a secure spot.

Intrepid boaters will find dozens of remote anchorages to explore and hide out along the 55-mile stretch north of San Carlos, far too many locations for this chapter. We highly recommend Gerry Cunningham's well detailed fold-out "Cruising Charts." They're available by writing to Gerry at P.O. Box 976, Patagonia, Arizona.

Port Clearance: Both marinas can handle your port clearance for a service fee, or you can do it yourself. The Port Captain and all port offices are located in Guaymas. Start with the Capitania, located on the street end of the ship yards in the northeast corner of the harbor. The Port Captain's offices are on the second floor. The nearest anchorage is between the ship yard and the Navy piers, in nine to 10 feet of water.

Fuel Stop: The easiest fuel dock for pleasure boats is at Marina San Carlos. The 80-foot dock with Pemex pumps and oil recycling is tucked in hard to starboard as you enter the marina's side bay off the

Haul-out Yards: Marina San Carlos's work yard has lots of laborers available, or you can do your own thing. Maximum size for the cama baja trailer is 60 feet or 60 tons.

For larger yachts, the only facility is the former INP ship yard in Guaymas harbor. They have a massive ways, crane and Travelift, and their services include shaft lathing and alignment, stainless and aluminum welding, and audio-gauging. To get a bid on your work list, fax it to INP Yacht Division at 011-52 (622) 2-80-77. This is the only haul-out facility for larger vessels between Puerto Penasco and Mazatlan.

Local Services: Two small grocery stores and cafes are within easy walking distance of Marina San Carlos, because most of this end of the town of San Carlos is quiet residential. The more commercial part of lies to the east, along the sandy shores of Bahia San Francisco. Although one hardware store and two outboard repair shops near Marina San Carlos, most groceries, mechanics, marine supplies and spare parts come from Guaymas, a 13-mile bus ride east.

You can rent a car through the Plaza las Glorias or Howard Johnson hotels or at the Guaymas airport.

Sea of Cortez Overview

Now that we've covered the major cruising ports on this side of the Sea of Cortez, let's get an overview for the purpose of planning your circular itinerary.

Lay of the Land: This elongated body of water is surrounded on three sides by semi-tropical Sonora Desert and coastal mountains. Nearly 1,500 miles of shoreline stretch along its 600-mile length. Only 50 miles across at the stepping stone Midriff Islands, the width of the Sea of Cortez flares to 150 miles between Baja's East Cape and Mazatlan on the mainland.

In the entire Sea of Cortez, pleasure boaters will find only about eight town harbors with docks or marinas, but there are at least six reliable diesel docks, at least two reliable haul-out yards, more than 100 friendly fishing villages, a dozen sizable islands – and at least 75 pristine but remote anchorages with names – more without names. Most of the facilities for cruising and sportfishing boats are located on the Baja side of the Sea of Cortez.

Many of the nearly 2,000 recreational boats that visit the Sea of Cortez each year don't explore farther north than San Carlos/Guaymas on the mainland side or farther north than Santa Rosalia on the Baja side.

During the winter and spring boating season in Mexico, the entire lower half of the Sea of Cortez enjoys warmer and more settled weather than does the northern half, which gets swept by Northers. (See Chapter 25, Weather and Routing in Mexico.)

During summer hurricane season, however, the slower or smaller boats that are going to summer over inside the Sea of Cortez will want to migrate farther north toward San Carlos or L.A. Bay and the upper reaches of the Sea of Cortez. Boaters who don't head north in the Sea of Cortez should stay close to the hurricane holes of Puerto Escondido on the Baja side or San Carlos on the mainland side - for shelter from any tropical storms that threaten the middle or lower Sea of Cortez.

Sea of Cortez Routing: If you're coming up the mainland coast from Puerto Vallarta, you have at least three options. Some boaters choose to jump off from Punta Mita and make the 225-mile offshore passage to the Los Frailes (The Friars) headland on Baja's East Cape region. (For more about this crossing, see Chapter 25.)

Los Frailes: East Cape of Baja, this whitish headland makes a good landfall and offers two anchorages.

Others opt to coast hop north on the mainland as far as Mazatlan, then cross over to Los Frailes. This route eliminates the long stretch between Mazatlan and Guaymas that has shallow waters and little to offer pleasure boaters.

Either way, after landing at Los Frailes, it's easy to visit La Paz and then work slowly up the Baja side. The most popular route for jumping back across to the mainland side is to depart Baja from Santa Rosalia and land at San Carlos, an open-water passage of only about 75 miles.

Cruising Ports

Another option for boaters coming up from Puerto Vallarta is to travel north along the mainland side as far as San Carlos, then cross over to Baja via the Midriff islands, landing in the L.A. Bay region. The Midriff Islands make good stepping stones providing short hops and some shelter from Northers.

Of course, boaters entering the Sea of Cortez from the outer or Pacific side of Baja simply round the East Cape. They can either continue up the Baja side of the Sea of Cortez or hop across to the mainland from Los Frailes or Santa Rosalia or via the Midriff Islands.

At any one time, there may be 800 to 1,000 long-term cruising boats in the Sea of Cortez, and many of those spend two to five years repeating these routes. The Sea of Cortez is a major cruising ground.

Trailer Boating: Pocket cruisers and trailerable boats seem to have been designed with Sea of Cortez-type cruising in mind.

Each year, more than 1,500 small power and sail boats are trailered down Baja's Highway 1 and Sonora's Highway 15, then launched into the smaller regional cruising grounds scattered along the Sea of Cortez. Pocket cruisers and folding trimarans can be trailered by their owners, put in at these same base camps and cruised regionally for weeks and months at a time, then moving to another region. Professional international boat truckers are available to and from San Carlos.

On the Baja side, the three primary cruising grounds for trailer boaters are between La Paz and Santa Rosalia, the L.A. Bay and Midriff Islands region. On the mainland side, the trailer-boat cruising grounds are from Puerto Penasco down to Kino Bay, then around San Carlos/ Guaymas.

Important launch ramps on the Baja side are found at La Paz, Puerto Escondido, Loreto, Bahia Concepcion, Mulege, Santa Rosalia, Gonzaga Bay, Puertocitos and San Felipe. On the mainland side, they're found at Puerto Penasco, Kino Bay, San Carlos, Mazatlan and San Blas.

But dozens more hard-sand beaches and remote ramps are available for the smaller boats, car toppers and kayaks. Most of these are located on the Baja peninsula and along the upper reaches of the mainland side.

Now that we're done over-viewing the entire Sea of Cortez, let's continue by looking specifically at the Baja side.

Chapter 36
Sea of Cortez: Baja Side

This chapter covers the Baja side of the Sea of Cortez and its six most popular boating destinations, starting in the north end and moving southward, plus many intermediate anchorages and points of interest en route:

1.) Bahia Los Angeles
   - Between L.A. Bay and Santa Rosalia
2.) Santa Rosalia
3.) Mulege and Bahia Concepcion
4.) Puerto Escondido and Loreto
   - Between Puerto Escondido and Espiritu Santo
5.) Isla Espiritu Santo and Isla Partida
6.) La Paz

Bahia Los Angeles

L.A. Bay and is an ideal region for pleasure boats to summer over in the upper reaches of the Sea of Cortez. The small desert town has sufficient services, and nearby are a dozen interesting islands and at least 14 getaway anchorages. Most importantly, the natural hurricane hole of Puerto Don Juan is right here.

Superb year-round fishing and semi-sheltered waters are what created this small oasis at the foot of the desert mountains. Similar to Kino Bay on the mainland, more than half of L.A. Bay's population is made up of retired gringos and Baja buffs who have built vacation homes here. A long rough paved road connects this region to Highway One.

Located on the Baja California side of the Midriff Islands region, L.A. Bay lies 50 miles northwest of Bahia San Francisquito, 110 miles northwest of Santa Rosalia, and 155 miles southeast of San Felipe.

Hurricane Hole: The Window at Puerto Don Juan near Bahia Los Angeles

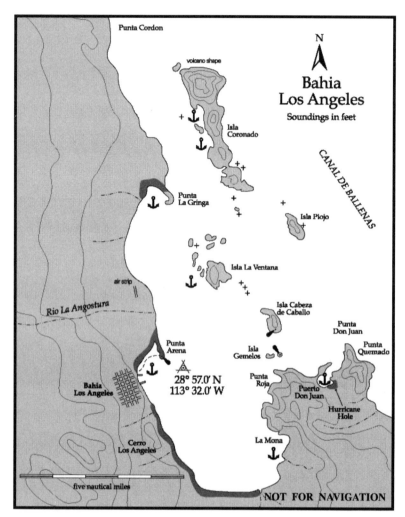

Bahia
Los Angeles
Soundings in feet

CANAL DE BALLENAS

Punta Cordon

volcano shape

Isla
Coronado

Punta
La Gringa

Isla Piojo

Isla La Ventana

air strip

Rio La Angostura

Isla Cabeza
de Caballo

Punta
Arena

Isla
Gemelos

28° 57.0' N
113° 32.0' W

Punta
Roja

Punta
Don Juan

Punta
Quemada

Puerto
Don Juan

Bahia
Los Angeles

Hurricane
Hole

Cerro
Los Angeles

La Mona

five nautical miles

NOT FOR NAVIGATION

Coronado (distinctive 1,500-foot volcano cone) and Isla Angel de Guarda (Guardian Angle Island, the 2nd largest island in the Sea of Cortez). Some folks spend months exploring just Guardian Angel Island. La Unica Bay and Bahia las Animas (Spirit Bay), both to the southeast of L.A. Bay, have additional anchorages.

Off the town of L.A. Bay, you can anchor almost anywhere you want between the northern launch ramp and the rock groin south of town. Anchor about 100 yards off the beach in 18 to 25 feet of water over sand and rock. Our GPS waypoint on this anchorage is 28°56.93'N by 113° 33.34'W.

TIP: The tidal range in this region is 11.5 feet.

Approaches: Most boats enter the bay of L.A. Bay by rounding Punta Quemada (burned point) which is reddish and burned looking. On the southwest side of this major headland is the entrance to the hurricane hole called Puerto Don Juan (See below.), but continue west between the lighted islands of Cabeza de Caballo (horse head) and Los Gemelos (the twins). The town of L.A. Bay lies south of the low sandy Punta Arena (sand point). Our GPS approach waypoint for the town anchorage is 28°57'N by 113°32'W.

Anchorages: There are probably a hundred places to anchor in this immediate vicinity, mostly on the tiny key-hole islands and Isla La Ventana, Isla

Hurricane Hole: This natural harbor is the finest all-weather anchorage in the upper Sea of Cortez. Although it's called Puerto Don Juan, so far nothing port-like has been developed here; it's still a natural beauty. The narrow, steep-sided entrance to Don Juan bay lies about six miles east of the town of L.A. Bay, about ½ of a mile west of the 500-foot Cerro Punta Quemada.

After entering, you pass on your left hand an enclosed but shallow side bay called the Bath Tub. The main bay then opens up with room for more than 100 boats to anchor. The middle of the bay is only 30 feet deep.

The Window is a low shale bar or shingle that forms part of the western perimeter of Puerto Don Juan; you can anchor off the Window in about 25 feet of water – and see out to Islas los Gemelos and Bahia de los Angeles.

Midriff Islands Crossing: From here, boats planning to cross the Sea of Cortez to the mainland (and vice versa) can use the stepping-stone islands of San Lorenzo (Larry), San Esteban (Steve) and Tiburon (shark) to create short hops to the Kino Bay region. Kino Bay, which is very popular with trailer boaters and fishing enthusiasts, lies about 70 miles northwest of San Carlos. Tiburon Island (the largest island in the Sea of Cortez) and the area north of Kino Bay are the home reservation waters of the nearly extinct Seri Indians, famous for their ironwood carvings.

Between L. A. Bay and Santa Rosalia

We know of no harbors and only a few anchorages along the remote 75-mile coastline immediately north of Santa Rosalia. These few roadsteads and "small hopes" include Caleta Santa Maria, Bahia Santa Ana, Punta Trinidad, Cabo San Miguel and El Barril.

Elefante Winds: This stretch is where you may encounter the "Elefante" winds, which occasionally sweep down the mountain passes and fan out across the sea, sometimes as far as five to 10 miles. *How can you tell if an Elefante is about to start?* They're often preceded by a small but tightly packed Tootsie Roll-shaped cloud forming along the crest of the mountain pass. This weather phenomena was named for the signature cloud, which some think looks like the trunk of an elephant. Either way, if you see it forming, head offshore.

Bahia San Francisquito: However, at Bahia San Francisquito, you'll find a 1-mile wide bay open to the northeast. Our GPS approach waypoint just outside the entrance to Bahia San Francisquito is 28°27'N by 112°52'W.

In the far western corner, an anchorage off the beach (12 to 36 feet of water) has pretty good shelter from north winds. In the bay's southeast corner you'll find a tiny enclosed side bay called Caleta San Francisquito, but the entrance channel is reported to be only four to six feet deep. We've seen shrimpers inside here, but we've not anchored inside.

A better choice in northerly weather may be to anchor not inside Bahia San Francisquito, but outside it and to the south, in the lee of a sizable headland called Punta Santa Teresa. We've anchored off the north end of this beach in 18 feet of water. Some charts call this area Bahia Santa Teresa, but it's not a deep indentation.

Santa Rosalia

The town and harbor of Santa Rosalia is 33 miles north of Bahia Concepcion and Mulege, and about 220 miles north of La Paz, and about 80 miles across the Sea of Cortez from San Carlos and Guaymas.

Santa Rosalia's small harbor is enclosed by a riprap breakwater on the north and east sides, opening to the south. Built to shelter fishing boats and the car ferry to Topolobampo on the mainland, this harbor also provides recreational boaters with an anchorage and a very small marina. The Port Captain's office is inside the ferry terminal.

The town grew around a copper smelting works owned by Bolero Mines, a French company; sooty industrial ruins and smoke stacks litter the steep hillsides. The company built houses of wood, rare in Baja,

Marina Santa Rosalia: anchorage and entrance.

and a few of the original wooden structures remain. An ore train monument graces the entrance to Santa Rosalia's downtown streets.

Approaches: From Mulege and Punta Chivato to the south, the island of San Marcos lies on your route northeast to Santa Rosalia. The south tip of San Marcos has Lobos Rocks and a shoal extending another half mile south. If you're south of

the island, hug the mainland side about half a mile off. The gypsum quarry on the southwest side of this island is active, so you'll see some commercial boats. About one mile south of the entrance to Santa Rosalia, the shoal at Punta Santa Agueda is marked by buoys and a navigation light that is well maintained.

The wide, south-facing entrance to Santa Rosalia's breakwater enclosed harbor is lighted by non-flashing red and green navigation lights. Our GPS approach waypoint just outside the entrance to Santa Rosalia harbor is 27°20'N by 112°15.6'W.

Marina Santa Rosalia: The only place for recreational boats to get a slip is he 18-boat Marina Santa Rosalia, found in the northwest quadrant of the harbor. As you transit the harbor, stay closer to the outer wall. On your port side, you'll pass the big ferry dock and ferry terminal, then a shoal, then several rusty commercial docks. The building for the marina is usually painted bright turquoise, a definite landmark in contrast to the dingy surroundings.

Although it isn't a pretty harbor, surrounded as it is by industrial ruins, the people are friendly and a little awed by yachts; the Port Captain of Santa Rosalia runs a tight ship, so security has not been a problem. The north wall is

Map of Santa Rosalia harbor. Labels include: Navy, Pesca, foundry, marina office, Migracion, ferry terminal, Port Captain, Highway One, ferry basin, shoal. Soundings in feet: 22', 24', 12', 15', 24', 30', 15', 22', 24', 11', 17', 18', 24', 17', 18', 24', 18', 27', 11', 18', 14', 27', shoal, 30', 33', do not anchor here, 21', 33', 13', 14', 9'. 27° 20.0' N 112° 15.6' W. N. Santa Rosalia, Soundings in feet. one quarter nautical mile. NOT FOR NAVIGATION for the Navy base and commercial fishing boats.

There's a sign over Marina Santa Rosalia's floating docks, and a ramp to the sea wall. Highway One runs close by. Call "Marina Santa Rosalia" on VHF channel 16 to ask their English-speaking dockmaster about slip availability. Their phone is 011-52-(115) 2-00-11. The largest boat we've ever docked here was a 62-foot power boat.

Ashore in the marina office, you'll find a cooler full of sodas, a small library and several easy chairs in the shade. The service was friendly and efficient, and the price was quite reasonable. This marina is expanding but it gets filled up during the summer, so plan ahead. The only disadvantage here is that, when the wind is strong from the northwest, black grit blows off the land onto your decks.

Port Clearance: The marina can do your paperwork clearance for you, for a small fee, or you can do your own. The Port Captain and Aduana's office is inside the big ferry terminal at the southwest corner of the harbor. Migracion is half a block south.

If you plan to leave your boat here and take the ferry over to the mainland, be sure to tell the Port Captain and the marina of your plans before leaving.

Fuel Stop: Marina Santa Rosalia can order fuel for you. They keep a small tank on the premises, but larger quantities usually come from a tank truck brought to the seawall. This is the last fuel dock in a long way.

Anchorages: The only place to anchor inside the harbor is off the marina and a little farther south, in 15 to 22 feet of murky water over rock and rubble. Don't anchor outside the harbor entrance, because old cables foul the bottom and gobble up anchors.

Bahia Concepcion and Mulege

Bahia Concepcion (Conception Bay) is a sea within a sea. The entrance to this lovely bay lies right next to the service town of Mulege, pronounced "moo-lah-HAY." Together, they are about 33 miles south of Santa Rosalia, 70 miles north of Loreto and about 80 miles across the Sea of Cortez from San Carlos and Guaymas.

This elongated bay runs about 21 miles from northwest to southeast and between two and 3.5 miles wide. Its upper end is somewhat open to northeast wind, and most of the anchorages lie along its northwest and west shoreline, which is backed by steep volcanic hills. Concepcion is a favorite destination of trailer boaters and RVers, thanks to its close access off Highway One, many concrete or hard sand launch ramps, and plenty of campgrounds and user-friendly beaches. Concepcion was made for kayaking; a couple outdoor training schools are based here.

Approaches: From Santa Rosalia or the north, come inside Isla San Marcos (least depth 21 feet) and give Punta Chivato a ½-mile clearance. If you come west of Islas Santa Inez, be sure to clear the adjacent shoals.

When entering Bahia Concepcion, steer right down the center of the passage between Punta Las Ornillas (tallest peak on the outer arm) and Punta Arena (a low, cactus covered point about four miles down on the west bank), thus avoiding a shoal ledge off Punta Arena.

If you're coming north from Loreto, some of the nicer intermediate anchorages are found at Punta Mangles, San Juanico,

Punta Pulpito and Caleta San Sebastian, providing more than enough small steps north. To enter Round Punta Concepcion and Punta Aguja (needle) about ½ mile off.

Of the anchorages mentioned above, San Juanico is our favorite. It's most remarkable for its bizarre spires and geological oddities; it's in the lee south of Punta San Basilio and offers five different areas (including False Cove to the north) in which to anchor and explore ashore. Our GPS approach waypoint for San Juanico is 26°22'N by 111°25'W.

Anchorages: Mulege is on the Rio Santa Rosalia, and there's an open roadstead (18 feet, mud and rock bottom) just north of the river mouth, off Punta Sombrerito (little sombrero, aptly named) that serves for taking a dinghy up the river to town. You'll find lots of docks for smaller boats and dinghies lining the south side, and a few on the north side, which is much closer to Mulege.

Punta Aguja and Santo Domingo on the outer arm has a small but welcome shelter from north wind. Anchor in about 15 feet of water. This spot is within sight of Mulege but very isolated at the end of the peninsula.

West of Pitahaya's lighted shoal, the 5-mile long Bahia Coyote is the first real cove on the west side with shelter from north weather. Its first two northern lobes, Playa Santispac and Playa Posada, each have several anchoring spots between shore and Isla San Ramon. Anchoring depths range from 16 to 39 feet. Ashore are a small convenience store and a cafe/bakery called Ana's. The twisty highway winds along the hilly shoreline, and some trucks make racket during the night. Although the beach gets crowded with trailer boaters and campers, especially on long holiday weekends, it's rare to see more than a half

dozen long-range cruising yachts anchored in here at one time, and there's plenty of room. This end of Coyote Bay has the best attractions for novice kayakers and snorkelers. Farther south in Coyote Bay, the larger Isla Coyote and Playa Coyote each provide two beach-front anchorages.

EcoMundo and Mulege Kayaks give lessons, rent novice kayaks and provide naturalists for group kayak tours of the bay. Their juice bar, cafe and nature interpretive center are well worth a visit. EcoMundo and Mulege Kayaks are located in the quieter south end of Coyote Bay called Playa Posada.

About half way down Bahia Concepcion, little Isla Requeson sand spit is a popular camping spot. Requeson is pronounced "ray-kay-SOHN."

In flat calm or slightly southerly weather, the whole south end of Concepcion could provide anchorage, but its subject to stiff chop in the slightest northerly breeze. A small road passes close by here, leading east and out to Caleta San Sebastian.

Mulege by land: The town of Mulege is 10 miles up the two-lane highway. This small fishing town is a natural date-palm oasis mostly behind the north bank of Rio Santa Rosalia that flows down from San Ignacio, sometimes underground. The river is mostly a tidal estuary, and the first mile or two is navigable at high water by small boats. The first docks inside the river are for the Serenidad hotel and air-strip on the south bank, and a half dozen Mom 'n Pop RV parks amid the trees with small docks and launch ramps line the south bank all the way west to the bridge.

Neither Mulege nor Concepcion have a diesel dock, but there's a Pemex diesel and gasoline station just south of town and another on the right side of Mulege's narrow one-way inbound street.

Puerto Escondido: (front to back) inner bay, semi-circular basin, entrance channel, Waiting Room, approaches.

Two small grocery stores are well stocked, but limited. We found good eateries west of the square, and on the two blocks east of the square, and on the out-bound street, up stairs.

Puerto Escondido and Loreto

The next major recreational destination 115 sea miles north in the Sea of Cortez is Puerto Escondido, and the town that services this popular anchorage is Loreto, which lies 12 miles farther north. Puerto Escondido is a large natural harbor, almost landlocked, that shelters more than 100 anchored cruising boats and sportfishers for months on end.

From south to north, Puerto Escondido is comprised of an outer bay with a tall concrete commercial dock, a narrow channel leading north into the large inner bay, and the large inner bay that measures about a mile long and ½ mile wide.

The southwest corner of the inner bay contains a concrete boat-launch ramp, a water spigot, a semi-circular seawall, a rickety but still floating dinghy dock, and a series of dead-end concrete channels – all the result of long-halted construction on a proposed marina, hotels, etc.

Approaches: Puerto Escondido lies below some of the most jagged of the peaks in La Giganta (the giant, feminine) mountain range. The small entrance channel is open only to the south, but it's hidden behind the outer hills. There's a light on Punta Coyote, the south end of the outer hills, but it's not always operating. Our GPS approach waypoint just outside Punta Coyote and the entrance to Puerto Escondido is 25°48.8'N by 111°17'W.

Anchorages: The first anchorage you come to is a smaller outer bay called the Waiting Room, because deep-draft ships used to wait for high tide to enter the larger bay. You can anchor in 24 to 50 feet of water in the east corner.

Inside Puerto Escondido, you can anchor almost anywhere along the irregular shoreline which has three sort of coves. The middle of the bay is only about 48 feet deep, and it's littered with old moorings, engine blocks, etc. A silty shoal juts out from the seasonal river on the west side.

Juncalito is a fishing village a few miles north of Puerto Escondido, and you can anchor there on very settled summer days. Clamming has been good here.

But everyone's favorite place is called Honeymoon Cove or Lovers' Cove on the northwest end of little Danzante Island, only about two miles offshore of the entrance to Puerto Escondido. Two boats is a crowd here. All three lobes are open to the southwest; there's nice snorkeling around to the north on Danzante.

Carmen Island is the 17-mile-long island offshore of Loreto, shaped much like the Southern Cross. A small cove called Balandra lies on the northwest side, and the huge bay and ghost town of La Salina is on the northeast side of Carmen. La Salina has plenty of room and shelter from the north wind.

The volcanic island of Isla Coronado lies about six miles northwest of Carmen, and you can anchor off either side of the pretty sandspit on its southwest corner.

Port Clearance: As we go to press, you still must go to Loreto to clear in with the Port Captain, Migracion and Aduana. The Capitania is one block inland from the panga darsena, on the south side of the street. It's easier and safer to drive 12 miles

into town, but in very calm weather some boats anchor off Loreto – in 20 to 50 feet on the open roadstead off the riprap panga darsena, or just south of there. A small Navy battalion based inside Puerto Escondido sometimes checks boaters papers.

Local Services: Water is sometimes (not always) available at a household-type spigot just west of the concrete pilings and the launch ramp. The Puerto de Loreto people in the old stone building control the water and the launch ramp, and, after you've cleared in, they can order a fuel truck brought down from Loreto to the Waiting Room's commercial dock, which is also used by shimpers.

One mile inland, where the broken paved road meets Highway One, you'll find a large Vagabundos RV park with showers, an air conditioned restaurant, a pool, a coin

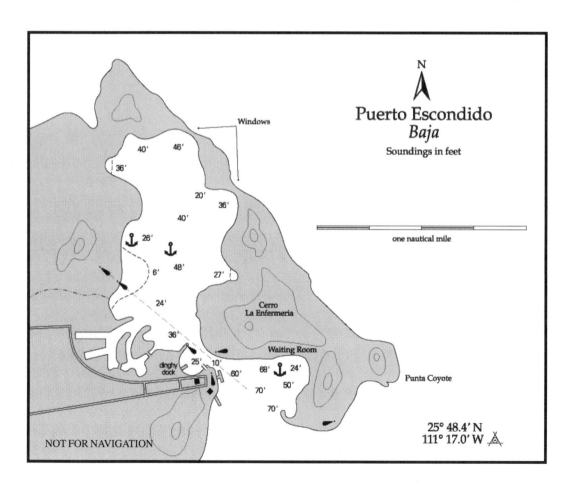

laundry and sometimes a grocery store. Boaters can pay a small fee to use these services. The RV park office can send and receive faxes for a fee, too.

During the winter and spring cruising season, farmers from Ciudad Constitucion bring their fresh fruits, veggies, eggs, tortillas and tamales down to Puerto Escondido to sell to the gringo boaters and RVers. This is a wonderful service.

Getting to Loreto: Because so many boaters spend so much time based around Puerto Escondido, and because it's 600 miles to the U.S. and 12 miles to the nearest town, many boaters buy cheap beater cars in San Diego for use here – and they pass them along to fellow boaters before shoving off. The parking lot is full of such clunkers, which of course infuriates the local taxi drivers.

Loreto: The riprap enclosed darsena for pangas also has a dinghy landing, and the entire waterfront seawall has been raised and bolstered against summer storms. Loreto's claim to fame is the Mission de Loreto, the first in Fra. Junipero Serra's long chain of missions that continues into Upper California. A pretty "paseo" or pedestrian street runs from the mission to the main plaza or "zocalo." Loreto is the most sizable town on this side of the Sea of Cortez north of La Paz, and it's growing.

Sport fishing and diving are the biggest industries here, so those shops abound. It has several good and inexpensive hotels, plus the required Pemex and bus station. Loreto's not a good place to provision, but it has two fairly decent grocery stores, one on the main drag from Highway One into town, the other north of there. If you like seafood restaurants, Loreto is tops. The international airport is a few

miles south of Loreto, and it has daily flights to Los Angeles.

Puerto Escondido to La Paz

We highly recommend that boaters take their time moving between Puerto Escondido and La Paz, because this passage contains some of the most beautiful and remote anchorages in the entire Sea of Cortez. The craggy mountains are always changing color, and the sea surface is often broken by enormous schools of porpoises or pods of whales. Look for giant but docile manta rays and sun fish on the surface, too.

Underwater, the colorful tropical reef fish and other flora and fauna are rivaled only on the Great Barrier Reef. We expect the entire Sea of Cortez soon to be designated a natural preserve.

Along this stretch, our favorite places to hang out on the hook are:

⚓ Agua Verde offers a tiny isolated village and cove, at least three pretty places to anchor (two of them are open to northerly weather), and the unofficial Agua Verde Yacht Club camps out ashore north of the village. We think of Agua Verde when we read Gene Kira's great little novel, "King of the Mountain." Agua Verde, is only 22 sea miles south of Puerto Escondido.

Agua Verde Yacht Club

⚓ Los Gatos, about 15 miles south of Agua Verde, is spectacular in calm weather, offers at least two small anchorages.

⚓ Timbabichi, two miles south of Gatos is a fair weather anchorage.

⚓ Punta Nopolo, one anchorage, about 17 miles south of Timbibichi, seven north of Evaristo.

⚓ Evaristo village and cove, two pretty anchorages 45 miles north of La Paz.

⚓ Isla San Jose, southeast quarter, has three good anchorages, diving, kayaking.

⚓ Isla San Francisco 20 miles north of Partida Cove at least one anchorage.

Isla Espiritu Santo & Isla Partida

These two nearly uninhabited desert islands are so intimately connected, that we think of them together as Espiritu Santos, plural, a 12-mile-long paradise destination only about 15 to 27 miles north of La Paz. Partida means parted, and Espiritu Santo means holy ghost. The reddish volcanic landscape and the turquoise waters make these anchorages seem sort of mystical.

Espiritu Santos has a dozen deep indentations (or cuts, or "caletas") along its eastern side, and each caleta provides several places to anchor – but they're all somewhat open to the west. The largest and most popular is Caleta Partida, where the two islands are joined at a low sandspit – which is divided by a narrow twisting passage usually navigable by dinghy.

Our GPS approach waypoint just outside Caleta Partida is 24°31.5'N by 110°24'W. In the northwest corner is the inner cove, and a tiny seasonal fish camp sprouts on a narrow shingle below the cliffs. The north and east sides are obviously shallow, but you can anchor almost anywhere along their edges in from nine to 46 feet of crystal clear water over brilliant white sand and shell – hence the turquoise color.

Don't be satisfied to follow the flock out to Partida Cove. Other great anchoring possibilities on Espiritu Santos are: Caletita El Embudo, Ensenada Grande, Caleta El Cardonal, Caleta Candelero, Caleta Ballena, Puerto Ballena, Islas Gallo and Gallina (rooster and hen), and Caleta San Gabriel. The wedge-shaped island off the east side of Isla Espiritu Santo is called Isla Ballena.

Isla Los Islotes, the white pinnacles located ½ mile off the north tip of Isla Partida, is a great place for scuba diving and to watch the sea lion colony.

La Paz

The port of La Paz is the largest city in southern Baja California, and it's the largest recreational boating destination in the Sea of Cortez. La Paz lies about 150 nautical miles around the East Cape from Cabo San Lucas, 240 miles across the Sea of Cortez from Mazatlan, and 130 miles south of Loreto. More than 100 U.S. registered yachts call La Paz their "home-away-from-home-port." It offers them a variety of marinas and anchorages within Bahia La Paz, easy fueling, good provisioning, and lots of getaway anchorages.

Los Islotes pinnacles at Espiritu Santo north end are good diving spot.

Approaches: When crossing from Puerto Vallarta or Mazatlan, the best East Cape landing spots are Los Frailes (north and south anchorages) and Cabo Pulmo (spectacular coral reef for scuba diving).

The next great East Cape anchorage is at Muertos, a pretty bay just south of the Cerralvo Channel that offers good overnight shelter from northerly weather. From there, it's about 35 miles northwest to clear the San Lorenzo Channel, where you'll turn south toward La Paz, 15 miles farther.

Our GPS approach waypoint just outside the entrance channel into La Paz harbor is 24°13'N by 110°20'W. Stay within the marked channel as it skirts close to the eastern shoreline, because shoals abound well offshore of El Mogote peninsula.

Marina Palmira:
One of the first things you see upon entering La Paz Channel is Marina Palmira, the newer of the two larger marinas. In fact, Marina Palmira (pronounced "palm-EE-rah") is encircled by a riprap breakwater that's adjacent to the city's entrance channel before you enter the main harbor. Marina Palmira contains 140 full-service slips for boats to 150 feet in length on floating docks. It has metered power (30-, 50- and 100-amp), filtered water, dock boxes and carts, locked gates, showers and laundry, 24-

hour security, ample parking and a launch ramp. The busy (sometimes noisy) road between Pichilingue and La Paz runs next to the marina; it's a 15-minute taxi ride into town from here. Nearby are some upscale restaurants and hotels. Marina Palmira's phone is 011-52 (112) 1-62-97, and their fax is 1-61-42.

Many sportfishers favor Marina Palmira, because it's so close to open waters and has the easiest access fuel dock, immediately on your left as you enter the marina's breakwater. The Moorings

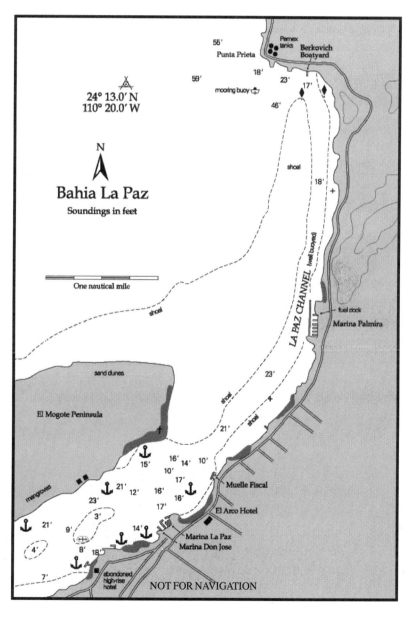

24° 13.0' N
110° 20.0' W

N

Bahia La Paz
Soundings in feet

One nautical mile

NOT FOR NAVIGATION

operates its bare-boat charters from Palmira – its only location in the Sea of Cortez.

Marina La Paz: After passing the main downtown anchorage, the next marina you come to is Marina La Paz, owned by the Shroyer family. (Mac Shroyer practically invented the panga; Mary and son Niel run the marina.) Their comfortable marina contains 90 full-service slips for boats up to 70 feet in length, plus outer end

Marina La Paz: closest to town. Dinghy dock is handy for anchored boats, too.

ties for up to 200-footers. Marina La Paz has 30- and 50-amp power, potable water with good pressure, hot showers, dock boxes and carts, trash pickup, oil recycling, locked gates, 24 hour security and a launch ramp. Marina La Paz also operates a fuel dock, just east of the slips. Call on "Marina La Paz" on VHF. Their phone is 011-52 (112) 5-21-12 or fax 5-59-00.

Marina La Paz is within walking distance of the center of town, and it's favored by long-term cruisers. Most of the boats on the daily VHF net are here. Club Cruceros clubhouse is inside the marina office building – a good rendezvous spot for ride sharing and mail drop. There's a little dock cafe here too.

Marina Don Jose: Also known as Big Abaroa's marina, it's immediately west of Marina La Paz and has about 20 slips. The Abaroa family has a long history in La Paz fishing; Don Jose is the family patron, and you'll see many big boats carrying an Abaroa name. Marina Don Jose has a secured gate and gated parking. On land, it's at the foot of Calle Encina, easily reached from the main drag. The phone for Marina Don Jose is 011-52-112-2-08-48.

Port Clearance: La Paz has the only Port Jurisdiction (Port Captain, Aduana, Migracion and SCT) between Cabo San Lucas and Loreto. All the marinas in La Paz have port clearance services, or you can do your own. Start at Migracion (and Aduana) on the "malecon" just north of the fiscal pier. The Capitania and SCT are a mile inland. La Paz is also a Port of Entry. SCT is the Secretary of Communications and Transportation. Some ports have one, some don't.

Anchorages: The primary anchorage is right off the downtown "malecon" or waterfront street, in 18 to 23 feet, along the stretch from the Muelle Fiscal south to the big pink hotel on the point, staying out of the main channel. Sometimes visiting yachts are allowed to anchor north of the pier, too.

This whole anchorage area is infamous for the "La Paz Waltz," meaning that when the strong current and variable winds are coming from different directions, all the boats swing like dancers around each other. It's a daily study in hydro- and aero-dymanics. This anchorage has the easiest access to shore.

Alternately, you can anchor off the low, sandy El Mogote peninsula in 15 to 23 feet. However, vandals have been known to hassle boats and dinghies here, so ask around first.

Several other anchoring options are found farther down the bay (off Abaroas, off the tower, off La Posada, etc.), and outside the harbor at Bahia Falso, north of Pichilingue Bay, Caleta Lobos and Balandra Bay. Balandra has more room, but plan to visit here during the week; weekend beach traffic and PWCs make it less pleasant. This is one of the few reasons you'll have to keep track of what day it is.

Fuel Stop: The two main fuel docks are at Marina Palmira, right off the entrance channel before you get into La Paz proper, and at Marina La Paz, just past the malecon anchorage. Prices are reasonable and the service is efficient.

However, when the ferry from the mainland fails to bring the necessary number of diesel or gasoline tanker trucks, there's sometimes a fuel shortage on the Baja side. One of the last places to run out is La Paz - usually.

Provisioning: In the whole Sea of Cortez, La Paz is probably the best place to provision. You'll find three large air-conditioned grocery stores in town, complete with a good carniceria and delicatessen. Which one has the best prices seems to vary from season to season, but this is where you stock up. The selection of canned foods and dry staples is good, and the fruits and veggies that come over from the mainland on the ferry are excellent.

There's also a traditional Mercado Central or farmers' market in the up-town area of La Paz, but the stalls have become dark and not as clean as we'd like, and the quality varies.

We like the bread recipe for bolellos (pronounced "boh-LEE-ohz) at La Paz bakeries better than that of Cabo. This is a great place for breakfast pan dulces and birthday-type cakes.

Hurricane Hole: About six miles north of the malecon anchorage, Pichilingue Bay offers steep-walled protection on the west, north and east quadrants, and the southeast has some benefit from Punta Colorado. You can anchor in 18 to 32 feet. Our GPS waypoint just outside the entrance to Pichilingue Bay is 24°15'N by 110°20'W.

History: Hernan Cortez is thought to have landed in 1535 at what is now called Pichilingue (pronounced "pee-chee-LING-way") Bay, then a detached island. Padre Kino landed on El Mogote in 1683 but fled the hostile natives.

The first European settlers arrived in 1811, and La Paz became famous for its pearly buttons drilled from clam shells, until a blight killed off the clams in 1940. Piles of drilled shells can still be found disintegrating in the desert around La Paz.

Chapter 37
Cabo San Lucas

In this chapter, we'll closely examine Cabo San Lucas and some of the East Cape region of Baja California, the northwesternmost state in Mexico.

Cabo San Lucas

This major cape (cabo) named for Saint Luke (San Lucas) is strategically located at the tip of the 700-mile-long Baja California peninsula, which runs northwest to southeast. Cabo San Lucas is 720 miles southwest of San Diego, 155 miles southwest of Magdalena Bay on the Pacific side of Baja, about 140 sea miles southwest of La Paz on the Sea of Cortez, and about 290 miles northwest of Puerto Vallarta on the Mexican mainland.

Because of its close proximity to the U.S., Cabo San Lucas – or "Cabo" as it's often called – is a major sportfishing and yacht cruising destination for more than 2,500 Californians each year. Besides world-class marlin fishing, Cabo San Lucas provides everything a recreational boater could want: diesel and gasoline docks, full-service marina slips, moorings, anchorages,

dinghy docks, a haul-out yard, launch ramps, provisions, diving supplies, marine stores – and plenty of swanky resort stuff like disco clubs and barefoot beach bars.

Cabo San Lucas means different things to different people. To the annual fleet of sailing yachts migrating south, the outer bay is their first taste of tropical sun and crystal clear waters. To the marlin-crazed sportfishing fleet, Cabo is their private gold-plated year-round fun zone. To the average land-based tourist, Cabo Wabo is just another gringo-style party town with T-shirts, beaches and fishing thrown in for diversions.

Approaches: From the south or east, Los Frailes is the most functional recreational anchorage between La Paz and Cabo San Lucas, and it's also the primary landing point for boats crossing from Puerto Vallarta. Los Frailes is 44 miles northeast of Cabo San Lucas. (See East Cape below.) Stay two miles off shore while rounding the East Cape to avoid rocks and shoals. San Jose del Cabo's city lights are 15 miles northeast of Bahia San Lucas, then Cabeza

257

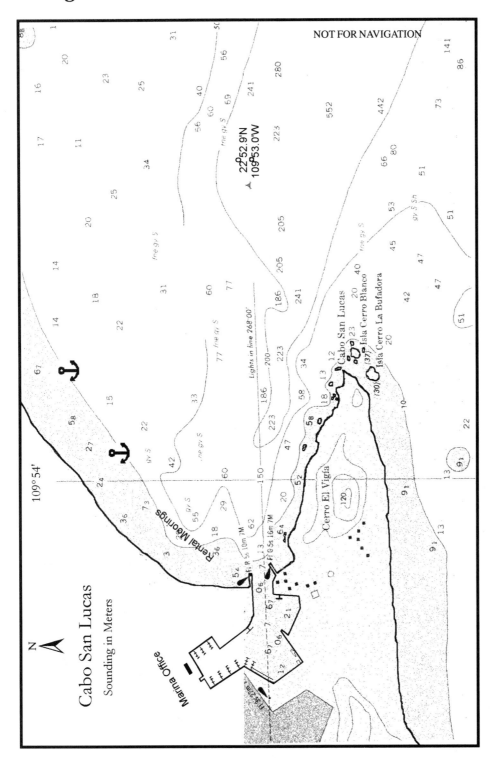

NOT FOR NAVIGATION

22°52.9'N
109°53.0'W

Cabo San Lucas
Sounding in Meters

N

109°54'

Cabo San Lucas

Isla Cerro Blanco

Isla Cerro La Bufadora

Cerro El Vigia

Rental Moorings

Marina Office

Ballena Light marks the eastern side of San Lucas Bay. Don't be surprised to see a cruise ship or two parked in the deep outer waters of the bay.

From the north, you'll find no respite between Magdalena Bay (150 miles up the Pacific coast of Baja) and Cabo San Lucas. Only the panga beach and shore lights at Todos Santos (39 miles northwest) and the loom from La Paz break this uninhabited stretch of the lower quarter of Baja.

Land's End at Cabo San Lucas.

Our GPS approach waypoint off Cabo's famous arches is 22°52.9'N by 109°53'W. Think of Cabo San Lucas's waterfront as two distinct parts: the natural outer bay called Bahia San Lucas, and the man-made inner harbor.

Bahia San Lucas: During the normal winter and spring cruising season, this beautiful natural outer bay is well protected from prevailing northwest weather, thanks to the rocky prominence called "Land's End," the photogenic arches that seem to march down into the sea. During heavy weather, big swells can make their way into the less sheltered eastern end of the bay. Unfortunately, the entire outer bay is wide open to the east, southeast and south-southeast, making it vulnerable to any southerly weather, especially to the ravaging storms of hurricane season during the late summer and fall months.

Bahia San Lucas has a lovely long beach along its north and northeast sides. Hotels, palapa cafes and palm trees dot the shoreline. However, because this bay is very deep at its center (+ 200 feet), the narrow sand shelf adjacent to the beach drops off very steeply into the abyss. The moorings on this narrow shelf are anchored in shifting sand.

In the western corner, the abandoned cannery building and old fuel pier are immediately west of the entrance channel (red and green lights) into the inner harbor.

Cabo's Inner Harbor: The man-made inner harbor has an older outer section and a newer inner section. Generally, the whole inner harbor is offers good shelter during the winter, spring and early summer. The narrow riprap lined entrance leads to the wide outer section, lined by high concrete seawalls. Around this perimeter you'll find the newer fuel dock, the Navy docks, a new "T" shaped breakwater, many fish/dive charter docks, some of the marina's big-boat fingers and another fuel dock. Also, the main dinghy landing lies just to starboard after you enter this outer section of the inner harbor; panga shore boats and taxis pick up and drop off passengers here.

The newer inner section of the inner harbor is further to the north, and it's filled with docks and slips from the marina, plus another concrete launch ramp. Surrounding the seawalls are 3- and 6-story hotels with restaurants and shops, including the marina office and a ship chandler.

Neither part of the inner harbor is a good place in hurricane season. The wind and swell enters through the breakwater entrance, causing considerable wave action and surge inside. The marina basin lies at the mouth of a seasonal river which gushes during flash floods. Many local charter boats haul out at the first posting of a hurricane watch. We do not recommend summering over in Cabo San Lucas.

Cruising Ports

Anchorages and Moorings: The first anchorage is in the outer bay, off the beautiful white sand beach in very clear water. Two-point moorings line the preferred western end of the beach, and anchoring is permitted east of the moorings all the way out to the end of the beach. To get a mooring, call "Cabo Moorings" on VHF channel 16; don't just grab one, because someone may just be out fishing or fueling. Though these moorings are very handy, we don't trust big boats on them in anything but light winds. The comfortable depths for the free anchoring area range from 36 to 45 feet over sand and gravel. You need a considerable amount of chain or rode to anchor farther offshore if the good places close in are taken. It is a long walk or long dinghy ride to town from this anchorage, but it is quieter at night than anywhere else in town. Shore launch service to and from the inner harbor is available.

Dinghy landing: You can land and leave a dinghy either at the Hacienda Hotel's dinghy dock or across the harbor near the ferry terminal. The older concrete boat launching ramp is in the northeast corner of the inner harbor. The newer one is adjacent to the Cabo Yacht Services haul-out yard on the other side of Plaza Las Glorias.

Marina Cabo San Lucas: The main marina in the newer section of the inner harbor is Marina Cabo San Lucas, and they have more than 300 full-service slips at floating docks. Slips here range from 20 to 140 feet, and nearby, yachts up to 200 feet can Med-moor between dolphins with stern access to floating docks. Amenities include shore power, filtered water, showers and laundry, satellite or cable TV, trash pick up, storage lockers, 24-hour security, locked gates, dockside delivery of parts from the nearby chandler, and access to the marina's swimming pool. An open slip in Cabo during cruising season is as scarce as hen's teeth, so it's best to make a reservation and then call within VHF range for a final slip assignment. Often they'll have a staffer or guard take your lines. The marina's phone is 011-52 (114) 31-25-1, and their email is cabomarine@cabo.net.mx The office is at the north end of the inner basin, and they can do your port clearance for you if your last port was in Mexico.

Ship's Agent: You don't have to hire a ship's agent to clear your normal ship's papers in Cabo, but if you even think you may have unusual circumstances or problems, it's a good idea. Cabo is infamous for "emergency" changes to the Crew List – usually when someone flees to the airport with his or her passport before the boat has been cleared into port.

We recommend Victor Barreda and his "Sea Preme Yacht Services;" he and his staffers are efficient and speak perfect English. Call "Sea Preme Yacht Service" on VHF

Marina at Cabo's inner harbor.

channel 88. Victor's office building is one block west of the inner harbor at the foot of the Pedregal. He also owns the adjacent marine hardware store and Penguino ice cream shop. The phone for Barreda's agency is 011-52-(114) 3-02-07, and the fax is 3-00-02. Their office hours are from 0800 to 1800 weekdays and 0900 to 1700 on Saturdays.

Port Clearance: You may clear your own papers if you wish. Or – if this is not your first Port of Entry in Mexico – a marina service can do it for you.

If you handle your own port clearance, you start with the Port Captain's office, which is three blocks north of the Mar de Cortez Hotel. Migracion is on the edge of town next to the Pemex station. The Aduana is in the southwest corner of the town plaza next to the church. Many of the officials speak some English and all are friendly and helpful. There are small service charges for all this paperwork. It's a good idea to hire a taxi to run you around Cabo, because the offices are spread out and the side streets are dusty.

Fuel Stop: Diesel fuel, gasoline and municipal water (water sometimes requires treatment) are available at the 100-foot-long floating fuel dock, located immediately to your left as you enter the inner harbor. This is a vast improvement from the rickety old pier off the abandoned cannery, but you need to fend well against wakes from passing boats. You can pay by credit card if it's arranged in advance.

Another fuel dock lies at the southeast end of the Plaza las Glorias hotel.

Water Warning: Tap water in Cabo needs chlorine or other treatment, especially after heavy rain. Ironically, this port had been prized as a reliable source of

Haul-out facilities at Cabo San Lucas.

pure water for five centuries, but recent urban growth overwhelmed the natural aquifer's ability to filter out salt and contaminated ground water.

Haul-out Yard: The only boatyard here is Cabo Yacht Services (formerly Nielsen and Beaumont), and it has a 70-ton sling hoist. The yard is in the far north end of the inner harbor, adjacent to Marina CSL's office, a Coast Chandlery store and the main launch ramp.

Local Services: Cabo's tourist district wraps itself around the inner harbor, so it's almost in the middle of town. A small grocery store on the corner of Matamoros and the malecon has a good selection of produce and staples at fairly decent prices, and Aramburo's larger grocery a few blocks east is also good. But prices for food and provisioning in Cabo San Lucas are among the highest in Mexico.

The Taqueria San Lucas south of the plaza is good for an inexpensive breakfast or lunch. The Mar de Cortez is a reasonably priced hotel with an excellent restaurant. The Giggling Marlin across the street is famous for boisterous drinking. We recommend the sundowners on the patio bar of the Hotel Finesterre, overlooking the broad expanse of the Pacific. It's well worth the trek up the hill.

Renting bicycles and small scooters is a good way to get around in town. Car and jeep rentals are available at all big hotels and, often less expensive, at the international airport east of San Jose del Cabo. From the airport to Cabo is a very expensive 45-minute ride in the van taxis, and it takes longer if you have to stop at each hotel along the way. But it's usually much less expensive if you can find a VW bug taxi.

History: This cape was marked on the earliest Pacific charts as a reliable source of pure water. English corsairs anchored in Bahia San Lucas and waited to ambush the Manila galleons. John Steinbeck first described the town as a tiny collection of grass huts from which the Port Captain paddled out in a dugout canoe wearing a ragged uniform shirt to greet visiting boats. Much of Sea World's original aquatic collection was gathered in the then-pristine outer harbor. Cabo of the second millennium is a posh resort teetering on the brink of disaster by hurricane or over-development, and its Port Captain runs a pretty tight ship.

East Cape

Everything between Cabo San Lucas and La Paz may be considered the East Cape region, and there are no true "cruising ports" on East Cape. But we'll look at the places of significance for long-range vessels, going east and north toward La Paz.

Punta Palmilla: This small point 12 miles east of Cabo San Lucas offers only scant shelter for anchorage east of the reef in about 20 feet of water. Only hotel boats

are allowed to use the landing for their charter passengers.

San Jose del Cabo: This nice town 15 miles east of Cabo San Lucas doesn't have a good anchorage, but it's an interesting side trip.

Gordo Banks: Off Punta Gordo about 25 miles around the corner from Cabo San Lucas, the inner and outer shelves provide excellent fishing. We've taken mucho marlin, wahoo, dorado and grouper here.

Los Frailes: The first good anchorage area on East Cape is 45 miles around from Cabo. Both the north and south sides of this landmark headland provide good anchoring alternatives, so you're covered whether the wind is blowing from the north, south or west. Of course, it's wide open to the east.

The only living coral reef system in Mexico is the lovely Cabo Pulmo Reef, and it starts just about two miles northeast of the anchorage on the north side of Los Frailes. Small diving hotels are ashore. Our GPS approach waypoint a mile off Los Frailes is 23°23'N by 109°24'W. Los Frailes makes the best jumping off and landing spot when crossing the Sea of Cortez.

Punta Arena de la Riviera: About 65 miles northeast of Cabo San Lucas, this low sandy point of land provides marginal anchorage in prevailing weather south of the point. Several small sportfishing hotels are within sight.

Muertos: A good overnight anchorage lies on the south side of Punta Perico in the bay called Ensenada de los Muertos – Muertos for short. RVers camp on the beach, and you can anchor off the ruins of an old wharf, dropping the hook in 13 to 20 feet of crystal clear water over white sand. This anchorage is about 100 miles around East Cape from Cabo San Lucas, and about 50 miles from La Paz harbor. Our GPS approach waypoint a half mile off the anchorage is 23°59'N by 109°49'W.

Cerralvo Channel: The 15-mile-long mountainous Cerralvo Island lies about five miles off the sandy shore between Punta Arena de la Ventana and Punta Gorda (both common names), and the channel running northwest to southeast is affected by tides and winds.

San Lorenzo Channel: This 3-mile-wide passage between the south end of Isla Espiritu Santo and the La Paz headland is marked by shoals and lights. Bajo Scout Light on the shoal on the south side of the passage stands at GPS position 24°22.10'N by 110°18.53'W. Pass just north of it. From here, La Paz harbor is only 15 miles south.

Cruising Ports

Navigating Baja's Pacific Coast

Use this **Planning Chart** for Chapters 38 through 41

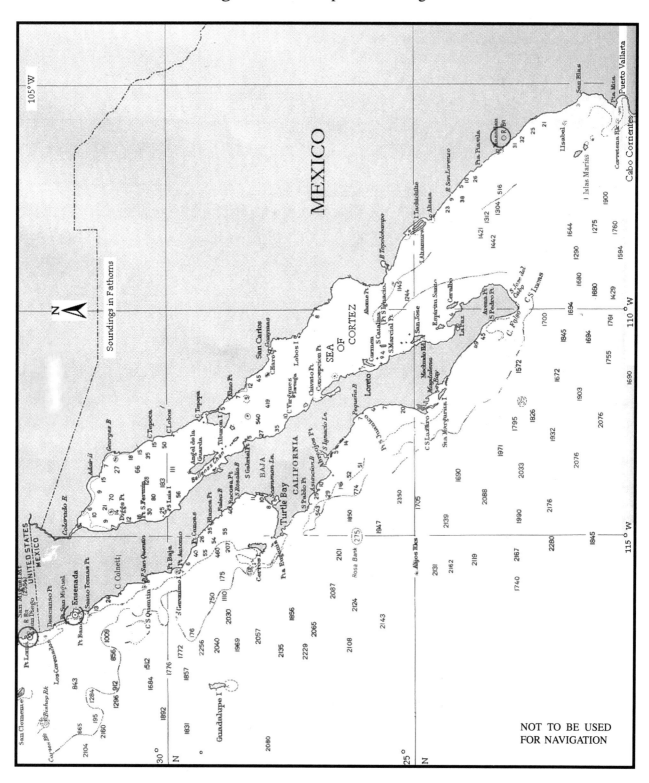

NOT TO BE USED
FOR NAVIGATION

Chapter 38
Navigating Baja's Pacific Coast

The Pacific coast of Baja California is mostly a wilderness of dry rugged terrain marked by very few navigation lights. Comfortable anchorages are few and far between. After having skippered more than 100 different yachts (power and sail) up and down Baja's Pacific coast between Cabo San Lucas and San Diego in all seasons, we've learned quite a lot. In this chapter, we'll share our local knowledge of this notorious passage – for boaters traveling in either direction.

For a much more detailed description of local weather and where to get WX-radio information for this complex leg, read "MexWX: Mexico Weather for Boaters" by Capt. John E. Rains.

Northbound Bash

Although we refer to this as the Northbound Bash, you're actually moving in a northwesterly direction. This 720-mile passage is mostly against the prevailing Northwesterly winds. How long this takes depends on many factors: your boat, your immediate weather, which courses you lay, and where you anchor – for starters.

Whenever these winds are light, we prefer to run a straight rhumb line up the coast, passing a few miles off the major capes. If the weather is heavy, we anchor more frequently and run closer to shore to take advantage of night and morning calms. (Occasionally, you'll encounter almost no wind on the outside coast of Baja, but you can't bet your life on it.)

Cabo San Lucas to Mag Bay

Departing Cabo San Lucas can be harrowing, because winds pile up and howl around Cabo Falso (22°52'N by 109°58'W), though they typically die down 10 miles farther on. If possible, ask for a weather report on VHF or SSB from any boats already 10 to 15 miles up the line. It's best to depart Cabo San Lucas during the early morning calm, well before the afternoon sea breeze fills in. The weather for this first leg from Cabo San Lucas to Cabo San Lazaro is generally mild. If winds are predicted to be strong, parallel the coast within five miles.

The first landfall about 135 miles up the coast is Punta Tosca (24°18'N by 11°43'W), a dominant land feature at the south end of Isla Santa Margarita, the barrier island that forms the outside of the southern half of Bahia Magdalena (Mag Bay). Don't attempt to enter Mag Bay east of Punta Tosca, because it's shoal and not an entrance. From Boca Flor de Malba, head due west to Punta Tosca to avoid this shoal area. However, Punta Tosca is a good land feature to use for a sextant altitude for distance off. (Also, bearings on Punta Entrada (24°32'N by 112°04'W), the north side of the real entrance into Magdalena are good.) About 45 miles northwest of Punta Tosca, the major headland of Cabo San Lazaro (24°48'N by 112°19'W) marks the northwest end of the barrier islands forming Mag Bay.

Magdalena Bay

Inside Mag Bay's true entrance, you'll find anchorages and good protection from Northwesterlies at Belcher's Point and Man o' War Cove. Mag Bay is a huge protected sea of a place. You may also get fuel and supplies at Puerto San Carlos, Mag Bay's main port, but we don't recommend it except in emergencies.

Puerto San Carlos lies 15 miles inside the northern half of Mag Bay, and the final approach is up a long narrow zigzag or "N" shaped channel through shoal water with heavy current. Puerto San Carlos has a Port Captain and all the other officials, so you must go through formal port clearance procedures in order to stop here. You fuel at the busy, dirty commercial pier. The concrete is rough, and the current is heavy. It's not a place for a yacht. The town of San Carlos is dusty and uninteresting.

The rest of Mag Bay is an interesting place to explore, and other anchorages are found at Puerto Alcatraz and

Puerto Cortez, both just south of the true entrance into Mag Bay.

Bahia Santa Maria

Santa Maria, a large bay outside of Mag Bay but still in the lee of Cape San Lazaro, is another very good anchorage in prevailing weather. Whenever we have to choose between Mag Bay and Santa Maria as an overnight anchorage, we pick Santa Maria because it's an easy in and out anchorage. The afternoon seabreeze can be strong and gusty in this anchorage, but there's no fetch and the holding ground is excellent.

Mag Bay
to Turtle Bay

If you have reliable reports of light winds from Cape San Lazaro northward, then head straight for Turtle Bay (27°40'N by 114°53'W), allowing five degrees left for set.

Too many times we've found ourselves pushed toward Abreojos (26°42'N by 113°34'W) by the current. The name Abreojos, which translates to "open your eyes," is appropriately named – because of the many reefs off this point. We've heard too many horror stories of wrecks and near misses in this area.

The prevailing wind north of Cape San Lazaro is usually too strong for comfort, so we regularly head due north toward San Juanito (good anchorage), and then when we reach lighter wind conditions, we parallel the coast, usually about five miles off shore. The wind and sea condition will be lighter than offshore. Good anchorages in northwesterly weather are Abreojos (above) and Asuncion (27°07'N by 114°13'W). The rest are marginal.

Turtle Bay, the next stop, can be missed in spite of its size. Make a landfall near Asuncion Island (the light is often extinguished) and keep a good DR plot going. The land features are difficult to discern because of rugged topography. When approaching Turtle Bay from the south, beware of a false entrance south of Thurloe Head. The beach is low and you can see the loom of the village lights over it at night.

Chapter 39 describes Turtle Bay in detail.

Turtle Bay
to Isla San Quintin

Leave Turtle Bay via the Dewey Channel between Isla Navidad and Punta Eugenia (27°51'N by 115°05'W) at first light, in order to get through this channel before the afternoon sea breeze builds. Currents mixing here contribute to its turbulence, setting you off course rapidly.

Along the east side of Cedros Island you'll find a welcome respite from the prevailing Northwesterlies. Enjoy it, because when you arrive at the north end of the island (28°23'N by 115°13'W), it is not uncommon to be greeted by 30- to 40-knot winds and high seas. Often calmer seas are encountered away from the island.

If Mother Nature is struggling to win, turn back and anchor in the lee of the island, south of the tiny settlement near the lighthouse on the north end. Often so many boats are hunkered down here awaiting their chance to head north that it's been dubbed the Cedros Island Yacht Club.

In heavy winds, some skippers prefer to head toward something called Fondeadero San Carlos (San Carlos anchorage) (29°37'N by 115°29'W). This course puts the wind a few points off your port bow and closes with land sooner, where the wind should abate somewhat. However San Carlos is a very marginal anchorage, and we have been blown out of it several

times. North of San Carlos, all vessels should pass well outside of the dangerous Sacramento Reef and its neighbor Isla San Geronimo. Other skippers tell us they pass between the reef and shore, but the area is clogged in kelp.

In light winds we head straight across from the north end of Cedros toward San Diego. We've laid a course for a point 15 miles off Sacramento Reef and still have been set within five miles of the reef by heavy current.

The lights on Isla San Geronimo, Isla San Benito and the north end of Cedros are not apt to light up your life. If you assume that all Mexican lights are extinguished and plan accordingly, you will rarely be disappointed.

The lee of Cabo San Quintin (30°21'N by 115°52'W) has good protection in prevailing weather. Breakers and migrating shoals block the entrance to Puerto San Quintin, which is inside the estuary, but local pangueros know the best path between them, at least for that day. Hire a panguero as a guide. Do not attempt to go inside the estuary without local knowledge or in a deep-draft vessel.

Chapter 40 covers more details about San Quintin.

San Quintin
to San Diego

Isla San Martin (30°29'N by 116°07'W) is the next landmark north of San Quintin, and this small island has two marginal anchorages: south of the island or inside the lagoon. However, south of San Martin Island, beware of Ben's Rock, a ship-killer pinnacle that breaks only occasionally. This stretch north of San Martin Island parallels a more regular coastline. We give Point Colnett a wide berth and pass 10 miles off Puerto Santo Tomas. Be careful of Soledad Rock which lies 1 1/4 miles west of Santo Tomas Point.

South Todos Santos Island (31°48'N by 116°48'W) has two sheltered coves on its northeast side, but they are too often filled with aqua-culture buoys that restrict anchoring. In heavy weather the next good anchorage is inside Ensenada (31°52'N by 116°38'W) harbor.

Ensenada harbor is covered in Chapter 40.

If the weather is good north of Santo Tomas, pass five miles west of the Todo Santos Light and finally sail between South Coronado Island (32°24'N by 117°15'W) and Rosarito Beach. Favor the island side of the channel to avoid one or two large offshore mooring buoys abeam of the generating station at Rosarito Beach.

Finally Point Loma (32'40'N by 117'15'W) and its welcome shelter come within sight. However, pass outside the north-south submerged Zuniga Jetty that frames the east side of the buoyed entrance channel into San Diego Bay.

Southbound Express

In all our trips, which have been made in both power boats and sailing vessels, we have enjoyed most the non-stop southbound sailing route from San Diego to Cabo San Lucas. This fast trip gets you into warmer weather much more quickly. How long this takes depends on many factors: your boat, your immediate weather, which courses you lay, if or where you anchor.

From South Coronado Island Light, we head due magnetic south until we're about 100 miles off shore. Sailboats find this is normally a beam reach and at times a little uncomfortable, because wind and seas continue to build as they break out of the lee of Point Conception. Outside, a 20-knot wind often blows out of the northwest,

day and night. We turn downwind, running before huge majestic seas.

Our course then parallels the coast, passing 50 miles outside San Benito Island, 50 miles off Cabo San Lazaro, and then heads directly for Cabo Falso at the very tip of the Baja peninsula. Having only two course changes makes dead reckoning much easier.

We're normally not coast huggers, but many people choose to transit this coast by day hops, anchoring each night. Coast skirting requires much more vigilance, because many of the anchorages are barely protected from the northwest and are open to the south and west. Coastal traffic is heavy, especially in the main shipping lane clearly defined on a pilot chart. Merchant vessels have a difficult time spotting small craft. Cruising the outside route avoids shipping-lane traffic but is still within VHF range of radio assistance.

We've often enjoyed the solitude of three days spent without seeing another vessel. However, your routine of standing good bridge or helm watches should not be relaxed; we've also had close encounters with fishing vessels 100 miles off shore.

Because power boat skippers aren't looking for wind, they should head between the Coronados and shore, then straight to the north end of Cedros Island, passing down its eastern side and through the Dewey Channel. From there, they can head straight to Cabo San Lazaro north of Mag Bay, then straight to Cabo San Lucas.

Most pleasure boats these days have GPS, and some still have satellite navigation systems. However, we don't recommend going off shore without knowledge of celestial navigation. Weather should be monitored closely, no matter which direction you're heading. Winter can generate violent southeasters in northern Baja, and summer brings hurricanes to southern Baja. Being fool hardy is dangerous to your health.

If a strong storm with southerly winds is predicted, head for a safe anchorage. Magdalena Bay, Turtle Bay and the east side of Isla San Matin provide the only protection from southerly weather on the Baja coast. However the anchorage in the cove on the east side of Isla San Martin is often full of buoys.

Landfall on Cabo San Lucas is easy thanks to high mountains visible from well out to sea. Cabo Falso Light is very powerful and the most reliable we've seen in Mexico. It has a racon, a radar identification beacon, for ease in identification as do Todo Santos, San Benito and San Lazaro.

If you don't want to make the trip non-stop, break it up by stopping only at safe anchorages. My suggestions: San Quintin, Turtle Bay, Asuncion, San Juanito, Santa Maria or Bahia Magdalena. All anchorages of course are subject to weather conditions.

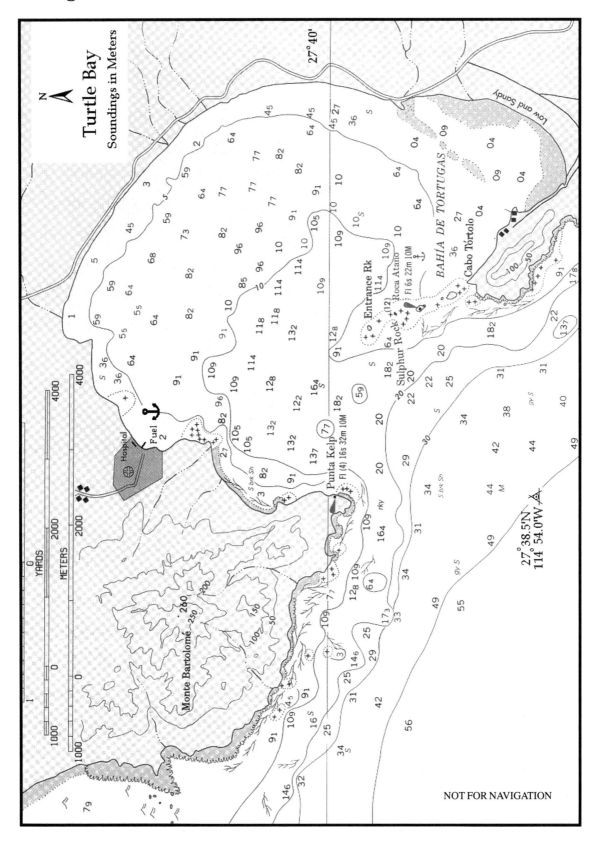

Turtle Bay
Soundings in Meters

NOT FOR NAVIGATION

Chapter 39
Turtle Bay & San Quintin

∿∿∿∿∿∿∿∿∿∿∿∿∿∿∿∿∿∿∿∿∿∿∿∿∿∿∿∿∿∿∿∿∿∿

In this chapter, we'll look at Pacific Baja's important cruising port of Turtle Bay and the smaller anchorage north of it, San Quintin.

Turtle Bay

Often considered to be the half-way point on the 733-mile-long Baja California peninsula, Turtle Bay (27°40'N by 114°53'W) is a large natural harbor located about 395 miles north of Cabo San Lucas and about 338 miles south of San Diego – plotting the coastal course. Turtle Bay offers boaters the only all-weather harbor between Ensenada and Bahia Magdalena, plus the only fuel pier between those locations, plus a small town with some emergency services, a bus connection through the barren desert to the highway, and some needed respite from the arduous Baja passage.

Turtle Bay's older names are Puerto San Bartolome or Bartoleo, and on some charts it's called by its Spanish name, Bahia Tortuga. The town's sole reason for existence was fishing, but the cannery it was built to service has been closed for years.

Approaches: When you're coming up to Turtle Bay from the south, a false entrance east of Point Thurloe allows you to see the town – but you're actually looking at it across a low stretch of beach. This is especially deceptive at night when the town's few lights appear close to the waterline. The real entrance is three miles to the northwest.

When approaching from the north, you should swing around Punta Sargazo to avoid the kelp beds. Be careful of a submerged rock called Roca Entrada, which you can see breaking in the daytime.

Anchorages: The main anchorage is on the north side of the bay fronting the town, in 18 feet of water on sand that makes good holding ground. Almost no swell makes it into the harbor, so if there's no wind, it can be a quiet anchorage. If you wish to get away from town, you can also anchor at the southeast end of the bay. During Santa Ana-like winds from the east, we've anchored safe and snug along the eastern side of the bay in the lee of a desert shoreline, but we got coated with orange dirt.

Fuel Stop: Jutting out from in front of the blue canning ruins you'll see the tall fuel pier, usually painted neon green or yellowish orange. Don't attempt to come alongside this pier. The fueling procedure here calls for Med-mooring. The water is eight feet deep at low tide.

Someone is generally on the pier from 0800 to 1700 Monday through Friday. If not, they will soon show up when they see someone Med-mooring. On weekends you may have to go ashore to ask around, and you may have to pay overtime. You'll need help to secure your lines to this high pier.

Head into the wind (usually on the east side of the pier), set your anchor and back toward the pier, sending up two stern lines. Sometimes they toss down a monkey fist; if not, dig out your own. You can criss-cross your stern lines and also secure long spring lines aft on each side of your boat, to help keep you from twisting.

Freddy or Maria or other of Gordo's offspring have the concession to operate this fuel dock, and they have many helpers. The fuel is delivered from tanks through a liter-measuring pump.

TIP: You need to be sure the numbers on the meter are zeroed out before anyone starts pumping. This avoids disagreements after you're done fueling. You also need to be competent at converting liters to gallons and pesos to dollars – talents southbound boaters may not yet have honed.

If you want only a smaller quantity of fuel, you may not have to Med-Moor to the pier. Some of Turtle Bay's pangueros will pick up your jerry jugs from your boat in the anchorage, take them to their pick up truck and out to the Pemex station by the road, fill them and deliver them back to your boat.

Of course, there's a small fee for such service. We think this is a great idea. An entrepreneur named Jorge was the first panguero to set this up, and others have followed suit.

Although it's been years since fuel at this pier was delivered directly from rusty barrels, you're more likely to received dirty or water laden fuel here than anywhere else along this route – simply because the fuel is trucked so far over bumpy gravel roads in order to get here. The proverbial "Baja fuel filter" may come in handy.

The fuel bill is payable in U.S. dollars or Mexican pesos, cash only. Put your money in a plastic bag, and they'll pass you a coffee can on a rope to put it in.

Dinghy Landing: You can tie a dinghy at the foot of the metal stairway on the southeast side of the pier. If it's full or unavailable, the west side of the pier has two very rickety ladders, but be careful of the barnacles. Otherwise, surf landings are usually drier northwest of the pier.

Turtle Bay fuel dock: Gordo's daughter and sons run this fueling operation, on the end of the old cannery's tall pier.

Port Clearance: Turtle Bay has no Port Captain, and it is not a Port of Entry. Ensenada and Cabo San Lucas are the nearest Ports of Entry. (Turtle Bay is part of the Santa Rosalia port jurisdiction.) A small detachment of marines that is stationed in Turtle Bay and Cedros Island occasionally checks the papers of visiting boats. If they're in the mood, they'll come looking for you; you do not have to go to them. The papers clearing you out from your last Mexican port are all that's necessary.

If you're southbound and didn't clear into Mexico at Ensenada, then have a Crew List, Fishing Permit, Fishing Licenses and all your other papers ready to show them. If your stay is only a day or two, you might have no contact with the officials.

Local Services: If you have electrical or mechanical problems that you can't fix yourself, ask the fuel attendants if they can refer you to the right repair people. Locals are self-sufficient; at times Turtle Bay has had diesel mechanics, electricians and welders, but they don't speak English.

Food supplies are very limited. A few small "tiendas" carry canned goods and a sporadic selection of limp vegetables. Don't buy raw meat here. As in most Mexican towns, the bakery and tortilla shops are excellent. Fish are available from the local fishermen, and some would rather trade than sell for hard cash. The cooperative members are forbidden to sell or trade lobster, shrimp or shellfish to anyone, so don't ask.

Scuba divers should keep in mind that a decompression chamber used by the old cannery was moved to the little clinic in the middle of town. Chambers were also located at Cedros Island and Abreojos, but the once flourishing abalone industry is extinct here.

Regular bus service connects Turtle Bay to Highway One at Vizcaino. The small bus that covers this 135-mile quasi-graded road gets filled up fast, so you need to make a reservation at the bus office in the east quadrant of the village.

Long stretches of the desert road into Turtle Bay get wash out by flash floods during each rainy winter and each summer storm season. If the road's open, you could make it in a passenger car, but the car will never be the same again. If the road is closed, it's likely to take a week of dry weather before repairs can be made.

Several telephone offices and a few pay phones are scattered through town.

Turtle Bay's small airstrip just north of town has an asphalt runway with many patched cracks. The cannery that built and maintained it closed several years ago. Occasionally a charter airplane flies down from Ensenada's municipal airport.

TIP: If you have to fly out of Turtle Bay – or land here – you're in for an experience. John once had to fly up to the states for parts, and he was lucky to get aboard an overloaded DC-3. He flew seated on a gunny sack of live lobster, sans seat belt of course. People were standing up in the aisle during take off, and the pilot had to take off down wind over the bay, because there wasn't enough room to clear the hills at the far end of the runway to windward.

When they landed safely in Ensenada and the pilot shut down the engines, you could hear the lobsters making a clacking sound. Since then he chuckles when the airline stewardesses give the spiel about buckling seat belts. And we always keep our seat belts fastened.

Turtle Bay has no tourists and therefore has no tourist amenities. (Pat wants to make picture post cards and donate them to the town of Turtle Bay, to raise

273

funds for the medical clinic or a new spay clinic.) However, the green restaurant on top of the highest hill in town has good seafood and traditional Mexican dishes. There's a tiny hotel in back where, if you really really need one, you can sometimes get a hot shower.

Church of the Sea at Turtle Bay.

The church you can see from the pier and anchorage here has an interesting story. About 30 years ago, three sailors from Southern California wrecked their boat on the rocks well outside the entrance, and the some fishermen plucked the sailors out of the water, got them medical attention, and then put them up in their houses for several weeks while they recovered.

One of the survivors spent many hours praying in the tiny, ramshackle building the townsfolk used for a church, even though it was practically sliding down the berm into the bay – even though he wasn't Catholic. When both survivors returned to the states, they raised a couple thousand "thank-you" dollars and sent the money back to Turtle Bay. The town decided to use the money to lay the foundation of a real church. The large building you see today looks quite prosperous.

Between Turtle Bay and San Quintin

The previous chapter on Navigating Baja's Pacific Coast gives waypoints and explicit details about this stretch from Turtle Bay to San Quintin.

Cedros Island: This 20-mile-long island is located about 50 miles north of Turtle Bay. Cedros Island has a real town at the south end, and its tiny fishing harbor is protected inside a riprap breakwater. Cedros Island Village has its own Port Captain and Navy base, but due to heavy commercial traffic (barges, freighters and tugs) going in and out of the salt factory docks just south of the town, all recreational boats are urged to use Turtle Bay instead – unless of course in case of emergency. The west side of Cedros Island is usually its weather side. The 5-mile-wide bay on its southwest side can provide some shelter between the reefs on its western side.

Instead, many boats hang out at one or two small anchorages on the northeast end of Cedros Island below the navigation light, usually waiting for better northbound weather. Whenever a few boats gather, they dub themselves the Cedros Island Yacht Club. This island was named for the forest of cedar trees that formerly covered it.

Fondeadero San Carlos: Also called San Carlos Anchorage (to differentiate it from the port inside Mag Bay or the marina in the Sea of Cortez), this marginal anchorage lies 53 miles southeast of San Quintin and 78 miles north of the north end of Cedros Island. When crossing the Bay of Vizcaino northward, we often think of Fondeadero San Carlos as a tiny light at the end of the dark tunnel. It's more a target to aim toward on land than a place to anchor. We've been blown out of here and had breakers start closing in behind us, so stay alert if you anchor overnight.

Punta Baja lies 28 miles northwest of Punta San Carlos. But en route lies the infamous Sacramento Reef.

Sacramento Reef: Between Fondeadero San Carlos and Ensenada, watch out for two major hazards: Sacramento Reef and Ben's Rock. Both these hazards have claimed many ships and lives – a few more each year.

The infamous Sacramento Reef covers an area almost four miles square, so give it lots of room. Our GPS waypoint about two miles outside Sacramento Reef is 29■44.0'N by 115■50.0'W. The south end of the Sacramento Reef lies about 16 miles northwest of Fondeadero San Carlos, so to travel between San Carlos and San Quintin, you must go way out around the reef – giving Punta San Antonio at least a 7-mile berth. If you're coming south, be aware that Sacramento Reef lies about two miles south-southeast of Isla San Geronimo.

Ben's Rock: This nasty pinnacle is only occasionally awash, but its primary danger is a set of huge breaking waves that erupt sporadically within a 1-mile radius, known to capsize large commercial fishing vessels without warning. Ben's Rock lies about 1.25 miles south of Isla San Martin, which is on the northern approach to San Quintin.

San Quintin

Cabo San Quintin (pronounced "keen-TEEN") is the south-projecting headland forming the north end of Bahia San Quintin, and although sheltered anchorage can normally be found in the lee east of this point, first-time visiting boats should not attempt to enter the large shallow estuary that runs northeast from this point.

Cabo San Quintin lies about 110 miles down the coast from Ensenada harbor and about 180 miles up the coast from Turtle Bay. Five large volcano cones (610- to 876-feet-tall) are distinctive landmarks forming the west side of the estuary. A low sandy peninsula runs eight miles south from the taller volcanoes, ending in the 1.5-mile-wide Cabo San Quintin. The smaller cone of Mount Mazo (160-feet-tall) stands on Cabo San Quintin, along with buff sand dunes and black lava flows. San Quintin Light stands on the outside of the Mazo cone. Migrating sand bars and breakers block the entrance to the estuary, which is fine – because it's only for local pangas or shallow-draft vessels with local pilots.

Anchorages: The anchorage for heavy northwest weather is tucked up inside, east of the rocky reef-strewn Punta Entrada, in 18 to 25 feet of calm water, south of the breakers. Our GPS approach waypoint ½ mile south of Cabo San Quintin is 30°21'N by 116°00'W. From here, round the low black reefs at least ½ mile off.

Punta Azufre (Punta Azufre Light) is the low sandy arm at the northwest end of the long beach lining the eastern shore of Bahia San Quintin (not the estuary). About three miles east of Punta Azufre, you can also anchor off the big hotel or just about anywhere along that regular beach where you can find shelter, usually in 24 to 40 feet of water. The hotels launch pangas across the beach, but dinghies need to be locked up. The hotels usually welcome yacht guests at their restaurants, if you don't show up too grubby.

San Quintin Estuary: By dinghy (and with a local panguero to act as your guide), you can negotiate the breakers and outside sand bars – in order to enter the estuary. Once inside, the narrow channel winds around for nine before arriving at a launch ramp and the outskirts of the town of San Quintin. If you can hitch a ride into town, it has a daily bus link to Ensenada and a few small grocery stores. The Pemex station is out on Highway One.

If you dinghy adventure up inside the estuary, don't forget that, when you are ready to exit, the tide will have radically changed the breakers – so you'll probably need a guide to get out as well.

Every year, some unknowing first-time cruising boat or sportfisher blunders inside this estuary in the dark, bumping several times going in. In the morning, after they've discovered where they are (and after their hearts start beating again), they have to call for a very expensive rescue service to tow them out. And the rescue service always hires a local panguero to guide the operation. Our advice is, *no vale la pena*: It's not worth the effort.

Isla San Martin and Ben's Rock: Only 9.5 miles northwest of Cabo San Quintin (a couple miles due west of the five big volcano cones), the small island of San Martin (pronounced "mar-TEEN") is marked by a 500-foot-tall "Chinese hat" in its center. Isla San Martin has a small cove on the east side, thinly enclosed in a low rock perimeter that leaves it open to the north and east. This cove is called Hassler's Cove, and you can sometimes find room amid the aqua-culture buoys and fishing boats to anchor inside, in about 24 feet of water. Our GPS position inside Hassler's Cove is 30■28.83'N by 116■06.20'W. The small village ashore has no services.

But between San Quintin and Isla San Martin, beware of Ben's Rock. Ben's Rock lies about 1.25 miles due south of Isla San Martin. This nasty pinnacle is only occasionally awash, but its primary danger is a set of huge breaking waves that erupt sporadically within a 1-mile radius, known to capsize large commercial fishing vessels without warning.

TIP: Due to the danger of Ben's Rock, avoid the area within two miles south of Isla San Martin. Between San Quintin and Isla San Martin, either hug the coast or go well outside these points.

Cabo Colnett: This distinctive mesa headland (Cabo Colnett Light) offers a decent anchorage in northerly weather. Cabo Colnett lies about 30 miles northwest of Isla San Martin and about 65 miles southeast of Ensenada harbor. The anchorage lies about 2.5 miles east of the tip of Cabo Colnett, just east of the notch (30°57.64'N by 116°17.63'W) in 25 to 35 feet of water.

On radar, Cabo Colnett looks like the profile of a nose. This analogy holds true, because the notch or nostril is infamous for snorting or gusting. A small breeze up on the flat plateau gets amplified and directed down the notch. We've seen a good sized sailboat get knocked over sharply when it was peacefully anchored directly below Colnett's notch.

Chapter 40
Ensenada

〜〜〜〜〜〜〜〜〜〜〜〜〜〜〜〜〜〜〜〜〜〜〜〜〜〜〜〜〜

For southbound boaters, Ensenada is their first taste of foreign cruising and often their Port of Entry into Mexico. Southbound boaters use this guidebook in reverse order to make the 5,000-mile route to Miami.

For northbound boaters, Ensenada is their last stop before returning to the United States – after a 5,000-mile adventure from south Florida.

Ensenada

This thriving port town of Ensenada (31°52'N by 116°38'W) lies only about 60 miles south of San Diego, California, making it Mexico's closest port to Southern California. Ensenada's proximity makes it useful to Southern California boaters as:

✓an increasingly popular marina and offshore delivery spot when purchasing a recreational vessel in California.

✓an increasingly popular haul-out port to take advantage of lower labor rates.

✓ a good shake-down cruise destination to prepare for a longer cruise through Mexico and beyond.

✓a first (or last) stop in a long cruising itinerary where you can take care of last-minute items.

✓an easy in, easy out fuel stop.

✓an interesting cruising port for sportfishing, great Mexican restaurants.

In the past few years Ensenada's Port Captains, marinas and downtown businesses have really cleaned up the harbor and made a big push to develop its busy, colorful waterfront in a way that is harmonious with both pleasure boaters and the town's thriving industries of fishing and shipping. Cruise ships call here, and many sailing regattas from California yacht clubs finish here. Land tourists arrive by the hundreds even on week days, yet the quaint town retains its rural character, unlike its neighboring Tijuana which has no port.

Ensenada's weather is very similar to Southern California's. The main hazard is frequent dense fog created when cold currents well up. Every few years or so in the winter or early spring, strong southeast gales sweep the harbor. The southern breakwater protects the harbor from that direction only slightly.

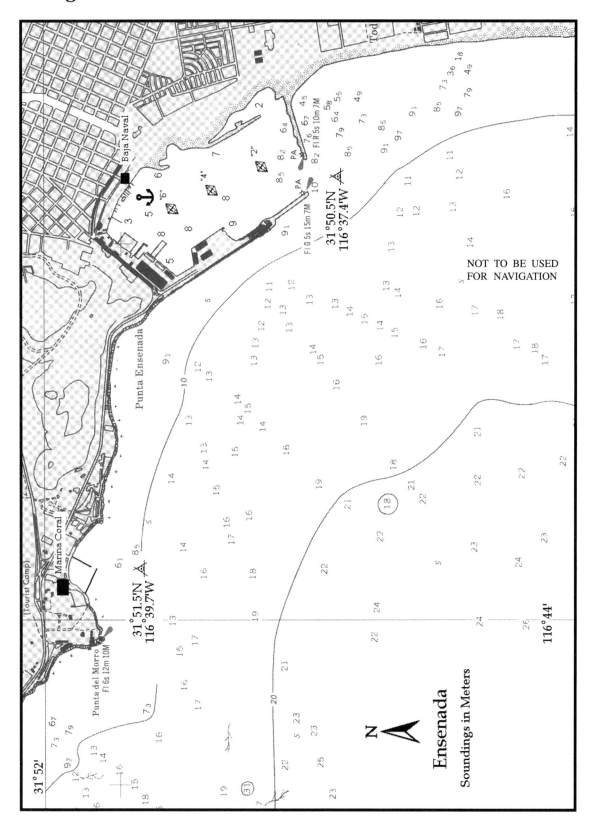

Ensenada
Soundings in Meters

NOT TO BE USED
FOR NAVIGATION

Approaches: From the south, after Cabo Colnett (See previous chapter.) the next headland is Punta Santo Tomas, 22.5 miles south of Ensenada, and its off-lying danger of Rocas Soledad. In northerly weather, anchorage may be found southeast of this rocky point, off the tiny fishing village called Puerto Santo Tomas. We've anchored among the kelp patties and panga moorings at GPS position 31°33.16'N by 116°40.69'W, but there's not shelter from westerly swell or southerly weather.

The southerly approach to Ensenada passes through the 2.5-mile-wide channel between Punta Banda and Islas Todos Santos. The main hazard is a reef that extends one mile to the northwest from Punta Banda. Often a strong current sets toward this reef. Therefore lay a course through the half of the channel toward the islands.

Anchorage in the tiny coves on the northeast side of the larger Isla Todos Santos Sur (south) is too often prohibited, due to seasonal aqua-culture buoys. If the buoys aren't present, you can anchor in the second cove from the north end, usually bow and stern. This is good shelter from the northwesterlies, but it's wide open to the east. Our GPS

approach waypoint just outside this tiny cove is 31°48.2'N by 116°47.2'W. But don't count on it.

From the north, the Coronado Islands 15 miles south of Point Loma provide a marginal anchorage on the southeast side of the largest and most southerly island. Somewhat better than an open roadstead, this anchorage below the "scar" lies at GPS position 32°24.35'N by 117°14.35'W. This is about 10 miles northwest of Rosarito Beach on the mainland which shows landmark smoke stacks, antenna, ship mooring buoys and a rock just off the hotel-lined beach.

El Sauzal: About five miles northwest of Ensenada harbor, this small breakwater enclosed harbor formerly was restricted to the local commercial fishing fleet, but some larger yachts occasionally find alongside berthing.

Marina Coral: This large recreational marina located 2.75 miles northwest of Ensenada harbor lies inside its own lighted riprap breakwater, on the east side of Punta Morro (Punta Morro Light). Fog often affects this area. Our GPS

Marina Coral: Nice new marina is 2.75 miles northwest of Ensenada harbor.

approach waypoint just south of the entrance to Marina Coral is 31°31.5'N by 116°39.7'W. Enter by swinging close around the east end of the southwest breakwater.

´Marina Coral (pronounced "coh-RAHL") has 150 full-service slips on floating docks for boats up to 150 feet. It has shorepower up to 3-phase, filtered water, dock boxes and carts, 24-hour security guards, parking, a launch ramp and a fuel dock. The dockmasters can handle port clearance papers through the Port Captain, Aduana and Migracion offices in Ensenada. They're also experienced in paperwork documenting California's SBE exemptions. The Hotel Coral ashore has two eateries, plus a pool and gym available to marina guests for additional fees. A shuttle bus takes guests into town. Marina Coral's phone is (800) 862-9020.

Ensenada Harbor: Skippers approaching (or departing) Ensenada harbor tend to hug the shore too much and end up in the kelp beds off Punta Morro. To avoid this hazard north of Ensenada, head first to the buoy on Bajo San Miguel 2.5 miles north of Islas de Todos Santos, then head 080° M for another 10.1 miles to the Ensenada breakwater. (Of course, use the reciprocal course when leaving for the north.) This dog leg course keeps you farther offshore so you just nick the south edge of the kelp beds, in an area where it's not usually too dense.

Our GPS approach waypoint about half a mile southwest of the entrance to Ensenada harbor is 31°50.5'N by 116°37.4'W. Enter the harbor between the two lighted breakwaters and then head approximately 000° M. This takes you between the two buoys marking the inside ship channel and points you toward the harbor's smaller marina area.

Anchorage and Moorings: Inside Ensenada harbor, the crowded municipal anchorage is anywhere not inside the buoyed ship channel, but pleasure boats usually prefer to anchor or pick up a mooring in the northeast corner off the older marinas. Launch drivers can rent you a mooring, but be careful in a blow as the ground tackle is suspect. You can make use of the launch drivers' shore boats, rather than leave your dinghy ashore.

Moorings belong to the smaller marinas that line the northeast shoreline: Baja Naval Marina, Bandito's Marina, Juanito's sportfishing and Gordo's Sportfishing. Of these four, we prefer either Baja Naval or Juanito's. Many "sub-contractors" in little boats will approach you as you enter the harbor, each hoping to lead you to a mooring they "manage" for Bandito, Juanito or Gordo. If you accept a mooring, be sure to agree on the price and then the sub-contractor is supposed to supply you with shore boat service.

Baja Naval Marina: Recently remodeled, this 50-slip marina and 75-ton haul-out yard are both just north of the giant Mexican flag, immediately south of the huge pink shopping center. The town's "malecon" walkway divides the slips from the yard, but the marina office is in the 2-story building inside the walled boat yard. Baja Naval's two docks have secured gates and shorepower. The dockmasters can clear papers for their guests, and they also have experience with California's SBE exemption requirements. A tank truck or barrels of diesel can be arranged and brought to the concrete pier north of the slips. Anchored or moored boaters can make arrangements to use Baja Naval's secure dinghy docks. Most of the floating slips are rented year round by California boaters, so to check on availability, call

Baja Naval Marina: Located inside Ensenada harbor, it has boat yard and smaller marina.

"Baja Naval" (pronounced "nah-VAHL") on VHF channel 16 or 09. The phone for Baja Naval is 011-52 (667) 4-00-20.

Immediately north of Baja Naval are the orange docks of Bandito's Marina. Bandito handles these 10 slips, which are often taken up by local fishing and excursion boats, and also about half of the moorings in the open harbor. Call "Bandito's Docks" on VHF channel 06.

Juanito's Sportfishing Docks: Juanito's 25 blue and white floating docks are just north of Bandito's, in front of the pink Plaza Marina shopping center. Juanito's docks keep more of their sportfishing docks available for visiting yachts, and they run almost the other half of the moorings. "Juanito's Boats" answers on VHF channel 18. Owner Luis Cordona speaks perfect English and can arrange fuel and other boat services for you. The phone for Juanito's Sportfishing Docks is 011-52 (667) 4-09-53.

Call "Gordo's Moorings" on VHF channel 06 for availability of his moorings. Gordo is well-known to veteran trailer boaters, and his ancient launch ramp and two-boat yard are still visible behind the new developments – but very little used.

Baja Naval Boatyard: Baja Naval Marina also has a large boatyard with a 75-ton travel lift, a huge covered shed and a good-sized walled yard that is patrolled 24 hours. You can do your own work and/or use Baja Naval's yard staff. Their rates are so reasonable that many San Diego boatyards are nervous.

Small to mid sized recreational boats favor this haul-out yard, while larger yachts often use the other haulout yard in Ensenada, I.N.C., discussed below.

Port Clearance: You should check in with the authorities immediately after your arrival. If Ensenada is going to be your last port call in Mexico, you'll need to get a Zarpe before you head to the U.S.

If this is your first entrance into Mexico, called your Port of Entry, take your Crew Lists, tourist cards and passports, documentation or registration, boat fishing permit and fishing licenses. Start at the Port Captain's office, then Immigration. You may not need to visit the Aduana's office here if the Port Captain can take care of that. To clear into Ensenada takes about half an hour.

When you wish to leave, visit these same offices with your filled in Crew List

Cruising Ports

forms. If you wish to clear in and out within 48 hours, you can do it all at one time, saving time and money.

Ship's Agent: However if you wish to use an agent to have them do the clearance for you we suggest Agencia Gil Ojeda (phone 8-36-15, fax 8-30-27). Or it can be done through the marina office at Marina Coral and Baja Naval.

Fuel Stop: Diesel and gasoline are available at the floating fuel dock in the north end of Marina Coral, and this is the easy in, easy out choice. If sportfishing tournaments or yacht races are in town, you may need to reserve a large quantity of fuel in advance.

Alternately, you can take diesel by tank truck at a concrete pier at the north side of Baja Naval. You do need a fuel permit from the Ensenada Port Captain, which the marinas can arrange.

Local Services: If you need marine parts or supplies, check with Agencia Arjona directly across the street from the Port Captain's office. Also, Baja Naval and I.N.C. regularly bring marine parts down from the states.

I.N.C. or Industrial Naval de California (phone 81901, fax 40478) has taken over the two ship yards (formerly Unidos and Rodriguez) east of the big cruise ship pier. This enormous yard hauls up to 200-foot yachts on its vintage marine railway, and its 200-ton travel lift and 1,000-ton cranes handle big ships. Like Baja Naval, the yard rates and labor are very reasonable. Because the yacht portion of this big industrial yard is difficult to find from the water, scope it out from the shore side first. The blue and white exterior is easy to find, across from the Port Captain's office and west of the Immigration office.

The third launch ramp is inside Bahia Estero, at the Estero Beach Resort south of Ensenada, and the entrance to the estero is so shallow and froth with breakers that it's good only for skiffs and Hobie-type catamarans.

Three additional marinas in the Ensenada vicinity have yet to materialize. Marina Posada may be a way off yet. The San Nicolas Hotel planned to build a large marina and resort inside one of the protected basins you passed to starboard as you entered the harbor. About 10 miles north of Ensenada, a small-boat harbor for hotel boats is planned. Plaza Marina, the two-story peach-colored shopping center lining the harbor north of Baja Naval, hopes to offer slips soon, and the initial structure is in place.

No scheduled airlines fly into Ensenada from the U.S. The only way to get back and forth by public transportation is on the bus. Take a short cab ride to the bus terminal and take Tres Estrellas to Tijuana. It's very inexpensive and buses run about every half hour. In Tijuana you can connect to Greyhound in the same terminal to downtown San Diego. Or you can take a cab to the U.S. border, walk across, and catch the red trolley in San Ysidro.

Ensenada has some excellent Mexican and seafood restaurants, including an annual 7-day festival with international judges.

For moderately priced seafood, our favorite place is the Bahia de Ensenada about two blocks inland from Baja Naval. A few blocks south on Madero is the Cafe El Rey Sol with excellent French food, elegant ambiance and higher prices. (The founding family of this unique restaurant and the nearby Travelodge were settlers in the mining town of Santa Rosalia on the Sea of Cortez.) Las Cazuelas is another moderately priced restaurant about a mile south of Baja Naval, just past the big turn in the Malecon. The Cueva de los Tigres sits right on the beach but is a long cab ride south of town. Try the cut-with-your-fork abalone Cordon Bleu.

Side Trips: Many U.S. visitors come to Ensenada for vinyard tours and wine tasting at the newer L.A. Cetto vineyards, the older Santo Tomas winery or the Domeq distillery. The tasting rooms are downtown, and the hills inland and south of Ensenada are where the grapes are cultivated.

Punta Banda, the major point of land south of Ensenada, has a blow hole that visitors like to watch. Take the turn off west at the south end of Maneadero.

A hot springs camping park called Uruapan is about 30 minutes south of Ensenada on Highway One.

Returning to the U.S.

If we're heading to U.S. Customs from Ensenada, we often distribute our remaining fresh produce and uncooked meats and eggs to locals on the docks; otherwise many of these items are confiscated by the agriculture inspectors when you clear into the U.S.

Confiscated items must be incinerated at great expense, in order to prevent disease infestation of healthy U.S. crops, poultry and livestock. You can obtain a list of prohibited items from U.S. Customs.

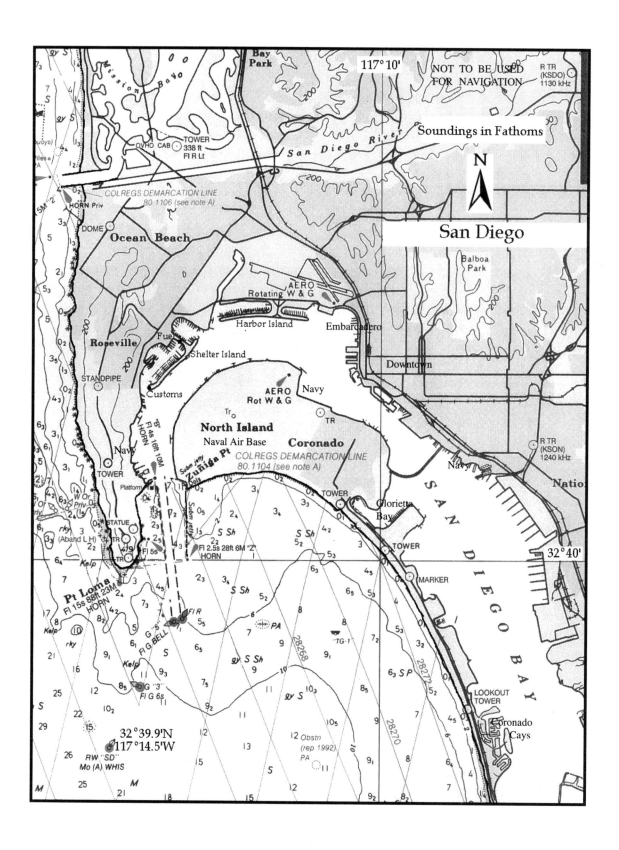

Chapter 41
San Diego

〜〜〜〜〜〜〜〜〜〜〜〜〜〜〜〜〜〜〜〜〜〜〜〜〜〜〜〜〜〜〜〜〜〜〜

This chapter covers San Diego – both as a final cruising port, and as a jumping-off point for southbound boaters.

If you're preparing to shove off south, into the blue world between California and Florida, San Diego is the traditional stocking-up and jumping-off port, the springboard into adventure.

If you've just finished this route, like weary seabirds swooping into a safe rookery, you'll feel welcomed home by San Diego's stateside comforts – yet shocked by the fast pace of life. Each time we return to San Diego, we have a few minor wounds to lick and many exciting tales to share with our neighbors still in port.

San Diego

No matter which way your boat is headed, San Diego has lots to offer. San Diego Bay is a beautiful deep-water port, one of the finest natural harbors in the world. Point Loma rises just 15 miles north of the U.S. border with Mexico, and it forms the harbor entrance. (Mission Bay is accessed through a separate channel 5.75

miles northwest of the tip of Point Loma.) San Diego Bay's 25-mile shoreline touches five modern cities (San Diego, Coronado, National City, Chula Vista, Imperial Beach) that provide 14 marinas, several municipal mooring areas, a dozen chandlers large and small, a chart and nautical book store, many engine-repair shops, three haul-out yards, a dozen launch ramps, several sail makers, numerous electronics shops and specialized welders, an international airport and everything the Land of Plenty has to offer.

Weather Report: Coastal winds are generally light year round, and land-sea breezes predominate. The sea breeze is strongest in the mid-afternoon from the southwest to the northwest, dying near sunset. The night and morning hours are generally calm with a possible light breeze off the land. Summer months have the lowest wind velocities and warmer temperatures, though seldom reaching the uncomfortable stage. Winter brings occasional wind, rain and cooler temperatures. You even have to wear a jacket. Cold fronts moving in from the

Cruising Ports

North Pacific are often preceded by winds from the southeast (attaining gale force on rare occasions), then shifting around to the northwest, moderating and clearing. This can cause very choppy conditions in the bay, hazardous to vessels anchored off Shelter Island.

The primary weather hazard in San Diego is fog. December is the worst month. Fog and low clouds frequently roll in during the night hours and burn off around noon. Try for a mid-day arrival or departure to minimize the risk of this occurrence. When approaching San Diego from Mexico, pass through the channel between the Coronado Islands and the Mexican border. It is wide, free of hazards, and enables a good position fix prior to picking up Point Loma.

Approaches: When approaching San Diego from either direction, aim for the sea buoy (32°37.3'N by 117°14.8'W). Even though the town lost its Naval Training Center, the port still houses a large naval base; the main ship channel is well marked and used by such deep-draft vessels as the aircraft carriers "Kitty Hawk" and "Stennis."

Don't cut the corners. Never attempt to take a supposed short cut when entering San Diego Bay from the south. By going all the way to the sea buoy and proceeding up the main ship channel, you pass safely inside Zuniga Jetty, the partially submerged jetty that parallels the beginning of the main ship channel. Though marked by lights, Zuniga Jetty can be quite deceptive and dangerous. If you cut the corner from the north, you enter an area of breaking shoals disguised by kelp patties west of Point Loma's southern tip.

Following the channel buoys into the bay you pass Point Loma (the distinctive headland) to port, and Zuniga Jetty and North Island Naval Air Station to starboard.

Point Loma Light is powerful (23 miles, 15 seconds). There's a fog signal on Ballast Point and also south of Shelter Island. The San Diego Marine Operator's antenna is also located on the point (VHF channels 28 and 86). You will now line up (353°T) up on range markers that will take you to the entrance of the Municipal Yacht Harbor at Shelter Island, passing Ballast Point to port.

Ballast Point is still covered with round rocks that arrived here over the decades from the northeastern U.S. via Cape Horn. Just inside the point was the original harbor of San Diego. In the early 19th century, yankee traders often entered San Diego Bay to load up on cow hides. So many ballast stones were dropped inside the bay that it began to cause problems, until the port finally prohibited it. Instead, trading ships had to dump their ballast stones out near the tip of Point Loma, on a pointed little shingle of beach that became known as Ballast Point.

Richard Henry Dana, in his classic "Two Years Before the Mast," recounts a ballast discharging episode that took place in 1835. Dana lived for six months on this tiny beach – sleeping in a huge abandoned oven with several Hawaiian sailors. He told of feeling a very long way from his academic life at Harvard.

Beyond Ballast Point, the flanks of Point Loma are home to a submarine dry dock, the Naval Research and Development Complex, and the Scripps Institution of Oceanography's Operations pier. Just beyond that is Shelter Island, a T-shaped peninsula that is the vortex of yachting in San Diego. The second T-shaped island is called Harbor Island, and behind Harbor Island you'll see the international airport at Lindbergh Field. West of Harbor Island lies the U.S. Coast Guard station San Diego, and west of that is the area called the Embarcadero. San Diego's downtown

U.S. Customs dock: Tie up to this Harbor Police dock on the south end of Shelter Island.

skyline rises behind the historic Embarcadero. The land on your port side north of Zuniga Jetty as you continue cruising up the main ship channel is the city of Coronado, and that part of Coronado is called North Island, housing a U.S. Naval air station.

Port Clearance: Clearing U.S. Customs is easily accomplished in San Diego. Recreational boats clear in by first docking at the Harbor Police station on the southern tip of Shelter Island. As you leave the main ship channel and bear to port to enter La Playa yacht basin, the small white Harbor Police dock is the first one on your starboard side. Pull to the north end of this single dock, because police craft use the south end, painted red. (Commercial vessels must go to the Customs dock in the Embarcadero.) If you arrive at night and the Harbor Police dock is full, your only alternative is to take one of the three yellow mooring cans a few hundred yards to port.

The U.S. clearance procedure is similar to entering and/or leaving any foreign port. (But the procedure in San Diego is quite different from that of Florida.) After tying up to the dock, only the captain may go up to the Harbor Police office, where the officers will take basic vessel information. You are not allowed to leave the dock area or have visitors on board during this time. If you have arrived during normal business hours (Monday through Friday 0800 to 1700) and Customs officials have been notified, they will usually board you within the hour.

Normally one agent represents several agencies – Customs, Immigration, Public Health, and Agricultural. He or she will assist the captain in filling out the proper documents (including a Crew List), and they'll ask questions and inspect the vessel. Inspection can run the gamut, from a brief tour to a meticulous search of every inch of your boat and a chemical analysis. We've have seen as many as eight armed agents and a dog on board a 50-foot vessel.

If you arrive after hours (a high likelihood, since most mariners operate 24-hours a day), you'll either wait till the next morning or pay overtime. The Harbor Police will allow you to move to one of the nearby yellow Customs moorings for free until the officials arrive in the morning. Even if you opt to pay overtime during the night, you may have to wait several hours for an agent to arrive. When the agents are finished, you're allowed to go.

Cruising Ports

Marinas and Guest Slips: The Harbor Police administer the 20 guest slips in the municipal marina adjacent to their facility, renting them on a first come, first served basis. Guests are limited to a 10-day stay during any 40-day period, but with very reasonable rates (including water and electricity) of $5 per day for the first five days, $10 a day for the second 5-day period. Maximum slip length is 62 feet.

If all these slips are occupied, you can use the phone here to find a slip at one of the 14 marinas or five yacht clubs. The Port of San Diego (291-3900) also leases two-point moorings in the Commercial Basin, located behind the other end of Shelter Island.

Shelter Island: The Shelter Island is a first or more southerly of San Diego's two T-shaped peninsulas. Shelter Island was landscaped and built to look like a Polynesian village, with Spanish influence on the south end. The Shelter Island area contains almost anything a boater could want within walking distance: six well-stocked chandlers, repair facilities for everything from engines and inflatables to electronics and compasses, sailmakers, sign painters, three full-service haulout yards, a nautical bookstore, several banks, grocery stores, restaurants, hotels, two fuel docks, and innumerable yacht brokerages.

Shelter Island has six marinas: Shelter Pointe Hotel Marina (formerly Kona Kai), Best Western Island Palms Marina (formerly Shelter Inn Marina), Bay Club Hotel Marina, Half Moon Inn, Shelter Cove Marina, Sun Harbor Marina. It houses four yacht clubs: Southwestern Yacht Club, Kona Kai International Yacht Club, Silvergate Yacht Club, and the venerable San Diego Yacht Club.

The La Playa yacht basin's anchorage lies behind the south end of Shelter Island, between Southwestern and San Diego yacht clubs. La Playa is the most pleasant anchorage in San Diego, but you may anchor here only from Friday morning to Monday morning. It's a small area and gets filled up. Although there's no official dinghy landing, everything on Shelter Island is within walking distance of La Playa.

Proceeding along San Diego Bay's main channel, a mooring area lines part of the outer length of Shelter Island, which is a linear park. The boats moored here suffer badly from wakes and wind. However, the dinghy landing on the sandy beach offers access to Shelter Island's facilities.

Rock groins protect the municipal launching ramp on this side of Shelter Island, and just past this area, to port, are the entrances to the Americas Cup Harbor (formerly the Commercial Basin) and the Harbor Island yacht basin. Note the shoal marker, don't cut it too close.

Americas Cup Harbor, behind the northeast end of Shelter Island, is lined with haul-out yards for yachts and commercial boats, small marinas and sportfishing docks. The center is filled with Port-leased long-term moorings. Their floating dinghy landing is in the southwest corner of this basin.

Harbor Island: Harbor Island is the next man-made T-shaped peninsula northwest of Shelter Island. Harbor Island has no haul-out facilities, just marinas, hotels, restaurants and one fuel dock, all located behind the outer stretch of linear park. Tom Ham's Light House restaurant marks the east end, and behind it is the easy-in, easy-out fuel dock. The west end marinas are Harbor Island West Marina, Marina Cortez, Cabrillo Isle Marina and the Sheraton Harbor Island marina. Paralleling the main ship channel on the outside of Harbor Island is a measured mile. Only Sun

**Star of India: museum ship
in the Embarcadero.**

Road Marina is behind the west end. The view from Sun Road of the San Diego skyline is superb; it's said to resemble a tool box, because three buildings look like a philip's head screw driver, a chisel and a set of hex-head wrenches.

The Embarcadero: In the upper northwest corner of the bay is another frequently used moorage called the Embarcadero, operated by the Port of San Diego. Situated near the end of the airport runway, it gets aircraft and street noise, and the anchorage is exposed to southeast winds. The Embarcadero is close to downtown but busy with tourist coming to view the ships of the city's Maritime Museum: the Star of India, the Berkeley and the Medea. Also, many harbor excursion vessels and several giant cruise ships call at their berths on the west end of the Embarcadero.

Seaport Village is a collection of 1- and 2-story shops and eateries. Just beyond it is the chisel-shaped Hyatt Hotel, and then the twin Marriott Resort towers. The Marriott Marina is at the foot of the Marriott towers. Look for its entrance in the middle of the rip-rap breakwater that surrounds this private basin. (Sun Road Marina and the Marriott are your best bets for finding an available slip, because they have obligations to the city to maintain ample guest slips.)

South Bay areas: On the starboard side of the main ship channel, before you pass under the Coronado Bridge is the Glorietta Bay mooring area, and beyond it and under the bridge is Glorietta Bay, which offers Coronado Yacht Club, Glorietta Bay Marina and a municipal launching ramp. Don't cut the corner too close as it shoals.

Loew's Marina is further south, on the west side of San Diego Bay. This new resort hotel has 81 slips to 145 feet with all amenities. Some of the larger slips have 3-

phase power. To find Loew's Marina, stay in the main ship channel as far as the red buoy #26, then turn 155 degrees magnetic to follow the 12-foot deep channel to the resort. The marina entrance lies just past the cream colored hotel with orange tiled roof. Loew's monitors VHF channel 68.

The Coronado Cays, a residential complex with private slips, is just south of Loew's. "The Cays" has a fuel dock and an adjacent yacht club with extra slips sometimes available for visiting yachts.

On the east side of South Bay, Chula Vista's municipal yacht harbor is well marked on charts (off the lower right edge of the partial chart at the front of this chapter), but inside the basin's rock breakwaters you'll find the water crowded with two marinas and a launch ramp. Chula Vista Marina has several hundred slips, filling the north end. This boating community is one of the best deals in the city, and close to the open sailing of South Bay, but it is far from the sea buoy. California Yacht Marina is south of Chula Vista Marina. Several fine restaurants are located here, too.

Local Services: Dona Jenkins Vessel Documentation Service in the Shelter Island area will do the leg work for your Mexican fishing permits and licenses, Crew Lists, tourist cards and any vessel documentation problems. Their fee is moderate. They're located at 1050 Rosecrans, San Diego, CA 92106, and their phone is (619) 223-2279.

If you need charts and nautical publications, go to Seabreeze Nautical Books and Charts, 1254 Scott Street, conveniently located in the Shelter Island area. If they don't have some chart, owner Bill Swink can order it for you. The phone for Seabreeze is (619) 223-8989. Located well inland, The Map Center, 2611 University Avenue, also has a good selection of charts.

The Log Newspapers serve all of Southern California with their three bi-monthly waterfront newspapers. The news articles, features, columns and advertisements serve as a guide to local events and marine services.

Many full-service chandler stores dot the Shelter Island area. Downwind Marine caters especially but not exclusively to cruising yachts, located at 2804 Canon Street. Call (619) 224-2733. Owner Chris Frost is a veteran cruiser who sponsors cruising seminars throughout the year and an annual Cruisers' Kick Off Party in the fall. Otherwise, one of the West Marine stores is located at 1250 Rosecrans.

All of the haul-out yards are located in San Diego Bay, mostly along Shelter Island.

Mission Bay: Mission Bay's entrance lies 5.5 miles north of Point Loma. Good landmarks are Sea World's 338-foot lighted needle, 1.8 miles inland, and the Belmont Park roller coaster, which lies 0.3 miles north of the entrance jetties. Mission Bay's green 4-second bell buoy is offshore of the entrance.

This 4,600-acre city park has 27 miles of protected shoreline, including islands, beaches, water-ski zones, wind-surfing areas, bike paths, bridges, hotels, restaurants and shops. Nine marinas lie inside Mission Bay, and so does Sea World, the famous aquatic amusement park.

Mission Bay is entered between two rock breakwaters. Pass closer to the north jetty where the swell has less tendency to break. This south jetty is lighted with a red 2.5-second light. Don't mistake the south jetty for the north one, or you'll be aground in the San Diego flood channel. In heavy westerly weather, breakers may close out Mission Bay's entrance channel.

The Mission Bay entrance channel runs straight for about a mile, then bends north. After this bend, Quivira Basin lies to starboard, and Mariner's Cove lies to port. Quivira Basin houses the Mission Bay Harbor Patrol station. Its reception dock is a good place to stop if you need any local information. Quivira Basin has a fuel dock, haul-out facilities, marine supplies and four large marinas.

Immediately across the channel is Mariner's Cove with free 72-hour guest moorings and a brick shower house on the beach. Unattended boats are not permitted to spend the night. This pretty little cove puts you right in the middle of San Diego's most popular beach area. This end of the park is surrounded by the community of Mission Beach, a magnet for teens and colorful beach people.

Beyond these two basins is a fixed bridge with 42 feet of vertical clearance. Six more marinas, one yacht club, two fuel docks and four launch ramps are scattered throughout Mission Bay. Three more bridges further into the park have 43-, 36-, and 6-foot clearances.

History: In 1542, Juan Rodrigues Cabrillo, a captain and native of the Iberian peninsula sailing under the Spanish flag, was the first European to record entering San Diego Bay. Cabrillo's monument stands on the peak of Point Loma overlooking the harbor's entrance. Two flags, Spanish and Mexican, flew over the port until the eventual Stars and Stripes.

For centuries the town remained isolated and small in population. Yankee immigrants began to see California's potential, and San Diego became part of the United States in 1847 after Mexico's defeat in the Mexican-American War.

The city's growth was slow until World War II when U.S. Navy contracts created a local population explosion. Dubbed "America's Finest City," it's the nation's ninth largest. More than 2.5 million people live in the cities surrounding San Diego Bay. The county of San Diego stretches north to Oceanside Harbor, and west deep into the mountains and desert.

Appendices Contents   page

Charts & Publications

Here are the charts and government publications covering the areas in this book. This is the bare minimum; gunk-holers will need more extensive coverage. Charts represent quite an investment. These chart numbers and areas covered are constantly being revised, which makes selecting and ordering charts a challenge. So check with your local chart dealer before ordering.

Chart	Title and area covered
145	All of North and Central America
400	West Indies
28006	Caribbean Sea, Southwestern Part
28004	Caribbean Sea, Northwestern Part
11013	Straights of Florida and Approaches
11467	Miami to Fort Lauderdale, Intra Coastal

Yachtsman's Chart Book: Mexico to Panama. Mariner's Ink Corp. (707) 827-5400. This large format spiral-bound book contains all the charts you need to get you to Panama.. However, because many of the coastal charts are cut in segments, having the whole coastal chart is helpful.

Maptech Compact Paper Chart Kit Florida Keys. Maptech 888-839-5551.

Reed's Nautical Almanac North American West Coast.
Reed's Nautical Almanac Caribbean. Thomas Reed Publications, Inc. (617) 268-0500 The above two Reed's books can save you quite a bit of money. They contain the nautical almanac, sight reduction tables, tide tables, current tables, Light List, Coast Pilots and Sailing Directions as well as harbor charts. The North American West Coast goes only as far south as Puerto Vallarta so you should also have:

–.*Sailing Directions for the West Coasts of Mexico and Central America,* Defense Mapping Agency, Hydrographic Center.

MexWX: Mexico Weather for Boaters, Capt. John E. Rains. Contains all the weather information and radio schedules necessary for the whole route including the Caribbean. ($19.95 plus 4.05 shipping and handling) Order from Point Loma Publishing, P.O. Box 60190, San Diego, CA 92166, or order it with a credit card by calling toll-free (888) 302-2628.

Waypoints

Global Positioning Systems (GPS) have made many of our charts obsolete, because the best surveying technologies available when our paper charts were created have been surpassed. This doesn't mean that we should attempt to navigate with electronics alone, it merely emphasizes the age-old axiom that the prudent mariner will not rely on only one method to verify his or her position. With the extensive use of electronic navigation, latitude and longitude positions have become even more useful. You can plug them into the computer's waypoint memory and tell at a glance their range and bearing, and your ETA.

When GPS is connected to the autopilot, the pilot will automatically steer you directly to the waypoint, correcting for the effects of wind and current. This may be okay after much testing for mariners who must constantly retrace their courses, like lobster fishermen returning to their pots regularly. But I discourage this practice for readers of this book -- who are venturing each day in unfamiliar waters.

The following waypoints are laid out in Florida-to-California sequence, except where alternative routes have branched. This format uses degrees, minutes and tenths of a minute (rather that seconds). These positions are given as a planning convenience only. Most of them were taken from the gazateer section of the DMA Sailing Directions. Those marked with an asterisk are positions that come from the approach waypoints marked on the charts in this book. If a position is given without a decimal point in the minutes, it has been rounded off to the nearest mile. If the position contains a decimal, it has been measured to within .1 of a minute.

Use extreme caution when navigating in the vicinity of these waypoints. Most of them are on land, so a course laid directly from one waypoint to another may well ground you; the actual turning point may be a mile or two offshore. The prudent navigator will always double check these latitudes and longitudes with the chart and lay his or her courses and distances manually on the chart.

Atlantic Ocean

Use special caution when using the waypoints along the Florida Reefs. A course laid directly from one point to another may well carry you on the reef. You should pass about 1 mile off each of these turning points and the actual course paralleling the reef is a series of many small courses changes. See page the chapter on the Florida Keys for more detail.

Ft. Lauderdale, "PE" (26°05.5'N, 80°04.8'W)
Miami "M" (25°46.1'N, 80°05'W)
Fowey Rocks (25°35.4'N, 80°05.8'W)
Truimph Reef (25°28.6'N, 80°06.7'W)
Pacific Reef (25°22.3'N, 80°08.5'W)
Carysfort Reef (25°13.3'N, 80°12.7'W)
The Elbow (25°08.7'N, 80°15.5'W)
Molasses Reef (25°00.7'N, 80°22.6'W)
Davis Reef (24°55.5'N, 80°30.2'W)
Alligator Reef (24°51.1'N, 80°37.1'W)
Buoy R "18" (24°47.5'N, 80°41.6'W)

Tennesee Reef (24°44.7'N, 80°46.9'W)
"20" (24°40.5'N, 80°57.4'W)
Sombrero Key (24°37.6'N, 81°06.6'W)
Big Pine Shoal (24°34.1'N, 81°19.6'W)
American Shoal (24°31.5'N, 81°31.2'W)
Pelican Shoal (24°30.3'N, 81°36.1'W)
"32" (24°28.4'N, 81°44.5'W)
*Key West "KW"(24°27.7'N, 81°48.1'W)
Sand Key (24°27.2'N, 81°52.7'W)
Satan Shoal (24°26.6'N, 81°58.8'W)

Western Caribbean
Offshore Route
Wpt #1, Cayo Jutias, Cuba (23°06'N, 84°21'W)
Wpt #2, Cabo San Antonio (21°52'N, 85°16'W)
Cape San Antonio (21°52'N, 84°57'W)
*Grand Cayman (19°17.7'N, 81°25.0'W)
Swan Island (17° 25'N, 83°56'W)
Wpt #3, Nicaraguan Bank (15°45'N, 81°00'W)
*Panama, Cristobal (09° 23.8'N, 079° 55.1'W)
Cruising Route
*Isla Mujeres (21°16.6'N, 86°45.1'W)
Cancun (21° 05'N, 86° 47'N
Cozumel, Isla (20°30'N, 86° 58'W)
*Rio Dulce (15° 50'N, 88° 44'W)
Roatan, Coxen's Hole (16°18'N, 86°35'W)
Wpt. A Nicaraguan Bank (16°20'N, 82°35'W)
Wpt B Nicaraguan Bank (15°25'N, 81°38'W)
Cayo Vivarillo (15°50'N, 83°18'W)
Cabo Falso (15°12'N, 83°20'W)
Cabo Gracias a Dios (15°00'N, 83°10'W)
*Providencia, Isla (13°23.95'N, 81°23.75'W)
*San Andres, Isla (12°32.2'N, 81°41.2'W)

Pacific Ocean
Panama
*Panama Canal, (8°51.5'N, 79° 29.0'W)
Taboguilla, Isla (8°49'N, 79°31'W)
Taboga, Isla (8° 47'N, 79°33'W)
Bona, Isla (08°35'N, 79°36'W).
Mala, Punta (7°28'N, 80°00'W)
Jicarita, Isla (7°13'N, 81°48'W)
Montuosa, Isla (7°28'N, 82°15'W)
Costa Rica
Burrica, Punta (8°02'N, 82°52'W)
Golfito (8°38'N, 83°11'W)
Blanco, Isla Cabo (9° 32'N, 85° 07 'W)
Cano, Isla del (8°43'N, 83°53'W)
Quepos (9°24'N, 84°10'W)
*Puntarenas (9°58'N, 84° 50'W)
Guiones, Punta (9°49'N, 85°44'W)
*Marina Flamingo (10°28'N, 85°48'W)
Playa del Coco (10°34'N, 85°43'W)
Guatemala
*Puerto Quetzal (13° 54.8'N, 90° 46.7'W)
Offshore turning point (14°04'N, 91°52'W)

Mexico: Mainland
*Puerto Madero (14°41.7'N, 92°24.8'W)
Puerto Arista (15°56'N, 93°50'W)
Boca de San Francisco (16°13'N, 94°45'W)
*Salina Cruz (16°09.0'N, 95°11.6'W)
*Huatulco (15°44.5'N, 96°07.0'W)
Puerto Angel (15°39'N, 96°31'W)
Puerto Escondido (15°50'N, 97°04'W)
Punta Galera (15°53'N, 97° 50'W)
Punta Maldonado (16°20'N, 98°35'W)
Rio Papagallo (16°35'N, 99°29'W)
*Acapulco (16° 49.0'N, 99° 53.2'W)
Zihuatanejo (17°37'N, 101°33'W)
Isla Grande (17°40'N, 101°40'W)
Punta San Telmo (18° 20'N, 103°31'W)
*Barra Navidad (19°12.0'N, 104°41.4'W)
Tenacatita (19°15'N, 104° 15'W)
Carreyes (19°25'N, 105°02'W)
Chamela (19°33'N, 105°07'W)
Los Frailes (19°18'N, 104°57'W)
Ipala (20°14'N, 105°36'W)
Cabo Corrientes (20°24'N, 105° 43'W)
Yelapa (20°30'N, 105°27'W)
*Puerto Vallarta (20°39.1'N, 105°15.0'W)
Punta Mita (20°46'N, 105° 33'W)
Cabo San Lucas to San Diego
*Cabo San Lucas (22°52.9'N, 109°53.0'W)
Cabo Falso (22°52'N, 109°58'W)
Cabo Tosca (24°18'N, 111°43'W)
Punta Entrada (24°32'N, 112°04'W)
Cape San Lazaro (24°48'N, 112° 19'W)
Abreojos (26° 42'N, 113°34'W)
Asuncion (27°07'N, 114°13'W)
*Turtle Bay (27°38.5'N, 114°54.0'W)
Punta Eugenia (27°51'N, 115°05'W)
Isla Cedros, north end (28°23'N, 115°13'W)
San Carlos anchorage (29°37'N, 115°29'W)
Cabo San Quintin (30°21'N, 115°52'W)
San Martin Island (30°29'N, 116°07'W)
Todo Santos Island (31° 48'N, 116°48'W)
*Ensenada (31°50.5'N, 116°37.4'W)
*Marina Coral (31° 51.5'N, 116° 39.7'W)
South Coronado Island (32°24'N, 117°15'W)
San Diego "SD" (32°37.3'N, 117°14.'W)

Distances Between Ports

The distances (in nuatical miles) shown in the chart on the next page are intended only for planning purposes. They are taken from small-scale charts, and therefore they are approximates. To find a distance between ports, look up the starting port and the next port below it. The distance is in the column to the right of the lower port. For instance the distance between Golfito and Balboa is 335 nautical miles. The cumulative distance from either San Diego or Fort Lauderdale is to the far right. The cumulative distance is as if you went in and out of every one of these ports. If you do not, then the actual total distance will be less than the cululative distance. For instance the distance between Cabo San Lucas and Turtle Bay includes the 30-mile round trip required to enter Bahia Magdalena and go all the way to the port of San Carlos. If you bypass this port (something we highly recommend), then subtract 30 nautical miles from the cumulative distance between San Diego and Cabo San Lucas.

West Coast to East Coast				East Coast to West Coast		
Place	Miles	Cumulative		Place	Miles	Cumulative
San Diego	0			Fort Lauderdale		
Ensenada	60	60		Miami	20	
Turtle Bay	278	338		Key West	142	162
San Carlos, BCS	255	593		Marina Hemingway	90	252
Cabo San Lucas	170	763		Isla Mujeres	275	527
Puerto Vallarta	295	1058		Cozumel	40	567
Manzanillo	156	1214		Livingston	295	862
Zihuatanejo	175	1389		French Harbor	135	997
Acapulco	110	1499		Providencia	365	1362
Huatulco	285	1784		San Andres	55	1417
Salina Cruz	61	1845		Cristobal	217	1634
Puerto Madero	183	2028		Balboa	50	1684
Puerto Quetzal	116	2144		Golfito	335	2019
Corinto	233	2377		Puntarenas	165	2184
Flamingo	145	2522		Flamingo	116	2300
Puntarenas	116	2638		Corinto	145	2445
Golfito	165	2803		Puerto Quetzal	233	2678
Balboa	335	3138		Puerto Madero	116	2794
Cristobal	50	3188		Salina Cruz	183	2977
San Andres	217	3405		Huatulco	61	3038
Providencia	55	3460		Acapulco	285	3323
French Harbor	365	3825		Zihuatanejo	110	3433
Livingston	135	3960		Manzanillo	175	3608
Cozumel	295	4255		Puerto Vallarta	156	3764
Isla Mujeres	40	4295		Cabo San Lucas	295	4059
Marina Hemingway	275	4570		San Carlos, BCS	170	4229
Key West	90	4660		Turtle Bay	255	4484
Miami	142	4802		Ensenada	278	4762
Fort Lauderdale	20	4822		San Diego	60	4822

Selecting a Delivery Skipper

Boat owners hire professional captains to move their boat for a variety of reasons. Most boats represent a huge investment, so an owner should want the best skipper available to protect his or her investment. This is not the kind of job that should go to the lowest bidder, because, generally speaking, you get what you pay for. Less experienced people may charge less, but after the boat owner pays for the damage, needless port stops and mistakes, then any savings is negated. Inexperienced skippers are far more likely to damage vessels.

Here are several methods of finding a good skipper. Most yachting areas have professional groups that can recommend several licensed skippers who have experience both with your type vessel and with the intended route. Marine insurance companies are the best place to begin. Many yacht delivery firms advertise in the classified section of boating magazines and newspapers. Local boat brokers who do business with larger yachts can refer you to reliable captains with whom they have worked.

Your initial contact with a potential skipper should be conducted like the job interview that it is. Interview several to find what their qualifications, experience and terms are. Ask for several references from people for whom they have recently done deliveries. Call each reference, and ask particularly about integrity. On long trips a captain will be handling large sums of expense money for which he or she must account, so be sure your captain is indisputably honest and a good record- keeper.

The skipper should have a Coast Guard license. This is not yet a legal requirement, but most insurance companies insist on it. Having earned a license shows that the skipper has verified a minimum amount of sea time and has been able to pass an examination. It also indicates a higher professional attitude toward the profession. The Coast Guard can revoke this license for any number of reasons, so a licensed skipper isn't likely to do things that could jeopardize his or her livelihood.

On the other hand, a license is no guarantee of competence or integrity. I know of licensed skippers who don't know how to navigate offshore, can't program a weather fax machine, and couldn't bleed an injector if their lives depended on it. That's why you should check reference thoroughly.

Once a skipper has been selected, you should use a written contract to set the terms of the agreement, so there can be no misunderstandings later on. The delivery contract should spell out all wages, what expenses covered or not covered, the method of payment, any preparation charges. After it is signed and witnessed, both parties should keep copies.

Going rates for deliveries are computed on a mileage basis (approximately $3.50 per mile) plus all crew expenses such as flights, food, and fuel. Some experienced owners do not like this method, because they fear a skipper will drive the boat to hard. The faster the skipper goes, the more money he makes. This could be true of a disreputable captain. Some captains and crew can be hired on a daily basis ($400 to $500 per day for a total crew of four inclusive of Captain) plus expenses and daily rates for each additional crew member. Another method is to have the job done for a flat fee that includes expenses. This usually proves to be the most expensive, because the captain has to make allowance for weather delays and any possible breakdown.

If proper precautions are taken when selecting a delivery skipper, any vessel can be moved competently, professionally and painlessly.

WX Radio Broadcasts

Explanatory notes to broadcasts:

1. Unless otherwise noted, all broadcast are Greenwich Mean Time, 24-hour clock (0000-2359). Frequencies listed are carrier frequencies.

2. Emission Classification is shown in parentheses immediately following the frequency. A3J—Single sideband, suppressed carrier.

3. Contents are indicated as follows:

A—Analysis	**F**—Forecast	**P**—Prognosis
S—Synopsis	**SR**—Synoptic reports	
W—Warnings	**G**—Gulf Stream Analysis	

WWV National Bureau of Standards. Fort Collins, CO

Broadcast from Colorado and Hawaii, this SSB station's primary function is giving the "time tick," which is indispensable for accurate navigation at sea, but it also gives abbreviated Atlantic weather at 8 and 9 minutes past the hour and Pacific weather at 10 minutes past each hour. The WWV report is limited to severe weather warnings such as gales in the Gulf of Tehuantepec and elsewhere, tropical depressions, tropical storms, and hurricanes. It is also a source of checking radio propogation conditions and the latest status of the GPS navigation system.

Broadcast Time	Frequency (kHz) (A3)
H+10	5000
	10000
	15000

NMC U.S.C.G. San Francisco -- **Voice**

Area:

(a) North Pacific, Equator to 30°N, east of 140°W.

(b) North Pacific, north of 30°N, east of 160°E.

(c) Offshore Waters, 20 to 250 miles from shore, Mexican Border-Cape Flattery, Wash.

Broadcast Time (UTC)	Frequency (Khz) (A3J)	Channel	Contents
0430, 1030	4426	424	W, F
	8764	816	
	13089	1205	
1630, 2230	8764	816	
	13089	1205	
	17314	1625	

WX Radio Broadcasts

USCG Master Station Atlantic, Chesapeake, Virginia-- **Voice**   **NMN**

Area (a) has the most thorough forecast.

Area:

(a) The National Weather Service forecast for the offshore waters consists of the west central North Atlantic offshore waters between 32° North and 41° North and West of 65° West, the southwest North Atlantic, the Gulf of Mexico, and the Caribbean Sea and, with the exception of the 0330 UTC broadcast, the offshore waters east of New England north of 41° North and west of 60° West. The offshore forecasts are given at :

Broadcast Time (UTC)	Frequency (kz) (A3J)	Channel
0330, 0930	4426	424
	6501	601
	8764	816
1600, 2200	6501	601
	8764	816
	13089	1205

(b) The high seas forecast consists of the North Atlantic waters north of 03° North and west of 35° West including the Gulf of Mexico the Caribbean Sea. The high seas forecast is given at:

Broadcast Time (UTC)	Frequency (kHz) (A3J)	Channel
0500	4426	424
	6501	601
	8764	816
1130, 2330	6501	601
	8764	816
	13089	1205
1730	8764	816
	13089	1205
	17314	1625

Amateur Radio Nets

Amateur Radio Nets	Freq.	Time	Area	WX
Sonrisa Net	3.968	0630 PST	Baja California	yes
Central American Breakfast Club	7.083	1300 Z	Central America	no
California Baja Net	7.238	0800 PST	Baja California	yes
Waterway Net	7.268	0730 EST	U.S. East Coast/Bahamas	yes
Maritime Mobile Net	14.313	24 hours	World Wide	no
Manana Net	14.342	1900Z	U.S. West Coast/Mexico	no
Halo Net	21.390	2100Z	U.S./South America	no
Pacific Maritime Mobile Net	21.402	2200Z	U.S. West Coast	no

Notes: All frequencies below 10 Mhz are on the lower sideband. Nets listed in local times, PST and EST keep their nets at the same local time during daylight savings time. Nets on commercial SSB frequencies for usage by non-hams are informally formed around the times and areas covered by the nets below 10 Mhz. They come and go. Check with other boaters when entering a new area for the latest times and frequencies.

WX Radio Broadcasts

SAN DIEGO TO PUERTO VALLARTA -- WX FAX

NMC PT. REYES, CALIFORNIA, U.S.A. (SAN FRANCISCO)

CALL SIGN	FREQUENCIES	TIMES	EMISSION	POWER
NMC	4346 kHz	NIGHT	F3C	10 KW
	8682 kHz	CONTINUOUS	F3C	10 KW
	12730 kHz	CONTINUOUS	F3C	10 KW
	17151.2 kHz	CONTINUOUS	F3C	10 KW
	22527 kHz	DAY	F3C	10 KW

TRANS TIME	CONTENTS OF TRANSMISSION	VALID TIME	MAP AREA
——/1415	TEST PATTERN		
——/1418	96 HR 500 MB PROG	0000	1
——/1428	96 HR SURFACE PROG	0000	1
*——/1438	SATELLITE IMAGE	LATEST	5
0245/——	TEST PATTERN		
0248/1449	SATELLITE IMAGE	LATEST	7/6
0259/——	SATELLITE IMAGE	LATEST	5
——/1500	SEA STATE ANALYSIS	1200	8
0310/——	SEA STATE ANALYSIS	0000	1
*——/1510	TROPICAL SURFACE ANALYSIS	1200	4
*0320/1520	SURFACE ANALYSIS (NE PACIFIC)	00/12	2
0333/1533	SURFACE ANALYSIS (NW PACIFIC)	00/12	3
0345/1545	(REBROADCAST OF 0320/1520)	00/12	2
0358/1558	(REBROADCAST OF 0333/1533)	00/12	3
0410/1610	500MB ANALYSIS	00/12	1
0815/2015	TEST PATTERN		
*0818/2018	24HR SURFACE PROG	00/12	8
0828/2028	24HR WIND/SEAS PROG	00/12	8
0838/2038	48HR 500MB PROG	00/12	1
*0848/2048	48HR SURFACE PROG	00/12	1
0858/2058	48HR SEA STATE PROG	00/12	1
0908/2108	SATELLITE IMAGE	06/18	7/5
0919/2119	SURFACE ANALYSIS (NE PACIFIC)	06/18	2
0932/2132	SURFACE ANALYSIS (NW PACIFIC)	06/18	3
0944/——	SATELLITE IMAGE	0600	5
——/2144	TROPICAL SURFACE ANALYSIS	1800	4
0955/2154	(REBROADCAST OF 0919/2119)	06/18	2
1008/2207	(REBROADCAST OF 0932/2132)	06/18	3
1100/2300	TEST PATTERN		
1104/——	BROADCAST SCHEDULE (PART 1)		
——/2304	SST ANALYSIS	LATEST	9

Continued on next page.

WX Radio Broadcasts

Continued **NMC**

1115/——	***BROADCAST SCHEDULE (PART 2)***
1126/——	REQUEST FOR COMMENTS **NMC Continued**
——/2335	BROADCAST SCHEDULE (PART 2)
1137/——	PRODUCT NOTICE BULLETIN
1148/——	(REBROADCAST OF 2304) LATEST 9
1158/——	(REBROADCAST OF 2314) LATEST 6

MAP AREAS:

1. 20N - 70N, 115W - 135E   2. 20N - 70N, 115W - 175W
3. 20N - 70N, 175W - 135E   4. 20S - 30N, EAST OF 160W
5. 05N - 60N, WEST OF 100W   6. 23N - 42N, EAST OF 136W
7. 05N - 55N, EAST OF 130W   8. 25N - 60N, EAST OF 155W
        9. 40N - 53N, EAST OF 136W

NOTES: 1. CARRIER FREQUENCY IS 1.9 kHz BELOW THE ASSIGNED FREQUENCY.

PUERTO VALLARTA TO PANAMA -- WX Fax

NEW ORLEANS, LOUISIANA, U.S.A.   **NMG**

CALL SIGN	FREQUENCIES	TIMES	EMISSION	POWER
NMG	4317.9 kHz	CONTINUOUS	F3C	10 KW
	8503.9 kHz	CONTINUOUS	F3C	10 KW
	12789.9 kHz	CONTINUOUS	F3C	10 KW

TRANS TIME	CONTENTS OF TRANSMISSION	VALID TIME	MAP AREA
0000/*1200	TROPICAL SURFACE ANALYSIS	18/06	1
0030/*1230	24/36 HR WIND/SEAS FORECAST (2 charts)	00&12/12&00	2
0050/*1250	HIGH SEAS FORECAST (IN ENGLISH)	22/10	5
0115/*1315	0/12 HR WIND/SEAS FORECAST (2 charts)	00&12/12&00	2
0135/*1335	U.S. SURFACE ANALYSIS	18/06	3
0150/*1350	GOES-8 IR TROPICAL SATELLITE IMAGE	2345/1145	4
0205/1405	REQUEST for COMMENTS/PRODUCT NOTICE		
0600/1800	TROPICAL SURFACE ANALYSIS	00/12	1
0630/1830	*BROADCAST SCHEDULE*		
0650/1850	HIGH SEAS FORECAST (IN ENGLISH)	04/16	5
0715/1915	0/12 HR WIND/SEAS FORECAST (2 CHARTS)	06&18/18&06	2
0735/1935	U.S. SURFACE ANALYSIS	00/12	3
0750/1950	GOES-8 IR TROPICAL SATELLITE IMAGE	0645/1745	4
0805/2005	(REBROADCAST OF 0030/1230)	00&12/12&00	2

NOTES: 1. CARRIER FREQUENCY IS 1.9 kHz BELOW THE ASSIGNED FREQUENCY
     2. THIS BROADCAST ORIGINATES FROM THE TROPICAL PREDICTION CENTER

MAP AREAS: 1. 05S - 35N, 0 - 120W   2. 10N - 30N, 55W - 100W
       3. 15N - 50N, 65W - 125W   4. 12S - 44N, 28W - 112W
          5. 3N - 32N, 35W - 100W

Spanish Lexicon

General Boating Terms

Anchor (to): fondear
Anchor: ancla
Anchorage: anclaje
Arrive (to): llegar
Beam: manga
Boom: botavara
Bow: proa
Cabin: cabina
Captain: capitan
Cook: cocinero
Copies: copias
Customs: Aduana
Deck: cubierta
Deckhand: marinero
Draft: calado
First Mate: Segundo a Bordo
Halyard: driza
Helm: timon
Helmsman: timonel
Hull: casca
Immigration: Migracion
Jib: foque
Jibe (to): virar
Launch (to): botar
Launch, skiff: lancha
Leave port (to): embarcarse
Line: linea
Mast: mastil, palo
Oar: remo
Oarlock: chumacero
Papers: papeles, despachos
Pleasure craft: yate de placer
Port Captain: Capitan de Puerto
Port Captain's office: Capitania
Port hole: tromera
Port: babor, puerto
Power yacht: crucero
Propellor: helice
Sailboat: velero
Sailor: marinero
Screwdriver: tornillador
Sea sick: mareo
Starter: arranque
Tool: herramiento
Winch: molinete, winche
Wrench: llave

Mechanical Terms

Battery: bateria, pila
Bearing: cojinete
Bolt: tornillo
Breakdown: parada
Cable: cable
Diesel: diesel
Engine: maquina
Exhaust: escape
Fuel: combustible
Gasket: empaquedura
Gasoline: gasolina
Grease: grasa
Head: cabeza
Hose: manguera
Injector: inyector
Mechanic: mecanico
Nut: tuerca
Oil: aceite, lubricante
Piston: piston
Pump: bomba
Row: (to): remar
Rudder: timon
Screw: tornillo
Sea level: nivel de mar
Seamanship: marineria
Sheet: escota
Ship: barco, buque
Speed: velocidad
Starboard: estribor
Stern: popa
Tank: tanque
Tiller: cana del timon
Tow (to): remolcar
Tugboat: remolcador
Wharf: muelle, embarcadero

Marine Meteorology

Barometer: barometro
Breakers: rompientes
Breeze: brisa
Calm: calma
Clear up (to): aclarar
Cloud: nube
Degrees: grados
Ebbtide: marea menguantes
Fog: niebla
Forecast: predicion
Front: frente
Gale: viento duro
Gentle breeze: brisa debil

GMT: hora media de Greenwich
Gust: rafaga, racha
Haze: calima
High pressure: alta presion
Horizon: horizonte
Hurricane: huracan
Light air: ventorina
Mist: neblina
Moderate: brisa moderada
Norther: nortada
Rain: lluvia
Shower: chubasco
Squall: turbonada
Surf: resaca
Surge: oleadez
Thunder: trueno
Tide: marea
Trade winds: vientos alisos
Wave: ola

Navigation Terms

Altitude: altitud
Barometer: barometro
Bearing: orientacion
Breakwater: rompeola
Buoy: boya
Chart: carta
Chronometer: cronometro
Compass: brujula
Course: rumbo
Depth: profundidad
Deviation: desviacion
Dividers: compas
East: este, oriente
Fathom: braza
Knot: nudo
Lighthouse: faro
Magnetic: magnetico
Meridian: meridiano
Observation: observacion
Parallel: paralelo
Position: posicion
Radar: radar
Reckoning: estima
Reef: arrecife
Sextant: sextante
South: sur
Star: estrella
Track: trayectoria
West: oeste, poniente

Index

We want to hear from you!

The world is always changing. When you arrive in your next cruising port, if you find significant changes that other boaters should know about, we'd appreciate hearing about them. Any corrections, updates, additions, photos or general feed-back that you can send to us, we'll really appreciate, and we'll try research these changes before including them in the 5th edition of *"Cruising Ports."* Tell us:

What's new or changed? _____

_____

_____

_____

Where is it? _____

_____

_____

Who should we contact for more information? _____

_____

_____

When were you there? _____

_____

_____

Why is it important for other boaters? _____

_____

_____

GOT MORE NEWS??

What else is new or changed? _____

_____

_____

_____

Where is it? _____

_____

_____

Who should we contact for more information? _____

_____

_____

When were you there? _____

_____

_____

Why is it important for other boaters? _____

_____

_____

Your name _____

Boat name & kind _____

Mailing address _____

Book Ordering Form

"Cruising Ports: Florida to California via Panama"   *$ 34.95*
4th edition, by Captains Pat and John E. Rains
      Either direction, this +300-page nautical guidebook covers the 5,000-mile
      route with better charts, more ports and anchorages, now including
      the Sea of Cortez. This is the "Bible" for long-range cruisers.

"MexWX: Mexico Weather for Boaters"   *22.95*
2nd edition, by Captain John E. Rains
      If you're boating in Mexico's Pacific waters, you need this 112-page
      book. Concisely presented data for each region, plus radio frequencies for
      WX-fax, ham radio nets with weather reporting, SSB weather sources.
      Tactics for avoiding bad weather and hurricanes, where to
      summer over safely.

"Boating Guide to Mexico: West Coast Edition"   *39.95*
by Captains Pat Miller Rains and John E. Rains
      The authors still have a few copies of this spectacularly beautiful
      278-page cruising guidebook to Mexico's Pacific Coast and
      Sea of Cortez. Lots of color photos & harbor charts with GPS positions.

Please send me the following books:

		shipping	CA tax (if applicable)	subtotal
____ **Cruising Ports**	$34.95	$3.00	$2.71	_____
____ **MexWX**	22.95	2.50	1.78	_____
____ **Boating Guide Mexico**	39.95	3.00	3.10	_____
			TOTAL	_____

NAME _____

PO Box / Street Address _____ Apt._____

City _____ State _____ Zip _____

Mail your check or money order to: ***Visa, MasterCard, American Express***
Point Loma Publishing   ***Call 24-hour toll-free to order books:***
P.O. Box 60190   (888) 302-BOAT
San Diego, CA 92166   (888) 302-2628

Thank you very much for ordering our books!

Book Ordering Form

"Cruising Ports: Florida to California via Panama"   *$ 34.95*
4th edition, by Captains Pat and John E. Rains
        Either direction, this +300-page nautical guidebook covers the 5,000-mile
        route with better charts, more ports and anchorages, now including
        the Sea of Cortez. This is the "Bible" for long-range cruisers.

"MexWX: Mexico Weather for Boaters"   *22.95*
2nd edition, by Captain John E. Rains
        If you're boating in Mexico's Pacific waters, you need this 112-page
        book. Concisely presented data for each region, plus radio frequencies for
        WX-fax, ham radio nets with weather reporting, SSB weather sources.
        Tactics for avoiding bad weather and hurricanes, where to
        summer over safely.

"Boating Guide to Mexico: West Coast Edition"   *39.95*
by Captains Pat Miller Rains and John E. Rains
        The authors still have a few copies of this spectacularly beautiful
        278-page cruising guidebook to Mexico's Pacific Coast and
        Sea of Cortez. Lots of color photos & harbor charts with GPS positions.

Please send me the following books:		shipping	CA tax (if applicable)	subtotal
____ **Cruising Ports**	$34.95	$3.00	$2.71	_____
____ **MexWX**	22.95	2.50	1.78	_____
____ **Boating Guide Mexico**	39.95	3.00	3.10	_____
			TOTAL	_____

NAME _____

PO Box / Street Address _____ Apt._____

City _____ State _____ Zip _____

Mail your check or money order to: ***Visa, MasterCard, American Express***
Point Loma Publishing   ***Call 24-hour toll-free to order books:***
P.O. Box 60190   (888) 302-BOAT
San Diego, CA 92166   (888) 302-2628

Thank you very much for ordering our books!

Book Ordering Form

"Cruising Ports: Florida to California via Panama"   *$ 34.95*

4th edition, by Captains Pat and John E. Rains

> Either direction, this +300-page nautical guidebook covers the 5,000-mile
> route with better charts, more ports and anchorages, now including
> the Sea of Cortez. This is the "Bible" for long-range cruisers.

"MexWX: Mexico Weather for Boaters"   *22.95*

2nd edition, by Captain John E. Rains

> If you're boating in Mexico's Pacific waters, you need this 112-page
> book. Concisely presented data for each region, plus radio frequencies for
> WX-fax, ham radio nets with weather reporting, SSB weather sources.
> Tactics for avoiding bad weather and hurricanes, where to
> summer over safely.

"Boating Guide to Mexico: West Coast Edition"   *39.95*

by Captains Pat Miller Rains and John E. Rains

> The authors still have a few copies of this spectacularly beautiful
> 278-page cruising guidebook to Mexico's Pacific Coast and
> Sea of Cortez. Lots of color photos & harbor charts with GPS positions.

Please send me the following books:		shipping	CA tax (if applicable)	subtotal
____ **Cruising Ports**	$34.95	$3.00	$2.71	_____
____ **MexWX**	22.95	2.50	1.78	_____
____ **Boating Guide Mexico**	39.95	3.00	3.10	_____
			TOTAL	_____

NAME _____

PO Box / Street Address _____ Apt._____

City _____ State _____ Zip _____

Mail your check or money order to: *Visa, MasterCard, American Express*
Point Loma Publishing   *Call 24-hour toll-free to order books:*
P.O. Box 60190   (888) 302-BOAT
San Diego, CA 92166   (888) 302-2628

Thank you very much for ordering our books!

Book Ordering Form

"Cruising Ports: Florida to California via Panama"   *$ 34.95*
4th edition, by Captains Pat and John E. Rains
> Either direction, this +300-page nautical guidebook covers the 5,000-mile
> route with better charts, more ports and anchorages, now including
> the Sea of Cortez. This is the "Bible" for long-range cruisers.

"MexWX: Mexico Weather for Boaters"   *22.95*
2nd edition, by Captain John E. Rains
> If you're boating in Mexico's Pacific waters, you need this 112-page
> book. Concisely presented data for each region, plus radio frequencies for
> WX-fax, ham radio nets with weather reporting, SSB weather sources.
> Tactics for avoiding bad weather and hurricanes, where to
> summer over safely.

"Boating Guide to Mexico: West Coast Edition"   *39.95*
by Captains Pat Miller Rains and John E. Rains
> The authors still have a few copies of this spectacularly beautiful
> 278-page cruising guidebook to Mexico's Pacific Coast and
> Sea of Cortez. Lots of color photos & harbor charts with GPS positions.

Please send me the following books:		shipping	CA tax (if applicable)	subtotal
____ **Cruising Ports**	$34.95	$3.00	$2.71	_____
____ **MexWX**	22.95	2.50	1.78	_____
____ **Boating Guide Mexico**	39.95	3.00	3.10	_____
			TOTAL	_____

NAME _____

PO Box / Street Address _____ Apt._____

City _____ State _____ Zip _____

Mail your check or money order to: ***Visa, MasterCard, American Express***
Point Loma Publishing   ***Call 24-hour toll-free to order books:***
P.O. Box 60190   (888) 302-BOAT
San Diego, CA 92166   (888) 302-2628

Thank you very much for ordering our books!

Book Ordering Form

"Cruising Ports: Florida to California via Panama"   *$ 34.95*
4th edition, by Captains Pat and John E. Rains
>Either direction, this +300-page nautical guidebook covers the 5,000-mile
route with better charts, more ports and anchorages, now including
the Sea of Cortez. This is the "Bible" for long-range cruisers.

"MexWX: Mexico Weather for Boaters"   *22.95*
2nd edition, by Captain John E. Rains
>If you're boating in Mexico's Pacific waters, you need this 112-page
book. Concisely presented data for each region, plus radio frequencies for
WX-fax, ham radio nets with weather reporting, SSB weather sources.
Tactics for avoiding bad weather and hurricanes, where to
summer over safely.

"Boating Guide to Mexico: West Coast Edition"   *39.95*
by Captains Pat Miller Rains and John E. Rains
>The authors still have a few copies of this spectacularly beautiful
278-page cruising guidebook to Mexico's Pacific Coast and
Sea of Cortez. Lots of color photos & harbor charts with GPS positions.

Please send me the following books:		shipping	CA tax (if applicable)	subtotal
____ **Cruising Ports**	$34.95	$3.00	$2.71	_____
____ **MexWX**	22.95	2.50	1.78	_____
____ **Boating Guide Mexico**	39.95	3.00	3.10	_____
			TOTAL	_____

NAME _____

PO Box / Street Address _____ Apt._____

City _____ State _____ Zip _____

Mail your check or money order to: ***Visa, MasterCard, American Express***
Point Loma Publishing   ***Call 24-hour toll-free to order books:***
P.O. Box 60190   (888) 302-BOAT
San Diego, CA 92166   (888) 302-2628

Thank you very much for ordering our books!